the sympathy of tl

to J. B.

V2_Publishing
NAi Publishers

the

sympathy

Ruskin and the Ecology of Design

of

things

Lars Spuybroek

contents

preface   7

the digital nature of gothic   11
    Ruskin: The Nature of Gothic · 17
    Craft and Code · 48
    I Believe in Things · 61
the matter of ornament   75
    Ruskin: Wall Veil and Earth Veil · 78
    An Abstract Materialism · 89
    Tessellation Ornament and Ribbon Ornament · 102
    Some Hints on Pattern Designing · 134
abstraction and sympathy   145
    The Mosaic of Experience · 148
    The Fabric of Sympathy · 159
    Lipps's Sympathy and Worringer's Empathy · 177
    The Veil is the Anti-Eidos · 201
the radical picturesque   207
    Forms and Forces · 210
    Ruskin: The Parasitical Sublime · 222
    Sublime Things · 243
    The Technological Wild · 261
the ecology of design   269
    Ruskin: Beauty is the End · 280
    A Veil of Strange Intermediate Being · 306

acknowledgments   335
list of illustrations   336
notes   339
bibliography   367
index   386

John Ruskin. *Entrance to the South Transept of Rouen Cathedral* (1854).

preface

There are two ways of revitalizing a historical figure. One is to expand the study of his or her relationship with contemporaries, to find more links and with any luck make unexpected discoveries, and to see whether you can reconstruct the person's main inventions in another light – in short, to make the person more historical. The other is to wrest the figure from history, to see whether you can filter out the typical statements of the day and discover what is left on the table, and, out of these parts, construct a creature we can recognize as one of our own, while hoping you are not creating a ghost version of the original.

   The book before you attempts to do the latter. It takes John Ruskin and places him primarily in the context of historical figures that have appeared *after* him. It is like a history written backwards. While the technique is not uncommon among those seeking to prove a particular subject should be viewed as an influence on others who followed, that is not my aim here. My ambition is to update Ruskin, not to see him diluted in the countless streams of diverging trends. Many of the figures I have him meet on his way to the present never referred to him, nor can they be characterized as followers, though I make them forge alliances with Ruskin because of deep theoretical affinities. This is quite an ahistorical approach, one that looks more like a design or construction project, certainly if we understand a project in the literal sense, as a projectile. Think, for instance, of the animated diagrams of the Voyager probe's launch into space: we see the projectile sweeping around Mars – not landing there but merely using the planet's gravitational field to increase its own speed – and then, some years later, around Jupiter and Saturn, ever faster; then, it makes one more turn around Neptune before being ejected from the solar system, at a speed now approaching that of light, and straight into the dark beyond. In the same way, I let Ruskin encounter William James, revolve around him, and absorb some of his thought, but not enough to slow him down; sweep around Henri Bergson, acquiring more speed; and again around a few Germans (Theodor Lipps, Wilhelm Worringer and even Martin Heidegger); eject him over the twentieth century (which at several points in the book I call the dark age of the sublime), with its world wars, its minimalism and its deconstructivism; and stop him so that he appears suddenly in our own age, like Doctor Who, meeting the likes of Bruno Latour and Peter Sloterdijk. One could hardly call this project historiographic – but it is not pure science fiction either, since we are bound to make the creature from the past speak in words both he and we understand.

Though we do see Ruskin encountering some of his contemporaries – less affectionately in the cases of Charles Babbage and Charles Darwin but much more so in that of William Morris – this project follows a tradition in which every twenty or thirty years a new Ruskin is sculpted out of his huge volume of work. The Ruskins of Marcel Proust, Patrick Geddes, the Guild Socialists, Kenneth Clark, Raymond Williams, Richard Sennett – to name just a few, dispersed over the breadth of the spectrum – are all shaped according to what they saw as the needs of the times. In this sense, this book fits an established custom: to create a Ruskin object, a probe sent from the past to shine light on our own times. It should come as no surprise that has happened with Ruskin more than with other historical figures, since he was so outspoken and often so angry that his voice was fated to be heard for centuries. More than a cultural commentator or art critic, he was an agitator, even a castigator at times, and a merciless one at that.

My Ruskin will be a rather confusing one to many, since the version I create does not condemn machinery – digital machinery, to be exact. This must sound awkward at best, if not completely illegitimate. How can one make the aesthetic philosopher (as Edmund White correctly qualifies him) of variation, imperfection and fragility into one of machinery? This question brings me to my second project: I will argue that our contemporary tools of design and production should be understood in a framework not of modern times but of premodern ones – not only of Ruskin's age of the picturesque and ornament but also of the pre-Renaissance era his own century tried to recreate: the age of the Gothic. John Ruskin's Gothic, either misjudged as sheer ethics or aesthetically not taken entirely seriously, turns out to be such a radical concept of design that I do not hesitate to call it a Gothic ontology, a notion that fuels the rest of the book.

In Chapters One and Two, Gothic ontology is defined as a special re-lationship between figures and configurations, in which the figures are active parts that have a certain freedom to act, though only in relation to others and in order to form collaborative entities. This concept transcends the aes-thetic opposition of structure and ornament, making the Gothic "a beauty that works," one that leads to a much broader notion of an aesthetics based on sympathy. Sympathy, in my briefest definition, is what things feel when they shape each other. In Chapters Three and Four, sympathy is first elab-orated in the context of the work of James and Bergson; then inserted back into aesthetic theory via the German category of *Einfühlung*, which we de-velop through Lipps and Worringer; and returns to Ruskin's hands in the fourth chapter. It is here that he fights his duel with Heidegger over care and concern, but also over sacrifice and gift, veiling and unveiling, and beauty and the sublime. For Ruskin, the sublime is what things grow away from as they take on the form of flourishing beauty, while for Heidegger it is what things open up towards. Finally, in Chapter Five, I arrive at an ecol-ogy of design in which sympathy becomes part of a universal aesthetics, in-volved not only in the production of artworks but that of all beings, animate and inanimate, human and nonhuman. So, to summarize the book, what seems to begin as a history of art quickly becomes an aesthetic theory and, step by step, turns into an aesthetic ontology.

I will discuss how we might adopt Ruskin's concepts from a digital per-spective in only a few instances, refraining from exploring it further. I believe the transformation of history into theory must be limited by rigor; if the exercise were taken too far, it would turn the book into one with a double agenda – transforming a historical Ruskin into a theory of digital design –

and would degrade his position into a mere legitimization of our own. When we stop at the moment of transformation itself, his way into a future becomes our way back into a past, and, instead of visiting our times, Ruskin lures us into his own. I think that if there is one thing we can learn from John Ruskin, it is that each age must find its own way to beauty, and in our case, this means finding our way *back* to beauty, since we seem to have lost sight of it completely. One cannot simply hope to survive a hundred-year obsession with fracture and fragment by accident. As I say at one point in this book, so much has been destroyed that to have any hope of repairing it, we must learn a forgotten language, make it new and speak up until we are heard.

Rotterdam/Atlanta, June 2011

chapter one

the digital nature of gothic

Ruskin's *The Nature of Gothic* is inarguably the best-known essay on Gothic architecture ever published; argumentative, persuasive, passionate, it's a text influential enough to have empowered a whole movement, which Ruskin distanced himself from on more than one occasion. Oddly enough, given that the chapter we are speaking of is the most important in the second volume of *The Stones of Venice*,[1] it has nothing to do with the Venetian Gothic at all. Rather, it discusses a northern Gothic with which Ruskin himself had an ambiguous relationship his whole life, sometimes calling it the noblest form of Gothic, sometimes the lowest, depending on which detail, transept or portal he was looking at. These are some of the reasons why this chapter has so often been published separately in book form, becoming a mini-bible for true believers, among them William Morris, who wrote the introduction for the book when he published it with his own Kelmscott Press.[2] Morris's is a precious little book, made with so much love and care that one hardly dares read it.

Like its theoretical number-one enemy, classicism, the Gothic has protagonists who write like partisans in an especially ferocious army. They are not your usual historians – the Gothic hasn't been able to attract a significant number of the best historians; it has no Gombrich, Wölfflin or Wittkower, nobody of such caliber – but a series of hybrid and atypical historians such as Pugin and Worringer who have tried again and again, like Ruskin, to create a Gothic for the present, in whatever form, revivalist, expressionist, or, as in my case, digitalist, if that is a word. Each of them bends, distorts, and plunders the history of the Gothic, but invariably uses it as a weapon against that other architecture of the south. Pugin, in *Contrasts*,[3] rescued the Gothic from its phase of folly, the phase of the *Gothick* (which was nothing but a dark Rococo), took it into the top league and pitted it against classicism, calling the latter "pagan" on page after page, denigrating it as a white, marbleized ghost of an essentially wooden architecture. Ruskin, no less subtly, kept calling classicism "Greek," meaning not-English or worse, not-from-the-North. Another nationalist from the other side of the North Sea, Wilhelm Worringer, preferred to label the Gothic as "Nordic";[4] Nordicism then wasn't as bad as its 1920s variant (with aviator Charles Lindbergh as one of its chief straight-nosed, high-foreheaded champions), but this nonetheless signaled a serious disqualification of Mediterranean architecture. Gilles Deleuze, who is known as a vitalist, was the last proponent of the Gothic, but in a barely recognizable manner, never giving it serious historical attention save for making a repeated reference to Worringer's Gothic line[5] and borrowing from him the concept of nonorganic life, in which free, proliferating curves are equated with deterritorializing barbarians, nomads and vagabonds breaking away from the state, whether Greek or Egyptian.

We – for I have joined that partisan army now too, so from here on it is "we" – do not need to designate Gothicism as a stylistic entity like classicism, which keeps throwing the same columns, the same Corinthian or Ionic orders, the same universal whiteness in our faces age after age, and in its latest postmodern version has shown its true nature by jumping directly into the laps of the world's developers and dressing up modernist skyscrapers and building fake Arcadias on top of five-story underground parking garages (I am writing this in Atlanta, itself currently trying to become a resurrected Atlantis). The Gothic, by contrast, is like a barbarian guerrilla force, constantly changing its face and adapting – fitting itself into a bourgeois niche, as in Art Nouveau; becoming historically self-evident, as in the Victorian revival; taking the form of the metallic, magnetic storm of its digital incarnation.

Hundreds, if not thousands, of books have been written about John Ruskin, a man to whom an entire library containing his manuscripts is now dedicated, but one searches in vain for any reference to *The Nature of*

Gothic in any scholarly book on the Gothic. There is none in Focillon,[6] nor in Jantzen,[7] and only a few pages in Frankl[8] who characterizes Ruskin's thought as "utter vagueness and dilettantism" – though thousands, if not hundreds of thousands, more people have read Ruskin's book than Frankl's own. Clearly, it is unnecessary to read Ruskin as if he is a historian of the Gothic; he is an advocate of it, of which Gothic exactly, neither he nor we come to know. He argues a case for his time, terrified by the state of the empire as he watches it slowly being engulfed in iron and shrouded in smoke. His way of working certainly should have stimulated more historians, who undeniably would have profited from its empiricism: lying on scaffolds for days drawing a detail high up in some forgotten corner, sketching capitals bathed in shadow, painting watercolors of inlaid marble baking in the sun, taking exact measurements, drawing up tables – things we do not get from the Frankls and Focillons. Ruskin is a hero of architecture, feeling it, smelling it, noting it down in its every detail, drawing its minutest part for us. In *Stones*, we get a complete archaeology, the actual stones of Venice dug out from reality, drawn, measured and categorized, not a single plan, not a single section of a building, only stones and members. We get them as they were carved and as we see them, nothing bigger, no system, no "metaphysics."

In *The Nature of Gothic*, Ruskin sets up a grand rhetoric to state his case, with a cascading list of "characteristics," all of them exclusively anti-classical, dramatically building one argument on top of the other. Since there have been so many books on Ruskin, books on every aspect of him, and books comparing every aspect of him and every other Victorian, it will suffice here to briefly summarize the six characteristics before I begin mobilizing the most important ones for my own case.

The first one, a close relative of the picturesque, is savageness – a delightful term in itself, which Ruskin does not use in the same way as Owen Jones in his reference to "savage tribes" in *The Grammar of Ornament*,[9] but nonetheless equates with a form of primitivism. "Savage" describes the workmen, the rough northern laborers, with their hands freezing, their heads in the mist and their feet in the mud, inevitably making "mistakes" in their carving because of their "rude" nature but also because of the open design system of the Gothic, which at certain points leaves them to decide what to do, or to hesitate suddenly, and ultimately present us with "failed, clumsy" ornament. All the same, it is the more beautiful because such savage details are markers of who the workers are, where they live and what they do:

> Imperfection is in some sort essential to all that we know of life. It is the sign of life in a mortal body, that is to say, of a state of progress and change. Nothing that lives is, or can be, rigidly perfect; part of it is decaying, part of it is nascent.[10]

If there ever was a vitalist, it was John Ruskin.[11] Some might be inclined to contest this statement and argue that he was a Christian (long periods of doubt and a significant "unconversion" notwithstanding), and a pious one at that. This is true, but he was usually a Christian at the *end* of an argument, never at the start; that is, after all thoughts had been thought. With Ruskin, a line of reasoning never relies on his Christianity, but it does heavily rely on his vitalism. He sincerely despises everything about Greek and Renaissance architecture, the form, the structure, the details – it is "an architecture invented, as it seems, to make plagiarists of its architects and slaves of its workmen,"[12] who are forced merely to copy and repeat a single detail, one curve after another, without ever adding anything of their own, clumsy or otherwise.

The second characteristic, changefulness, if not a more admirable term than the first, does not, like savageness, indicate anything about the nature of the stonemason's execution of his craft but rather signifies a broader sense of variety in *design*, that is, the work of the architect, the master mason: "The vital principle is not the love of Knowledge, but the love of *Change*."[13] Such variety is demonstrated in the curvature of the moldings, the bundled grouping of the shafts, the tracery of the windows, the pointedness of each arch, and the meshing of the ribbed vaults. The third characteristic, naturalism, is an index of the "intense affection" of the Gothic workmen for living foliage. Previously, Ruskin had called the Gothic a "foliated architecture"[14] that "has been derived from vegetation," which gives it a natural component. This is a category we might expect from the author of *Modern*

John Ruskin. *Ornaments from Rouen, St. Lô, and Venice*. Plate I from *The Seven Lamps of Architecture* (engraving by R. P. Cuff, 1880, orig. 1849).

15

Painters, who taught us to draw every twig, every cloud and rock as unique and filled with personality. The fourth, grotesqueness, occurs in extension of savageness, taking imagination into the domain of fancy, humor, and often the burlesque. It is the best-known feature of the Gothic, with its pagan gargoyles, and Ruskin covers it in just three sentences. The fifth, rigidity, is especially interesting because Ruskin has been accused more than once of not appreciating structural notions of architecture. In this section, he explains in detail how we should understand the Gothic as an active form of support and transfer of loads rather than a simple form of resisting forces. The sixth characteristic, "redundance," relates to "an accumulation of orna-ment" that expresses "a profound sympathy with the fullness and wealth of the material universe," a logical final category since redundancy directly op-poses the classical reductionism Ruskin so despises.

The six are closely related – redundance to naturalism, naturalism to changefulness, grotesqueness to savageness – and intersect at the point of rigidity, but for us the relationship between savageness and changefulness is the most relevant since it raises the main question: How does the Gothic succeed in converging existing forces into form? If there are forces of per-ception and of social organization alongside the forces of gravity, how are all these channeled into form? Ruskin's deeply philosophical answer is "through variation," the Gothic takes variation as its main formative drive by acting changeful at the level of design and savage at the level of execution. In alignment with Ruskin, we must first ask ourselves what exactly consti-tutes each quality, and second, how the two relate to each other. How does changefulness contain, permit or give rise to savageness, or vice versa? Many authors on political economy have devoted their share of thought to the notion of savageness – though the architectural historians have not – espe-cially because of its ethical and social consequences. Few art historians have devoted serious thought to changefulness either, much less to its reciprocal connection with savageness, though the two are expressed at completely dif-ferent levels. In the course of this essay, we will find that each operates by different types of variation, one smooth and delicate, the other rough and incremental, but we will also find that together they aggregate not only into an amalgam of forms but also one of organizations of work. We will find that fields of changeful smoothness contain not only hard little bits of savageness but themselves develop hard edges that allow the structure to grow, to transform or even to be broken off.

In this chapter, we will encounter various types of hands, which turn up one after the other – not only Ruskin's workman's hands chiseling stone and the craftman's hands of Sennett's Chinese butcher Chuang Tzu, but angels' ethereal hands, and little girls holding hands during a dance, and a master mason's hands scissoring compasses, and robot hands operating with magical dexterity, and even objects taking matters into their own hands, literally self-assembling. We'll see activity and work take on an abstraction, either occurring in small amounts distributed over the various stages of the process or concentrated into a single phase. In whatever form, work cannot be isolated or definitively located; even when done by a group, it is activity to be passed on. The notion is one of physical work being as much part of the design as drawing and tracing are part of cutting and carving; in short, *work is in design, and design is in work* – and thus savageness is in changefulness, and vice versa. This makes our argument specifically one of the digital, since the digital constitutes the realm of self-generating and self-drawing form.

ruskin: the nature of gothic

Let us now start to investigate Ruskin's characteristics of the nature of Gothic more closely, while concentrating in particular on savageness, changefulness and rigidity – not because the other three are of no importance, but because they are subcategories of the first set.

Not surprisingly, the argument for savageness has met with vehement ridicule.[15] Take one look at the cathedral in Reims and you will immediately understand that savageness cannot be called a main characteristic of the Gothic. The building is completely designed, and with a precision that continues to baffle us today. For some reason, there still exists a widespread misconception that the Gothic was an era without architects. In fact, the inverse is true, it was the time of their definitive ascent after a millennium's absence.

Architects, mostly from northern France – men who had exchanged their hammers and chisels for compasses and rulers – traveled around Europe from one project to the next. The eleventh and twelfth centuries saw the emergence of master masons who no longer concerned themselves with personally carving the stone but with drawing it, a practice that was not always met with equal acceptance. According to a sermon from 1261:

> In these huge buildings there is an architect who directs by word alone and who seldom or never dirties his hands; however he receives much higher recompense than the others. (Nicolas de Biard)[16]

What is most important for us, however, is to understand the distance and the stages between the drawing and its executed form. When an architect today makes a drawing, it has all the details worked out; the drawing is *prescriptive*: different scales, front and side views, and cross-sections together geometrically determine the whole object. The architects of the Gothic, however, had only recently said farewell to pure craft, and hence we see drawings not only marked on paper but also cut into wood and carved into stone floors. Most drawings were made (in so-called trasuras – tracing houses or drawing offices) on paper that perished fairly quickly, but some have been preserved on parchment, and one can see that in the main they were overall designs. Not everything that was ultimately built would have been included in a drawing, since drawings were mostly *descriptive* in nature. In the stone floors of a few Gothic buildings, so-called tracings have been found, deeply incised full-scale schematic drawings of parts[17] such as window traceries in the form of a horizontal *plan*. In addition, there were so-called templates that provided information about the *cross-section* of an object; these wooden models were mainly used by stonecutters to determine the profile of a molding, base or rib. Dozens of these templates can be found in the famous remaining books of Villard de Honnecourt.[18] We should keep in mind that any outline can be extruded over any centerline. Together, the stone incision showing the overall geometry and the wooden template of the selected contour provided all the information a stonecutter needed to make a part of a column or window tracery. Thus we find drawings on paper, but in a way also in wood and stone, and each of these techniques is embodied by a group, a guild with its own laws and opinions; and neither these groups nor their techniques fit hierarchically together.

It is in no way true that the higher group only actively performed and the lower receptively and passively executed; there was some space between drawing and execution, enough for individual details, though not as much as Ruskin hoped. For him, architecture chiefly belonged to the domain of ornament, and ornament was small, so it was mainly in the capitals and added images, such as the famous gargoyles, that his savageness appeared. Of course, a project's success depended on a continuous flow of information supported by the necessary legal remedies and financing – in short, by a high level of organization – but this is not to say there was no room for invention and imperfection. Later in this chapter, we will see that savageness appears to a much more significant degree on the collective scale.

Variability's greatest influence in the Gothic, however, was determined by something else, not incomplete execution but changefulness, the second characteristic on Ruskin's list – the idea of variety, in which the wide applicability of the rib as the driving design principle leads to an incredible multitude of solutions. Variation thus lies much more in design technique than in manual labor. Ruskin's argument is therefore closer to that of Hogarth, who, in *The Analysis of Beauty*,[19] states that beauty needs that specific tool of variety, the serpentine line, as well as the nesting of it in various ways of interconnection. Ruskin devotes a wonderful long paragraph to the principle:

> … They were capable of *perpetual novelty*. The pointed arch was not merely a bold variation from the round, but it admitted of millions of variations in itself; for the proportions of a pointed arch are changeable to infinity, while a circular arch is always the same. The grouped shaft was not merely a bold variation from the single one, but it admitted of millions of variations in its grouping, and in the proportions resultant from its grouping. The introduction of tracery was not only a startling

change in the treatment of window lights, but admitted endless changes in the interlacement of the tracery bars themselves.[20]

Ruskin is often cited at length, but nowhere do we come across this section, a paragraph that fully demonstrates the penetrating insight with which he analyzes the Gothic. He insistently writes of "millions" as opposed to "a few," and variation as opposed to uniformity. In the third volume of *Stones*, entitled *The Fall*, he expounds at length on why the Gothic differs so strongly from the Renaissance, which knows no variation, or only *proportional variation*, where an element remains constant when the whole is scaled up or down, so that the proportions are changed but not the element itself. In the Gothic, the element is changed through the ever-shifting combination of the subelements which are in themselves also variable and flexible: the ribs.[21] We will call this *configurational variation*. Ruskin tells us exactly which configurations are those of variation: the grouped shaft (generally known as the compound pier), the webbed or net vault, the pointed arch, the traceried window, and a bit later savage massing – none of which are in fact elements but rather combinations in context, configurations, collective patterns of figures. Each has its own variations, its own way of putting ribs together to yield new results, new designs, again and again, with a variation of "perpetual novelty." On this point Ruskin's observation is critical: to keep getting new configurations, one needs both different figures and different combinations of figures. This means that in the Gothic there exist two related areas of variability; first, a set of figures each of which has its own range of variability, and second, the combination or configuration of these figures into a larger entity. Generally, a combinatorial art is understood in terms of nested scales of sets, based on the fixity of the element, but the moment the smallest entity is capable of deforming the set of outcomes on the highest scale becomes inexhaustible and unpredictable. It is this relationship between figure and configuration that makes the Gothic unique. While other architectural styles often revolve around elements and form, the Gothic is much more about relationships, and how they are expressed in members themselves, not just in the spaces between the members. Most theories of the Gothic are still elementarist, though, infected as they are by classical analysis, and concern themselves solely with the resulting members, sometimes so much so that they get called "membrology," e.g., by Thomas Rickman and Robert Willis, early historians of the Gothic. Such element-focused analysis completely disregards the fact that in the Gothic the relationships are formed by something that moves through all the members: the linear rib.

Every rib is formed by linear figures in which every point on the line is active. In the Middle Ages, these were more often than not combinations of straight lines and arcs, exactly as Aristotle had prescribed – third-degree curves did not yet exist, so everything was linear or quadratic, and every curve was an interplay of the two. In the Gothic we can distinguish a number of curves or motifs, which from now on we will call *figures*. At the beginning of this analysis, it is important to establish that the underlying circles we often see in diagrams of the Gothic[22] are not, strictly speaking, figures. Such circles merely help to organize the figures and are not themselves visible. Figures are the combinations of lines that move over such circles and straights, and thus take on something of both. We see S-curves, J-curves, C-curves – not the ogives, pinnacles, tiercerons, liernes, ogees, crockets and trefoil of typical Gothic nomenclature – for the figures we distinguish are more fundamental within Gothic grammar, because they are relatively independent of the member or component embodying them. A figure is neither an architectural member nor its underlying geometrical schema but something closer to what we know as a *motif*, an abstract entity that has a certain freedom to adapt and change while interacting with other motifs. Crucial in the concept of changefulness is that the variation of the individual figure is linked to the possible configurations that can be formed of multiple figures. In short, the line is active and shows *behavior*. It can stretch and contract, not merely changing in scale but altering while still remaining itself; in short, it can be modulated. It can be a J-figure with a long or short shaft, including a wide or narrow arch, making up one half of an ogive; or a C-figure with various sizes of opening, which together form the familiar cusps of the trefoil; or an S-figure, which we know in the arch as the ogee – a curve that can be flattened but can also appear as a deep wave, such as we encounter in many traceries.

In fact, this is the first argument for why Gothic patterns are essentially digital: the fundamental variability of all figures. Secondly, though, the fact that the figures are relational makes the Gothic even more digital. Changes in a figure occur in relation to another figure with which it crosses, merges or collides; a wide spectrum of effects flows from this collective behavior of figures. This dynamic, interactive relationship between figure and configuration is at the conceptual heart of Ruskin's remark about "millions" and the "infinite number" of variations. A figure is a formal organization of variable points, not a fixed form. The organization is fixed, but not the form. With Bergson, we could say they vary both in degree (for instance, the possible modulations of a J-figure) and in kind (the distinction between the J-figure, C-figure, S-figure, etc.). This is not almost but exactly how the digital is defined today. Fairly simple behavior by individual members resulting in complex and irreducible collective behavior is a form of computation, which finds its most fundamental form in the digital, though not necessarily electronically. We often understand "digital" as meaning "electronically computed," but the speed of those electrons is actually irrelevant to the notion of computing, which refers solely to the method of calculation, a stepwise procedure of iterative adjustments based on the minimization of difference. Some might argue (after pointing out that there weren't any computers in 1280) that while these relationships are indeed mathematical in nature, comparably to Arabic patterns, they are not specifically digital. Of course geometry does play a role in both, but with Arabic patterns the effect never contributes to the pattern on a larger scale, and certainly not to its form. Of course they are also configurations, but they lack hierarchy and thus more often have the character of wallpaper, i.e., pattern independent of form. They do not *form* a column, window or vault but are applied to it later.

By contrast, Gothic patterns are very efficient at filling large geometric frames. The curves usually form smaller groups of five or six, resulting in a leaflike contour, a kind of mini-configuration, which then often, through different proliferation techniques such as translations and rotations, forms larger configurations bound together by a heavy frame. These might consist of high, pointed gables such as we see in portals, or the big, round circles of rose windows, or the ogive of a pointed arch. Though framed, all are constructed out of mini-configurations without any overly complicated addi-

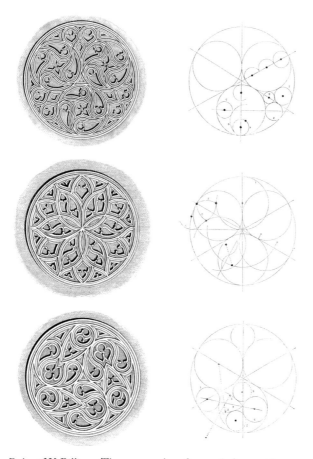

Robert W. Billings. Three examples of rose windows with
their corresponding geometrical diagrams. Plates III, XXXVII,
XLIII from *The Power of Form* (1851).

tional figures becoming necessary. Each of these combinations gives a specific expression to each of these elements; thus, a rose window can be completely static like a spoked wheel, or floral like a chrysanthemum, or radiant
like a flaming sun, or winding like a yin-yang design. The figures' movability
on a small scale results in a stable tracery structure, but the configuration's
expression on the larger scale is also one of movement, which in turn relates
to other loci of action.

As I argued earlier, Ruskin's concept of changefulness evokes Hogarth's
serpentine line, but it relates as strongly to Worringer's concept of the

"Northern line," with its "ceaseless melody" in which linear figures that seem to have come to life connect to each other and form patterns. For Worringer, an even more extreme expressionist than Ruskin, the Northern line is a line that both possesses abstraction and arouses empathy. In *Abstraction and Empathy* (1908), the famous thesis he wrote at the age of twenty-five (which had enormous influence on people as diverse as Franz Marc, T. E. Hulme, Vernon Lee and Herbert Read[23]), he develops this distinction as a fundamental one, in which abstraction identifies with the mechanical forces in the world, with structure, while empathy identifies with organic form and ornament. According to Worringer, the Gothic occupies an in-between position, which makes the world of forces palpable:

> Here they run parallel, then entwined, now latticed, now knotted, now plaited, then again brought through one another in a symmetrical checker of knotting and plaiting. Fantastically confused patterns are thus evolved, whose puzzle asks to be unravelled, whose convolutions seem alternately to seek and avoid each other, whose component parts, endowed as it were with sensibility, captivate sight and sense in passionately vital movement.[24]

He is referring to Karl Lamprecht's *Initial-Ornamentik*,[25] a late-nineteenth-century book on the aesthetics of illumination and interlaced decoration. According to Worringer, the lines seem to possess a life of their own, and an inclination to constantly keep copying and proliferating, without forming a finite organic body,

> ... far outstripping any possibilities of organic movement. The pathos of movement which lies in this vitalized geometry – a prelude to the vitalized mathematics of Gothic architecture – forces our sensibility to an effort unnatural to it. When once the barriers of organic movement have been overthrown, there is no more holding back; again and again the line is broken, again and again checked in the natural direction of its move-

ment; again and again it is forcibly prevented from peacefully ending its course, again and again diverted into fresh complications of expression, so that, tempered by all these restraints, it exerts its energy of expression to the uttermost until at last, bereft of all possibilities of natural pacification, it ends in confused, spasmodic movements, breaks off unappeased into the void or flows senselessly back upon itself.[26]

And here, he is even more clear:

> In short, the Northern line doesn't get its life from any impress which we willingly give it, but appears to have an expression of its own, which is stronger than our life.[27]

This life is not corporeal, and hence it is nonorganic, and "of a spiritual vitality." It is no longer the classical interplay between element and form that is operating here but one of figure-relationship and configuration-expression. In short, it is not the case that the theories of Ruskin and Worringer apply only to ornament (although they seldom articulate this themselves); rather, the behavior of the lines, however small and thin they are, displays a structural and connective logic. The division between structure and ornament we know from classicism is eliminated in Gothic architecture. When there is no fundamental distinction between mechanical laws and organic curves, because, for example, curves can interweave with each other into a straight, strong braid, or straight ribs shoot out of a column and subsequently transform into arched fans, or snaking curves spring from the straight mullions of windows, we suddenly find ourselves in an in-between world, one David Channell calls the world of the "vital machine,"[28] where the one is merely a gradation of the other.

It is not only a changefulness of columns, vaults, or traceries in themselves, but also one in which *columns transform into vaults into traceries*. Variation frees the column not only from the classical formal canon but also from its own definition, thus making it possible for it to change into a fan, and from a fan into a vault, of which no two are the same. Variability *within* an element leads to variability *between* elements. This makes the Gothic more radical than any other architectural style up to the present day. The Gothic has movement, but it does not result in either an image of movement or a vague amorphic mass, because it converts this physical movement into abstract structure. It does so with the most precise articulation, by counting, grouping, unraveling, regrouping, precisely in the manner of textile techniques that previously had been normally found only in ornament.

In *The Stones of Venice, I: The Foundations*, Ruskin does nothing more or less than look very closely at these column-bundling techniques, which he calls "grouped shafts." Actually, in imitation of him, we can look just as precisely at window traceries or networks of vaults, because these too are morphologies specifically consisting of configurations of ribs. And these ribs are flexible – not literally, *after* they have been carved from stone, but *before*, during the design phase, when changefulness is in charge.

Let us look a bit more precisely at the intriguing plates that deal with the grouped shafts. We see pages of a kind we are only accustomed to seeing in natural history books, filled with various kinds of flowers or insects, something like the famous plates of Ernst Haeckel, who grouped radiolaria taxonomically with multiple varieties on a single sheet. In a similar vein, I was also put in mind of Bentley and Humphreys's beautiful photo books exposing the morphological richness of snowflakes.[29] The grouped shaft is a splendid discovery, in the same category as the tracery window, rose window or net vault (a complex variation of the earlier rib vault). Instead of understanding it as a single heavy column with many thin colonettes added as ornament, like the Doric fluted type, we can see it as a collective bundle articulated in a way that allows it to do much more than merely shoot straight upward. The column is freed from its constructional unequivocalness, since the grouping makes the shaft immediately related and gives it a context. All members exist only in context, never in advance. On either side of the main shaft there is usually a lower arch, and since in the Gothic the arch is continuous with the column, two smaller columns are needed on either side of the main one. In addition, the main shaft has to split into two or even three again at the top, by the main vault, since the cross vault consists of multiple ribs. So we already need three rib columns at the front and two on both

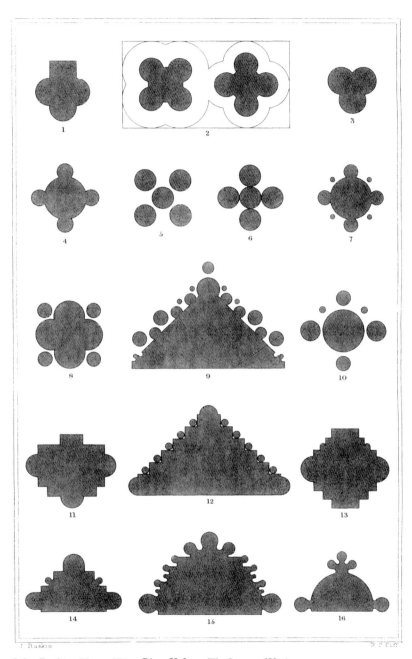

John Ruskin. *Plans of Piers*. Plate II from *The Stones of Venice*,
Vol. 1: Foundations (1851).

W. A. Bentley and W. J. Humphreys. Example from *Snow Crystals* (1931).

sides, and behind, two or three more that also comprise part of the lower cross vault in the aisle. This already makes eight rib columns, which, although they require a cross-shaped distribution over the shaft, do not have a fixed morphology. This results not in a fixed circle on which eight smaller ones are distributed but in a free grouping, in which the eight – or, often, as many as twelve or even more – thinner rib columns can merge but also break free again of the main group. Like the braiding of hair, it's simply a re-arrangement of material into strands, in which one is continually able to decide whether to combine the strands into a single heavy line, i.e., a thick braid, or to let them fan out over the head and then make them into smaller braids further on. None of the Gothic members are elements that can be shown separately and in isolation on the page; they exist only in context, are created out of relationships with each other, which is precisely why Ruskin's plates became taxonomies.

We can make a similar argument, with plates of variations, for window traceries, net vaults and pointed arches – though Ruskin does not do so for any of these three in *Stones I* – and for moldings, which he does elaborate, following Pugin, for whom the direction in which rain drips from the profile is just as important as the beholder's viewing angle. They are directions, me-chanical and organic forces that find their nexus in a morphology (we will not call it a typology), which has its hallmarks and is constructed according to certain rules but has no fixed form. These hallmarks are operational and procedural; they include bundling in columns, interweaving in tracery, meshing in vaults, and, in moldings, a protruding, a flaring out from and rejoining with the wall. And these are the sources of Ruskin's "perpetual novelty" born of the "millions of variations" the Gothic has for each mor-phology, as an "expression of life."

By this reasoning, we understand better and better what the role of work is and how, in the process of forces concentrating at a nexus, it ultimately finds expression in stone, in a specifically surfaced stone. Very early, in 1848, Ruskin wrote:

> Now I think that Form, properly so called, may be considered
> as a function or exponent either of Growth or of Force, inherent
> or impressed; and that one of the steps to admiring it or un-
> derstanding it must be a comprehension of the laws of forma-
> tion and of the forces to be resisted; that all forms are thus ei-
> ther indicative of lines of energy, or pressure, or motion,

variously impressed or resisted, and are therefore exquisitely abstract and precise.[30]

I think it is clear from this quote why Ernst Gombrich calls Ruskin a proto-expressionist,[31] since expressionism directly relates force to form. So we proceed stepwise, from kneading, constitutive natural forces to human action and work, first design work and then execution work, towards a sociocultural form-expression, a long string of mapping and passing on of forces toward a form, with an indexing at each level that expresses itself on the next. Design is work too, since it consists of the handling and processing of forces, and the realm of changefulness channels life as much as savageness does. Every stage receives templates from the previous one, and some of those templates are more rigid than others. When a twelfth-century architect designs a column, it will take on the morphology of a column and nothing else, but therein lies his freedom, because he takes the column for granted, since it will not materialize as such anyway; he is merely interested in an expression of the bundling. And so a wooden template of the column's profile is made, with some room for the mason to carve his own pattern behind the template. In this sense, the wooden templates used in Gothic building should not be confused with, say, the molds contemporary architects use in prefab; the Gothic mold is not filled with inert matter but elaborated to a subsequent, more detailed level. We should try to understand this as a savageness that runs through all stages of changefulness, becoming more intense at each, and leaving more and more room for mistakes, fancy, and grotesquerie. But let us now study savageness again in another context.

The movement that Worringer describes in such flowery style is that of a living line, but this does not mean it gives rise to an architecture of proliferation, stopping only at the point of exhaustion. The "nonorganic" behavior of the Gothic figures that Deleuze so appreciates in Worringer's descriptions we find only in the smallest ornaments – and probably not even there, since they so neatly form knots and nets. Yes, the Gothic line does exist as a living line, though not as one that simply overgrows structure but as one that produces it. It is actually at these moments when the geometry, i.e., the structure, comes alive, or, as Worringer says, is "vitalized." Deleuze tends to read a movement in Worringer's figures that is metastatic and de-territorializing, and there we must disappoint him – the Gothic is much more intelligent, it uses movement not to break away from form but to actually create it – though a specific, "nonformal" form results from it. The movements are choreographically related in such a way that together they form a system, and although implicitly restless and unending, it generally results in balanced, symmetrical forms. The movement that endlessly swarms over some capitals is in no sense the same movement as that of window traceries, which habitually move in mirror image, very precisely coordinated with each other, and fit within the heavy framework of the ogive. But this does not do Worringer's analysis an injustice; the variation of the *Nordische Linie* is still the agent of all variability in design; moreover, the fact that such complex choreographies yield an infinite variation in traceries and net vaults is actually evidence of its productivity. Life mirrors and segments its endless variation, and this makes it not vague but precise. The mirroring and segmenting of the body plan actually ensures that variation continues to function and does not merely lead to shapeless piles of matter. *First there is variation, then there is differentiation* – and then there is more variation, and again differentiation.

It is no accident that when biologists are explaining these principles of body plans and their phyla, they often reach for Gothic floor plans and not Greek or modernist ones. First there is the nave, then the transept, and if the nave is long enough a second transept if necessary, then a Lady Chapel, and the Cloisters, and then an octagonal Chapter House (always with that splendid single column in the middle). They extend and stretch, yes, but only *to a certain point*; then they sprout off sideways, on either side of the nave, and stretch again, once more *to a certain point*; then more additions are made perpendicular to the transepts, a chapel here and another one there, hexagonal or octagonal, single or multiple, but again *to a certain point*; and then it grows some more, vertically, once again *to a certain point*.

The Gothic body is what these days we would call a fractal body, a body of splittings, extensions and continuous breaks. Of course, the Gothic *Trieb* is nonorganic, an unstoppable *flow* and irrepressible urge to multiply, but its expression is not simply nonorganic and certainly not antiorganic; it segments, and keeps *tending* toward the making of a body. It has the necessary instruments for doing so, but the result need not be the body of Christ; the *nave* can become as long as a snake, and even bend and twist if desired, zigzagging over the field; but then you get more than one transept, and multiple spires of different heights at every crossing – not a problem, but it will invariably subdivide and segment. Gothic logic is like that of an ice crystal branching out to propagate itself over a cold windowpane, reorganizing water vapor by giving it form.

In light of this, it does not make much sense to radically oppose the organic and nonorganic, as Deleuze does, because the rules that lead toward the making of a body in no way imply that that body will always be finished, as if it were to run up against the wall of an invisible mold and find itself unable to keep mutating. Yes, the organic, or, more precisely, organicism, makes the moving parts meet up so blindly in an unavoidable whole that their movement becomes futile, but, on the other hand, to deny the existence of wholes at the cost of losing sight of their variation is just as useless. In short, if movement of figures did not lead to quasi-stable configurations, change and development would never occur. Movement and change need to alternate. If movement did not lead to organization, it would simply exhaust itself, like a primordial soup never coming to life. Life is first and foremost the power of organization; it continually segments and divides itself.[32] And although the existing Gothic cathedrals do not feature examples as extreme as those described in the previous paragraph ("zigzagging over the field" with "multiple spires"), great variation is ever present. The well-known historical fact that construction was constantly being halted, delayed and interrupted cannot account for this. Gothic architecture has the continuous urge to mutate, and even when a floor plan is completely symmetrical, the spires need not follow that symmetry.

This picture, which we know from Chartres, seems an all-too-familiar one, and when we are confronted with two unmatched spires, which may not even share the same composition, we all too quickly blame it on some medieval lack of organization, funds, or political will. But if we assume that such a thing was done relatively willfully, that the cathedral was deliberately designed that way by a collective, not an individual, then it suddenly starts to make sense to us. In other words, the asymmetry of Chartres is not simply a nonsymmetry; on the contrary, it is much more complex than that, the symmetry of the plan and the symmetry at the base of the towers both allow for an asymmetry at the top. Again, it tends toward the making of a body but does not necessarily lead to it. The asymmetry would never exist if it did not tend toward symmetry. This is the way it was, or, if not, mismatched spires were at least acceptable to the late medievals, which is enough for me to accept it as design. Of course, an entire community that has invested an amount of time, money and work beyond our comprehension does not decide at a certain point to simply halt construction or change its mind – that the steeple may as well be left off, or one tower may as well be this way and the other one that way. Rather, something totally different lies behind it, namely, self-segmentation and limb formation. The variation occurs *after* the body has been segmented and *after* the segments have been segmented again in turn. This means, in opposition to what architects are taught, that symmetrical organization does not necessarily lead to symmetrical form. Here we see Ruskin's primary argument, savageness, returning on a different scale, not the scale of individual work but the largest scale of collective execution, in which groups and guilds together, along with the patron and possibly his successors, allow imperfection.

We may as well get used to it, the concept of symmetry in the Gothic is completely opposed to the Greek one. It is a symmetry that guides and channels growth rather than checking it. The process is filled with obstacles ("problems," as Worringer fittingly calls them), but they do not block things, only structure them, not unlike a system of locks, which is dynamic and functions on different levels using thresholds and channels. Each reservoir can hold only a certain amount of variation. Growth never works when there is a lack of differentiation; it is absolutely impossible for a system to increase in scale without segmenting, because, as Galileo demonstrated, simply enlarging the same form leads to something that very quickly collapses under its own weight. No, growth is the redistribution of material, not blind excrescence; it is continual reorganization, not continual enlargement of the same form of organization.

Here, we seem to arrive at some essential point. Whereas before, we

observed the complex relationship between changefulness – smooth variation of design – and savageness – rough variation of execution – proceeding
downward in scale, we now see that it proceeds upward as well. Changefulness needs savageness in all directions; nothing can grow or shrink without
cracks in the fields of smoothness. The Gothic requires smooth variations
of woven tracery and bundled columns together with as much crudeness in
the capitals as in the massing of the whole building.

To imply that multiplication and growth are the opposite of organization and constitute a nonorganic force is a gross misconception of life and
movement. It is to confuse organization with finalism, because life thrives
on organization, which is not what stops growth but what actually encourages it, and encourages change, since when something mutates it is *some
thing* that mutates. We must emphasize, though, that Worringer's and
Ruskin's understanding of the Gothic as fundamentally non-classical, as an
architecture that denies finalism, is completely correct. From this perspective, Alberti's organicism seems fatally flawed, a misunderstanding of matter
if not a complete misunderstanding of nature. What we see in nature is a
continuity of elements and a discontinuity of bodies. What we find in Classicism is a discontinuity of elements and a continuity of bodies.

When we keep in mind that Worringer makes his theory of the Gothic
a racial one (I wouldn't say racist just yet), constantly referring to "das
Nordische," the *Nordic*, not "the Northern" – the word that regularly pops
up in the mellowed English translations of his books – we can understand
why his conception of the Gothic is so influenced by Norse and Nordic ornament, the most twisted and serpentine (often literally featuring snakes
and dragons) ribbon decoration in history, which runs over door frames,
rune stones and capitals alike. Granted, the notion is rather an uncomfortable one, but viewing the Gothic within a framework of migration and population politics can be taken unusually far. The classic theory is that Gothic
patterns came about when holes were drilled in Romanesque arches.[33] That
may be, but the great disadvantage of such historical explanations in general
is that the way something evolved is not the same as its concept; that is, the
predecessor never serves as the content, much less the design method, of
the successor. It explains how an idea arises, but not the idea itself. It may

well be that the Gothic wall sprang from a Roman wall that was hollowed out step by step, but this does not at all mean that it is one. The drilled circles of the early trefoils and quatrefoils very quickly became virtual ones, drawn on paper, then on stone, and the circles touch at the tangents perpendicular to their diameters, and inevitably the figures begin moving over these virtual trajectories.

We should notice how the status of the lines keeps changing, a continuous line one day is a dashed line the next; what is physical one day is schematic the next. If you make the holes big enough, lines will remain between them, and these tangents turn the previous completely upside down; suddenly, it no longer changes from a solid wall into a porous screen but begins immediately with fibers, with ribbons and stalks, and now it is these that are drawn as continuous, and the circles as dashed. This transition from what art historians call plate tracery to bar tracery (as it flourished during the French *Rayonnant* and the English *Decorated* style, the so-called mid-Pointed) is essential, for suddenly the holes in the wall, high in the spandrels between the arches, are able to forge links with the columns rising up from the wall below; two separate design problems are suddenly related, part of the same family, not through proportion but through form and methodology, through being made to share a part more fundamental than themselves, not even a part but a subpart: the rib. This is exactly the kind of thing biological evolution comes up with all the time, the invention of nonparts, or almost-parts, parts that are neither brick nor wall but kind of a bit of both – which is why Stephen Jay Gould was so interested in the spandrel. This is how the Gothic should be understood, as the *genetic engineering* of architectural language. From the early twelfth century all the way to the late fourteenth, a recoding was constantly taking place, bringing the majority of elements into the same family, a northern invasion conducted not by the earlier methods of violence but via the much more effective means of viral transmission, so that everything came to share the same DNA. All work – the concentration of forces in a column, the distribution of forces in a wall or vault – was done via the constant reorganization of ribs.

As they carved out the walls, the *Norsemen*, the Norman master masons of the Somme valley, must have recognized their own ancient weaving, their insanely complex knotwork, their leather belts and bronze clasps, their straw baskets and red braids, more clearly with every step. And their work is linked not only to Norman weaving techniques but also to the older Insular illuminations found in the Book of Kells and the Lindisfarne Gospels, in which spirals and cat-headed snakes fill the initials, gradually interweave and become long straight bands that clasp the text, only to explode again and swarm across the empty margins of the page. If one looks closely at illumination patterns, one sees that, just as in the Gothic, everything is continually subdivided into ribbons – straight bars as well as initials and tendrils – and these ribbons can connect to each other again and again in new variations, solving new problems, such as variable amounts of white on the page, blocks of text of different widths, different numbers of columns, initials and subheads, and so on. Celtic knotwork, by contrast, is even more exact, more mathematically complex, and at all times symmetrical, with an intelligence far beyond that found in the Norse snake pit, braids not only run freely under and over each other but loop back to form increments, small woven units that can split off from each other, in a technique that makes it possible to fill the discontinuous figure of a cross in a continuous way, just as later in Gothic illumination it would be possible to fill a capital T or G with weaving as easily as an O. This does not, perhaps, mean there was a linear historical evolution from (Celtic) *knotwork* to (Insular) *illumination* to (Norman) *tracery*, but a meshed, conceptual relationship certainly exists.[34] From a historical point of view, it is true that the Celts traveled from France to England centuries earlier and the Gothic arrived centuries later in England by way of French Normandy, but we are speaking of similar styles, in which separate ribbons were woven together into complex configurations, in a decorative technique that could avail itself of individual tendrils on the one hand and tightly packed surfaces on the other, and in fact everything in between. In this sense, Norse weaving techniques are more closely related to the Gothic than the Gothic is to its predecessor the Romanesque. Worringer in effect expands Lamprecht's theory of northern ornament from the clasps and initials to the Gothic. Ruskin devotes a paragraph in *The Flamboyant Architecture of the Valley of the Somme* (1869) to the comparison but unfortunately does not elaborate it further:

Second initial page of the Gospel of Matthew, or the *Chi Rho* page from the Lindisfarne
Gospels (680–720 AD).

You are doubtless all aware that from the earliest times, a system of interwoven ornament has been peculiarly characteristic of northern design, reaching greatest intensity of fancy in the Irish manuscripts represented by the Book of Kells – and universal in Scandinavia and among the Norman race. But you may not have considered – that, disguised by other and more subtle qualities, the same instinct is manifest in the living art of the whole world. This delight in the embroidery, intricacy of involution – the labyrinthine wanderings of a clue, continually lost, continually recovered, belongs – though in a more chastised and delicate phase – as much to Indian, to Arabian, to Egyptian, and to Byzantine work, as to that of Norway and Ireland – nay, it existed just as strongly in the Greek.[35]

To put it ahistorically: Ruskin is in full agreement with Worringer's theory of early medieval ribbon ornament being related to the Gothic, and partially with his view of it as a style specific to the north. To be sure, Gothic ribs, even Flamboyant ones, never behave in as complex and pliable a manner as the ribbons in knotwork, but both the rib and the ribbon are distinct abstracted elements that create larger wholes by bending, braiding or webbing that are as structural as they are ornamental. What makes the comparison of the Gothic to knotwork so significant for us is that it enables a different kind of fusion of savageness and changefulness than the one Ruskin had in mind, something we have hinted at previously: when design technique is influenced by craft, a fundamental displacement occurs. Since design customarily retreats from the material into the abstract world of drawing, while craft maintains a one-on-one relationship with matter, bending every twig with its own hand, at first sight the two appear to lie as far apart as possible. But when the line of a drawing is directly informed by that pliable twig, and thus an entire design by the craft of weaving and knotting, then the argument gradually changes: in the Gothic, *work, activity and craft were taking place at the design stage*, rather than only appearing on the scene at the execution stage. This may not be exactly the handwork Ruskin imagined, with bad Mondays, mistakes and earthy Gothic stonecutters, but his concept of work was ultimately a strongly ideologically tinted one. The fact remains that handicraft and design mingled because the drawing – later to be carved in stone – was informed by a world of interweaving twigs, leather handles and bundled hair. Although the whole logic is one of the assembly of flexible elements, this is not a case of *skeuomorphism* (as developed by Semper), in which stone often much too literally seems to weave, intertwine and knot.

John Ruskin. *South-West Porch of St. Wulfran, Abbeville* (1848).

The fact that Gothic tracery, even Flamboyant tracery, treats mullions as if they are flexible does not mean the final pattern mimics fabric – which Ruskin, none too flatteringly, liked to call "cobwebs." No, the tracery's flexibility, though material, is abstract, not literal or imitative. In a way, this makes the twin phenomena of savageness and changefulness more reciprocal than his class-driven view of the draughtsman and stonemason suggests, since *the former draws as if he is weaving and the latter carves as if he is drawing.* Yet we should not brush aside Ruskin's vision of labor as obsolete, since for him, aesthetics is at all times related to work, and work to aesthetics; mountains and clouds are as much the result of construction as are paintings and buildings.

At this point, we should make a radical distinction between labor and work (or craft), a distinction Ruskin perhaps does not always pursue terminologically but certainly does conceptually. Labor, in the sense of John Stuart Mill and David Ricardo, is a provider of exchange value weighed against the use value of a product or service, a concept Ruskin strongly disapproves of. First, objects' value cannot be simply economically determined by usage, since so much of an object's value is based on uselessness, e.g., ornament or beauty in general. Second, the concept of labor cannot simply explain the work done, since a portion of it is extra work, a form of sacrifice even, which Ruskin compares later, in *Unto This Last,* to the overtime work done by a physician or the life-threatening risks taken by soldiers.[36] There is an intensity to work, as well as a sense of duty, that cannot be calculated in terms of extra hours. These two concepts appear in the first chapter of *The Seven Lamps,* which starts with an exposé on the main characteristic of architecture, "The Lamp of Sacrifice," considered as both useless ornament and extra work. The quality of a stonemason's work in Gothic times would have been based on the enjoyment he experienced, not on the hours he spent on the job. Mind you, we must consider this a joy related to work and tasks, not to the state of exaltation we find in leisure. Work and the objects created through work, in Ruskin's mind, circulate for a larger or smaller part in a *gift economy,* not the market economy of mere supply and demand.[37]

Labor is based on the minimum we can do, work on the maximum we can give. Needless to say, Ruskin did not propose a tribal, free distribution of goods without any renumeration, either, though at a certain point in his career the hybrid of labor and work did lead him to defend fixed wages and prices. Contrarily to our contemporary intuition, such fixity precisely allows the worker freedom to make mistakes (which have to be limited by a solid training system, such as that provided by a guild). We will encounter this seemingly paradoxical situation several times in this book, and it must be conceived as the most fundamental Gothic principle: the freedom of work (be it of stone figures or flesh-and-blood people) is never a quality in itself but is strongly bound to collaboration; it is a freedom that leads to collaborative entities and also sprouts from them. Fixity leads to movement, and movement leads to fixity. We find this jerking, jolting style of the Gothic in its architecture, with as many sharp cusps as it has flowing lines;[38] in its paintings, which depict as many folds in clothing as they do stiff postures underneath; even in the *poulaines*, the famous shoes with elongated toes,[39] which seem to intensify movement as much as obstruct it – the Gothic is an art of flowing as much as an art of stopping.

In this sense, work is the gathering of forces, their convergence or intersection, instigated not by a person or a deity but by the forces themselves, unanchored, turning work into an act of the mind as well as the body, into something Ruskin tends to call "noble"– the same phenomenon that makes Worringer plead for the Gothic as spiritual and not sensuous, and the reason Focillon's description of the Flamboyant as "Baroque" is so terribly off the mark.[40] The French consider the early High Gothic and Flamboyant to run in parallel to the Renaissance and Baroque, probably in an attempt to make the Gothic acceptable, but one which fails utterly time after time. There is nothing sensuous or Baroque in the intertwining of mullions, because, as Worringer says, there is nothing organic – referring to the classical realm of imitative ornament – about it. The Gothic whole is frayed, created by parts strangely both abstract and alive, by flexible ribbons that interlace, connect and bundle together, their work is like that of ants, their behavior like that of bacteria, leading the simple life of intuition.

Here, we must recall the short-lived collaboration between Ruskin and Millais. Under striking (and rather humorous) circumstances during a vacation in Scotland in the summer of 1853, Millais was working on a portrait of Ruskin as well as *A Waterfall in Glenfinlas,* which featured Effie Gray, Ruskin's then-wife. Millais and Gray, whom Ruskin was completely ignoring, fell for each other, so much so that a divorce from Ruskin would soon result, followed by a marriage with Millais, which eventually produced eight children. Amid this situation, the two men were trying to develop a "new style" together, for the only time in their lives – Ruskin by talking, Millais by drawing. While his wife was slowly falling in love with the artist, Ruskin was having a wonderful time, since he felt he and Millais were on the verge of inventing a new Gothic.

Only one known sketch by Millais representing this episode exists, but it is a truly remarkable one, which had Ruskin "beside himself with pleasure," "slapping his hands together."[41] In the positions of the two lancet arches and single quatrefoil that would form a Gothic window, ethereal beings join hands at the points where the ribs would come together to form the pattern's figures and switches. (And they kiss on the lips, and above each kiss, there flares a flame!) In other words, the tracery is replaced by angels, in a seeming attempt not only to revitalize organic ornament within the domain of the Gothic by leaving vegetal and animal figuration behind but, moreover, to express the status of work, to render stone carving equal to design and handicraft to thought, and to visualize lines and fibers that seem to have a life of their own. If we concentrate on the positioning of hands for a bit longer, we can envisage the rough craftsmen's hands transforming into the delicate angels' hands. Suddenly the hands of craft are attached to matter itself, enabling it to act and grab onto itself. Ruskin's and Millais's image beautifully shows this self-crafting capacity of matter, or better, the self-designing capacity of things, ribs only move and vary to connect to other moving and varying ribs.

Now imagine a building made entirely of angels. All the material is animated, not by souls inhabiting matter but by flexibility living within rigid matter, textile inhabiting stone, weaving inhabiting carving, carving inhabiting drawing. Again, work is not located – not in a class, or a pair of hands, or even in human beings; work is continuously displaced, and boundaries blur; it is omnipresent, and therefore spiritual. And the angels and agents not only work, they collaborate. Agents make agency. The flexibility of the

John Everett Millais. *Design for a Gothic window* (1853).

elements in the Gothic is radically opposed to that found in the Baroque; there, structure comes first, and *then* movement is added. The relationship between columns, beams and pedestals does not change at all; they only bend *afterward*, after they have connected. The Baroque is merely distorted classicism. It sticks to the classicist elements but soaks them until they are bent and twisted, and however distorted they become, they remain simply capitals, pedestals, flutings, friezes, all dipped in the same eternal white of uniformity and universality. All the bending does not change the internal relations one bit. In the Gothic, the bending creates the structure; it is the actual agent of rigidity. In the Gothic, nothing is distorted; the elements are free – free *beforehand*, not in the sense of being loose but in the sense of being free *to find each other* – and when they do, they build, they hold onto each other.

To explain using our earlier terminology of the figure: Greek architecture, or better, Greek *ontology* (how things come into and remain in existence) consists of a set of I-figures that fit together, as in a post-and-beam system, which William Morris derogatively calls "lintel architecture."[42] Baroque ontology follows the same schema, but after the straight elements have configured, they are bent into ellipses, ovoids or any combination of these forms (it is a formalist technique). The Gothic, however, starts with J-, C-, O- or S-figures – ribs – that act and vary not to simply move about but to form groups – configurations – which at that point become fixed and start acting in relation to other configurations. The mereology of the Gothic is the reverse of the Greek and Baroque versions. We see the most complex relationships: mergings, braidings, splittings, crossings, branchings, overlappings; and these forms of collaboration lead us to the following unusual conclusion: in the Gothic, *ornament acts like structure and structure acts like ornament.* This has a number of important consequences. One is that in the Greek system the scales of structure and ornament are completely severed, since the large scale is occupied only by structural parts and the small scale only by ornamental features. In the Gothic, such separation never occurs so prominently; wooden fences can act as mini-structures and webbed vaults as mega-ornaments. Moreover, tracery is capable of hovering in between scales, as we see in the use of fans that prevent sudden jumps between column and vault, while a garland or volute is never capable of filling the space between elements. The Baroque tries to correct the problem by adding movement, but the operation is a mere illusion, an image of movement, a three-dimensional photo.

The historicizing opinion on Gothic architecture still prevails that, because Romanesque columns were chronologically first smooth and only later "covered" with ribs, structure and ornament are theoretically separate, à la Alberti. One does the work, the other provides the beauty; one is mechanical, the other organic; one calculable, the other valuable. What a grave misconception of both work and beauty. It may be true of Greek ornament, where the organic oozes out like marmalade from between rigid structural parts. But this theory fatally separates empathy from abstraction, and worse, *Kunstform* from *Werkform*; and even more fatally, it causes most historians to think of ornament as an excrescence of the joint, the *knot* as a *Naht*, to put it in Semperian terms, which are, in fact, opposing concepts and not related ones.

In the Gothic, as Worringer emphasizes with his notion of vitalized geometry, the figural ribs have properties of both structure and ornament, but the one enhances the other, merged into a state that can suddenly flex and move or just as easily freeze and petrify. Seen from the angle of structure, which in other architectures is considered crystalline, the curved parts of each figure increase the potential for the line to orient itself to others. A straight line can only be scaled up or down or be rotated, while a curve can vary in direction between beginning and end. Seen from the angle of ornament – which in most architectures is chiefly arabesque – each curve has a straight element attached to it, whether an actual straight aligned with the axis of gravity or a virtual straight in the form of a tangent that helps regulate contact. Naturally, in the Gothic we find some ornament playing a role similar to that in classical architecture, such as moulded pedestals and even even capitals articulated with foliage, but these are more often conceived as bands tying up bundles of ribs than as actual terminations of columns. Other small-scale, refined ornaments, such as finials, crockets and pinnacles, are mostly designed as extensions of local movements, and never as termini. In most architectural styles, structure is conceived as big and ornament as small, but, again, in the Gothic, the ribs exist on an in-between scale, too thin to carry weight and too thick to be delicate. Pragmatically, it solves the former problem by bundling ribs and the latter by interweaving and splitting them, obtaining more and more vertical articulation through molding. Hence, aesthetically, it elevates structure from an expression of strength to one of *delicacy*. It is a beauty that works. It is a flexible rigidity, which Ruskin, describing his fifth characteristic of the nature of Gothic, calls

> an *active* rigidity: the peculiar energy that gives tension to movement, and stiffness to resistance, which makes the fiercest lightning forked rather than curved.[43]

And, probably already thinking of Millais's angels, he writes:

> Egyptian and Greek buildings stand, for the most part, by their own weight and mass, one stone passively incumbent on an-

other; but in the Gothic vaults and traceries there is a stiffness analogous to that of the bones of a limb, or the fibres of a tree; an elastic tension and communication of force from part to part, and also a studious expression of this throughout every visible line of the building.[44]

This is a completely different Ruskin from the one who is habitually ridiculed for not being able to handle a structural analysis of the Gothic. First of all, he does not reduce the complexity of the relations between ribs to pure thrust and load; for him, the notion of force is as aesthetic as it is constructive. Second, when he does analyze mechanical forces, he does not do so in terms of passivity, balance and rest, as is the custom in statics, but as an ongoing activity. Generally, the whole debate around the structural properties of the Gothic rib vault merely oscillates between two types of rationalism. On one side, we find Viollet-le-Duc, who reduced the Gothic elements to structurally determined ones;[45] on the other, we find his critics, such as Pol Abraham,[46] stating that the rib vault is an illusion and that the rib has no actual structural properties. Both lines of reasoning are faulty, because both are based on exclusively structural principles. The Gothic has never been concerned with the rationalism introduced by Viollet-le-Duc nor with Abraham's denial of it. Reading ribs as primary structure with secondary filling is thoroughly inaccurate (as if one is comparing them to modernist paneling![47]); the Gothic has nothing of the engineer's art, nor of some transparent pre-high-tech, because it treats structural forces as equal to compositional ones it regards as just as real and powerful. All forces are real, all things are

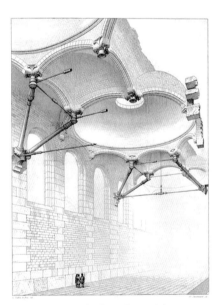

Eugène Viollet-le-Duc. One of the exemplary iron-masonry structures of the twelfth lecture in *Entretiens sur l'architecture*. Plate 22, *Maçonnerie* (1863).

real, not just material ones. Again, the Gothic is *configurational, not simply structural*, and being configurational means it operates via interconnection, via patterning; all this is materialized, yes, though not solely for the transfer of loads. In a sense, the Gothic is even more materialist than the engineer's approach, since it extends the thinking in forces to the realm of the social, aesthetic and religious.

Viollet's addition of the iron rod – proposed in his famous *Entretiens* – to replace the flying buttress is nothing but a purification and cleansing of the Gothic, forcing the stone ribs into a network of thick compression elements and thin tension elements, replacing Worringer's vitalized geometry with a purified, crystalline, mechanical geometry.[48] In the Gothic, the weak, delicate elements interact and build structure, actively creating rigidity, and the final strength is the result of a collaborative effort. The problem with engineers is recurrent, since they know that material systems undergo compression as well as tension and

Gloucester Cathedral, view of the south cloisters (1351).

that structures need strength as well as stability, they believe design should follow such distinctions, and design procedures merely enact the analysis by putting in the columns first and then adding the bracing to stabilize them (and decorate – if compelled to – at the end). But the Gothic refuses to separate a system into such predetermined states; the verticality of gravity is simply married with the horizontality of the wind from the outset, which is exactly why the ribs tend to become curvilinear and interlace. For engineers, elements can only exist as determined, while the Gothic is perfectly happy varying gradually between vagueness and finality and exploring every possible state in between. All the life and movement of the ribs is transferred to the structure, and this makes it beautiful. Life and beauty are not added to a column afterwards, like classical acanthus leaves; they are effectively what produces that column. The standard opinion on Ruskin's theoretical development has been that he started out with aesthetics and proceeded to political economy and social criticism, but he never made such distinctions; for him, mountains, churches and paintings were the result of what he calls "help" and collaboration, and so should they be for us.

The truth is, *life is abstract*; it pervades organic things as much as inorganic ones. And it is this abstract life of agency that makes the nature of Gothic fundamentally digital.

craft and code

Let us not get into a retrospective discussion of what John Ruskin – a man who hated the railways, every cast iron column, and basically every piece of machinery, steam-blowing or not – might have said to such a remark. But the machines he hated so intensely are the ones that spat out the same things over and over, the same profile over the length of a beam, the same ornament cast again and again, the same five million bricks or sugar cubes every day. They made the same thing every time they were operated, and worse, they operated in the same way over and over, turning their operators into machines too. Well, digital machines are different – they thrive on difference. They are something else altogether.

When you print out a piece of writing, is it your work? Was it written by you? I am sure that you are as proud of the page that comes out of the printer as if you had written it in longhand – even if we disregard the now not-very-useful metaphysics of tools, which separate the pen from the typewriter, and from the laptop computer, with its inherent notion of copy-paste.

Richard Sennett believes we should write in longhand first. In *The Craftsman*,[49] he claims that Renzo Piano's architectural designs are proof of the hand's primacy over computing because Piano sketches them by hand first – which is absurd. Sennett's book is generally admirable, he elegantly lays out the various states of work, from the operation of dumb assembly-line machinery to the highly charged flashes of brilliance of artists like Cellini and Stradivarius, while gradually carving out a middle zone for craft and pragmatism. Disappointingly, though, in his conclusion he takes a position of moderation – not the radical middle of our radical picturesque, *the middle as a way out*, but a middle that is stuck between extremes. Our preferred option of implanting craft into machinery is not the same as having little islands of craft surrounded by a vast ocean of machines. We come across the same erroneous idea time and time again, be it in Lewis Mumford, E. F. Schumacher, Jacques Ellul or Ivan Illich: the belief that we can humanize machines by slowing them down, refraining from their continuous use, alternating their use with authentic home- and handcrafting, or using them on a less massive scale. Finding a way to use them more slowly or less often is no good; such theories are generally ones of abstinence, which propose a kind of technological diet. Believe me, diet is not the issue; the point is not to make the same machine *do the same thing more slowly,* at a human pace or in a friendlier way, but to make machines do things differently. The issue is not technology itself but how it relates to human perception and action, whether it renders them extinct or causes them to proliferate – life or death, as Ruskin would say. We should look carefully at how human action organizes itself around machinery, how machinery organizes and even institutionalizes action, and how it slowly takes away or enables freedom. And though the sociological aspects of technology are beyond the scope of my argument, I want to make clear that the machine-work relationship is never predetermined in any way; the extinction of one type of human activity can – and generally does – make another flourish, and must at all times be studied ecologically, not ideologically.

The oldest forms of technology are tools, like the hammer and the sword; they are operated by hand, and interwoven with complete ecologies of action, with a much wider network of activities than simple use. Tools have persistently been misrepresented through the notion of use, which defines action as fixed purpose. For example, let us observe how a butcher dismembers a carcass. See how he points his razor-sharp knife away from him, how he turns it with his elbow and not his wrist, and how he spins and flips the piece of meat simultaneously with the rotations of the knife. See how the knife slides into the unresisting layers of fat, between the layers of muscle, the joints; see how everything falls apart, with apparent effortlessness.

Is this "use"? The gracefulness of the actions, the way the butcher's flowing attention accompanies them without interrupting, is something very different from following the instructions in a manual. The example, which originated with Chuang Tzu in the twelfth century and was used by Baudrillard[50] and then by Sennett as an example of the path of least resistance, is a good illustration of how we work, namely with a complex *motor schema* in our heads – not a mental image of an end product (a tableful of sirloins, tenderloins, prime ribs) or a drawing but a series of actions we know by heart, which have a rhythm as much as an order. It is much more like a tune than an image. Cutting, slicing, paring, the work is always the same and yet always different, the same organization of actions under ever-changing circumstances. Work takes place in time, as a process, and the mental-motor schema determines its order; concentration accompanies action, to prevent it becoming a pensiveness that interrupts the flow.

Let us conduct a little experiment, much simpler than the one with the carcass. Take a sheet of paper and write ten separate *a*s in a row: *a a a a a a a a a a*. Unlike the printing in this book, your handwriting will contain no identical letters, many small differences will occur in various places, though with luck, all the *a*s will be legible. Bringing in the argument from the preceding paragraph, we could say they invariably have the same motor schema of an *a*: curve down, curve up, go down sharply, go sideways. Activated by the fingers and thumb, with a bit of wrist movement and a small amount of corrective feedback via the eyes, the schema turns out a different actual letter every time it is written. The execution or activation of the schema is based in variation; the loops can be thinner, wider, closed or open at the top, though there is a powerful constraint to this variation: legibility. It would be impossible to make every *a* the same, even if one wanted to; the schema is not like a mold, fixed and geometric, but flexible, it does contain points on lines, but those points are movable in the surrounding space to make the lines bend. The schema represents an organization and a procedure more than a description or drawing of an actual form.[51] It is a guide for all the minute muscular forces involved, which works from the inside out (each letter must be "enacted" more than executed), not a negative form casting a positive one.

To extend the experiment somewhat, let's write another ten lines of ten *a*s each. In my own handwriting, two out of a total of 110 *a*s look like *u*s, and two others look like *d*s (which would be rather embarrassing if this weren't being done in the name of science). While the ten *a*s in the first line were mere variations, these four new ones are mutations, what the reader would call "mistakes" and John Ruskin would probably deem "rude" or "savage," and certainly imperfect. Nonetheless, changefulness and savageness are completely continuous. We have seen how changefulness can never be fully isomorphic, and starts to break down on both the small and large scales. And, more importantly, we have also seen that savageness does not come out of the blue; it is not a streak of genius breaking through a system. Rather, it needs changefulness, variation pushed to the limit and beyond. A system not based on variation does not accept imperfection; a Greek, state-run controlling mechanism of elements that are preconfigured and of fixed proportions, and refer constantly to authorized examples, would never be able to absorb crudeness; it would be like a single handwritten *a* amid clones. Since changefulness is a highly coordinated system of movements, of figures channeling force and balancing with other figures, it tries to include everything, but *only up to a point*, when the pattern starts to crack, which does not mean the system is failing but that the pattern is reorganizing itself on another scale. When we step back, we see that another pattern has emerged, which contains the first. Here we arrive at a seemingly paradoxical conclusion: systems based on joints, on elements, do not allow for imperfection and breaks, but continuous systems do.

Again, what did we conclude changefulness was? The coming to life of a motif via figuration, that is, a line with active points on it, a line that, when those points are moved, still runs through all of them, in a new expression. In his explanation of the expressionism of the figure, Worringer constantly refers back to the gesture, to the biomechanics of elbow, wrist and hand and how their collaboration gives us an infinite variety of expression:

> If we trace a line in beautiful, flowing curves, our inner feelings
> unconsciously accompany the movements of our wrist. We feel
> with a certain pleasant sensation how the line as it were grows

out of the spontaneous play of the wrist ... If we meet such a line in another composition, we experience the same impression as if we ourselves had drawn it.[52]

The Northern line has – or better, *is* – a motor schema, and just like the *a*, which is many *a*s and becomes *d*s and *u*s, it is nothing more or less than what today we would call a *script*, or a code, which in the case of handwriting cannot be exact, since we never write a letter by itself but positioned within a word, meaning the letters must adapt to each other's variations. The code itself, then, needs to be flexible, the formula not of a single line but of many lines drawn simultaneously, by many hands acting likewise, coordinated like a flock of birds; and those lines – traceries and tracings – interact, find common points at which to link, merge, cross, form cusps, whatever, as long as the free action results in a structural entity, be it a bundle or a web, a fan or a rose. A computer is not an outgrowth of the hammer, like the four-stroke engine, amplifying the lever that is the human arm; it is not even a tool or an extension, in fact hardly even a medium – it is simply the conflation of design and work. A computer is not a machine that replaces hand-drawing or handicraft; it is *handicraft taking place at the level of drawing and design*, a way of positioning any possible motor schema inside matter itself.

Such a historically strenuous, if not impossible, merging of opposites brings us to an illuminating comparison between John Ruskin and one of his Victorian contemporaries, the two of whom were among no more than a dozen pillars holding up nineteenth-century culture, but positioned as far apart as possible. On the one hand, we have Ruskin's nonnegotiable repudiation of machinery, accompanied by an acceptance only of things that were as natural as possible, in all their uniqueness, all their variation, each crafted by hand, on a certain day in a certain place, under a certain light. Then, at the other extreme, we find Charles Babbage, the inventor of the Difference Engine – no less than the first computer – but also a perceptive critic of Victorian economics. The two men were as antipodal as can be imagined. Whereas Ruskin was against the division of labor, Babbage was emphatically in favor of it, not only because he supported utilitarian laissez-faire economics but especially because he was a radical abstractionist.

Instead of conceiving of machines as simply iron versions of human labor, Babbage understood the whole industrial revolution as a transformation of "making" into "manufacturing" – that is, the making of real things into the abstract organization of that making. Or, in the words of Henry Colebrooke, on awarding Babbage the Astronomical Society's gold medal in 1823: "In other cases, mechanical devices have substituted machines for simpler tools or for bodily labor. But the invention to which I am adverting comes in place of mental exertion: it substitutes mechanical performance for an intellectual process,"[53] therefore not just replacing human labor with mechanical power but mechanical power with the abstract processing of digits. I need not emphasize that this represents John Ruskin's worst nightmare, a world in which "working" becomes "tasking," the execution of labor not only by a machine but by a set of instructions, a code, a punched card read by the movable pins of a machine. The punched card had been invented a few decades earlier to program a Jacquard loom, which – recalling our own notion of changefulness being akin to weaving – directly informed Babbage's steam-powered Difference Engine and, later, his improved Analytical Engine, which he called "a manufactory of figures." As Ada Lovelace said: "We may say most aptly that the Analytical Engine weaves algebraic patterns just as the Jacquard loom weaves flowers and leaves."[54] What makes Babbage's "contrivances" so useful for our thesis is that he saw his engines not simply as devices for doing calculations but as the foundation of a larger machinery for producing material forms, if not the whole material universe.

Firmly remaining on Ruskin's side, however, we should stress that Charles Babbage mistook such abstraction for the production of inevitably pristine objects, manufactured with "unerring precision"[55] and thus without variation, perfectly uniform. Though the formative, organizational forces behind every shape are abstract, as Babbage correctly asserted, this does not mean the real object is not concrete, or lacks specific aspects or unique traits. He simply mistook his Difference Engine for a Platonic cave, in which "the industrial arts realize identity by the unbounded use of the principle of copying."[56] To upgrade the Difference Engine with a capacity for variation, however, one would have to convert its singular, mechanical schema into a biomechanical, multiplied motor schema, to make its punched card flexible and soft, thus making the engine truly differential and allowing the abstraction to be concretized differently each time a product is created, so that the variation of handicraft would become part of the mechanical abstraction – which, all in all, makes a good definition of digital computing.

This is precisely the point at which Sennett's examples run aground. With all due respect, Gehry and Piano are examples of how *not* to use computing. Piano takes a completely gridded, Greek, industrialized system and adds a swoosh by hand, just a single humanized stroke, a gesture that does not configure with anything (often simply resting on top of the structure, in the case of a roof, or wrapping around it, in the case of a wall), that does not result in pattern and becomes an unintentional sign of failing humanism and pragmatism. Gehry's designs consist of large, handmade models of curved surfaces, which are digitally scanned three-dimensionally by a free-moving robot arm. All these warped planes are smashed blindly into each other on every corner of the volume, light-years away from Gothic grace and coordination. The only thing Gehry and Piano have to offer us is quasi-variation, because their introduction of craft into design lasts for but a single, artistic moment, in opposition to the complex, elaborated methodology of Gothic interweaving and braiding. If instead we had such multi-handed craft working at the core of design today – and the digital is the first unified medium of our time to allow for it – it would mean a fundamental displacement not only of work but of the designer's relationship to matter. The equal relationship between craft and matter has inherently been challenged by the designer, who tries to control and impose form on matter but, even acting in good faith and in possession of the right techniques, cannot fully inhabit matter and must assume the position of the mold. If we view the situation in this way, our question becomes how to combine mold and craft in design, at a point when design technique and technology are converging.

Ruskin's strongest criticism of nineteenth-century industrialism concerning the relationship between aesthetics and work invariably focused on the casting of matter into molds, with its implied notion of Babbage's mechanical copying: the handwork of carving only occurs during the making of the mold and is undone by the subsequent repetition and "the unbounded use" of identical castings. Seen from this angle, Ruskin's criticism applies mostly to the problem of the copying, because of its intrinsic lack of variation, and not so much to the operation of carving in one material and casting in another, as is customary in the production of bronze sculpture, for instance. The act of casting in itself, according to Ruskin, only becomes questionable when it approaches a form of deceit, when one material is used to imitate a second. Hence, even in the notion of casting, some carving is still present; the carving of the original negative form (from a block into a designed shape), followed by the casting of the final material (transformation from liquid to solid) in the mold. In short, casting consists of two types of work, not one. Evidently, the creative, qualitative work, the carving, is completely "outnumbered" by the machine work, the casting-copying, which is pure quantity. To better understand this problem, we must pose the question of how work relates to the production of forms in terms of technology, and how such technology relates to matter and to activity.

Adrian Stokes, in his Ruskinian *Stones of Rimini*,[57] distinguishes between two types of sculptural techniques: *carving*, which is stereotomic by nature and works from the outside, and *modeling*, which works from the inside out, building up form through the addition of material. Between the poured liquid state of cast materials and the solid state of carvable materials like marble and even wood, there is a third kind of material, soft and malleable, such as clay or wax, that can be modeled and elaborated during working. In both sculptural techniques, the statue's final contour is the end product of a process. In neither does a mold blindly create a form; in both cases, an active process of formation takes place. In the early eighteenth century, seeking to conceptualize the growth of an embryo, Comte de Buffon came up with a similar idea,[58] a merging of the concepts of carving and modeling, so to speak, when he decided embryos were molded from the inside. Though seriously flawed scientifically, this idea of an internal mold should interest us, especially because it is so contradictory. While a negative form has to be positioned on the outside of the material, in Comte de Buffon's mind, it needed to nestle inside matter to facilitate the principle of a form growing over time rather than being cast in a single moment; therefore, the form needed to be cast in parts, internally, at different moments during a process of formation. Something was at work inside matter. Or, in Ruskin-ian terms, carving and casting operated on a more equal basis than had been thought. Buffon, though, reasoned that the observed biological variation in the world was a case of increasingly bad copies of that first mold, and was therefore gravely mistaken. We would need to understand such an internal mold as staying active during the time of formation, as a mold that is itself variable, undergoing what the French technology philosopher Simondon called "continuous temporal modulation."[59] He reasoned that a triode, for instance, was continuously molding variable electrical information by in-serting a third electrode between the cathode and anode. Simondon termed this variable molding "modulation." The in-between electrode "molds" and modulates a given flow of matter, which means the output exists within a certain range, varying between minimum and maximum states.

Potentially, when seen from a broader perspective that does not only include electrically charged matter but all materials, variable modulation liberates the mold from the doom of identical copies, in which the design work is done once and execution is purely atemporal. Simondon's variable mold would combine a continuous supply of matter, such as we find in in-dustrial casting, with the variable carving of handicraft. The action that is needed during every second of carving – whereas in casting, action is needed only for a single moment – is here called for again, to continuously instruct the mold how to vary. Such a set of instructions, which we characterized earlier as a motor schema, is what today we would call digital code, and also similar to what we know of genetic code, which is precisely such a temporal modulator in a flow of ever-replicating matter, running activation and in-hibition scripts in a variable manner. We should keep in mind that in growth (or decay), there is copying going on; the creativity lies in the stopping and allowing of such copying at certain positions in certain modalities. Quality is the modulation of quantities. Again, with genetic code, the material ac-tivity of multiplication is a given; it doesn't need to be inserted or inspired, but it does need to be regulated, corrected and informed.

Theoretically, the dual relationship between drawing and carving is combined in the concept of digital code, in which each element is fed a coded motor schema, i.e., a set of instructions for how agents should behave in various situations. If we observe many elements behaving simultaneously, a general behavior emerges out of the interactions. We call this generalized, collective behavior a pattern. Again, this does not take work out of the equation. Naturally, programming itself is a complex craft, but that is not what I mean. It is the operational, procedural logic of the Gothic which makes it code-dependent, its relational approach to problems of design – its manner of knitting its way through every question by separating the figural behavior of agents from configurational effects, and its rule-based consistency. Since the early 1990s, if not before, the most persistent misunderstanding about the digital has been that it is somehow "immaterial," even "gnostic."[60] The fact that code is written doesn't make it immaterial or linguistic; on the contrary, the language we speak every day is descriptive, while programming language is instructive. Code talks to things just as things talk to things. If that, do this. If this, do that. Code is not immaterial; it speaks the language matter speaks. This means its instructions tell matter not just to do something but also to stop doing it at a certain point. But speaking a simple language does not result in a simple outcome – far from it. Babbage already grasped this fundamental trait of computing, proposing a transformation of skillful work by individuals into a complex "manufactory" of mindless computation by a large group of clerks, identical to the simple behavior of our changefully tracing angels, which through interaction creates myriad crystalline configurations of incredible beauty and complexity.

Within the framework of human design and production, such a shift means not only the transformation of design from hand-drawing to code-scripting but a move from hand-carving to the laser- and water-cutting of glass and metal sheets under the guidance of numerically controlled machines, and the milling by free-moving robot arms of volumetric blocks of foam and wood to be used as cores for panelwork or unique molds for casting liquids such as concrete. Just as digital code can bring life into elements, instructing them to self-assemble into patterned structures, it can also tell machinery to print, cut, or mill, i.e., to stereotomically carve any given shape at any moment, at the right speed and, more importantly, as a unique part. This technological argument brings us to the following, again seemingly contradictory conclusion: if we want to bring craft to design, that is, move design from the single-swoosh artistic approach to the complex interlacing and interweaving of craft – which is an aesthetics of the elaborated, if not the laborious – all actual manipulation of materials needs to be transferred into the hands of machines. Or, to use a subtle distinction: *as all craft moves toward design, all labor must move toward robotics.* Changefulness, savageness and imperfection evolve during the design stage; the final execution must be perfect – and done by slaves of steel. Our age can expect a totally unforeseen convergence of John Ruskin and Charles Babbage.

Now that we have refined our insight into the nature of digital, we can rephrase Ruskin's list of the characteristics of the nature of Gothic, keeping the same properties, but inevitably changing their order. Whereas his list was arranged ideologically, ours needs to have a more procedural, computational logic, in which each property is actively dependent on the one preceding it. Code often consists of a set of smaller packages of code, activated one by one at different moments during the procedure; again, instead of a single formula there is a strategy of incremental actions, and one package is necessarily activated after another. In short, this code is an algorithmic, stepwise procedure that works over a period of time, in which certain actions are initiated, executed and then stopped, to be overtaken by the next set of actions, and so on, until completion – if any.

Let us observe how this works in the design of a Gothic cathedral according to a coded, digital methodology. Imagine lines on the screen, not stiff and dead but able to stretch, bend, interlock and connect, as if made from that malleable, vital, codified material, all according to Gothic rules, each line straight or circular. Step by step, we will try to describe how each level becomes responsible for tackling a set of design problems within the morphology of the structure:

1. *Redundancy:* Though Ruskin lists this characteristic last, it would be much more correct to start our Gothic operation with redundancy and abundance. Most importantly, we will not define it as the extra ornament left over from all executed operations but as an initial indeterminacy of the available ribs.

Redundancy in information theory is defined as a basic noise permeating all things, an overall relationality that after a program has been run results in effects (grouped shaft, traceried window, webbed vault), but also in-between effects (fan vault) and aftereffects (reticulated walls, pinnacles).

In Gothic digital design, redundancy means the availability of an enormous, but not infinite, number of ribs, organized at first in row-like fashion, which are willing to interact. Usually found in opposing pairs, they are initially straight verticals that start to copy two by two, in fixed increments, when we push the start button.

2. *Changefulness*: Every figure is variable in its own way; it consists of lines activated by points that can be moved sideways, up or down. Such movements – motifs – are limited, however, by the definition of the figure. In short, its variation is parametric, controlled by a continuous function.

Depending on how one sets up the operational systemacy to generate the Gothic cathedral, the bundles of lines will start copying in the longitudinal direction of the nave while at the same time growing upward and, as they bend inward, interlacing into a vault, while the column does the same at the opposite side of the nave. The nave will keep growing until a certain length is reached (checked by the surrounding buildings), when it will turn ninety degrees to create the transepts, though not at all times, and the nave will only be copied sideways to the aisles. Meanwhile, the spaces in between will be filled on the exterior with finer tracery movements.

3. *Rigidity*: All free movement of figures settles into configurational patterns; hence, the Gothic is characterized by a flexible rigidity, a concept not far removed from Ruskin's concepts of help and crystallization. Such rigidity has two modalities, one structural and one ornamental; the former relates rigidity to the actual transfer of loads to the earth, while the latter remains solely configurational, a patterned outcome of line interaction.

In our digital procedure, we can observe three different stages on the screen: in the first, all the lines are straight and unbent; then they bend as they interact; and then they come to a stop after their interaction. They can only stop when ribs either cross diagonally, merge like railway switches, or bifurcate to form liernes and tiercerons. After the aisles have been formed, flying buttresses form as a function of the outer columns.

4. *Naturalism*: Though the figural movement and configurational pattern are not necessarily "natural," they are certainly not alien to us. Such behavior by figures does not mimic human or animal movement, nor does the pattern of configurations mimic crystalline or biological structures, yet there is a fundamental sympathy between the two.

Looking at our screen again, while we would not say our digital lines grow like trees, since they do not bifurcate as branches do, their movement looks familiar, or at least not unnatural. This is not the same as natural or representational, but it is not purely abstract either.

5. *Savageness*: Though Ruskin placed this at the top of his list, I think it is the result of the other operations, not their basis. Yet imperfection is essential, it means that a system that nests figures in all kinds of configurations must meet its limit at several thresholds. Such points appear as heterogeneous breaks in fields of variation. Therefore, systems that don't allow for much changefulness have more breaks and cuts than ones that allow for more variability. These breaks occur on two levels, the smaller-scale level and the larger-scale level of massing. The latter, in particular, makes a Gothic building what it is, with its broken symmetries, sudden additions and unfinished parts.

In our digital breeding box we see thick lines emerging on the growing object, at right angles to the general movement of the figures. Sometimes new spires shoot up following the formation of savage ridges; sometimes they do not because the threshold value has not been met.

6. *Grotesqueness*: When savageness goes further over the limit, the result is a grotesqueness that can be either humorous or monstrous. Since it is a subset of savageness, one encounters it even less often than the previous category.

At the end of our digital Gothic experiment, very strange excrescences may appear at certain points. We do not remove these.

I believe in things

Surprisingly enough, we can thus manage remarkably well with Ruskin's list of characteristics when we look at it from a digital and operational perspective. I can imagine that a number of historically inclined readers will think that I am pushing reality over the limit here, but bringing a historic argument into our own age is impossible without recasting it as a purely conceptual and theoretical one. I am trying to revive Ruskin's argumentation, and to follow it as far as I can, though in another age it seems to lead us into another domain. Today, hundred and fifty years later, it would carry no weight to start advocating a return to handicraft; our world is covered with more ugly buildings every day, there are more unbearable DVDs, disaffected design and useless printed matter than ever. Would it help to start another Guild of St. George colony where we all – all thirty-seven of us – worked by hand, as the world around us was swamped in generic sameness? I don't think so; sharing the same ethics need not result in the same action. Ruskin's morals are unfailingly valid today, although we need them for other reasons, just as he needed the Gothic to save his era from the division of labor, we need it in order to unify design, so architects can be anonymous again, designers can move away from product and commodity, and artists can leave the museums and start occupying real, everyday spaces. The return to variation, more precisely to configurational variation, including a material understanding of it, that I am commending necessarily implies another, more forward-looking Gothic, which probably won't even look Gothic to most of us but nonetheless will show the same rigor, the same changefulness and savageness: an art of digital, configurational variation. Handicraft, while offering variation, cannot provide us with nearly enough continuity; and inversely, industrial casting (prefab) offers continuity but no variation. By bringing the concept of handicraft into the very heart of molding technology, we can have both variability and continuity. Code and modulated fabrication give us exactly that, but let us not forget that code specifically demands an art of configurational variation (be it architecture, design, music or something else) – that is, *a digital Gothic*, not the digital swooshism of a Frank Gehry or the generations following him, which we are supposed to believe defines coded architecture today. My claim is that the Gothic is more digital than any random example of contemporary digital architecture. The problem, the insuperable problem of the contemporary digital Baroque, is its unobstructed ontology, i.e., the fact that it is structured and related before it is formed. Things are already related before they can act, or, in other words, before they can take on form. We see nothing but a persistence of the same old Beaux-Arts, purely artistic modeling in digital plaster of Paris, merely a digital Arts without Crafts, the exertion of sheer technological control over a design that is itself out of control. Of course, it is possible to code anything; one can even code the design of a Greek temple or Miesian skyscraper (recommended only as a freshman assignment), but take a good look at what happens on the screen when you do. All the elements fly in as if from out of the blue, appearing on the screen as if popping out of hidden drawers, stiff and preformed, seemingly moved into position by some exterior force; nothing "forms," nothing bends or interlaces.

What a profound correlation between the vital machine of the Gothic and the vital machine of the digital! Coded properly, the digital could establish a type of formation that is neither completely abstract nor completely organic, because the two states collaborate without a direct, linear relationship. It is mechanical, all right, but only on the lower, molecular scale of the figure; it tends toward organic form on the larger, configurational scale. It is an abstraction that never fully retracts from the real, and an organicity that is never fully accomplished – never completely organic, never completely mechanical. "Then we really may believe that mountains are living?" asks one of the young girls in *The Ethics of the Dust*. "Things are not either wholly alive, or wholly dead. They are less or more alive," responds Ruskin's Lecturer, and he has the girls – not unlike Millais's angels fifteen years before – walk around and grasp each other's hands, as in a dance, creating *"crystals of life,"* to empirically teach them the configurational nature of things.[61]

Less or more alive! Nothing inanimate, no mountain or cloud, can be considered completely dead, and nothing organic can be described as being fully alive at every scale.

My earlier fantasy of a Gothic crystal with a nave proliferating across

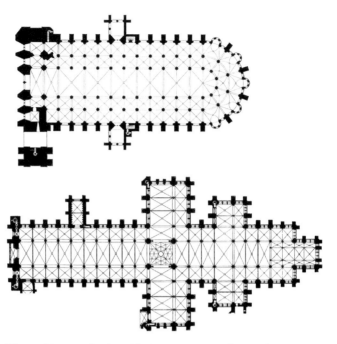

Plans of Bourges (top) and Salisbury cathedral (bottom).

an open field, zigzagging and producing multiple spires and transepts, shows how such vitality depends both on the copying mechanism and the organic tendency toward form, though the final result necessarily depends on context. Obviously, the edges have to tell the copying to halt. This is the sole reason why the English Gothic differs from the French: English cathedrals are exceptionally long because they were generated in open fields or on lawns, while French ones mostly occur in dense urban areas, where proportions were often inflexible. The two are definitely products of the same code. For instance, Salisbury has grown such a long nave that the transept has had to branch off twice, while Bourges has no transepts at all. Instead of making the structure grow into an elongated morphology, the same set of instructions can just as easily generate a short, fat volume; when a site has little depth but plenty of width, the algorithm simply starts adding more aisles instead of transepts. The whole secret is that the algorithm is coded in packages, incrementally, with each section containing a certain amount of variation. And if the content were something other than a church, and the urban environment was different, such a system could generate an endless number of forms most beautiful (as Darwin would have said), varying depending on which problems needed tackling. Ruskin, as well as Revivalist architects like George Edmund Street and George Gilbert Scott, stressed the fact that the Gothic dealt with problems in a relaxed way, which later historians confused with the methodology of functionalism. Obviously, the Gothic system allows for an extra spire, or an extra stair or turret, but not because it resorts to amorphism and simply aggregates accidents. Accident – though it is the motor of the picturesque, according to Ruskin in *The Seven Lamps of Architecture*[62] – is here absorbed by a flexible, relaxed systemacy, which constantly adapts to change rather than exposing accidents as mishaps. When a system adapts to accident, that accident changes from the random to the variable.

Gottfried Semper was the first theoretician to remark that the Gothic was "Scholasticism in stone,"[63] and though he meant the comment to be derogatory, the idea was elaborated and transformed by Worringer in *Form Problems in Gothic* (slightly mistranslated as *Form in Gothic*), and again by Erwin Panofsky – who fails to mention Worringer, by the way – in *Gothic Architecture and Scholasticism* forty years later.[64] Worringer's thesis, though not as precisely formulated and referenced as Panofsky's, is the more interesting of the two, because he takes the supposedly negative aspects and turns them into favorable ones. The well-known criticism that Scholastic thought only convolutes and never reaches a moment of knowledge, Worringer argued,[65] is exactly what makes it so powerful, and Gothic. He affectionately calls it "the ornamental stage of thought."[66] More methodological than epistemological, Scholasticism is a mechanical way of thinking that circumvents problems – *quaestiones* – with a strict, if not Boolean, logic. Its understanding of form as a set of problems, ones not to be resolved but to be handled according to Aristotle's law of non-contradiction, is precisely the logic of Gothic continuity and connectedness. With Scholasticism, we enter a world of things, not of language, and things simply cannot contradict each other. It attacks the problem of the column, just as it attacks the problem of the vault with the invention of the continuous rib, but such problems must be reformulated over and over, until the variations are exhausted. But to be able to be reformulated, both vault and column must share the rib's grammar. Is there a better way of explaining the digital? The digital is a totally Scholastic, numerical, programmatic way of thinking. Not really even mental but much more material, it is a way of thinking akin to the way hands treat matter, as an object. The digital nature of Gothic should be taken literally, it not only offers a new way of rethinking the Gothic in our own time, but it also means the Gothic was already digital (and expressionist) in the twelfth and thirteenth centuries.

Computing in stone is not fundamentally different from Babbage's computing in steel or today's electronic computing, just a lot slower. When, in 1950, Alan Turing[67] repudiated Ada Lovelace's assertions that a digital machine "cannot do anything new" and "cannot do anything that we have not told it to do," he points out that novelty can be conceived as inherent to digital machinery, not external to it. Instead of viewing calculations as an excrescence of the machine's universalism, Turing postulated a machine prone to pure accident. The intelligent machine spans hundreds and hundreds of years of history. At first sight, Leibniz's combinatorian proliferation would seem the likeliest source of our contemporary digital version, were it not for its axiomatically uniform and infinite substance, akin to the white stucco of the same period. Such topological smoothness can only be actualized when it finds no obstruction in matter.

When we look back much further, however, we encounter the Scholastic obsession with defining everything as being made of something. For medieval philosopher John Duns Scotus, general universals were as real as individual particulars ("the universal as universal does not exist"[68]). The intellectual goal of Scholastic thought was to construct a faith in God through a notion of things (not vice versa), making Him as actual as everything else. The Gothic universe is never smooth but granular. However, as with tracery, the granules operate smoothly and take on the form of fibers. The Gothic successfully combines the elementary and discrete state of things we find in Greek ontology with the flexibility and continuity of Baroque ontology, correcting the one with the other. In the Baroque operation, matter has to be ground into the finest powder before form can be explored in all directions, while in the Gothic, the material constituents stay present – in a nonmaterialist way, mind you, losing their mechanical rigidity along the way and exhibiting a pliability similar to, but not to be confused with, that of the Baroque fold. Both are vibrant worlds, though in the Baroque universe things emerge from an already structured, already coherent white paste while in the Gothic one they interweave and entangle. In the Deleuzian fold system,[69] continuity always precedes singularity, while in the rib system, entities precede continuity: Gothic things are thing-actions. Differently than in the billiard ball universe, however, such an action immediately divides itself up, splitting in two directions: the figure changes form (what else is an act?) while at the same time relating to other figures. The figure does not change by itself, nor can it act on others without changing. And, differently than in the white-fold universe, things stand on their own and have the freedom to change sympathies and to engage with any of the other members. It is Gothic ribs vs. Greek sticks vs. Baroque folds.

One has to understand that in the Gothic world of design, ribs are not like components as we understand them today, like bolts or screws predestined to fit only in one way, existing in relations of necessity. A rib more resembles a twig in a bird's nest, what we have previously called a "nonpart," which ascends to the role of part only through relationality, through shared action, a form of connecting that can be manifested in acts as various as stacking, interlocking and entwining, where sometimes the whole length of the member is used and sometimes only a single point, or a set of points, or shorter increments of the length. Though the physical connection can be a close one, the relation between such components is not fixed. At first, the twig is enveloped by a range of actions, a fundamental freedom, which is sacrificed to become part of a nest of twigs. Each of the twigs acts in its own specific way, and together these acts produce an overall stability, which is again the way the nest acts. Stability is not a form of rest or balance at all. We marvel at the design of a nest when we find an abandoned one; it is clearly no less intricate and delicate than, say, Rouen cathedral, and maybe even more so, since its level of imperfection is much more developed than Ruskin could ever have imagined possible. It would be nonsensical not to call this myriad of twigs a design, since it has more than enough aspects of one (it is a brilliant compound of ornament and structure, it is very well and consistently articulated, and it cleverly serves multiple purposes, such as stability, insulation and protection), but surely we cannot assign these qualities to the bird and proclaim it the designer. There is intelligence in the making of the nest, and there is design, but these occur *between things*, not behind or above them. This is exactly why it is computable. The natural theologist William Paley could not have been more wrong when he compared design without a deity to the miraculous finding of a watch on a heath,[70] as if things resembled wholes with predefined parts, each restricted to a single act. Wholes do not look as if they have been designed by someone, they look much better and much more intelligent.

To clarify further, I disagree both with commentators who deny the existence of design by saying that all wholes simply "emerge," in nothing less than a miraculous plopping into being, and at least as much with those who say design is simply the sign of a benevolent designer, a plopping as miraculous as pure emergence. Though wholes are tinkered and Gothic, frayed, full of redundancy and contingency, this does not mean their existence is mere coincidence. In the process of interaction between things, the initial amount of freedom of action starts to slowly dissipate as more structure is acquired. That is *Gothic ontology*: there is plenty of accident, yes, but accident leading to substance, and there are huge amounts of flexibility, but flexibility leading to rigidity. Things do not miraculously meet in a single moment, either through magical emergence or magical intervention; rather, they settle step by step, in a process that takes on more direction the more it progresses, trading the initial vagueness for increased determination. The secret, though, is that this trade is never fully closed, with only finality remaining, the process ending and the thing happily persisting ever after.

With Gothic ontology, things not only add up through enumeration but internally – and accidentally – change as they do so, combining the discrete state of number with continuity. And, if there is still room left for a distinction between substance and accident after such a remark, it would be purely one of nuance, no greater than that between, say, maroon and mahogany. Let us keep in mind that the one-dimensionality of the rib, as much as the notion of the figure, solves the apparent paradox of discreteness and continuity, similar to that of particle and wave. Viewed in this way, Gothicism is the *string theory* of aesthetics, dissolving the opposition of part and relation. Unlike Roman bath houses and Romanesque churches, Gothic cathedrals *are made not of stones but of ribs*. Stone would be passive if not shaped by forces into a rib, and the ribs channel the forces, enabling the stone to act. Unlike in stone architectures, in the Gothic the positioning of the joints between the carved blocks is totally irrelevant and often hardly visible, while the grooves between the ribs are extremely articulated and visible. It is the ribs that organize the stone (not stones), and therefore it would not be right to consider them as merely a formal tool functioning apart from matter; by their nature, they act in a constructivist or, as we have defined it, configurational way.

I am not sure if this describes a universe that *ends* with God, as opposed to one starting with God – that would sound more like science fiction than theology – but it certainly looks like it. It is an intriguing thought, and one that goes completely against the second law of thermodynamics (entropy).

Perhaps you are wondering whether rewriting Ruskin's notion of the Gothic with digits is not merely another all-too-timely and fashionable project, but it was absolutely inevitable that a machine thriving on configurational variation would one day meet its aesthetic ally. It was bound to start exploring its own nature, which is simply *the Gothic nature of the digital*. It is Gothic not because of the stained-glass window foreshadowing the glowing screens that today cover whole buildings, as Virilio once suggested, but solely because of its vital materialism. Combinatorial machines understand all form as calculated (almost an exact quote from Leibniz), while configurational machines distinguish their universal computing power from what is actually calculated. Ruskin's "perpetual novelty" is truly a radical concept. Gothic things stand out as purely accidental substance, of which the form *escapes* its calculation. Therefore, the universalism of the device does not render the formal result equally universal and indifferent; rather, it turns it into something fully unique and, well, beautiful.

Why does the Gothic seem to be best understood in art and architectural history by "dilettantes" (Worringer and Ruskin, both expressionists) and so much less well by the official spokespeople (Frankl, Jantzen, Von Simson, Panofsky)? It seems to me that this is mainly owed to the structure of historiography. Much too often, architectural history is about that vague modernist concept, "space," or worse, "meaning," or, worst of all, "iconology"; such terms are wholly irrelevant to the Gothic.[71] A cathedral is hardly interesting in spatial terms; iconologically, it is ridiculous (except for the statues and the stained-glass windows, which are meant to be read) and in terms of meaning, incomprehensible. And the argument of the microcosm is also continually resurrected, the idea that Gothic "represents" the world, or the universe, and naturally God too. Of all the arguments, this is the worst – as if the world, and the universe, are anywhere other than where you are right now. I would rather hear Ruskin saying the Gothic embodies "a profound sympathy with the fullness and wealth of the material universe" than Panofsky explaining to us what it means. There is no meaning, just construction.

Why does architectural history not simply work with techniques, materiality and morphologies? By techniques, I mean those of design as well as building; materiality is what the two have in common, and the concept is thus a much broader one than structure. The third, morphology, is the final effect, the result of the other two, and covers a much broader idea than the familiar term "typology" (but much narrower than the vague "form"), because typology is fixed in advance and is not active on every scale of the building. Each of the three has its own history, and each of the three affects the others. This classification makes no a priori distinction between ornament and structure, nor between structure and form. Forms evolve, and consist of tendencies of continuous transformation, for none of the three elements are ever in balance. It is never the ideas that change; if there are ideas, they follow the above three. If there is one thing that cannot be cast in stone, it is an idea. Language simply never precedes form, for it is not instrumental, and if it is, it is code, not language. Unfortunately, only a few biologists have ventured into art theory, but one of the best is Alfred Haddon, whose *Evolution in Art*[72] simply looks at forms as forms, made by groups of people, using certain materials and techniques, and with a certain morphological history. One must look at forms as if one does not understand them, simply observe what they do and how they do it. Of course, Focillon's *The Life of Forms in Art* formulates a clear program for such an approach ("That our idea of matter should be intimately linked with our idea of technique is altogether unavoidable"[73]), but not the method itself. And his *The Art of the West* (one of whose two volumes discusses the Gothic in full) can hardly be described as exemplary of such a program and is still full of references to meaning.

What good to us are Sedlmayr's baldachin, Jantzen's diaphanous structure, and Panofsky's Scholasticism if we get to hear nothing about the techniques by which these effects come about? All of them surely exist, but they can be achieved just as well through other means besides the Gothic rib. None of these concepts comes even close to explaining the specific figural-configurational nature of the Gothic, as Ruskin and Worringer do. It is the means and techniques that determine the idea, not the other way around. And then, when one thinks one has distilled an idea, one can be certain it is the wrong one. In the Gothic, the means are specific and unique, and it is these means, set in train by design and building techniques, that make the Gothic what it is.

The effect is "diaphanous," of course, but the word does not capture the true theoretical crux of the Gothic – namely, that *walls and windows are of the same order*. This can be done only through study of the connection between the design techniques (reticulation, articulation, interweaving, molding) and material building techniques (carving, stereotomy). The perfectly reasonable, commonplace conclusion that windows are open and walls are not does not apply in the Gothic. In the Gothic design technique, the fact that the ribs weave the building is primary; how and with what (glass or stone) the interstitial openings are eventually filled is secondary. Its fabric doesn't make the cathedral "transparent" – certainly not "phenomenally transparent,"[74] in the modernist sense of an object penetrated by an exterior world – but it does make it delicate and fragile. This tendency in the Gothic is generally viewed as anti-wall or pro-window ("an architecture of light"); neither notion draws attention to what is actually going on: all the elements are turning into relationships, into threads and fibers. It is its overall delicacy, rather than light as a form of antimatter, that makes the Gothic so "spiritual," the word Worringer and many others after him have used to describe the Gothic. The term has some uncomfortable connotations, which shouldn't deter us from using it; on the contrary. In the first place, this spirituality has nothing to do with religion or Christianity. Gothic cathedrals are Christian churches, of course, but that doesn't mean the mental structure of Christianity automatically explains the Gothic in any way; even Ruskin knew that. Secondly, the notion of spirituality replaces that of "idea."

The Gothic is *an architecture of spirituality, not of ideas*. Idea stands in opposition to materiality, transcending it; spirituality stands on the same side, sympathizing with it. Or, to word it more strongly, idea exists outside materiality, in antithesis to it, while spirituality takes place within it, inhabiting it; this is why an architecture of heaviness suffices for the former while the latter requires that everything be thinned out, made delicate and movable. The act only looks like one of "dematerialization," but that word is a major philosophical trap if ever I saw one. No such thing is taking place (how could it?). The fact that the building gets lighter does not mean it becomes less material; less material is merely needed to build it. The material becomes more active and less inert. The Gothic provides an *improved view of matter*, not an antimaterial one. But although material, the Gothic offers no direct bodily experience of materiality; again, it is no Baroque, no Rococo, not sensual and physical; it is not happiness, ecstasy or theater but a perfectly ordinary everyday relationship with … well, everything. It is not about forming an idea of the world (*Weltanschauung*) but about being connected. Hence, the Gothic is an architecture of *relationality*, of entanglement, an architecture that constantly forges new relationships and expresses them in every possible form and shape.

This actually makes it ecological and topological rather than organic, as William Morris thought.[75] The Gothic makes this-place-here into every place, and this-moment-now into always. Maybe not everything-everything, but everything-enough, and maybe not always-always, but always-long enough. Enough so that you start caring about other things. As you see this thing here and now, in fact you are "seeing" all things, or, as Ruskin says, you are experiencing "a sympathy" with everything. But "seeing" is not the right word; it is not about an image. "Believing" is actually much better –

another uncomfortable word, like "spirituality," although it too refers not to something transcendent but to things. *I believe in things.* Seeing becomes saturated with believing. How else can we orient ourselves in this "mighty Commonwealth of things," as Wordsworth called it? One might ask: Is that not a bit weird and unnecessary, believing when you can actually see things? Well, the issue is precisely that you cannot see them, for they lie hidden behind the horizon, or are too tiny, or lie under your feet or behind your back, but you believe they are there – not as a collection of objects but in all their connectedness; that is, in their relatedness to this thing here. It is not that we imagine them but that we *feel* them, we stretch one thing out spiritually across all the others, by an act of sympathy. Seeing is a concrete experience in which we single out one object amid our basic relatedness to things. Yet this doesn't mean our background relatedness disappears; the selected thing is still tied in with the others. Between concrete experiences, we still experience abstractly; even without an object, we are still ready, so to speak. Even without content, experience is charged. We could see this readiness as belief or spirituality – not faith, hallucination or even imagination but more of an awareness; a basic, given involvement of ourselves with things. To believe in things is to be prepared to be involved.

And, by the way, belief in things stands in diametrical opposition to what today we call "the media." There, you see everything and believe nothing.

Monet's Rouen series. I keep looking at them all the time, one page after another. He has painted the same façade of Rouen Cathedral over and over – warming up in the morning light, ice-cold in December, on a gray afternoon, in the morning fog, in a glorious summer sunset. Thirty amazing paintings, all from the same angle but all in different light, at various times of day, various times of year. Compare them to Ruskin's plates, his pages filled with moldings, and all the grouped shafts. Monet's paintings show a single Gothic thing over time, Ruskin's plates all the different variations of one Gothic thing; I see the two as reflections. Formation and experience mirror each other; first, time is reflected in form, then form in time. Monet's light immediately overwhelms us; of course, it is much thicker and more

Claude Monet. *Rouen Cathedral. The Portal, Morning Fog* (1894).

viscous than light as we know it. No southern sun brightens up this northern church; light is not cast on it. Rather, the stone itself seems to shine, completely reversing the notion of the Gothic as transparent, and also reversing the experience of the stained glass in the interior, making the whole building radiate light.

Monet's Rouen glows – which is perfect. There is no chiaroscuro in the Gothic, no white marble, no contours, except the fractal one of the roof, which is not a roof but a landscape of spires, pinnacles and buttresses that dissolves anything defining a volume, such as a cornice. The northern Gothic is one of deep grooves, ribs and moldings, the southern Gothic one of marble paneling. Why is the northern mostly viewed from the interior and the southern from the exterior? Why, furthermore, is the northern Gothic always treated as if it scarcely has an exterior at all (Semper considered it naked and uncovered), as something turned inside out? The Gothic amalgam of stone, light and rain mixes dirt with design, as we can see in Pugin's diagrams, with all that water dripping off the moldings and intersecting with the eyes' gaze upward, as both enjoy the profile. It is the light that dresses the building, not the shadows; the numerous stone dressings cause it to nestle in the countless profiles; everything seems to absorb light and radiate it back. Again, wall and window are of the same order, both expelling light outward as much as they drink it in.

This light is decidedly different from that of the Mediterranean sun, which outlines things against a blue sky; this light is diffuse and opaque, mixed with clouds, with limestone, with the dirt in all the profiles. This is animism as opposed to metaphysics. All things Greek drop out of the blue, from a cloudless sky of idealism, finished, pure and polished; nothing is grown, no work or sweat required. In opposition to this, we find no metaphysics in the northern Gothic, the spirits enter from soaking wet ground, out of mud and dirt, not immaculate sky. It is sky against ground, beach against forest, and hence gods against spirits, or as we know them, ideas against things, ideas thought against things made.

chapter two

the matter of ornament

At the start of the twenty-first century, having passed through the twentieth and its fatal obsession with the sublime, we can hardly imagine any longer how unthinkable it was a hundred and fifty years ago to leave the surfaces of things – vases, walls, chairs – as plain and bare as we know them today. We must be the first generation of Homo sapiens to know objects only in their naked state. To us, a wall without wallpaper, bas-relief or wood panel-ing, a wall that has simply been painted – white, more often than not – is normal. Our cars are as smooth and undecorated as if they had been pol-ished, as are our razors, refrigerators, television sets, laptops and mobile phones. Today, we live in a vast universe of smooth, polished objects. And it is not only machines made by machines that are bland but our cups and plates, too; our paintings come without frames, our buildings clad in smooth concrete or steel panels, our bathrooms tiled in shiny monochrome. All our objects are treated in such a way that, were we to show them to John Ruskin, Owen Jones or Gottfried Semper (the main protagonists of the present chapter), they would recoil in horror, ashen-faced, with their hands covering their eyes and their heads bowed in total disbelief. To them, seeing an object of design bare would have meant being confronted with a thing untreated, or worse, treated without care or feeling, like a thing thrown in their faces. It would have been unspeakably rude.

Theoretically, such a gaping cultural divide is not at all a bad position to start from, since today we so completely and fundamentally lack tech-niques of ornamentation that we must conceptualize it in full before we can even begin to reconsider it. We will do so, automatically, without nostalgia or the need to recreate, since our quest will have to take us from specific examples of ornament to a general theory. If we can find a way to reconstruct the reasons why ornament has always been so evident, then we can hope to retrieve it without a need to copy, comment or historicize. In a similar vein, we will have to retrieve the steps of its disappearance in order to ensure we do not follow the same path again.

I have always believed the disappearance of ornament was related to a matter of scale, and more precisely, to scaling up, because around a century ago the problems of design began to shift from the domain of surfaces to that of volumes. We needed to house more people in more and more buildings that got bigger and bigger, to produce more objects for more people, to move them more quickly from one place to another, to print them more books, more magazines, more newspapers. This certainly could have been one of the reasons behind the decline of ornament, the fact that massing – the composition of volumes – gradually became the primary focus of design, in place of the composition of surfaces. We have to keep in mind, though, that the aesthetic problem of massing is directly related to the social appearance of the masses, so we can never trace the disappearance of ornament back to a single event as primary cause. Both massing and the masses are highly industrialized products, so to speak, since they cannot exist without mass production, without cars, trains and televisions. Such a mass – for the moment I will not distinguish between the two types – must therefore be a homogeneous one, a substance without qualities, a machined mass that by its nature would have a shiny, smooth and polished surface, since it can only assume the qualities of the machine that produced it. In the end, the course of things toward abstraction, their shaking off of clothes step by step, is a process in which every influence is intricately related to every other. At some point, the concept of unformed, unarticulated mass, of pure substance, became the only option left, and the reason for the loss of ornament is found not so much in the metaphysical search for naked truth, as Adolf Loos[1] would have had us believe, but in the fatal disconnection of matter and form – or of substance and matter, since the former is abstractly raw and the latter necessarily formed. And at all times formed with texture, as we will see again and again in this chapter. By definition, matter, having passed through a continuous process of formation, takes on form and texture simultaneously, while mass lies passively in a reservoir, ground down to the smallest possible particles, waiting to be poured in some form or other. (It seems that I am already mixing up the masses in the streets and the semiliquid concrete that is poured into molds, both of which emerged during the same period.) In a sense, mass does not even have an outside, it is pure interior.

Ornament is profoundly related to matter, to the way it structures itself as it undergoes forces, be they natural or technological, which is a complicated way of saying that ornament and texture share the traces of being made, of the constant reconfiguration of matter. Our first task at this point becomes to resist thinking of ornament as applied, as stuck on a bland surface afterwards – to resist the thought of an underlying nakedness, and instead to see matter and ornament as mutually dependent. We will have to do so by drawing a clear line between mass and matter and following matter along its spectrum of different states of viscosity or aggregation. This path will, of course, lead us to Semper's *Stoffwechselthese*, which brilliantly mixes up physiology and architectural evolution into something not unlike Ruskin's amalgam of geology and architecture;[2] but it will also lead us to the broader concept of pattern, which will bridge the notions of natural texture and artificial ornament. We will find that pattern is the main expression of a self-abstracting capacity of matter, as we find it in the wrinkling of a face, the ribbing of sand, or the striping of a zebra, that is, the organization of surfaces by lines. In a sense, it comes down to a exchanging of positions: pattern in nature as self-abstraction, and ornament as abstract texture. Ornamentation, as we will see, approaches the problem of dimensionality from two opposite directions. One moves downward on the dimensional ladder, operating from *surface to line*; this is *tessellation*, or tiling, as we know it from Owen Jones's mosaics and encrustations. The other proceeds upward through the dimensions, from *line to surface*; we know it as weaving, the interlacing of *ribbons*, such as we find in William Morris's wallpaper designs or Celtic knotwork. Like earlier scholars, we will find that modernism was the result not of advancements in the fine arts of painting and sculpture but of discussions and developments in the decorative arts, in the world of ornament. And, not without shock, we will discover a terrifying monster hidden there, one that we know by the name of "abstraction" but John Ruskin disparaged as "cruelty," a characterization I have come to find astoundingly accurate. Sometime in the middle of the nineteenth century, an alliance was forged of abstraction, machines, grids and purism, leading us straight into a century of minimalism, world war and genocide. Needless to say, crime, savagery and primitivism have persistently been part of the discussions around ornament, but perhaps not in the way they should have been. Only at the end of our quest will we see Alan Turing take up Charles Babbage's main invention and turn it completely on its head, finding a way of abstracting not directed at a purified final destination but deployed at the start of a process of formation; a reverse abstraction that will guide us to pure variation, opening a new road to ornament and to an aesthetics of tenderness and sympathy, which we have yet to discover.

ruskin: wall veil and earth veil

Not surprisingly, we start our journey by consulting John Ruskin, again by reading *The Stones of Venice*. We turn our attention to a peculiar chapter in *The Foundations*, the first of the three volumes, entitled "The Wall Veil,"[3] which, like "The Nature of Gothic," is a bold piece of reasoning and rhetoric. As we follow Ruskin's descriptions of all the architectural elements, all the so-called members, such as bases, cornices and shafts, we find the description of the wall starting not with stones, stucco or symmetries, as one might expect, but with an elaborate three-page description of a mountain called Mt. Cervin, one of Europe's highest. We know it better by its German name, Matterhorn, located on the border between Switzerland and Italy and with a slope facing each country. Obviously, this is to be expected, given Ruskin's obsession with mountains (the extensive fourth volume of *Modern Painters* is completely dedicated to them, to peaks lateral and central, and their ridges, their "aiguilles," "crests" and "precipices";[4] and he continually compares architecture to mountains in *The Seven Lamps of Architecture*'s chapter "The Lamp of Power"). The narrative is breathtaking. Ernst Gombrich, who – like most twentieth-century scholars of art and architecture – is not particularly fond of John Ruskin, called him a proto-expressionist,[5] and that is exactly what he was, not only in his premonition of Bruno Taut's and Wassily Luckhardt's mountainous architectures but moreover in his perception of form as a material index of forces gathering and converging into a shape.

A mountain has faces; like a building, it orients itself in an environment; but it is simultaneously something that has been directed, vectorized, a cluster of many vectors making up the mountain as an architectural object:

> It has been falsely represented as a peak or a tower. It is a vast ridged promontory, connected at its western root with the Dent d'Erin, and lifting itself like a rearing horse with its face to the east ... The eastern face of the promontory is hewn down, as if by a single sweep of a sword, from the crest of it to the base.[6]

In short, Mt. Cervin is a mass sculpted by vast forces – not an undifferentiated mass but one layered out of courses of stone set down "in their suc-

John Ruskin. *The Cervin, from the East, and North-East*. Plate 38 from *Modern Painters*, Vol. IV, Part V: Of Mountain Beauty (engraving by J. C. Armytage, 1856).

cessive order," "of a thickness and strength continuously varying," "laid by snowy winds and carved by the sunshine – stainless ornaments of the eternal temple." And, Ruskin adds with more determination, it is a mountain that "should be to us an example of the utmost possible stability of precipitousness attained with materials of imperfect and variable character."[7] Slowly, he combines the savage, picturesque mass of the Matterhorn to a structuring and layering of that mass that is as least as wild and imperfect, and after introducing a geological aesthetics, he proceeds to put the final nails of architectural argument in the critical coffin. "I believe we may conclude with great certainty that it is better and easier to strengthen a wall necessarily of imperfect substance," he argues. And "the decorative reasons for adopting the coursed arrangement, which we shall notice hereafter, are so weighty, that they would alone be almost sufficient to enforce it: and the constructive ones will apply universally."[8] All the major Victorian architects, such as the amazing William Butterfield and George Edmund Street, started changing their designs after reading this sentence; no brick wall escaped variation in the colors of its courses and even the sizes of the stones themselves. "The Wall Veil" was hugely influential.

I believe this was the first, and probably the only, architectural theory to successfully relate massing to texture through interdependence. And it works from the inside out, making it a showcase for expressionism: as the mountain is being formed, it expresses its courses at the surface in a way that communicates the same set of forces. Massing and texture are created under the same laws, as they would have put it in Ruskin's day. The form of the Matterhorn cannot be understood without understanding the geological layering of sediment that channels and guides the forces. Forces operate here in two ways, from the inside out – constitutively – and from the outside in – erosively. However, the mountain's texture – the "wall veil" – is not merely draped but also encrusted, covered with its own material, in a self-draping, a self-adornment. Such a consistency of material generally leads to what modernists call transparency, since the internal structure is exposed at the exterior, but here that internal structure transforms while being exposed to new forces such as weathering and erosion, which turn it into drapery. The wall veil is pressed out of the mountain, not draped by snow falling on its slopes but by the stones themselves, covering it in layers and courses, guided by a system of breaks and fractures. Geological articulation, by varying the hardness and orientation of the stone courses, completely structures the generation of form; the promontories, the crests, the faces all result from the stone's qualities and composition. So the process also works upward in dimensions, texture guides the shaping of form.

Here we encounter a new theory of ornamentation, which is simultaneously a theory of construction, a "third way" of treating architectural surfaces. Let us, for a moment, consider the other two, which are much better known. One way is to leave the skin undraped, to expose the naked structure to the world, waving that modernist flag of transparency, either literally or phenomenally, as Rowe and Slutzky's theory states. The other is based in a theory of drapery, of draping as an act distinct from erecting the structure, with the drape being cast over from the outside and the structure in fact kept naked underneath the cloth, untransformed, simply given a (postmodern) mask. Mask and skeleton, having persistently defined the flimsy metaphysics of architecture's history, are merely two sides of the same coin. Ruskin's third way is different, proposing a kind of generative relation between the other two, a process that originates on the inside, as in the first approach, yet is dressed, as in the second. It offers the depth of structure, but without transparency, and the opacity of the mask, but without flatness. The structure is pushed outward, but as it is exposed it *transforms*, like the crust of molten lava, the canopy of a tree, foam on water, or the courses of a mountain. It is no accident that these are *fractal* examples; the transformation of structure into texture is one of refinement, a recursive scaling, such as from rib columns to rib tracery. The word "veil" is particularly well chosen by Ruskin. Ornament is a demonstration of *delicacy*, that is, the surface is not merely made of ultrathin and refined elements, but the elements configure, and, as delicate as they are, they could even carry load, because they configure collaboratively. Filigree, tracery, inlay, cloisonné, lacework, guilloché and fretwork are typical examples. Even the inventor of fractals, the late Benoit Mandelbrot, fairly early in *The Fractal Geometry of Nature*,[9] expresses a preference for Beaux-Arts ornament above Miesian reticulation because of its fractalism, i.e., its unstoppable urge to add another detail. Natural texture, and abstract texture, i.e. ornament, have a depth, not of space but of surface, which offers us a very precise definition of texture.

To clarify this relationship between encrustation and drapery, it might help to look briefly at Ruskin's ambivalent relationship to the northern Gothic and its southern, Venetian counterpart – it embodied a conflict that persisted all his life, and for good reason. We should recall his repeated travels through Europe, which invariably had the same, very symbolic structure: crossing the Channel by boat; arriving in Normandy, homeland of the Flamboyant (Amiens, Rouen, Abbeville, St. Lô, Beauvais); moving on to the Alps, where he stayed for a month or two, climbing and drawing; and then finally journeying to Pisa, Verona and Venice. In other words, the conceptual Alps are invariably divided up and balanced between the northern "linear" and the southern "surface" Gothic, the ribboned and the encrusted. I do not think we need to view this opposition as mutually exclusive, as so many have done, including Ruskin himself, often.[10] We can instead safely view them as two solutions to the same problem, proceeding from opposite directions; we can see the relationship between line and surface as a dynamic one of movement and transition. Both options are concerned with dividing up a surface, either by means of interlacing lines and ribbons or the breaking up of the surface into courses and ornamental layers or tiles. The northern way drives the columns into the wall, not simply to open it up but to weave a smaller-scale web of tracery, in which columns branch sideways to form windows, absorbing color with stained glass; the southern way encrusts the wall with patterns, whether horizontal layers of alternating colors or checkered patterns of inlaid marble. There is structure and ornamentation to both. All the other differences – the amount of openness, the amount of color – are, I think, mere climatic influences enlarging the difference between the two options, but operating according to the same rules of texture to turn the whole surface expressive.

Before we watch John Ruskin entering into a theoretical dispute (though at a polite distance) with Owen Jones, we should acknowledge that both moved the concept of ornament beyond an incidental meandering band here and foliate capital there – the Greco-Roman variety – toward entire textured or diapered surfaces from a drystone wall of extreme crudeness at one end of the spectrum to the most exquisite tiled pattern at the other, again navigating between savageness and changefulness.

We could label Ruskin's geological notion of ornamentation as "naturalist," but the reverse observation is as valid, or more so, and surely more interesting: nature shows an architectural tendency, and art occurs everywhere, not just as design but as a working collaboration between accident and structure, that is, an undivided aesthetics of pattern and texture. What does not have texture? Texture emerges at a point where surfaces start to show linearities, even actual lines, where they start to show themselves as being made up of lines – as, in a word, woven ("texture" stems from *texere*, "weaving"), or in another word, worn, and in still another, wrinkled – thus not necessarily made of fabric but occupying a zone of transition: are we seeing a system of lines or a surface? Our education is soundly unambiguous and Euclidean: lines exist as contours and edges, delineate things as objects, envelop them in universal three-dimensional space, release them from their backgrounds – but this idea is untenable. Ruskin shows time after time in *Modern Painters* that only gradations and variations exist, that is, gradations not only of hue and brightness but of dimensions themselves. Texture occurs – I will continue to describe it as an event – when enough lines combine to produce a surface, as when fibers nest and entangle, or when surfaces start to produce lines, such as ripples on water or cracks in drying mud. It seems that only the in-between of line and surface truly exists – all that is not Euclidean – and the finite dimensions are just illusory stations in active zones of transition.

Just look at Pre-Raphaelite painting, and more specifically at Millais's pictures such as *Ophelia*, *Autumn Leaves*, or the astounding *Mariana* from 1851, which modernist scholars somehow always dismiss as "realist," or even "photorealist," as if we were looking at the chrome grille of a parked truck in California reflecting a store window and neon advertising, which is not right at all. *Mariana* does not question the status of the real, simply because here the real is not haunted by its reverse, as in the mediated USA, but made part of an infinitely textured universe – "clothed," as Tennyson would say. This is a painting in which there is no fundamental difference between Mariana's velvet dress, the wallpaper, the metalwork of her intricate belt,

John Everett Millais. *Mariana* (1851).

the stained glass, her hair (each strand individually painted), the leaves, the trees, the bushes and, at the heart of it all, the almost-finished embroidery on the table: *everything is texture*, all is inextricably woven into the world-cloth. There is no space separating things, no visual depth; everything is filled in, knitted together. To make is to see, and to see is to make, in fact, Millais weaves his paintings, paints them so meticulously stroke by stroke that they become tapestries.

The autumn leaves and the creases in the white tablecloth are not, because of their minute detail, realistic or in any way photographically precise, but unique and particular. Every leaf is an individual, curling, drying and catching the light in its own way; nothing is the same, and everything has the right to be acknowledged. There is no transcendence, each leaf refuses to stand in for all the other leaves; it is just that one, at that moment, though without being "captured." There is no momentariness at all, Mariana is not caught in any act; she seems to stand there forever, with her weary eyes half closed and not looking outside or at anything specific, hands locked on hips, thumbs pointing forward, arching her back but hardly letting herself go. Though she has risen from her stool and put down her needlework, the transition is not completed, but suspended. In contrast, the numerous paintings of the Lady of Shalott, another Tennyson topic dearly taken up by all Victorian painters,[11] show the reverse: the subject jumps up, startled by Lancelot passing by on his horse. But Mariana seems to know what the Lady of Shalott, caught in the wires of her loom, does not know yet: there is no use extracting yourself from the texture of things. If there is no space, where can you run to? *Mariana* is painted as a *preservation*; it is a real that is not of the flesh but spiritualized, cast in colored stone, encrusted.

In Pre-Raphaelite painting things come to a stop; becoming textured is their end. When we look at the most stunning painting of them all, William Holman Hunt's *The Scapegoat* of 1854, in which a long-haired goat reaches the end of its life on the encrusted shores of the Dead Sea. You can almost hear the hooves puncturing the crust of salt as they take their final staggering steps. The secret communication between the undulating hairs of the goat's coat and that vast mineral world around it is of an absolute beauty. It seems unequal, but only the small animal is actively presented, being a sacrifice, while the surrounding world is completely passive and can only receive. How on earth can the offering of that small animal be sufficient, and can its life be weighed against the uninhabitability of the landscape? The equation can only be solved aesthetically, by giving the hairs extra length and extra undulation, adding extra holes in the crust, and including skeletons of previously deceased animals at left and right in the water. The delicacy of texture is enhanced by an increased fragility of the creature that is extraordinary.

Of course, Hunt, like Millais, often accompanies his paintings with lines of text – in this case, not Tennyson but the Bible.[12] However, we should not for a moment think that these lines provide us with the artwork's "meaning" – that horrible word that lets us believe the mind can trade aesthetics for textual interpretation. Here the artist has already done that for us, so to attach any meaning to the work would be futile. The biblical lines may be its subject, but they are not its object; the object – the end – is beauty itself. Subjects are merely vehicles; the painting is the destination, not the scriptural text, which is just a point of departure. In other words, the picture solves what the text cannot. In twentieth-century painting, the artist's main problem – when to stop[13] – remained unresolved, but in Pre-Raphaelite art it was solved again and again: things, fibrous things, collaborated with the shared aim of beauty. But note that this is not the beauty of things becoming drowsy and lethargic, as we so often observe in the Victorian classicism of Albert Moore and Frederic Leighton, who populated their works with endless slabs of marble and sleeping women – pointing the way to aestheticism and *l'art pour l'art* – but rather the beauty of the Gothic stopping *as an act* we are engaged in, not as a fact that is over and done with, which is the whole reason Ruskin's notion of active rigidity plays such a crucial role in its ontology.

In our study of ornament, we will constantly encounter this fusion of the petrified and the fibered, the mineral and the vegetal, of stillness and liveliness. "To dress it and to keep it." Ruskin begins the last volume of *Modern Painters* with another partial Bible quote[14] and proceeds with an exalted narrative describing how we inhabit our planet, sharing it less and less with rivers and foliage, with a surface of the planet he designates as "The Earth-Veil":

> The earth in its depths must remain dead and cold, incapable
> except of slow crystalline change; but at its surface, which
> human beings look upon and deal with, it ministers to them
> through a veil of strange intermediate being: which breathes,
> but has no voice; moves, but cannot leave its appointed place;
> passes through life without consciousness.[15]

A veil of strange intermediate being! Living but not alive, dead but not passive; an enormous sheet is stretched out over the whole surface of the earth, a horizontal wall veil composed of stone and foliage, encrusted and woven, ornate and alive, but also preserved and still. This is certainly the reason architecture and botany have enjoyed such a long-lasting relationship.

Now we have briefly touched on some of the main issues around ornament in order to obtain an initial overview of the field we must now explore more thoroughly, step by step, as we deploy a few of Ruskin's most enduring themes: the wall veil as a fundamental intertwinement of matter, massing and texture; the draped and the encrusted as the main protagonists of ornamentation; and his friends in the Pre-Raphaelite Brotherhood's mixture of live foliage and stone as an illustration of his notion of an "earth-veil," of the planet as an ornate crust, more specifically as a system of sympathetic relations. We will now leave Ruskin for a moment and bring in two other theorists of ornament, his fellow Victorians Owen Jones and Gottfried Semper (though the latter was merely a temporary Victorian[16]), and slowly stir and sort their arguments before combining them into a general, matter-oriented theory of ornament.

The very first image in Owen Jones's *The Grammar of Ornament*[17] must have come as quite a shock, certainly in 1856, to a man like John Ruskin. It is of a decapitated head, its eyes closed, mouth open with the teeth bared and its skin covered in tattoos. "Female Head from New Zealand, in the Museum, Chester," Jones wrote as a caption. We now know that it is not a woman's head but a male warrior's, preserved after death by the Maori, as many were. These *mokomokai* were boiled, smoked and dried, treated with oil and finally sealed with wax to be kept by the warriors' families, and later

Owen Jones. *Female Head from New Zealand, in the Museum, Chester.* Ill. on p. 14 from *The Grammar of Ornament* (1856).

often sold in desperate circumstances to European and American museums. But Jones is correct when he says that in Maori facial tattooing – *ta moko* – "every line upon the face is the best adapted to develop natural features,"[18] and in this sense it must be viewed as texture, a pattern emerging from the inside out, though it has been applied from outside. We see figural lines, *motifs*, or, as we called them before, *figures*, lines that act, and do so through variation.

The first thing we notice is that the lines – thin, continuous tattooed markings – are spaced apart, often in tiny groups of two or three, and then the spacing skips one position by leaving out one line, transforms and starts offsetting again into another group. This basic operation allows the figures to fill the facial surface without a need for too much detail and to maintain a certain clarity. The second thing we notice is that the lines have acquired a multiplicity of behaviors: they can *bend*, and do so variably; they can *merge* at a single point; they can bend in one direction and then *switch*, in an S-figure; or they can bend further and start *spiraling*, sometimes halting abruptly to end up as a J-figure and at other times bending more and more, logarithmically, to form a spiral that ends in its own center. Or the lines can be straight, and change direction by *zigzagging* and forming Z-figures, or *bifurcate* to form Y-figures. In short, this line work comprises a set of very precisely described figures, each with its own Maori name: kau-wae, perepehi, hupe, ko-kiri, and so on. These figures then *configure* to not only fill but almost recreate the surface of the face, while incorporating the inborn graphics of eyebrows and lips; and this game is not a simple one, this cloth not a simple one to weave. The configuration *fits*, it is a three-dimensional veil without folds or seams, made of line-threads that are highly precise, not only because they are directional tools but because their directionality follows the slopes of the facial topography, like traces of skis left behind in the snow. See how they gather along the nose, sweep away downward and spiral up onto the summit of the slope of the cheek, then break backward, split off from the initial spiral, and sweep downward again toward the chin to form little spirals below the lower lip. All the lines, with all their complex behavior, act in unison to form a nested set with no loose ends. Meanwhile, the pattern stays striped; the lines never intersect; all problems are solved in a way that makes features like the chin, cheeks and nose interrelate with the eyes, ears and mouth. The pattern is fantastically Gothic, though with a different set of figural and configurational rules; nonetheless, it makes a traceried volume of the head, draping it with a "face veil" not fundamentally different from Ruskin's wall veil.

The continuity of dimensions can only be established by ornament, that is, by ornamental veils, by figural configurations, made as if drawn and drawn as if made. The question is not whether we need to "return" to ornament, because that would implicitly historicize the issue, but we do need ornament, more than ever; now that we are just naked beings between naked buildings and objects, we need to drape ourselves and our things as if they have been grown, drape them as if they are textured, as if they are encrusted; we need to weave them as if they are tessellated. With respect to weaving, we should discuss Gottfried Semper first, before arriving at Owen Jones's tessellations.

an abstract materialism

Semper was one of the members of the advisory committee for the Great Exhibition of 1851 (where he met Jones, who was commisioned to decorate the interior). The same year, his *The Four Elements of Architecture*[19] was published in German, though he had written it in London, where he lived in exile in the early 1850s. It was in the Crystal Palace that Semper had seen the famous full-scale model of a Caribbean hut, an artifact of architectural anthropology that became central to his thinking and has been cited ever since in references to him. Architecture, he argued, consists of four elements,

elements that incorporate the materials as much as the techniques for processing those materials. Before getting involved further in Semper's thought, we should take note of the fact that his theory, though it deals with materiality, is paradoxically devoid of materialism. He does not speak of brick or limestone, nor of iron and glass, which would in fact support a materialist theory and immediately turn it into a theory of building rather than architecture (if we momentarily accept the definition of architecture as being the virtual organization of a building and not its actual structure). This is why Semper is so important to our thesis, he helps us to understand design in relation to matter in a way that does not end up in a fatal determinism but allows us to perceive design as occurring at a point of transition from mass to matter, from building to architecture, as a zone of transfiguration essential to the emergence of ornament.

Semper's four materials, the four elements as they would be used in an order of construction, are as follows: (1) earth mound, (2) timber frame, (3) textile membrane and (4) hearth fire inside. One begins building by first raising the earth to a level above the reach of water and animals; one then drives wooden piles into the mound at each corner (the hut will be rectangular) and builds a timber frame, which is subsequently closed with woven or plaited leaves and strips and then heated inside by a fire to create a comfortable environment. Semper does not, however, adhere to this sequence consistently in his writings. He often states that architecture began with fire, with the open hearth around which early humans would have gathered to warm themselves and cook their food. For the moment, the elements' order of placement is not critical; what matters more is their theoretical status. As I have said, the four materials and their implied techniques did not directly inform the building technology of Semper's day, nor did they take on a mythological, iconic status like Laugier's primitive hut. Rather, Semper constructs an evolutionary path in which techniques previously used for certain purposes are transposed to others, almost as a form of heredity but also as an example of what Gould called *exaptation* (the taking on of a new function during evolution) in which ornamental preservation turns mere building into architecture.

Of the four elements, one clearly plays the most important role in this evolution: textile, accompanied by techniques of weaving and braiding:

> *Decke, Bekleidung, Schranke, Zaun* (similar to *Saum*), and many other technical expressions are not linguistic symbols applied to the building at a later stage but clear indications of the textile origin of these building elements.[20]

And:

> It is certain that the beginning of building coincides with the beginning of textiles.[21]

The making of a building, or more precisely a wall, involves not merely stacked stones resulting in a solid wall (*Mauer* in German) but something else that incorporates its former function and texture:

> The wickerwork (*Flechtwerk*), the original space divider, retained the full importance of its earlier meaning, actually or ideally, when later the light mat walls were transformed into clay tile, brick, or stone walls. Wickerwork was the essence of the wall (*Mauer*)." And he adds in a note: "The German word *Wand* (wall), *paries*, acknowledges its origin. The terms *Wand* and *Gewand* (dress or garment) derive from a single root. They indicate the woven material that formed the wall.[22]

Semper's theoretical transition takes place twice, first from *Mauer* to *Wand* and then from *Wand* to *Gewand*. The first transfigures the solid wall into a fabriclike woven structure; the second considers that fabric a dress, a notion we know as Semper's *Bekleidungsprinzip*. In related twentieth-century architectural theories, which are generally based on his notion of tectonics (represented by wood) and not that of textile, the first transition has actually been used to cancel out the second. What Semper saw as a design technique, and specifically one of ornament, was turned into a building technique by modernism and its theorists. When we look, for instance, at our contemporary hollow dry walls with their steel or aluminum profiles finished with sheetrock, or at the typical Miesian reticulated curtain wall (a black, industrialized example of classicism), we can easily mistake them for Semperian *Wände*, because they seem woven, or at least composite and not monolithic. But this is not at all what Semper meant; he was talking about solid *Mauern* becoming *Wände* owing to the use of ornamentation, to *Bekleidung*, not to the restructuring of the wall into a composite set of hollow elements. Again and again, the Semperian elements have been taken literally, but modernist composite dividers and panelized cladding are conceptually as far removed as can be from adorned, monolithic *Mauern*. What has been used as a theoretical basis for shaking off ornament was *actually intended as a theoretical explanation of its emergence*, precisely because, at a certain point in prehistoric times, primitive open-wickerwork dividers no longer sufficed and had to be replaced by closed, solid stone walls, but these were considered acceptable only if the woven and braided patterns were retained, petrified in stonework. Why? Human cultural evolution became intertwined with architecture as an art not of space but of atmosphere, and one less of materials than of patterns and textures:

> Hanging carpets remained the true walls (*Wände*), the visible boundaries of space (*Raumbegrenzung*). The often solid walls (*Mauern*) behind them were necessary for reasons that had nothing to do with the creation of space; they were needed for security, for supporting a load, for their permanence and so on. Wherever the need for these secondary functions did not arise, the carpets remained the original means for separating space. Even where building solid walls became necessary, the latter were only the invisible structure hidden behind the true and legitimate representatives of the wall, the colourful woven carpets.[23]

In short, the transfiguration of weaving into stonework explains the two most important traits of ornamental surfaces: polychromatism and inherent structure, i.e., the fact that many ornamental patterns still feature the typical under-over interlacing of weaving or the meandering ribbons of knotwork. Of course, since *Gewand* means dress, we are talking about ornamentation as drapery, as a cloth cast over the body. Yet we are also talking about it as encrustation, since we are observing the hardening of wickerwork into stone – sometimes directly, as when early baskets were used as molds for ceramic clay (which automatically took on an impression of the weave) and wicker-work was covered with mud reinforced by plant fiber (while the underlying plaited structure remained discernible), and sometimes indirectly, by design, as in a painted or embossed pattern on a vase.[24] Drapery is conceived as a soft cloth hardening at the moment it touches the stone, while encrustation is to be conceived from the inside out, with the hard stone softening at the exterior to be chiseled. At this point in our argument, it is not so important to know exactly what Semper's position was, what is crucial is that he understood this transfiguration as a material one, which he famously called *Stoffwechsel*.[25]

He derived the terminology from his friend Jacob Moleschott, a Dutch physiologist who published writings in German on metabolism in plants and animals. The German term *Stoffwechsel* can specifically refer to metabolism as it occurs in living organisms, and Semper's usage is vaguely related to this, since in bodily processes chemical reactions constantly transfer matter into energy, but Semper's theory is not so much one of chemical transformations as of technocultural ones. What is so powerful about Semper's notion of the metabolic is that materials do not passively wait to be cast or chiseled but are a symbiotic part of activities, techniques and technologies. His theory does not make the stereotypical connections between the half-product clay, the product brick and the object of the wall, going from raw to finished in linear fashion; that would not explain anything. Rather, he understands the transition from architecture to building as proceeding from soft to hard. In this sense, his four elements resemble the four ancient Greek ones, fire, air, water and earth, which embody the four states of aggregation. The four categories of raw materials, as he lists them in *Style*,[26] corresponding to his four elements of a decade earlier, are: (1) pliable, tough, resistant to tearing, (2) soft, malleable, capable of being hardened, (3) stick-shaped, elastic, principally of relative strength, and (4) densely aggregated, resistant to crushing and compression. These still correspond to the four elements of the Caribbean hut but are now material attributes, states of aggregation from softest to hardest, which become activities through their respective technological classes: textiles, ceramics, tectonics and stereotomy. The first two categories are techniques of embellishment, as he calls them – textile drapery and mosaic encrustation – while the last two are categories of structure, embodied by wood and stone. Thus, in the transitory *Stoffwechsel*, two events occur: the object becomes adorned, and it becomes rigid. Or, more precisely, the object becomes adorned *while* it hardens. The fact that it bears traces of the soft and malleable connects it to life, while the fact that it is petrified makes it endure. It is an embellishment that has become structurally stable, not a petrified image (the patterns of weaving are never literal). During the change of material – literally, the *Wechsel* of the *Stoff* – a texture is left on its skin by a technology of weaving transformed into a technology of carving and painting.

> The question now is what became of our *Bekleidungsprinzip* after the mystery of transfiguration was complete: as the essentially material, structural, and technical notion presented by the dwelling assumed monumental form, from which true architecture arose.[27]

Normally abstraction leads to idealism, i.e., pure formalist principles independent of material notions. On the other hand, materialism generally leads to a theory of building or construction, in which everything is driven by the connections between materials, their structural properties and their expression as such, rather than a theory of architecture. Semper steered clear of both "speculative aesthetics" and "coarse materialism"[28] and took an in-between position which remains extraordinary today: architecture is abstract because it is the result of a transformation and material because it is informed both by textile weaving and stone carving. Since we cannot proceed directly from the materiality of weaving to that of carving, we need an abstraction in between, an abstraction that by its nature is technical. Architecture still suffers daily from the devastating chasm between the technical, as it was taught at the Polytechnique, and the artistic, as taught at the Beaux-Arts schools. Only a few convincing solutions transcend this inherent opposition, and Semper's is one of them; Ruskin's is another. Semper's theory is, in short, one of *abstract materialism*, something quite unheard of and not yet well understood. Scholars try to retrospectively correct Semper either at the symbolic level – like Alois Riegl in *Stilfragen* – by replacing his material evolution with artistic will (pushing him into the formalist corner), or at the material level – like Kenneth Frampton in *Studies in Tectonic Culture* – by stating that his theory is one not of the knot but of the joint, i.e., the joint between panels or building elements (pushing him into the structuralist corner).[29] But Semper's intermediary veil is like Ruskin's, both alive and still, a crust of ornamentation that becomes a membrane between forces, materials, techniques and forms.

What can one say about such abstract materialism? Clearly, it does not view substance as something to be cast in the mold of forms but sees matter as occupying fields of activity, as clustered and grouped with technical and aesthetic forces; it views matter *as being in transit*, as neither being raw substance any longer nor having yet entered the field of finalized forms. This notion brings Semper's abstract materialism close to expressionism, which is generally classified under the individualist *Kunstwollen* and not under the category of material skills and techniques. Techniques bring materials to life because they can dissociate themselves from a specific material but not from matter in general. In this way, they become living, abstract stations for moving materials into other domains. One can weave anything – a dress, a house, a car, a vase – as long as one only applies the abstract logic of weaving. This means that, just as Ruskin's stone courses are related to the form of the mountain, the woven pattern is necessarily related to formal aspects, i.e., in the case of a vase, its bulging and edges, and in the case of a house, its openings, corners if any, and massing.[30] So, as long as one applies that logic, the weaving never becomes metaphorical or "applied." Since ornamentation occurs in the transition, it manages the original textile pattern as well as its abstraction and transfer onto another object. It is a technique that nestles between two technologies, that of weaving and that of building. All the ideas and intelligence are located in it, not in the mind. Matter can think perfectly well for itself. Semper offers us an active alternative to mere subjective artistic will or the objective archive of forms. Forms are merely dead, things archived as thoughts, because they have retreated from matter completely. The game of design, whether in nature or in aesthetics, is played between matter and technique, with the latter located somewhere between Ruskin's craft and Semper's technology.

The textile *inhabits* the stone, not as a material but as a technique and a logic. Reciprocally, the stone also abstracts the textile, and the weaving can inhabit the stone only as ornament – how else? Since we cannot literally knit a building or a vase, the stone, and the carving, must transform the fabric too; therefore, the abstraction of materials works in both directions: stone abstracts textile and weaving abstracts carving. It is not as if one material is literally in another, as if two materialities were existing simultaneously; rather, one state of aggregation is transforming into another, going from soft to hard, from pliable to rigid. This can happen to a single material, too, as when water freezes, lava turns to stone, or a face grows old. A material that solidifies as it cools, a group of threads weaving together into a fabric, without exception takes on a pattern during the transition from pliable to rigid. *Nothing passes through undecorated.* All such configurations, in which materials are arranged through a history of forces, we have come to call patterns. Of course, it is no surprise that the term "pattern" comes up in a discussion of ornament – dozens of books on ornament use it in their titles[31] – but there is a much more profound connection at work than its mere graphical meaning, something truly material, and abstract.

Here is a well-known quote from Gregory Bateson:

> It all starts, I suppose, with the Pythagoreans versus their predecessors, and the argument took the shape of "Do you ask what it is made of?" or do you ask "What is its pattern?" Pythagoras stood for inquiry into pattern rather than inquiry into substance.[32]

The first question apparently fits with the notion of passive mass awaiting a negative form to be molded in, as if the "made of" can be separated from the "it," while the second question implies an appreciation of form in the manner of Ruskin's Matterhorn or Semper's *Stoffwechsel*: when matter transforms, undergoes a transition, it organizes itself by abstracting into a patterned state. Matter is both material and structure, which is not the structure of a final form but *the structuring of a zone of potential forms*. Seen from this angle, pattern is an abstraction that can never be idealized, never fully subtracted from matter; on the contrary, it gives direction to matter's potential to become many forms, depending on the actual forces at work during the transition. The moment things have taken on a form, they will also have taken on a pattern; there is no other way through. All things are made, and all things made are structured by the making. Every thing is a nexus of external forces and internal structuring.

So far, there is no difference at all between natural and technical patterns, which is fully logical, since natural patterns, too, occur in massive factories – of climate and temperature change, for instance – with a continuous supply of matter to be transformed and a tendency to spill out products in great numbers, be they mountains, snowflakes or waves on water.

Let us look at a few such patterns – call them what you like: natural patterns, matter-patterns, pattern-forms – and see what their properties are and how these properties might begin to drive our own technically produced patterns of ornamentation. For reasons that will become clear later, I would like to start with two that have some similar properties but occur in opposite circumstances of cold and heat: snowflakes and mud cracks.

In the previous chapter, we referred to Bentley and Humphreys's magnificent 1931 book, *Snow Crystals*, which depicts no fewer than 2,453 snowflakes, no two, of course, the same. We could call each one an individual, in spite of them all being hexagonal – in fact, *because* they are all hexagonal. If we look carefully, we see that the hexagons are actually hardly ever "filled" – only under very special conditions. We are not dealing with a hexagonal mold into which water is poured in some sky-high freezer. Only a few water molecules are needed to start the growth process that creates a snowflake, not as a liquid that freezes solid but as a tree of spicules or dendrites, linear elements that progress in a solid state by branching, exploring the abstract space of possibilities in a consistent sixfold symmetry. What is important to us is that: (a) the flakes consist of similar branching motifs, (b) the figures add up into a set of similar, i.e., patterned, configurations, (c) there are *many* flakes, i.e., the patterns are repeated; and (d) the configurations all come out different. It is undoubtedly a clear case of "uniformity amidst variation," the paradigm of aesthetics for hundreds of years. Or, in Owen Jones's words: "See how various the forms, and how unvarying the principles."[33] Evidently, principles do not operate at the same level of existence as forms, or else it would not be possible for the two to coexist. We see an "ordering" principle at work, but it does not result in order, or any type of finalized entity. Like a Gothic cathedral, a snowflake is never "finished"; it is purely the management of a supersaturation of cold air through the extraction of water vapor in the form of solid crystals. If the air cannot contain all the vapor at a freezing temperature, the vapor simply transfigures into snow and gravity does the rest.

Uniformity does not occur at the same level as variation. The variation is real; the uniformity is abstract. The actual forms are all different, while their organizations are all the same; that is, the production of each flake is driven by the same principles, which, however, operate locally, making each dendrite decide when to split off and when to proceed forward, rather than globally as a constraint to form. So, to define the difference more precisely, the variation is explained by a consistency of behavior (Jones's principle of unvaryingness), not a sameness of form. What we think happens in space ("form") actually occurs in time ("formation"). The consistency is periodic, recursive and rhythmic. Patterns are true expressions of formation as time-dependent; the spatial forms are only the final products of such periodicity, the remnants carrying all the information as a graph of the process. Many authors, and especially Ernst Gombrich (an art historian of the Vienna School, founded by Riegl) in *The Sense of Order,* have attributed our need for patterned ornament to a need for order, not only an order of matter but one inherent in perception – a *Gestalt*, more a cognitive projection of an order onto objects than something we actually see and feel. We notice the same danger in all such observations: applying a schematism to a material transformation as if using a template for producing wallpaper, repeating exactly the same motif. In wallpaper design, this problem appears in the realm of the technical, and more specifically in the use of the woodblock (in the nineteenth century, that is; we'll return to Jones's and Morris's designs later), which necessarily results in "unvarying principles of unvarying forms," to paraphrase Jones, since technically it has been impossible to produce multiplication without unvarying, *exact* repetition. As we all know, individual things in nature do not repeat exactly, though it would be ridiculous to say there is only variation, in the sense that all things are simply different from each other. Waves on water are similar enough that we can speak of a kind of *inexact* repetition, better known as iteration. The changes in the waveforms that appear during their repetition work iteratively to create more variation. Variation and repetition are interdependent, and, as such, they are more a form of multiplication than addition.

Now, it would be oversimplifying matters to state that since today we have digital techniques of production we can act like nature and concentrate solely on variation, because this is not the case: variation cannot exist without repetition. How else would it vary? To organize variation, we still need repetition, exact or inexact. Obviously, inexact repetition implies variation, but that does not mean exact repetition necessarily works without variation; on the contrary, there it only needs to happen *in* the tile, instead of *to* the tile. Ergo, it comes down not to a final choice of one or the other but to acknowledging that there are two effects occurring simultaneously, *the tiling and the tiled*, respectively, *how* it repeats and *what* it repeats; that is much more important than the actual form of repetition. In this sense, the problems of designers today are by no means lesser than those of Owen Jones or William Morris. If, for a moment, we imagine a room decorated with digitally produced wallpaper, varied like Bentley and Humphreys's photographs, with all the snowflakes carefully packed together like coins (each surrounded by six others) but each different from the next, would that make all the difference in the world from a single motif repeated exactly? It would surely raise some interesting issues, but I do not honestly think it would make a crucial difference, for the same reason that I called the twelfth-century Gothic digital: the issue of how to design variation lies not so much in the choice between the exact repetition of latticed order and the inexact repetition of recurrent variation but in the understanding of the *transition* between variation and uniformity, between concretization and abstraction, or mobility and stillness. I think pattern is not an index of order but the ex-

Example of cracked mud pattern.

pression of transfiguration. *It is all in the passage*. Pattern is something that *occurs*, not something that is. We will discuss what this means for design a few paragraphs down.

Let us first proceed with the inverse of the snowflake. When we look at the way a mud puddle dries up in the blazing sun, we see a similar tendency toward pattern, toward a certain configurational

schema that nonetheless never results in exactly the same patch of dried mud twice. A dried mud puddle is made up of mostly polygonal tiles, that much is obvious, but the tiles' edges are not very straight; they tend to zigzag, and some edges do not make it all the way but instead remain cracks in single tiles that end in a sharp tip surrounded by dried mud. But even if the mud were homogeneous and the cracks totally straight, the polygons would still all be different; that is, they would consist of different numbers of edges and angles between those edges. The consistency of such a pattern does not lie in the polygons but in the nodes, since they are all three-legged junctions, which I call Y-figures. Since the angles between the legs do not have to be the same all over to fill the surface, they are the place where variation is expressed. It is rather amazing (from a design-theory point of view) to see a clay surface "self-tile," forming a floor pattern as it dries. This configuration, which we perceive as tiles laid one after the other, as in a dry stone wall or pavement, starts with the whole and breaks into the parts. We find many similarities between the snowflakes and the clay tiles, but there is an important difference: while in the snowflake the hexagonal contour is never filled, in the mud it is precisely the contour that is constantly materialized, though variably, as the outline of the tile. What is a *continuous* outline in the dried mud tile is only a *dashed* line in the snow crystal limiting the growth of the continuous lines of the dendrites.

These two natural phenomena seem to present us with two different models of patterned ornament, each occurring in the transition from one material state to the other: water vapor into ice crystals and homogeneous mud into cracked, baked tiles. Suddenly, under critical conditions, a homogeneous materiality acquires a "graphic" (i.e., operating by means of lines), even diagrammatic, self-abstracted form in order to pass into another state. All pattern emerges in a space between dimensions. We generally see dimensions as stations of the extensive, but in pattern formation we continually encounter dimensions as expressions of intensive material properties, of transitional states within matter. Why? Because all the external forces operating on matter can *only be processed internally*, through a restructuring. The ice crystal starts with lines that multiply into a surface; the mud tile begins with a clay surface breaking into a network of lines – in each case, there is a passage from one dimension to the other, but they occur in opposite directions: the snow crystal moves from a lower dimension to a higher one, the clay tile from higher to lower. The latter, an encrusted pattern we call *tessellation*, consists of a system of *outlines*: the cracks, analogous to what we know in mosaic patterns as joints. The former proceeds by materializing not the surface patches but the lines, which we will call *centerlines*, which branch, weave, nest, or otherwise multiply into a surface, a system of networked *ribbons*.[34] So as ornamental systems, the two modes of multiplication, of moving between figures and configurations, are antipodal: the tessellated breaks, self-tiles, into polygons, because only polygons can fill a closed surface, while the ribboned operates by variable curving and branching ribbons that multiply into some variable interlaced group. In ornamental design, of course, both will have to repeat in some form, either as a single element or as a group of varied ones. This obviously applies to tessellated ornament but is also true of ribboned ornament, which can multiply only with the help of polygons, tiles with dashed, invisible outlines, as in the best wallpaper designs, where we want to see the field of interlacing vines and leaves but not the hidden tiles organizing the "repeat" of the pattern, as it is called in wallpaper design.

At this moment in our argument, however, after passing through Semper's domain of *Stoffwechsel* and entering the world of pattern, we must confirm that both the ribboned and the tessellated exist in this specific zone of transition or transfiguration, of movement not just from one material state to the other but specifically between dimensions: *the ribboned operates from line to surface, the tessellated from surface to line.* One is a world of weaving, the other of cracking. This is exclusively the *transdimensional* realm of pattern, because nothing else can emerge there but pattern. We must look carefully into these separate approaches, each of which became a separate school of design, with very different protagonists, evolving along a very different path. However, we will find that there was no deciding moment of either/or; one does not face a choice for either the *mosaic*, the tessellated system of outlines filled with patches of color, or the *fabric*, a woven, ribboned system of centerlines filled with gradations of color. We will see that both, when at their best, work towards each other, the tessellated toward the ribboned (or, as we called it before, the encrusted toward the draped) and the ribboned toward the tessellated – neither resulting in pure weaving nor pure tiles but again, as in the Gothic, working towards a *vitalized geometry*, where the movement of flexible figures merges with the hardness of the edges of the tiles, again in a merging of abstract structure with vital ornament.

tessellation ornament and ribbon ornament

We will first visit the world of tessellations and encrustations before immersing ourselves in the jungle of interlacing ribbons. We find all the richness and beauty of tessellated encrustation we can possibly imagine in Owen Jones's *The Grammar of Ornament* of 1856.

Its title is already extraordinary and telling – the *grammar* of ornament – since until Jones the only books on ornament had been handbooks, manuals, and books full of canonical examples. Though his book contains a comparative analysis of ornament, grouping styles by nation or people and appreciating all the differences between them, its goal is a new one: finding a universal logic of ornamentation. Such handbooks normally depict all the various objects – keystones, lions flanking doors, fences, ironwork, heraldry, guirlandes, capitals, and so on; members all – but Jones's does not. He concentrates on ornamental fields, on so-called diapers, mosaics, rugs and fabrics – in short, on surfaces, and how they are constructed according to the logic of ornamental figuration. These fields are structural; they are constructions, or, as we call them, configurations; and for each category, he finds new sets of rules, new types of figures that have various properties enabling them to make bands, corners, or, most commonly, complete fields.

Jones's focus on surfaces must certainly have been affected by his comprehensive studies during the early 1830s of the Alhambra in Granada with Jules Goury,[35] since Moorish ornament concentrates solely on the production of intricate diapers: complex, mathematical, even kaleidoscopic patterns of a tessellated geometry, a geometry of subdivided surfaces comprising polygonal patches fitted together in mesmerizing configurations. Looking at *Grammar*, we immediately notice the minimal presence of the Greek and Roman – a mere eight plates, and in the context of the whole book, they hardly seem to fit, decorated as they are only with a few scrolls and meandering bands and some grotesques, but grammarlessly; they are more like formal solutions, difficult to vary and certainly difficult to nest into a patterned diaper. They differ greatly from the Persian, the "Hindoo" (represented by all the fabrics Jones bought for the Great Exhibition), the Chinese, "Moresque," Arabian and Indian. Jones's is very much an Orientalist notion of ornament: stylized, networked and always polychromatic. Each chapter contains a number of full-page color plates in folio format and is introduced with an explanation of the figures, their rules of construction, and their historical background. These introductory texts are generally more interesting than the famous thirty-seven propositions at the beginning of the book, which lack precision in their attempt to abstract rules, which become so general that they lack the power of grammatical logic and are ultimately useless. In the chapter introductions, however, Jones uses text, annotations, numbering, diagrams (some large, some small enough to fit into a sentence), and illustrations, some very abstract, some very realistic, and all without color. The "Moresque Ornament" chapter is one of the best,[36] along with the previously mentioned "Savage Tribes," which starts with the decapitated Maori head.

Owen Jones. *Persian N° 2.* Plate XLV from *The Grammar of Ornament* (1856).

Owen Jones. *Celtic № 1.* Plate LXIII from *The Grammar of Ornament* (1856).

Here are a few of the rules of the Moresque as listed by Jones, in the form of instructions for Victorian designers: (a) we must decorate construction, not construct decoration (obviously, the whole book argues against this rule!), (b) lines should grow out of each other by gradual variation, (c) forms must be understood as subdivided, (d) one must properly balance the use of orthogonal, diagonal and curved lines; and – more interestingly and less geometrically – (e) every ornament must be traceable back to a root, (f) one should use radiation from a parent stem as much as possible, (g) junctions of curved and straight should be tangential, and (h) one must try to avoid schematizing curves into circle segments.

I have rephrased these rules somewhat, but they are clearly still quite formalist, though often something seems to emerge in Jones's analysis that takes his grammar beyond Semper's notion of weaving. (By the way, how Semper arrived at his *Bekleidungsprinzip* has never been clarified, but it is certain that very early on he talked to Goury and Jones, who compared the decorations of the Alhambra to weaving.) Let us not forget that weaving, because it is a material technique, is inherently structural; therefore, rules of ornament derived from textile techniques, whether knotting, plaiting or interlacing, are structural (i.e., connective) too, even when applied to chiseling or painting. As previously stated, the transfiguration of weaving gives textile-derived ornamentation a logic, a set of configurational rules, but of course it is the abstract rules of connecting, overlapping and merging that make such ornamentation work, not actual weaving. In short, weaving and knotting are only a class of a much broader range of configurational patterns. As long as there are figures, and a certain variation of these figures, accompanied by rules of interconnection, they will always result in configurations. Abstract materialism thus gained a level of abstraction in Jones's *Grammar*, and this form of abstraction became highly influential, to say the least; we will return to this topic later.

If we consider Jones's turn to abstraction within the definition of pattern we discussed earlier, however, as part of a passage from individual ("figural") variation to collective configuration, from a world of movement to one of stillness, his grammar is a syntax that looks at global states of final order more than local rules of connectivity. Jones was so affected by the Alhambra that his view of order became strongly influenced by the notion of tessellation as an overall harmonics of subdivision. We must keep in mind that in 1856 we were still half a century away from fully grasping the complexities of the various symmetries of tessellation, as worked out by Fedorov and Polya. There are seventeen different types[37] of symmetry in the Alhambra, operating through the translation, rotation and reflection of polygonal tiles, including combinations of different types of polygon.

Though tessellation does not in itself necessarily prefer the simple over the complex, Jones favored the more simply ordered types, such as grids and diagrids. It is important to note in advance that the reason I list tessellation as one of the two categories of ornamentation (the fact that it works from surface to line in its expression of interdimensionality) is not the same reason Owen Jones was interested in it. There is a "natural" schematism to tessellation, since it visualizes the lines of organization, though this does not mean that its way of configuring surfaces is inherently simplistic or without dynamics. Nowadays, we know of very complex, irregular, fractal and even aperiodic forms of tessellation. But merely because of its sense of schematism, in aesthetics tessellation tends to be associated with uniformity and the study of repetitive patterns, while the ribboned tends to be associated with an emphasis on variety.

If I were classifying different types of tessellation, I would put what we call (1) the grid at one end of the spectrum, as the simplest; then perhaps (2) the lattice, then (3) the Arabic lacework, then (4) the more modern network, which can occur in many forms, from something as simple as a triangulated mesh to what today are called small worlds, and finally, at the other end of the spectrum, (5) the contemporary notion of pattern, which can contain cuts and breaks, in contrast to the network. Jones, as a strong believer in "repose" (Proposition 3: "As architecture, so all the works of the decorative arts should possess fitness, proportion, harmony, the result of all which is repose."[38]) in both his own wallpaper design work and his analysis of existing diapers, floats somewhere between grids and lattices. His designs are very symmetrical and, depending on the degree of symmetry, more or less homogeneous. As we saw in the dried mud example, the consistency of a tessellated system arises, often confusingly, not from its polygons but from its

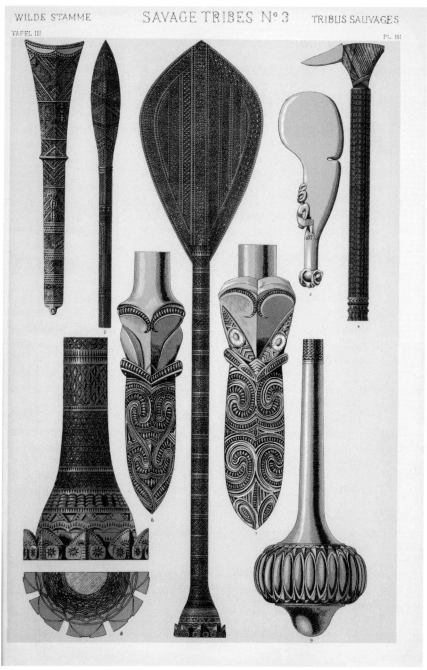

Owen Jones. *Savage Tribes Nº 3*. Plate III from *The Grammar of Ornament* (1856).

Owen Jones. *Moresque N° 5*. Plate XLIII from *The Grammar of Ornament* (1856).

types of nodes. For instance, the variety seen in the combination of hexagons and pentagons on the surface of a soccer ball disappears when we look at the nodes: they are all three-legged. In our analysis, we will therefore shift from studying the types of patch in a pattern to the types of node. Of all possible tessellations, the repetition of an X-figure (intersection), as in a checkerboard pattern, is the simplest, but it is also the most dangerous, since the X crossing does not allow for sliding, nor for a hinging of the four legs at the point of intersection. The X-figure can give us only *grids* and diagrids, i.e., grids made up of diamonds (as the legs do not necessarily cross orthogonally). Then there are grids of triangles, which are constructed by six-legged nodes, and hexagrids, created by three-legged nodes, which we have previously called Y- or T-figures; I would prefer to call them *lattices*, because their structure seems more refined, more delicate and more comparable to that of a typical Arabic screen, such as the Mashrabiya, carved from wood.

As stated, every mathematically possible type of tessellation can be found in the Alhambra, from simple checkered patterns operating on simple translations of tiles to much more complex patterns. For instance, beyond the simple X-, T- and Y-figures, we find overlapping geometries that, where they intersect, create two or sometimes three or four different polygons in a group to be repeated (rather than just one, as in grids and diagrids). Even when materialized by straight lines, such patterns create an effect that is less than reposed, especially when the joint of the tile transforms itself from a non-element into a band element with a width, changing the intersections into crossings, enabling the bands to slide over one another. The crossings can be aligned into a continuous band, and such bands can locally start to vary, to buckle or zigzag, creating tiles that have only one axis of symmetry left and are all of very different sizes. This type of pattern, which is a step beyond grids, diagrids and lattices, is much more like *lacework*, and moves closer and closer to the category of ribboned ornament. Yet these patterns are still very much of a crystalline, if not static, nature and made Owen Jones decide in favor of the harmonic, solid-state order, and – as Gombrich later did – Jones began to view ornament as a "sense of order." It is at this point – as Christopher Dresser, a follower of Jones, correctly saw – that decoration started to ignore feelings and became "an art of wholly mental origin." I, for one, do not believe in any sense of order; it is a pure Kantian trap, the mind's casting of a geometric cloak over the eyes, filtering out all variation, making a pattern a single global object instead of an interaction of multiple local effects. In the very first paragraph of the introduction to *The Sense of Order*, in fact, Gombrich states that he adheres to his friend Karl Popper's "search-light theory of the mind."[39] I am well aware that the term I have been using, "configuration," is quite common in the vocabulary of Gestaltists and radical constructivists, but I use it to refer to what figures *do* and how they *relate* to one another by acting upon each other, not to what the result – "order" – *is*, nor what the mind constructs cognitively. It might seem of trivial importance, but for Gombrich the object has come to rest and the activity is all on the side of the perceiving subject, while in my view it should be understood as shared. But let us continue and finish our list of tessellation typologies.

Only when we find truly small-scale polygons nested with bigger ones to create even larger gaps that radiate through the field like ripples in a pond do we get a glimpse of life in the Alhambra's tessellations. It seems that at these points more action and response occurs between tiles, that here, as in a *network*, all the elements are interdependent – especially when the colors start expressing movement in the context of the whole configuration. Looked at from a distance, some colors seem to merge and others stand out more, making the whole surface dazzle, in what Owen Jones called a "bloom."[40] It is no longer widely known, at least among designers, that Jones was in charge of the interior color scheme of the Crystal Palace (what's in a name?) – we somehow tend to think of it as painted white or some Norman Foster gray, but it was dressed in strong contrasting colors. Each iron column was painted with vertical red, white and blue stripes, so that perception of the structure changed completely between nearby and far away. With increased distance, the colors seemed to merge prismatically into a radiant white. Although color is not the topic of this chapter, clearly it influences the relationships between patches, making them move and change.

Is a life for the tile still possible? Of course, but we must first appreciate that both the ribboned and the tessellated are organized by lines of force, and that both, though inversely materialized, use the line as the active agent.

For tessellations, this means cracks form an infrastructural system that distributes forces over a surface; therefore, in design we can bring in all the complexities of different directions and edges as needed. The more we move away from grids and lattices towards our contemporary notion of pattern, the more variable they get. It is the consistency of the node, not as a fixed object but as something that can be varied – first in the angles between the edges, then in the length of the edges – that leads to great variation in polygons, such as that found in two-dimensional packing systems, like Voronoi diagrams. Nonperiodic tessellations, such as Roger Penrose's, are as interesting; though his only use two tiles, a kite and a dart, the patterns they create never repeat. Maybe more variation will also be possible when we become freer to use irregular polygons, somewhat as Haeckel suggested in his studies of radiolaria. But, as in the Arabian lattices, the tiles would have

Example of Penrose tiling, quasi-crystal structure made up of kites and darts.

to be kept relatively small, unlike typical large structural elements. But whatever we do, we should reverse the roles of patch and edge, the life should be in the line, not the patch, or move from the edge across the tile, because it is the line that transports force.

Ruskin was horrified at Jones's inclination toward perfection, order, structure, harmony and repose – and rightly so. Today Ruskin is often shelved away as a one-dimensional naturalist, a position considered to be acceptable for an artist, since he or she "sees and therefore can only feel" and necessarily must register the unique and the varied. But things are different with pattern design, which inherently has to deal with repetition, since, as we have explained, pure variation does not exist. Putting Ruskin at one end of the spectrum, however, on the side of empiricism as opposed to ordered idealism, would certainly oversimplify matters, and would not do him justice. He himself is partly to blame, however, as he so often took the liberty of changing his mind – "I am never satisfied that I have handled a subject properly until I have contradicted myself at least three times."[41] Therefore, if we want to get to the heart of the matter of ornament, we should quote him more than once, to be safe. First, here are a few lines from *The Two Paths*, specifically the chapter carrying the ominous title "The Deteriorative Power of Conventional Art over Nations":

> It is quite true that the art of India is delicate and refined. But it has one curious character distinguishing it from all other art of equal merit in design – *it never represents a natural fact*. It either forms its compositions out of meaningless fragments of colour and flowings of line; or, if it represents any living creature, it represents that creature under some distorted and monstrous form. To all the facts and forms of nature it wilfully and resolutely opposes itself: it will not draw a man, but an eight-armed monster; it will not draw a flower, but only a spiral or a zigzag.[42]

Without a doubt, this quote of Ruskin's only strengthens the accusation that he was a straightforward naturalist – if it is an accusation – and, perhaps worse, it supports the fatal opposition between abstraction and representa-

tion. We certainly will not argue here that instead of subordinating ornament to the orders of abstraction we will find a way out by rediscovering
representation! There is no doubt that Semper's motto is correct: we should
apply the methods of nature, not imitate nature. It must be, because a
painted picture of life is not identical to life at all, nor is a drawing of nature
identical to nature; it would simply makes us sad beyond words because
such art separates us from life, and traps us in a world on the other side of
the glass without hope of escape. If the answer does not lie in schematic
order nor in the representation of nature, where then? Fortunately, we need
not look far to find a contradictory quote by the same man in the chapter
from *The Stones of Venice* uncharacteristically titled "The Material of Ornament":

> For instance, the line or curve of the edge of a leaf may be ac-
> curately given to the edge of a stone, without rendering the
> stone in the least *like* a leaf, or suggestive of a leaf; and this the
> more fully, because the lines of nature are alike in all her works;
> simpler or richer in combination, but the same in character;
> and when they are taken out of their combinations it is im-
> possible to say from which of her works they have been bor-
> rowed, their universal property being that of ever-varying
> curvature in the most subtle and subdued transitions, with pe-
> culiar expressions of motion, elasticity, or dependence.[43]

And, a bit further on:

> … almost all these lines are expressive of action or *force* of some
> kind, while the circle is a line of limitation or support. In
> leafage they mark the forces of its growth and expansion, but
> some among the most beautiful of them are described by bod-
> ies variously in motion, or subjected to force; as by projectiles
> in the air, by the particles of water in a gentle current, by plan-
> ets in motion in an orbit, by their satellites, if the actual path
> of the satellite in space be considered instead of its relation to

the planet; by boats, or birds, turning in the water or air, by clouds in various action upon the wind, by sails in the curvatures they assume under its force, and by thousands of other objects moving or bearing force.[44]

"Lines that are expressive of action or force" – it could easily have been the maxim of expressionism. Using the terminology introduced earlier, I would say Ruskin here proposes replacing the *outline* of a leaf, which would depict its form and therefore be representational, with the *centerline* of a force. Object versus trajectory: we have definitely started to investigate ribbon ornament, that which works in the reverse direction from Owen Jones's tessellations. And here is the answer we were looking for a page ago: a line that abstracts from the real, but not by reduction; a line capable of precisely

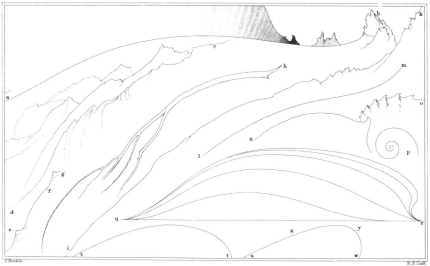

John Ruskin. *Abstract Lines*. Plate VII from *The Stones of Venice*,
Vol. 1: Foundations (1851).

registering the variation of the real – again, not unlike Hogarth's serpentine line, "the line of variety."[45] It is all in the quality of the lines, ones that manage transitions and guide forces. Ruskin actually indexes these in a diagram entitled "Abstract Lines";[46] to make these lines – abstracted from glaciers, ballistics, leaves, mountains – comparable, he draws them all at the same size, as single lines of a uniform thickness. I must emphasize that Ruskin's lines, though abstract, are not schematic. Since he uses a single line to express all the subtle variations in force and matter, it can never be a simplified curve like a circle. The diagram shows lines that are known mathematically as third-degree or cubic functions (circles, ellipses and parabolas are squared or second-degree); in physics, these are typically lines of not only varying *direction* but also varying *speed*. Change of direction turns (first-degree) straight lines into curves, but change in speed adds curvature to those curves.

Now, though Ruskin started thinking about such abstract lines as the source code of variation (instead of the source code of uniformity), he only applied that notion to S- and J-figures – again, very much in line with Hogarth. If we elaborate that concept of the abstract line, it should not be too difficult to produce a wider range of variation, based on a wider range of source figures. Let us look at a simple example first, one from Gombrich's *The Sense of Order*:[47] a twelfth-century wrought iron hinge on a wooden

door of the cathedral in Montréal in France's Yonne valley. We can see how the linear element of the hinge expands over the surface of the door in a typically Gothic manner, by branching off at specific points to then form curving, spiraling tendrils. To understand the complexity of such a line, let us imagine, in an abstract design space (a computer screen – why not?), that the hinge starts out as a single straight line, moving from

John Starkie Gardner. *Hingework at Montréal, Yonne*. Fig. 26 from *Ironwork*, Part I (1893).

the left side of the door to the right. We can imagine that the forces pulling on the linear hinge would be relatively strong and the local tension at the connection points between wood and iron would soon become too much; hence, the linear element of the hinge needs to spread itself out over the door, avoiding points of high tension. Logically, it must do so in continuity with the hinge point, by branching out (forming a T-figure), even bifurcating (into a Y-figure), perhaps ending in scrolls and tendrils (J-figures) that can spiral on as far as needed. The relationship among this set of figures would be similar to the abstract code of a tree branch, but that does not mean the hinge *is* a tree, nor is it mimicking or trying to represent one, though it certainly acts naturally. So, on our twelfth-century computer screen, we first see the initially straight line subdivide into a specific number of segments, and then, on each of the points between these segments, we see two lines sprout off diagonally, upward and downward, and then bifurcate, multiplying lines on each side of the middle lines, which then start to bend in opposite directions, continue to spiral inward, and then stop. Such a growth algorithm consisting of a whole set of variable figures with interrelated, and therefore configurational, behavior, allows a simple line to distribute itself over a surface, to almost become a surface *without* losing the continuity of the line. All these hinge patterns can be different, and, given the time and stamina, one could publish an immense volume – like Bentley and Humphreys's *Snow Crystals* – showing in the first part all the actual iron hinges produced for Gothic and neo-Gothic doors and in the second all the computer-generated mutations, exhausting the variations into the near-infinite.

While I lack the mathematical background to say precisely, I am sure the dimension of that resulting branching iron line is no longer a clean 1.0 but rather something moving in the direction of the two-dimensionality of a surface, perhaps 1.26: a fractalized, transdimensional number, a *relational* number. That is what makes it a pattern. The iron, still malleable and soft, starts to grow branches with tendrils sprawling out over the surface, and there it rigidifies to meet the door. A *Stoffwechsel* takes place, brought about by the behavior of *abstract lines* following the logic of a *grammar*. There is nothing lyrical or metaphorical at work here, nothing symbolic. There might well be a symbolic effect, for instance, the hinge could depict the "tree of life," but the symbolic can never be the driving mechanism. Language and meaning can never supply matter with the instrumentality of code. And it is pure, locally operating if/then code: if tension increases, then bifurcate outwardly; if it decreases, then spiral inwardly. Of course, the transformable condition of the iron is active during design and forging, but it is an abstraction that is not set apart from the real; it inhabits the real, like a genetic code of branching informing the still-hot iron. I would not even say that such code preexists the hinge, because the iron finds these points of abstraction while meeting the surface of the door. In that sense, the abstraction is a shared set of points between iron line and wooden door, and we are witnessing not a transition of abstract to concrete, which is so often proclaimed as the route of actualization, but of the reverse, from concrete material to abstract design. *The iron draws its own pattern on the door.* Frayed, unfinished, not fitting into any fixed format, the branching hinge simply manages forces and becomes ornate.[48] And I can imagine that if the wooden door became very large and heavy, the iron tendrils too would become enormous, like those on the door of Salisbury Cathedral, or the branches could reach further over the wood and start to touch each other, and begin to weave a net – no problem; such a code can tackle all such issues.

"Okay," you might say, "that example is a bit too easy. Since the hinge is structural, like Gothic ribbed columns swaying over a netted vault, it self-decorates because of the physical forces involved. Can you give an example in which there are no real forces involved, like wallpaper?"

"Well," I would answer, "why not take the hinges and place them vertically against the wall, like a grapevine shoot, and let them sprout over the wall from each vertical point?" Nothing could sound more like William Morris.

Detail of hingework at Salisbury Cathedral (mid-thirteenth century).

A thorough analysis of some of Morris's better-known ornamental patterns, especially the "floriated diapers," as he called them,[49] is imperative at this point. Morris, like Ruskin, is generally called an advocate of a naturalist theory of ornament, but it would be much better to look at the diapers of Morris's wallpaper designs, like Acanthus and Myrtle, as configurations of abstract lines. If we classify his diapers as ribbon ornamentation, they should operate from line to surface and, as such, invariably act to construct a surface, as a surface "in the making" (as James and Bergson would say, but we will save that for the next chapter). And, like the iron hinge, they should progress from movement to rigidity. Now, what are the constitutive elements of Morris's design? The twig, leaf and flower, always these three. Let us, for once, not look at these as representatives of absent nature but simply consider what they actually *do*, and study carefully the geometrical role each plays. The twig, of course, is linear and unidirectional, and plays the part of the ribbon, branching, bending and interlacing. The flower plays the role of the tile, a small surface patch radially pointing outward in multiple directions, in contrast to the twig. Between these two, we find the leaf, which displays both directional linear and expansive surface behavior. These three elements have two options for interacting: they can *nest* or *entangle*; that is, respectively, they can either fill a surface by dovetailing together, or they can overlap, leaves over twigs, twigs over twigs, leaves over leaves, and flowers on top. When they fill each other's leftover spaces, the surface becomes as flat as Flatland, a world without depth (such as we see in Jones's designs). Space is created by the contours of the elements. They nest, they pack together, and in doing so, they emphasize the flatness of the surface. The other option, entanglement, creates depth: elements overlap, and therefore a third direction becomes available for movement, though it is not completely perpendicular, like a Cartesian z-axis, but more of a thickening of two-dimensionality, a depth to a surface, since the leaves can overlap the vines and hide them momentarily but never try to bend out vertically, orthogonal to the wall, for that would cause too much distortion and destroy the illusion of thickness. As in *trompe l'oeil*, the illusion of tactility here is textural, intensifying the sense of surface, irresistible as a dog's furry coat; it is different from the stereoscopic effect of a pair of red-and-green glasses meant to create the illusion of space. Morris's entanglings, like Pre-Raphaelite paintings, are not about space but entirely about texture, depth of surface.

However, such complex behavior by interrelating twigs, leaves and flowers cannot be freely sustained over the entire surface, for obvious technological reasons. William Morris's main problem, like any wallpaper designer's, was the design of a *tile*, that is, in Morris's case, a *woodblock* that could be translated vertically, horizontally, and mostly diagonally, the (exact) repetition allowing the roll its required length and width. Being one of Ruskin's most dedicated followers, he strongly believed that for the production of wallpaper one should not resort to industrial techniques but instead revive the ancient technique of woodblock printing, using a stamp handcarved from pear wood, often applied in a diagrid or "half-drop" pattern, with each column of adjacent block prints staggering half a step. If one marked the center of each block on the wallpaper and connected these with a line, one would see such a Jonesian diagonal grid emerge. Of course, the whole point of Morris's designs is that one does not notice such a grid, and therefore, his woodblock is not your typical tile. Its edges follow the complex roughness of all the leaves and vines; it is not a square block at all but one shaped like a torn piece of paper, quite irregularly, except that the top edge fits exactly with the bottom edge and the left with the right, or, in the half-drop pattern, the top left with the bottom right. All wallpaper design show a double behavior, embodying two types of multiplication of the elements: first, on the small scale, the bifurcating, nesting or entangling of vines, leaves and flowers, and second, on the larger scale, the horizontal and vertical translations of that mini-pattern onto a large roll of wallpaper. To create a productive relationship between the two, the geometry of the tile should only be incidentally materialized by a major element; the curving vines only hit the edges every now and then, as if bouncing off. Nor should the flower occupy the middle of the woodblock, or one would immediately see the diamond grid jumping forward from all the complex entanglements. On the other hand, the pattern is not merely obscuring the hidden grid, either, but trying to merge, following the more general rule of vitalized geometry. Obviously, since the second multiplication operates by very simple geometrical rules of tiling, and the first by intricacy of entanglement, a wallpaper design is threatened by an internal separation capable of completely destroying its coherence. The main rule of wallpaper design becomes very apparent: do not fully visualize the edge of the tile or the edge of the roll, or else it will become a secondary system on top of another. Or, to use my earlier terminology: keep the edges dashed. Morris develops an active continuity between both types of multiplication, tiling and entanglement, which is essentially a Gothic principle, in which straight mullions and intricate trac-ery sprout from each other. I think there is a more profound grammar here than what we find in *The Grammar of Ornament*.

When we stand in front of a wall covered with Morris's Pimpernel or Myrtle design, we are immediately captivated by repetition without readable, clear joints, because the edges are axes of symmetry more complex than we would expect of simple re-flection. In the Myrtle pat-tern, the tile contains half-flowers that become com-plete when mirrored, but also single flowers that be-come two, so the pattern

J. H. Dearle for Morris & Co. Design for the *Golden Lily* wallpaper (1897).

as a whole begins to mix individuals with twins, making it unclear to the naked eye what is going on: which lines are materialized in a continuous ribbon, and which are virtualized in a dashed axis? Morris also found another even more innovative technique for captivating the eye. Looking at his amazing Acanthus wallpaper, for instance, astonishingly we find only leaves in the pattern, no flowers or twigs – and this choice of a single element is utterly daring, since it can make a design duller than a Corbusian wall. But see how the leaves behave, each has a thick main nerve, so it can act like a twig as long as it keeps its lobed contours close to that vein, but such large leaves often tend to curl away at the tips, so much so that they become rounded, pointing their lobed edges in all directions – in short, at that point the leaves behave like flowers. Simply by modulating the directions of the lobes of the acanthus leaf, Morris makes it act out all the complex behaviors of leaf, twig and flower. A zone of transition is created between line and patch, a zone of continuity, with lines constantly stretching out and curling up, animated by twisting lobes, in a way that is intriguing regardless of the repetitiveness of the guirlandes created by the leaves. Actually, the seriality (there are no balanced reflections in the Acanthus pattern) strengthens the rhythmicity of the whole design. The surface stays stranded and ribbed and hardly achieves two-dimensionality, but this is made up for by the plunging in and out of the densely packed leaves. The Acanthus wallpaper is one of the finest ever made.

Morris is crystal-clear in his *Some Hints on Pattern Designing* of 1881, in which he proposes a "new-born Gothic":[50]

> As to the construction of patterns the change was simply this: continuous growth of curved lines took the place of mere con-tiguity, or of the interlacement of straight lines.[51]

And, more theoretically:

> Rational growth is necessary to all patterns, or at least the hint of such growth; and in recurring patterns, at least, the noblest are those where one thing grows visibly and necessarily from another. Take heed in this growth that each member of it be strong and crisp, that the lines do not get thready or flabby or too far from their stock to sprout firmly and vigorously; even where a line ends it should look as if it had plenty of capacity for more growth if so it would.[52]

Is there anybody left who would label Morris a mere naturalist? I believe we have seen that such a designation does not begin to cover what takes place in his wallpaper design, and the same is as true of his book and rug designs. The quality lies in the lines, in the abstract lines of force. "Growth" is generally denigrated as "organic," but we must be careful with such disqualifications, because organicism would mean behaving like something organic, i.e., being representational, and here we are discussing *the abstract life of lines*. We are occupying some kind of new, middle ground here; yes, there are naturalist and organic features, but there are just as many mechanical and abstract ones. The last thing one would say, on looking at a wall covered with one of his designs, would be that it looked natural, since it looks as much like a machine has been working on it. We see organic iteration cooperating with mechanical repetition. Clearly, Morris has been able to solve the contradiction between Ruskin's abstract centerlines and his naturalist outlines by letting even the smallest leaf or flower play a role in the meshing and entangling of vectors. Morris uses mostly Y- and T-figures (specifically figures of growth) on variable curves, and offsets each figural line sideways with the most complex lobed or toothed contour – again, not merely to delineate a leaf but to elaborate on the line, to make it vary and fractalize. In short, the interplay between figures is only brought to a halt by internal coordination, never by an external, blocking force, and thus keeps that sense of potential, a "capacity for more growth," which is precisely the realm of the transdimensional, because it is a situation *in the process of crossing over but not arriving just yet*. When we compare Owen Jones's and William Morris's wallpaper designs, we can see they are not so far apart; certainly, Morris has borrowed some of Jones's innovations. His outlines often resemble Jones's abstract, thickened ones, just enough to take the realism out of the leaves. Jones's designs, though, decidedly lack the overall sense of potential of Morris's. It is not only that Jones mostly draws his flowers in orthogonal front or side views and usually reduces them to circles, but just as much because their stems are often cut off, the lines do not overlap, and there is no consistency of relationships between the flexible parts. And, though his lines are often flexible S-figures, they seem to have lost the capacity to vary. The difference is simply that with Jones we see the *end* of a process, it has reached that point of full repose, making the whole pattern fall back into schematism. Morris's diapers are without exception surfaces in the making, while Jones's are made and done with.

William Morris for Morris & Co. *Pimpernel* wallpaper (1876).

William Morris for Morris & Co. *Acanthus* wallpaper (1875).

Just to be absolutely clear: *we do need a grammar of ornament*; we need rules for the abstract life of lines (though for more complex behavior than Jones imagined). Ruskin's diagram of abstract lines of force and action should be expanded, not only to encompass a larger number of figures but to include configurational interactions with each other. All figures must interact, or, as Ruskin says elsewhere, "help" each other, and that interaction must be formative. We need S-figures for serpentines and J-figures for tendrils, C-figures for bending, Y-figures for bifurcations and T-figures for branching, and even X-figures for crossing and bouncing and Z-figures for zigzagging, and all of them must be able to deploy all possible variations in direction and speed, i.e., force and action, plus all possible forms of interaction enabling the formation of configurations. There must be variation *of* and *between* figures. Some ribbons should absorb the edges of the tiling, but not all the edges, nor all the ribbons. In the realm of linear ornament, we find a broad range of ways ribbons nest and/or entangle into a surface. The simplest are the Celtic bands,[53] which consist of pure intertwinement and in which the centerline is offset on either side by two parallel lines that follow its contours. In illumination, such offsets tend to get more complex, especially in the case of tendrils, whose outlines begin to acquire thorns and leaves. It is no accident that ribbons often take on a *vegetal* quality (tessellation is the *mineral* form of ornamentation), since plants' twigs are analogous to simple bands (as found in Morris's designs and elsewhere), while their leaves are offset into either smooth, lobed or toothed contours, and their flowers can form points of radiation, with many petals growing in different directions. Vegetal ornament combines the bifurcations and branchings we know from nature with crossings and interlacings familiar from textile techniques. The last type of multiplication, interlacing, in particular, saves a pattern from simple naturalism even when its elements are very realistic. When we look at the early woodblock printing of the Toile de Jouy, for instance, we see mostly vegetal motifs, but their internal structure does not collaborate with the exact repetition at all. That is not a pattern, they are merely pictures of rural scenes being repeated. *A pattern is never an image, nor a multiplication of images*; it is essential that the type of multiplication abstracts the images in the pattern or that the images abstract themselves

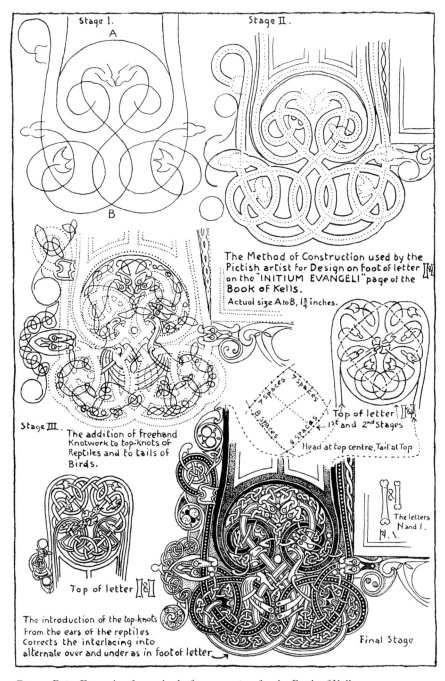

The Method of Construction used by the Pictish artist for Design on foot of letter on the "INITIUM EVANGELI" page of the Book of Kells.

Actual size A to B, 1¾ inches.

Stage I.
A
B

Stage II.

Stage III. The addition of freehand Knotwork to top-knots of Reptiles and to tails of Birds.

Top of letter — 1st and 2nd stages
Head at top centre, Tail at Top

The letters N and I.

Top of letter

The introduction of the top-knots from the ears of the reptiles Corrects the interlacing into alternate over and under as in foot of letter

Final Stage

George Bain. Example of a method of construction for the Book of Kells.
Plate R from *Celtic Art: The Methods of Construction* (1945).

127

enough to invent their own form of multiplication.

In ribboned ornament, all the movements together, from the interaction of smaller figures within the tile of the woodblock to the larger actions of repetitive printing and the translation, rotation or reflection of the block (the movements of tessellation), make up a package of abstract movements that ensure a pattern will never become simply naturalist or abstract. At this point, the game becomes different, the pattern is no longer solely a tessellation or ribboning but a meshing and nesting of the two. First comes the movement of the twigs, leaves and flowers *within* the template; then comes the movement *of* the template, feeding back into the first set of movements. In fact, it should not be too complicated, especially with digital tools, to upgrade the complexity of the underlying grid to that of the lattice or network, with two, three or more different tiles, and to invent for the dominant, interlaced ribbon ornament as many different woodblocks. In that case, since the tiles would now be rotating as much as translating, we would need to leave the notion of a stem, and the growth patterns would need to develop more radially. To conclude, the two sets of movements – within and of the tile – which have their own domains of variation, one of a ribboned and one of a tessellated character, always need to be calibrated and bridged; all movement should be passed on and shared.

Morris's wallpaper is not restless in comparison to Jones's reposed type; it is crucial to emphasize this. Ornament, especially in our times, is often associated with exuberance, lyricism or ecstasy. Again and again we encounter this Baroque notion of flesh and even voluptuousness, which is nothing but an obtrusive form of classicism in which all ornament is subordinated to abstract structure. There is no sensuality present in Morris's vitalized geometry, in this wallpaper whose purpose is not to create a sense of fun, pleasure, or anything like it, but a much more abstract joy. How else could you eat your breakfast in such a room? As with the Gothic, what needs to be established in ornament is simply a relatedness between us and things, *a fundamental sympathy*, which all design starts from. Such sympathy is *only* possible because of ornament. Ornament is an absolute condition for all things to be felt with the same immediacy as they are seen.

To elaborate a bit more, in the twentieth century we saw ornament replaced by texture, such as in the use of "natural" textures, often inspired by Japanese *wabi-sabi* design, or the use of "honest" materials such as brick or wood, and of less industrial craft techniques that intentionally leave traces on the surface of the object. This was not an improvement. In fact, it has made matters worse: the care necessary in design, or what Ruskin calls the tenderness of art ("the first universal characteristic of all great art is tenderness"[54]), has been obscured, because now the material and not the design takes responsibility for the sympathetic relationship, leading to a *naturalism without grammar* incapable of connecting the pattern to the form of the object. We have seen hundreds of buildings with copper cladding acquiring patinas, and modernist boxes overgrown with ivy or cladded with rectangular wooden panels with visible joints and strong visible grain – but does the grain in any way manage the tessellated geometry of the panel (let alone the windows)? No, not at all: it solves no problem; it merely replaces the sympathy lacking in the design with the psychology of naturalism. There is simply no *Stoffwechsel*, the sympathy is not in the architecture but all in the building material. Natural texture should always be transformed into artificial ornament.

Texture is what I would call *weak decoration*: no relation between pattern and object whatsoever. Weak decoration is simply applied independently onto a preexisting form and structure. In contrast, in *strong decoration*, such as Morris's, the pattern "builds" or "makes" the object, including all its characteristics, such as edges, corners and openings. Note that this does not mean that ornament literally predates the form or the surface, rather, *ornament is abstract making*, what I will call "fabricism" in the next chapter, i.e., it recreates the geometrical surface of, for instance, a wall abstractly, with rules of growth such as bifurcating, tendriling and the like. Why? Because a wall as a naked, Euclidean object with four static points in its four corners presents itself as finished, stable and at rest, in short, as something we cannot feel anything for but merely see. Sympathy can be felt only for things that are in the making or in transition, that have a life. Paradoxically, strong decoration is not an expression of strength and stability but of vulnerability and delicacy. In Semper's words, it is an expression not of *Mauer* but of *Wand* as *Gewand*. We should never make a fundamental distinction between the

Gothic iron hinge, which may chronologically precede the existence of the door, and Morris's wallpaper, which succeeds the surface of the wall. They are both abstract patterns to real things, following almost exactly the same set of rules. Just as the hinge is not a tree and does not naturalize the door, the wallpaper does not naturalize the room; rather, it abstracts the world. The flowers and leaves in his designs may well originate in his beloved Red House garden in Kelmscott, but that does not mean they "represent" it or any other splendid field of flowers; they extend into a much larger abstract cloth, that of the patterned earth veil, a world's wallpaper, a world made of the *abstract material* of ornament.

After Morris and Jones, both "trends" began to evolve in very different directions. Jones found his successor in Christopher Dresser, and Morris found his partly in Art Nouveau, where the Ruskinian notion of the abstract line hit the dead end of aestheticism. (Somehow, as a mirror image, I always have to think of the young Oscar Wilde, as a student of Ruskin's at Oxford in summer 1874, working on the construction of Hinksey Road, carrying rubble and sweating heavily.[55]) A strange thing happens in Art Nouveau: the lines, by now having turned into enormous water plant stalks, sprout from structural members – columns, doorframes, the edges of posters and menus – and move back and forth at their tops, as if under water, ending in the extraordinary tendrils of so-called whiplashes. They exist in an oneiric state of horizontal movement but build nothing, no new relationships, unlike the Gothic meshworks where the curves are inextricably part of the structure, they just sprout and then tendrilize. *Ornament has to work*, not lie idle on a sofa. In fact, Art Nouveau signaled the end of ornament. The fatal split had by then already occurred; the naturalists dozed off in their cocooned interiors, while the Dressers were becoming full-fledged abstractionists. Here is Christopher Dresser himself, speaking at the Royal Society of Arts in 1871:

> … Pictorial art can, in its highest development, only symbolize imagination or emotion by the representation of idealized reality … true ornamentation is of purely mental origin and consists of symbolized imagination or emotion only. I therefore

argue that decoration is not only a fine art … it is indeed a higher art than that practiced by the pictorial artist, as it is wholly of mental origin.[56]

As one movement was dreaming away, the other began to ignore the senses, heading straight toward conceptual art. Gombrich makes a particularly interesting observation in *The Sense of Order*, that "the theory of twentieth-century abstract painting owes indeed more to the debates on design that arose in the nineteenth century than is usually allowed."[57] No one should doubt where the origins of modernism lie, Mondrian found his predecessors not in Cézanne and Monet but in Jones and Dresser.[58] Decorative art began to supply the fine arts with order and abstraction – though an abstraction without making, without transition – taking a fatal turn against sympathy and tenderness. The abstraction of Semper and Ruskin is one in which materiality takes on the quality of thought; the abstraction of Jones and Dresser removes that thought and locates it in the human mind, severing it from all material encounters. This has had devastating consequences, while the first type of abstraction, always unique and temporary, was one of a specific meeting, such as between a hinge and a door, the second separates all things from each other since its source is a mental universalism. While the first is a movement of touch and tenderness, the second is one of repulsion and cruelty. That tendency toward generalized abstraction passed from Jones to Dresser and slowly became more schematic in its use of both line and color (Jones supported the aesthetic use of George Field's primary-color theory). Then it fell entirely into the hands of Mondrian and Doesburg, and ended in the black hole of Rothko and Judd. After that, we had the humor of Pop to play with, and the irony of postmodernism, but all such movements did nothing but dance on the smoldering ruins of modernism. Deconstruction, in particular, amounted to a plundering of the collapsed edifice of abstraction. The fine arts ran away with the decorative arts, and even now when artists try to return to some kind of world of feeling, for example, by decorating museum walls with teddy bears, or try to return to sympathy, hugging people on the street in little moments of art,[59] their actions are like those untreated wooden panels in architecture: nothing but psychotherapy after the trauma. Its effects have proven to be so persistent that to cure them we must resort to a more radical solution: a full return to decoration. Artists have no way to structure their sympathy anymore. Why? Because they are locked in the museum, the festival, the gallery, or worse, the transitory media, leaving us with the white walls and the empty squares. Art ran off with decoration and has not yet returned the favor.

Here, again, is John Ruskin in *The Two Paths*, in the chapter entitled "The Unity of Art":

> … No, it was an advised word – that 'detestable' ornament of the Alhambra. All ornamentation of that lower kind is pre-eminently the gift of cruel persons, of Indians, Saracens, Byzantians, and is the delight of the worst and cruellest nations, Moorish, Indian, Chinese, South Sea Islanders, and so on. I say it is their peculiar gift; not, observe, that they are only capable of doing this, while other nations are capable of doing more; but that they are capable of doing this in a way which civilized nations cannot equal. The fancy and delicacy of eye in interweaving lines and arranging colours – mere line and colour, observe, without natural form – seems to be somehow an inheritance of ignorance and cruelty, belonging to men as spots to the tiger or hues to the snake. I do not profess to account for this; I point it out, and you will find it true if you look through the history of nations and their acquirements. I merely assert the fact.[60]

If there is one paragraph that has earned him continual mockery, it is this one, and though it is hard to see through the racism, I can come to only one conclusion: he was right. Right, that is, on the issue of cruelty being innate to abstraction, not on cruelty being innate to specific peoples or nations. The main issue in design is the choice between cruelty and tenderness; there is no other. And if we want to begin to conceive what I would call an ecology of design, I think there is only one option, and that is the one for tenderness, or sympathy: a fundamental reaching out of things to things.[61] Let us remember, for instance, the concept of cruelty at the heart of Antonin Artaud's nihilism, developed in "The Theatre of Cruelty":

> Without an element of cruelty at the root of every spectacle, the theatre is not possible. In our present state of degeneration it is through the skin that metaphysics must be made to re-enter our minds.[62]

Metaphysics through the skin! I cannot imagine a worse nightmare; a pure form of art-torture. Even more explicitly a few pages later, Artaud claims to remove "the shroud that lies over our perceptions." He means Ruskin and Semper's veil. At least he is candid about his intentions, removing the shroud constitutes an act of cruelty and is typical of a century specializing in atrocities. John Ruskin was right, especially in hindsight, with the twentieth century between us and him: abstraction is cruel and perverse, because it wants to rip the clothing off everything, to present everything naked. First the Protestant iconoclasts destroyed the Gothic, making books more powerful than architecture (as Victor Hugo taught us[63]); then they destroyed ornamentation, in an effort to inject truth and meaning directly into the bloodstream. Obviously, since neither truth nor meaning exists, only the obscenity and cruelty of the act remains. Adolf Loos had it the wrong way around: *cruelty and criminality lie not in ornament but in its absence.* It is not that Ruskin only believes things should be dressed, but that our perception itself needs them veiled, because feelings of tenderness are impossible unless we see something in the making. Things cannot exist without clothes. For more than a century now, the metaphysicians have made us believe that the truth lies beneath, and each of us has run out to rip off our share of veils. We have taken part in nothing less than the rape of things. To let only the mind see, as Dresser foresaw, means to plunge directly into hysteria, to see with an unmitigated look, an eyeless look that immediately turns the face into a grimace. Things seen can now only leave a grimace of pain, because the bare object has a neurological hotline to the bare mind, waiting to be electroshocked by metaphysics. The whole twentieth century, from 1914 until 2001, to be precise, has been occupied with only one thing: the realization of the sublime, which is by default a strategy of shock and awe.

Of course, ornament is in itself a sign of caring and an act of sympathy; cruelty only surfaces when we are confronted with an absence of ornament. We must now correct him slightly: the presence of ornament is never a sign of cruelty, *in whatever form*, be it Arabic, Maori, English, Greek, whatever. Ornament represents care and tenderness, by its nature, because it is a form of sacrifice (as Ruskin titled his first Lamp), in the sense that it is uncompensated work, and without the return of user value. In a way, it is *pure* work, because it is perfectly useless; we only have "to dress it and to keep it." As I have said, ornament is often mistaken for a sign of exuberance, a kind of special treatment, a dressing-up for a special occasion, but in fact it is simply *dressing as keeping* – an everyday act of caretaking, calm and dutiful, like gardening. This is why Ruskin opposed tenderness to cruelty and why, in a similar vein, we should oppose sympathy to pity, with which it is often confused. While sympathy could be described as a form of resonance, a co-movement, pity by definition designates the feelings of the other as suffering. I would not be the first to define pity as an especially cruel form of contempt (Nietzsche gets credit for that), a degrading of the other through being overcome by feelings but not allowing them to cross over. It is a feeling that masquerades as a gift but in fact steals from the other. One person's feeling of pity leaves the other feeling humiliated. We need only think of Schopenhauer, the chief philosopher of *Mitleid*, who kicked a woman down the stairs, turning her into a lifelong invalid, and imagine him lovingly stroking the poodles he walked every day.

some hints on pattern designing

We have looked at the world of the tile and the world of what happens in the tile, in the respective domains of cracking tessellations and interlacing ribbons, and we have tried to unravel the conditions of exchange between them, one taking on traits of the other, one virtualizing the other, one being continuous while the other is dashed, one foregrounding itself and trying to obscure the other. We have also observed that we have come to live in the world of the pure tile, geometrized and abstracted. The abstractedness of pattern is obviously the home of mathematics, though it was not mathematicians that built our cities or started our wars (though they did join in the fighting) – architects and politicians did that. Abstraction made a pact with machines, with iron – imagine the last vitalist expressionists, such as Franz Marc and T. E. Hulme, dying, as they did, amid an orgy of iron in the trenches of World War I.

As the cloning devices of Henry Ford and the Bauhaus were taking over culture, fundamental changes were taking place at the heart of mathematics, not further toward the generic and the reductive, but in the opposite direction, towards the genetic and the generative. These changes reversed the notion of abstraction altogether, from one that reduced all variation to a uniform schema in order to produce sameness at the prolific rate of modernity to one of our abstract lines: living entities of minimal difference generating complex patterns, what we know as the world of code. The pivotal figure in this turn was a Charles Babbage who thought like a John Ruskin: Alan Turing. Not only was he the cracker of the Enigma code and one of the theorists of digital computing, he also wrote the seminal 1952 article "The Chemical Basis of Morphogenesis,"[64] which based a whole notion of natural patterns, such as zebras' stripes, on the relationship between two competing tendencies: one that activates the growth of an effect and one that inhibits it. Such a notion is inherently of a digital nature, since at each point a yes or a no defines the "difference that makes a difference," as Gregory Bateson characterized the smallest building block of information. The mechanism, called a reaction-diffusion system, begins by diffusing chemicals in a medium, in this case, an animal's skin, but this diffusion, i.e., the population of a *surface*, operates via a double chemical reaction – one that activates more of the same and one that inhibits it – which occurs in waves over the surface of the skin, thereby expressing a pattern of black and white stripes, i.e., *lines*. The skin is, of course, not a flat surface like a rug but is wrapped around the three-dimensional shape of the animal, its neck, legs and torso, in short, its *massing*. When we look carefully at zebras, we notice that, though they are all different, their patterns share some specific characteristics. The stripes are perpendicular to a centerline running through each of the more tube-like parts of the body: the neck, legs and middle part of the torso. The morphogenetic process runs quite uniformly over these more Euclidean areas, with black and white stripes alternating almost as if on wallpaper covering a cylinder. Obviously, a zebra is not made of pipes, and all its parts merge smoothly into one another, so the pattern on the zebra's back must transform from vertical stripes to horizontal ones that wrap the hind legs. It does so by bending the stripes into C-figures, by *de-forming* the pattern over the haunches. The front legs are more complex, since the horizontal stripes must be managed between the two vertical sets on the neck and torso; this can be done only by splitting the vertical lines, *transforming* them into Y-figures, which straighten out again on the legs. Basically, these play the role of the joints in the tessellated model, like the seams of a suit, being absorbed in a ribboned pattern that can only be stretched to a certain limit. The same also occurs in other areas, on the neck near the ears and on the legs at the protrusions of the joints: whenever the system cannot manage the changes in geometry by stretching and deform-ing the stripes, the pattern does it by inserting an extra stripe, i.e., trans-forming. (In truth, there are no "lines" – the pattern is made up of tiny dots of white and black, but their relatedness in the diffusion expresses them as lines.)

Incidentally, at the end of the paper, when Turing encounters problems solving nonlinear equations, he suggests that a "digital computer" might be helpful.

I would summarize by saying that in animal skin patterning we find an extremely close relationship between what we called texture and massing at the beginning of this chapter. The pattern is not like wallpaper stuck on a form (as most texture mapping in 3D modeling still is nowadays); rather, it must be constantly modified and adapted, deformed and transformed.[65] The deformations are, in Ruskinian terms, "changeful" (they vary), while the transformations are "savage" (they jump) – always a mixture of gradualism and incrementalism. To clarify, I am not arguing against wallpaper – a wall is flat and without massing and allowed us to closely investigate the rela-tionship between the tessellated and the ribboned – but at this point in the chapter we are returning to the wall veil, that is, to decorated mass. Funnily enough, Ruskin himself got this wrong when he used the example in *The Seven Lamps* of animal skin patterns to encourage the use of color and ornament:

> The stripes of a zebra do not follow the lines of its body or limbs, still less the spots of a leopard. In the plumage of birds, each feather bears a part of the pattern which is arbitrarily carried over the body, having indeed certain graceful harmonies with the form, diminishing or enlarging in directions which sometimes follow, but also not unfrequently oppose, the directions of its muscular lines. Whatever harmonies there may be, are distinctly like those of two separate musical parts, coinciding here and there only – never discordant, but essentially different. I hold this, then, for the first great principle of architectural colour. Let it be visibly independent of form.[66]

Here, Ruskin seems further removed than ever from his Matterhorn as a system of horizontal courses and vertical fractures, though in his mind the wall veil is as often a form of drapery as it is one of encrustation. In textile drapery, a pattern generally manages through a certain looseness and a capacity to deform, adapting locally to forces acting on its flexible systemacy. Only when the forces exceed a certain value do we observe a sudden change, a switch in direction, a seam or cut, a first crack. If we moved the concept of dressing from simply draping oneself with a flat cloth (hence containing only folds, like a poncho) to wearing a cut suit (containing both folds and seams), which is more than simply two-dimensional, to wearing, say, a stretch sweater, with a printed or woven pattern that both could deform and contained seams (but not folds), we would begin to close the gap between the two seemingly contradictory meanings of Ruskin's wall veil.

Between Turing's digital zebra and Ruskin's architectural Matterhorn, we find the same periodicity of pattern, a coursed system articulating the form, in a rhythm that can stretch, bend or deform and then, at a specific point, shift into another rhythm by passing through a transformation. The ribboned excels at the former, at gradual variation, deformation, stretching

– in short, the realm of changefulness. Tessellation is the realm of fractures *per se*, of cracking, or savageness. I think if we take our findings on zero-massing patterns – that is, wallpaper, including both Jones's and Morris's domains – and apply them to Turing's much more sophisticated concept of digital pattern emerging on complex massing, we should be able to map out a path toward contemporary ornament, combining the age of decoration with the one of massing, as it were.

Again, as in the case of the Gothic, we find ourselves entering the realm of digital machines, while we had started out on what seemed merely a historical journey. Before we proceed any further, let us retrace our steps for a moment. After acknowledging some landmarks in the field of ornament and texture (Ruskin's Matterhorn, Jones's Maori head, Millais's *Mariana*), we found Semper playing a pivotal role with his apparently paradoxical invention, abstract materialism, which stated that ornament was a form of making but necessarily an abstract form of making. This shift was similar to the one we noted in our discussion of the nature of Gothic, where the crafts of weaving, braiding and bundling nestled themselves in the design of windows, columns and walls. As is well known, Semper was creating an ethnological basis for the historical notion of design, and therefore he made no real use of abstraction; to him, it merely established a historical fact. To continue following Semper would have led us straight in the arms of historicism, however, since anything from the past can volunteer to become a sign to be imprinted on any contemporary material.

We moved further, searching for abstract activity, and found it in the behavior of matter itself, which demonstrates a tendency to self-abstract into pattern, to self-assemble and express texture and form simultaneously, either through the principles of tessellation or those of ribboning. This subsequently led us toward Ruskin's abstract lines and his expressionist concept of active lines, which, similarly to Gothic ribs, constitute centerlines of force and action. Making – and more specifically the making of ornament – does not occur in a zone between the drawn and the executed but between the concrete and the abstract. Seen from this point of view, it no longer matters if a blacksmith in the Yonne valley followed a design drawn up by someone or merely his own intuition, or if we imagine the iron crawling by itself over the wooden plane, fundamentally acting no differently from, say, ice crystals flowering over a windowpane. An abstract pattern is a form of agreement between concrete states, in which one conditions the other. A material can never meet another directly; there will always be the thinnest possible sheet of design between them. *Design is a veil between things*, whether they are organic or inorganic, artificial or natural.

While matter finds form, we will never come across any consciousness operating on the outside of matter. Human agency is just a way to speed up the process, a third material at best, acting as a catalyst. Again, we find technology acting on the inside of matter, and though we cut it, hammer it, forge it from the outside, our consciousness lives in the interior. We only have to sympathize with the technological tendencies present in matter itself. The branching and spiraling of the tendrils act abstractly, yes, but only – I emphasize – because the iron requires it. Though the rules are formal, the abstraction is not formalist, not generalized but specific. Semper's braiding of rope acts within the carving of stone, and the flamboyant "cobwebs" of the tracery in Rouen Cathedral were, as Ruskin explains, made possible by the soft limestone of northern France.[67] They never would have been conceivable in marble or granite. It is of the utmost importance to grasp this as fully as possible, because we are arriving at a point in our own times when Turing's "digital computers" can not only generate and draw such patterns but now also numerically steer the machines to carve and cut our ornaments. It seems as if we can generate any pattern and carve or cast it in any material, but that is not the case. Yes, we have found an *abstract* core in craft, be it the self-crafting of matter, the crafting of iron hinges or the drawing of intricate wallpaper patterns, but note that it is still *craft* and still deals directly with matter. Abstract, digital craft only abstracts to find *a way into matter*, to manage specific material problems, not a way out of it.

Saying that, I think we can now distill from our journey a set of requirements that we can perhaps use to create ornament for our own age. Decoration is not about play or fun, as I hope to have made clear; it is the most serious and rigorous part of design. It demands incredible precision and discipline. The first thing one needs is relatively small, flexible agents; call them *figures* or abstract lines, it does not much matter, but one precisely selects a number of them, and each of these has a certain amount of freedom to act, in what we call variation and changefulness, or, in digital speak, parametric behavior. All this behavior is rule-based ("if/then"). However, the pattern as a whole must be a system that can absorb every tiny eventuality, the edges of a menu, the concavity of a vase, a sudden change in width, or the windows and columns on a façade. In theories of texture, randomness or stochastics is often considered one of the most important properties, but in ornamental design this must be reevaluated as an inherent redundancy, or what Ruskin calls "richness." Though ornamentation is often considered rich, its richness is mostly misunderstood:

> Commonly it is said of all Gothic, that it rose in simplicity, that it declined by becoming too florid and too rich. Put that error at once out of your minds. All beautiful and perfect art, literature or nature, is rich. Titian is rich, Beethoven is rich, Shakespeare is rich, and the forests, and the fields, and the clouds are richest of all.[68]

Our second rule, therefore, is: when using ornament, use *many* figures. Decoration is an art of the many, and an art of elaboration. Etymologically, the term "elaboration" implies craft. The number of figures needs to greatly exceed the number of required elements, just as in the Gothic the number of ribs exceeds the number of columns and windows. The richness needs to be able to manage various problems from any angle.

Now, thirdly, these many figures need to be able to *configure*, to gather via the same or extra sets of figures, and to deal with design problems as they do so. For example, how does one break a text block? Use a large initial, let its tendrils spiral into the margins of the page, so the next block is automatically spaced and, if needed, shifted by the ornament. Again, ornament has to work. Ornament is structure, though often abstract structure or configuration. We need to understand how, in design, texture can never reach such a level of organization. When we look, for instance, at Mies's famous onyx-cladded wall in the Barcelona Pavilion, which has so often been hailed as an example of the perseverance of ornament in modernism, we notice that the curves in the material do not participate in constructing the surface of the wall. The lines of the marble have merely accessed the surface afterwards, not helped to create it, as does Gothic ribbon ornament, for instance, or Morris's wallpaper. Mies's onyx never reaches the abstract level of architecture, nor would any other cladding material. Again, we should call this weak decoration. Ornament is strong decoration, because it is able to exactly organize edges, openings, thickenings, corners, the whole volume, anything: it is articulation and elaboration. This is very different from a textured field with the windows and doors punched out afterwards, as we see on so many contemporary decorated boxes today. [69]

Let us proceed with our list. Fourth: the pattern must reenter the material domain. Along with managing design problems, our ornamental patterns should deal just as effectively with material issues. There is an inherent danger in splitting craft into design and robotics, because craft needs to deal with materiality, and since we are not holding the hot iron in our hands, the iron lacks the ability to talk back. The braiding informs the iron, but the iron also informs the braiding. How can we accomplish this with our contemporary materials, since we often lack direct contact with them? We need to organize our processes of fabrication in a manner that allows the materials to talk back. To make patterns integrate material issues (often represented by various specialisms), we must test and prototype and find solutions presented by both our ornate pattern and the qualities of the material.

Something I have done my utmost not to mention until now, because it is so overly obvious, of course, is that the age of intelligent machines allows us to return to ornament. As ornamentation was inherently part of an economy of manual labor and handicraft, it was completely excommunicated on technological and economic grounds (as well as Loos's moral grounds) in the last century. Today, it can return to center stage, since Charles Babbage's machines have converted into Alan Turing's machines, drawing and generating patterns and now, fifty years later, fabricating and producing them with the same ease. Nothing ever has to be smooth or bare again, since robot arms steered by digital information can cut, mill, press or paint anything. Most commentators argue that the fact that we *can* use digitally controlled machinery does not necessarily mean we *should*, but I disagree. Digital technology indisputably means a move away from uniformity toward variation; the only question remaining was *how* to design with variation. Contrary to the notion of an avant-garde, digital technology is taking us back in time, to the Ruskins and the Darwins, or, more generally, to the unique and the contingent, and, in a way, back to craft. We should reject both the default futurism associated with technology and the default historicism associated with ornamentation: we want to go back, yes, but not via history.

Once we have reestablished the unbreakable connection between massing and ornamentation, plus the fact that ornament is configurational, a form of work, not of leisure, and laid out the characteristics of both tessellated and ribboned ornament and how the two classes of objects relate to variability, the answer to the question of how to design with variation cannot be more obvious. We should challenge the appearance of metro cars, refrigerators, airplanes, DVD players, computers, cars, laptops, cameras, as well as houses, teapots, jugs, chairs, vases, suitcases, desks, if not also governments, companies, advertisements, television programs, and so on: Why are you so smooth and polished? Why do you not show wear and tear? Why are you not as excessively decorated as our beloved wrought iron hinge or Morris wallpaper? Why are cars not decorated like the bronze helmets made by Celtic craftsmen? Why are websites not overgrown by neighboring sites? Do we still believe every object should be tested in a wind tunnel, and be reflective like a pair of sunglasses and smooth as stones in a river?

To me, there is no question but that things should be jungles, overgrown by relations, woven, frayed, nested and entangled. I think a new form of ornament could lead us back into a certain wilderness – not that of pristine, authentic nature, heaven forbid, but another, maybe technological wilderness. We should not use our intelligent machines to return to nature (we would not be able to retrieve it anyway, since it was never there), on the contrary, we should make our machines go wild. Let us seek a way to send our postmodern tools back to premodern times. To some, such technoromanticism might seem preposterous;[70] for me, it is nothing less than an absolute necessity. My only question is: Can we, and will we, ever be Romantic enough? Will we ever be able to restore the feelings and care we had for things? We definitely need a *Naturphilosophie* for intelligent machines, since they have gradually become our natural environment. If the machines of modernism were meant to cleanse and purify, our machines will bastardize and hybridize.

I will begin to investigate this technological wilderness in the last two chapters, initially going back to the picturesque and then radicalizing it through several versions of the wild, and finally envisioning an ecology of design, in which things take on pattern and shape by conditioning each other. Things design one another through entanglement – this is the paradigm of Gothic ontology – continuously weaving Ruskin's "veil of strange intermediate being" between them.

But first we must descend deeper into the core of things and arrive at an understanding of how and why they entangle. In fact, they do so because of nothing but sympathy.

chapter three

abstraction and sympathy

We have arrived at a point where it all comes down to aesthetics. A digital Gothic as an architecture of relationality, a digital craft that opens a way to return to ornament, and, as we will see in the next chapter, a radicalized picturesque – fine, but why? We cannot answer this question in terms of "meaning," that much is certain. You cannot answer those questions at all in twentieth-century terms, I fear.

Meaning, language, criticality and semiotics have been standing over the grave of beauty for a hundred years now – there is no friendly way of saying it. Though it is not the topic of this chapter, it is clear that the battle between beauty and the sublime has been temporarily decided in favor of the latter. Not only have we lived through an age of what George Landow calls the "technological sublime,"[1] the age of Apollo and Auschwitz, but in art, too, we went from Zero's minimalism to deconstruction, all in the name of ultimate enlightenment through aesthetics. First art and architecture shook off all representation to reach a point of pure abstraction and structure, and then we either ironically reversed it (while it simply remained the same thing) or cut it into pieces, not to destroy it but to add more nodes in the structure, making it even more abstract. We reached a point where the body and its experience became totally irrelevant, merely an experience to personally "have," like a dirty secret. We have become completely alienated from the aesthetic in its original meaning, which simply concerns the feelings we have in the presence of designed things, be they paintings or teapots. There is no hope for a little repair work being enough. So much has been destroyed and neglected that we will have to reconstruct a whole edifice, and learn to speak a language nobody understands anymore, and simply keep on speaking it until we are heard.

In the following pages, I will argue that we must return to a notion of what has been heretofore known as sympathy – a term with a magical ring to it, indicating the deep-rooted engagement between us and things, deeper than any aesthetic judgment would allow. The word "sympathy" is not even used any longer in this context, and its later replacement, "empathy," though very popular today, is by now also out of use in aesthetics. Taste and judgment, generally the driving forces behind aesthetic theory, are not going to play any role here at all; sympathy revolves around a certain immediacy, not the neuroelectrical directness of sensation, however, but the more elastic immediacy of feeling. As we shall see, sympathy is as much a feeling as a form of thinking, but one that is especially present in aesthetics, meaning it specifically acknowledges a mental, but not psychological, and a bodily, though not sensual, reciprocity between us and things. It concerns both the resonance of two things and the synchronization of two activities, but it is certainly not a relationship of taste.

During this chapter, for once, we will not consult John Ruskin; of course, his name will inevitably cross our pages, but we will need to postpone his critical presence for a while. Not that sympathy does not concern Ruskin – on the contrary, his notion of vital beauty heavily relies on it, as has been shown by the same George Landow,[2] but the pure empiricism of David Hume that introduced sympathy to philosophy and the role sympathy plays in Adam Smith's economy of the "invisible hand" give it all the wrong connotations, especially because their notions of sympathy start out as ethics. And though I strongly believe we can derive an ethics from aesthetics, I think the reverse is highly problematic, and will lead us no further than ideas about the "good" and the "just" being beautiful. For the English, sympathy is mainly operative between people, not between things or between people and things, and to reinvestigate such a notion in the presence of the nature of Gothic, the matter of ornament and the radical picturesque would put us on the wrong foot. All immediacy would be lost forever, elastic or not. Actually, sympathy is such a radical concept in aesthetics that we can only revisit it by going to the end of our period of interest, the outbreak of World War I.

During the last quarter of the nineteenth century, sympathy and empathy played alternating roles in the cultural discourse and were often inextricably interwoven, flowing from German Romanticism on the one hand and French philosophy on the other, both of which were intensely occupied by what constituted a brotherhood of man as well as of things. As early as 1778, Johann Gottfried Herder spoke about aesthetics in terms of sympathy: "The more a limb [of a sculpture] signifies what it is supposed to signify, the more beautiful it is; and only inner sympathy, i.e., feeling and transposition of our whole human self into the form that has been explored by touch, is the teacher and indicator of beauty."[3] Later, such a feeling of transporting oneself into a sculptural form would be termed as *Einfühlung*, which was discussed extensively in the last century, invariably translated into English as "empathy" and used mostly in the context of psychology, i.e., something passing between two people but also between people and things. Yet German art and architecture found little use for it until Expressionism emerged, since so much of pre-Expressionist German art and architecture was based on Hellenism rather than the romanticist Gothic or picturesque, which hardly established themselves in Germany (all the romanticists there were scientists, all the artists classicists). *Einfühlung* reached its apex with the theories of Wilhelm Worringer, whom we have already encountered in our discussion of the Gothic, and Theodor Lipps, a psychologist with a strong interest in art and architecture, but by then we had already entered the early twentieth century. What makes Lipps so much more interesting than the theorists usually discussed in relation to *Einfühlung* is that he makes it a property of life (he is clearly a vitalist), not of objective proportions and space, as did Schmarsow, Wölfflin and Vischer.[4] From Lipps it is only a small step to Henri Bergson (another vitalist), and the connection between them is not so much historic (I have no idea if they even knew of each other's work) but certainly philosophical, with both sharing a strong interest in time and psychology.

Bergson cannot be understood, however, without investigating some of the penetrating ideas of American philosopher William James, which serve particularly well as an introduction – especially his notion of the "fringe" and his characterization of his own philosophy as "mosaic." As you will have come to expect of me by now, we cannot bring these authors together by generalizing their thoughts nor by laying them out in all detail and following them historically; we must construct a specific encounter, a precisely choreographed meeting point. Proceeding in this manner, we can hope to arrive at a better sense of what constitutes sympathy, how it can be understood aesthetically, and, more importantly, how it can be applied to art and design. We will slowly become acquainted with a form of sympathy that will seem more primitive with every step we take, a form in which things and people can no longer be distinguished, a realm where things feel for each other and people lose all personal traits and become wholly objectified. Gradually, we will come to see that sympathy is far more than a psychology bubbling up between two humans or a sublimated version with a human psychology at one end of the relation and a mute nonhuman object on the other; it can also be an aesthetics between inanimate objects. At a certain point, we will cease being able to distinguish between animate and inanimate, moving and still, form and action, and be left merely with things and feelings. Sympathy is what things feel when they shape each other.

And, if that is not strange enough, we will limit our discussion to the words written by the abovementioned authors in the space of the few years between 1903 and 1910.

the mosaic of experience

James writes a book of philosophy with such an ease of style that he might be writing a letter, speaking of "things," never of "objects," of "whats and that," never of "actual" and "virtual," of "stuff," never of "matter," calling things by their names in a way seldom seen in philosophy. Not the outright pragmatist he is often mistaken as – someone who brings all concepts to the brink of pure action – he is more occupied by real problems of thought, what a thought is and how it is sustained; what a perception is in itself, rather than as it relates to the material world, and how it is made to work.

His notion of cognition is one of a constant probing, testing and experimenting, of knowing as not a certainty but something constantly on the verge of being verified, or falsified if necessary. This practical notion of truth as more an invention than a discovery, as Bergson summarized it, allowed James to visit mediums, do research on hypnosis and write extensively on religious experience, from its quiet everyday forms to its exalted mystical ones. James shifted perception to experience, making it a philosophical concept rather than a scientific tool. Perception, feelings, thoughts, knowing, action – all are immediately present in experience, available to do their bit, entangled from the start, not to be activated in a specific order but lived simultaneously. James doesn't ask himself the classic epistemological question of what knowing is; rather, he asks how to live with knowledge – a practical, if not pragmatic, question, indeed, but one that inserts something between a perception and a thought: a transition, not necessarily a minute moment, but something that can even be postponed forever. For instance, we certainly know what anger is, but we never meet it in person, except in the form of "hurtful words," and we surely know what Memorial Hall is – in his example in "A World of Pure Experience," in which he describes himself sitting at a table in his library in Cambridge, thinking of the Hall[5] – but we have to walk over to it to verify our knowledge. Concepts are just contractions or summaries of actions that create local, lived connections, which James calls "relations." His whole philosophy, for which, at the end of his life, he coined the name "radical empiricism," is based on a notion of omnipresent relationality:

> To be radical, an empiricism must neither admit into its constructions any element that is not directly experienced, nor exclude from them any element that is directly experienced. For such a philosophy, *the relations that connect experiences must themselves be experienced relations, and any kind of relation experienced must be accounted as 'real' as anything else in the system.* Elements may indeed be redistributed, the original placing of things getting corrected, but a real place must be found for every kind of thing experienced, whether term or relation, in the final philosophic arrangement.[6]

This is radical, because before James it was supposed that we saw things with our eyes and thought relations with our minds. Or, more specifically, that we collected parts with our eyes ("sense-data") and constructed a whole ("cognition") with our minds. Obviously, this was somewhat arrogant, since we would have needed to have pre-cognitions of things as thoughts and then imprint or impose these on the things we saw. This would have been a form of blinding ourselves more than of actual seeing. But how can that actuality of seeing not be a being-thrown in a complete chaos of disconnected parts, like that of Oliver Sacks's patient who was operated upon after years of blindness in the hope of seeing again?[7] Of course, when he was finally able to see a walking cat, no flash of its fur, no movement of its legs or turn of its head ever made it into his mind as "a cat." Scientists studying perception would place a subject in a chair and a cat on the other side of a glass and make the patient push one of the buttons, but James's notion of perception is less isolated and more integrated into the way we live, replacing seeing with experience, a process that cannot be severed from life. Experiencing a cat is different from seeing one: between the perception and the thought or between the moment of merging between the knower and the known floats a suspense filled with feeling and movement. Things do not exist alone, they exist in relation with others. And they exist not only "with" others, as James says, but also next to, like, from, towards, against, because of, for and through them – in short, in a whole array of conjunctive relations of "ascending intimacy."[8] What a choice of words: things exist in intimacy. And, as we discover, not without shock, they exist not only with each other but also with us, with our minds.

A patterned materiality, a world organizing itself between form and force, between time and matter, no longer comes as a surprise to us once we have examined some of the configurational aesthetics of the Gothic and ornament, but postulating a mind that is directly involved, that both acts as matter itself and is intimate with matter, so to speak – this is something else. And this is exactly what James does.

Generally, in what he calls rationalism, and what we can call plain Kantianism, thought lies outside things, either "above" them and figuratively transcendent or physically "outside" them, since the mind is in our heads and the order between things between things. At best, it can only "reflect," and this is why the mind is considered a passive pond in which things are mirrored, keeping us at a distance from real, direct encounters. But James is much more radical than this – for him, we fundamentally cannot know whether the relations between things and between us and things are actually the same, whether the subjective experience we have of things is actually an objective one, since the experienced relation is a real one:

> In a world where both the terms and their distinctions are af-
> fairs of experience, conjunctions that are experienced must at
> least be as real as anything else.[9]

It is here that experience purifies itself, that is, shakes off that single, indi-vidual subject that undergoes it. The reality of both the terms and the ex-perienced relations can only be explained if these realities are not plurally coexistent but made of the same "stuff":

> My thesis is that if we start with the supposition that there is
> only one primal stuff or material in the world, a stuff of which
> everything is composed, and if we call that stuff "pure experi-
> ence," then knowing can easily be explained as a particular sort
> of relation towards one another into which portions of pure
> experience may enter.[10]

So our thoughts of things are actual relations, not mini-transcendencies but something that is both stuff-made and stuff-being-made:

> Knowledge of sensible realities thus comes to life inside the
> tissue of experience. It is made; made by relations that unroll
> themselves in time.[11]

Given the context of this book, the word "tissue" immediately jumps to the fore. Can it be that we have entered the domain of William Morris here as much as we have that of William James? Though we often encounter tissue or fabric used as a metaphor for life and experience, might we in this case be dealing not with a metaphor but with an organizational model, or even a real thing? If the world is one of intricate relations, of matter that is constantly on the move and producing forms, more precisely new forms, this world of pattern is not by accident the same one we care so much for, feel so strongly for, are so constantly engaged with? How does a world of what James calls pure experience exhibit the same patterned relationality as the world itself? In short, what does it mean to be in that world of pure experience? We are surely not Martians visiting earth; we are from the earth, part of it. The fact that we care is not something extra; it is intrinsic and innate. When I walk through a field and my attention is suddenly drawn to a few stones lying next to each other with a small plant growing between them, and I like what I see, what is that liking? Clearly the stones are lying there in a certain correspondence, if not accordance, because the wind and water have moved them, rolled them over the ground and made them find an impression, create a little group, a little nest where a plant could start growing and be protected – but where does my liking fit in? Is it merely in me, subjectively enjoying the sight, or is it something objective, an extended correspondence? I am with the stones and plant immediately, fitting in with them. Such a relationship need not be a liking per se; the same occurs with pain. A baby's hand and a flame are one when they unite in pain, as in James's troubling example of the baby in Boston hurting itself when it comes too close to a candle.[12] One as the stones and I are one, not as a unit but as a group. What fills the space of pain, which flows in and out, like the enjoyment of the stones? Feeling does. All relations are *felt* relations. The transitions are felt,[13] and the substances connected to us by feeling become known to us. The substantive and the transitive: through cooperation, these two create the tissue, or the "mosaic," of his philosophy:

> It is essentially a mosaic philosophy, a philosophy of plural facts, like that of Hume and his descendants, who refer these facts neither to Substances in which they inhere nor to an Absolute Mind that creates them as its objects.[14]

Though the mosaic consists of hard stones of knowing, it does not simply follow the tessellated model that we have come to know from the previous chapter, since in James's mind each stone has "fringes" – that famous word[15] he uses to designate the ins and outs of experience, its frayings, like those of a carpet. Since knowing is an act that takes time, it needs a preparatory phase, a flowing into, that he describes in terms of loose ends, threads, paths or lines. In one of his most memorable images, James compares his empiricist universe to:

> … something more like one of those dried human heads with which the Dyaks of Borneo deck their lodges. The skull forms a solid nucleus; but innumerable feathers, leaves, strings, beads, and loose appendices of every description float and dangle from it …[16]

One wishes there were more philosophers with such an extraordinary taste for imagery. There are solid, substantive nuclei – the mosaic tiles – and experience nests them together. Deleuze describes this model in terms of "the" American invention, the patchwork, in which the making of a cloth is similar to the making of "a wall of loose, uncemented stones,"[17] known as a drystone wall – it is an aggregate of patches of experience. While he denies that it is a whole, of course, such a wall is a configuration, and though full of chance and randomness, the stones fit together, and they do create a *wall*. I think Deleuze means to stress the looseness of the stones but forgets the stability of such a wall. He pushes James's image deep into his own century, the century of chance.

Gallery of a Dyak-chief's house, decorated with headhunter's trophies. North-east Borneo. Photo: J. Jongejans (mid 1920s).

153

This we see happen elsewhere – James's notion of chunks of experience is associated all the time with the rise of Cubism, with the paintings of Picasso, the writings of Gertrude Stein and the novels of John Dos Passos – but we must be very careful here. Organizationally speaking, I would compare such an early modernist painting or novel more to a bag than to a wall. A bag simply brings all kinds of stuff together due to its own external collecting efforts, unlike fitted stones, with their internal, organizational workings. In this aspect, a bag is not even close to a pile of stones, let alone a drystone wall, which is far more complex than a work of simple masonry. In masonry, the external substance of cement makes all the stones relate, while in a drystone wall the stones lock together, their complex, rough polygons finding a fit – a loose fit, yes, but not that loose. In fact, after the stones have nested and packed together, the wall is much stronger than any cemented one, because cement merely prevents sliding, while here, the stones lock together because of their diagonals (while bricks only have verticals and horizontals). A drystone wall is a complex version of the Voronoi pattern mentioned in the previous chapter, a tessellated system of polygons that can have four, five, six or more sides but always join up at three-legged nodes. The increased complexity lies in the fact that the nodes in the drystone wall can be opened; the stones do not entirely fit together, but they fit closely enough.

Drystone wall. Cotswolds, United Kingdom.

With James, we are not simply entering the age of modernism. His philosophy of the mosaic – or, in Deleuze's model, the drystone wall – is one of a complex whole, a nesting of mobile parts finding each other on their own terms, grouping and packing together. In short, his pluralism is a modernized monism, not a modernist fragmentism; his disjunctive cuts are connections, and consciousness is continuous and flowing. Again, we encounter a Gothic ontology: things act for themselves and are therefore plural, yes, but on the condition that they can all be experienced and are therefore made of the same stuff. The mind does not stop. So let us see what is going on with these fringes: are they just loose ends, like Art Nouveau's tendrils, or are they more substantial?

> … our experience, *inter alia*, is of variations of rate and of di-
> rection, and lives in these transitions more than in the journey's
> end.[18]

It might be that the fringes are actually longer than the stones they hang from, and become threads. Of course, there are microseconds of cognition – we know a cat when we see one – but does such a concept help us? Since we deal with the cat, feed it and pet it, it makes no sense to constantly refer to a hidden or even occult notion of it. We only experience cognition when we are separated from the known, just as James, when he leaves the library where he is writing his chapter on pure experience to go to the Memorial Hall, is guided by his knowing *of* that Hall. The knowing finally meeting the known through actual arrival is truly a matter of a microsecond, if not less; the walk over, however, is "a felt transition" and takes a lot longer. It is not so much the carrying over of a knowledge and a certainty but a guided progression, step by step, from point to point in the city, with the walker never losing track, more or less like a cat – he is not yet mentally projected in the Hall, not dragging bodily behind: he is at the Hall, but in a stretched manner, elastically pulled and pushed – in short, he feels and is connected, is not at all separate. Extensive space is exceeded by intensive feeling. The felt threads of transition are much longer than the known stones of sub-stance, really. We are weaving, though we do not have a loom to work from, just as the mosaic lacks a bedding; we weave from point to point, but not every thread stops at a single terminus,[19] some run through, or break away later and connect to new nodes. In this sense, experience should be consid-ered as *more of a fabric than a mosaic*:[20] it builds, but it has holes too, though they have no dimensions, and tears, though they have no length. Of course, as I said in Chapter Two, there is no qualitative difference between a tile mosaic and a ribboned fabric, because the tile is not smooth but patterned, and the ribboned fabric makes a cloth, which is a surface like any wall. But we need to expressly clarify here that, although James enlarged Berkeley's empiricist parts and transformed them from tiny sense pebbles into experiential stones, they do fit together – and they form something bigger than just a bunch of stones. In a Cubist painting, on the other hand, the loose shards of reality fit together only because they have been collected on a pre-framed canvas, which creates a more imposing whole than does a loom or even a mosaic bedding, because a canvas is completely preconfigured and secretly laughs at the randomness of the shards mixing.

My point is this: conceptually, threads hanging from stones are slightly off the mark – not dramatically so, perhaps, but being interested in the wallpaper of the mind, we should be as accurate as we can with such a model. When we consider the fabric as not so much a grid made from a warp and a weft but more a set of figural threads behaving as complexly as those in Morris's wallpaper designs or rugs – splitting, entangling, nesting, crossing, curling – then it becomes a field of various *speeds* of experience. The threads do not suddenly petrify to form a small monument of knowing, at least not in the sense of a dimensional, Euclidean jump, they remain threads, forming nodes through entangling and crossing. As in the Gothic, and as with Semper, the mineralization cannot be separated from the actual continuation of the threads. In this sense, it is much more a looping of feeling and memory than a jumping from feeling to knowing. The felt transitions keep on transiting; they form knotted mini-patterns, zones of change of direction, of slowing down: *stations, not termini*. Knowing is made up of felt experiencing; in this sense, we arrive at Memorial Hall in the same way as a cat would. We do not enter a discursive moment, nor do we jump from a feeling part of the brain to a knowing one, though our feelings naturally change in tone, mood and expectancy. But this does not mean feeling disappears in favor of something else. When certain feelings ebb away, that doesn't mean feeling itself ebbs away. Rather, it changes immediately to another mode, and – partially perhaps before we even arrive, locking into other matters – we are

being filled with hundreds of other threads of different lengths, simultaneously weaving different nodes. The tentativeness remains and is never interrupted by dead certainties; we are always shifting, overlapping, multi-
tasking, believing, hesitating. Perhaps instead of a Dyak's head the model
should be more like a piece of Celtic knotwork, neatly tied up like illuminated initials on the inside but fringed and frayed on the outside.

Let us try to go beyond the opposition of fabric and mosaic for a moment and ask ourselves a more important question: why do James's experiential models (the mosaic, and sometimes water with waves and crests) and,
following in his footsteps, Deleuze's (the drystone wall, patchwork, a harlequin's jacket – all purely tessellated, and more so than James seems to aim
for), consist of *surfaces*? As I said before, many recapitulations of James's
model stress its fragmentary state as an anticipation of modernism, but not
the fact that the tiles are many and configure into a single sheet. Why would
pure experience stretch out into a surface? Wouldn't it be more logical, if
one is introducing a model of irregular mosaic tiles or colored patches, to
think of these as strung in a linear structure – a line, a chain, maybe even a
necklace, or, more fittingly in our framework, a braid? Since James's fringes
are so strongly connected to a notion of time, which he frequently referred
to as a stream, such images would be the first to come to mind. But, since
such an idea implies an understanding of time as individualized, it would
be completely incapable of relating things that coexist extensively and three-
dimensionally. We are usually told to understand time as an *extra* dimension
added to space, but in pure experience things are products of time ("inventions"); therefore, time precedes space and has to consist of a dimension *less*
than space. Clearly, since pure experience is such a radical concept, individual, temporal experience must coincide with a generalized time shared by
all things and beings, and the time of experience becomes experience itself.
Spatial things – "whats," in James's words – are separated in space but connected by the continuity of pure experience, "pure in the literal sense of a
that which is not yet any definite *what*,"[21] that is, a pre-knowing, an "immediate flux of life"[22] that runs through all whats, a pre-knowing that is
lived *sectionally*. How else could things relate but by means of a sectional

plane cutting through all spatial three-dimensionality, through the *inside* of things? It comes quite as a shock to me, and to most of us, I guess, that a psychology living in us all can be directly connected to an ontology of all things, and placed in a time. On the other hand, how else can we live with things and with each other? I think what William James is saying is that when we know we are on the outside, but when we feel we are on the inside of things, because we only feel during transitions and in relations.[23]

Radical empiricism postulates a relatedness that exists before things are actually related, an awareness that is as yet without content, a readiness or interest:

> They would call it the *active* element in all consciousness ... whatever content his thought may include, there is a spiritual something in him which seems to *go out* to meet these qualities and contents, whilst they seem to *come in* to be received by it. It is what welcomes or rejects ... It is the home of interest, – not the pleasant or the painful, not even pleasure or pain, as such, but that within us to which pleasure and pain, the pleasant and the painful, speak. It is the source of effort and attention ...[24]

The mind is continuous in its engagement: the conscious is made of the same stuff as the unconscious; the foreseen is made of the same stuff as the unforeseen; the known is made of the same – experiential and primal – stuff as the unknown. But, to be fair, such a form of mind is as much a property of matter as how we spiritually engage with matter; it is not enough to make it a property of experience only, and though radical empiricism truly is great metaphysics, describing a complex philosophical problem in psychological terms is still difficult, as we have seen in the previous paragraph. The concept of experience has certainly broadened the scope of perception, and in phenomenology it has been well received and appropriated, but in its purified state it is not unproblematic. Though James's mosaicism is easily explained from the point of view of things, because they are chunky by nature, it does not follow how and why one stone would fit with the other unless the substantive is made of the same stuff as the transitive. Such a dissolution of the substantive into the transitive could be very convincing, but then we would need terms we could use for relations between things, between things and us, and between ourselves, and not terms that shift from one set of relations to the other. Do things experience each other? Do they share each other's time? Or do they share the same time? They certainly do, and if we were to proceed with such a thought, it would lead us to Whitehead's panexperientialism – a word, by the way, that he never used himself but that was invented for him by David Ray Griffin.[25] In addition, while things feel and experience each other, this does not explain why their mutual formation automatically follows. In short, we need a better word for it than "experience," but more on that later.

To find answers to these questions, perhaps we should explore the ideas of James's good friend Henri Bergson, who looked at matter as much as at psychology and reconceived experience as "intuition," a more creative, engaged form of life and living. While experience cannot be extended much beyond a broadened perception of things that are already there, intuition is an examination and embracing of an open-ended future and the unforeseen. By looking at it in this way, Bergson places intuition in the framework of a much older notion of sympathy, leading us directly into the realm of aesthetics.

the fabric of sympathy

Compared with James, Bergson sees things in a more fluid, elastic way. He often uses an idiom borrowed from thermodynamics, topology and other contemporary fields of science, in an effort not so much to update philosophy as to rethink scientific concepts like evolution in a contemporary, nondualistic philosophical framework. He often approved of the novelty of scientific ideas, but he just as often criticized science for using old Platonic notions of solidity and stability to explain those ideas. In his examples, things always stretch like rubber bands, melt like sugar cubes, heat up, expand; in short, they have an existence in time, not just in space. Things "reciprocally interpenetrate" and therefore differ strongly from James's mosaic tiles, even when these are softened by the "felt transitions of experience." Things, according to Bergson, are not surrounded by time but penetrated by it, and therefore they cannot be fully stable; their apparent solidity is continuously suspended:

> There do not exist things made, but only things in the making, not states that remain fixed, but only states in a process of change.[26]

The fringes of experience become the interpenetrations of intuition; Bergson expands James's concept into knowledge. It is now no longer *around* knowledge that things become blurred but deep inside it, at its very core. Things cannot definitely be known; for knowledge we would need to remove them from their existence in time, their duration, and isolate them in inert space. By nature, "intelligence" or the "intellect" needs to remove things from the flow of time, because it is "characterized by a natural inability to comprehend life."[27] The intellect has to stop or freeze-frame things to subject them to analysis, just as an anatomical dissection can be done only when the subject is dead. We cannot truly know them, because when we accept that life is inextricably bound up with matter, writes Bergson, we must at the same moment accept that its role is "to insert some indetermination into matter."[28] Note the word "some": he is not stating that things are amorphous; he is merely saying that if the mind is involved in the transformative state of things, knowledge is an inadequate concept, because it necessarily looks backward in time, using preconceptions, while "life is invention, unceasing creation."[29] If the mind wants to be involved in the process of making, it must be not only open but forward-looking, in the direction of as-yet-unknown creation; it cannot be satisfied by a (discursive) *moment* of knowledge but must be a process as well, acting in suspension. To return to the mosaic-fabric model for a moment, I would say that intuition is a knowledge that never solidifies, and it differs from experience for precisely that reason. In *A Pluralistic Universe*, James adopts some of Bergson's taste for interpenetration, and though he clearly admires him, he never seems fully convinced. Yet the concepts run in parallel: intuition is to knowledge what experience is to perception. Because the fabric of time penetrates things, or more precisely, because time itself "fabricates" things, knowledge has to deal with the unforeseen, and in that sense it has to go beyond what past experience can offer us or else it cannot act. Pure Jamesian experience can explain the part perception plays in our involvement with things, but not the part played by action. How could we act on things if our experience of things were not creative? This is where intuition appears, and it is not at all the irrational, unthinking, vague form of guessing it is often taken to be – on the contrary, it has precision, but a different kind of precision than intelligence has. Since intelligence anticipates outcomes and results, it needs to "mold" these for coming encounters, and its precision lies only there: the mold is exact but not the operation, which is properly speaking extremely blunt and imposing. Meanwhile, with intuition, the operation is everything; its precision lies not in its outcome, which is heterogeneous by nature, but in its process, its timing, what is generally called Bergson's "method" of intuition.[30] We now have a precision in space, which is geometrical, and a precision in time, which is operational. Clearly, when the outcome is suspended, the required exactitude cannot be epistemological but only methodological.

Intelligence operates by molds, "on the outside of things,"[31] while intuition discerns from within, in a distinction we remember from our discussions of Gothic craft and the internal mold of code. Bergson identifies intuition as *sympathy*, a form of feeling-knowing operating in the interior of things. "Sympathy" is a word we have used intermittently in previous chapters, but it is now in urgent need of closer investigation, because it has emerged at the very heart of our argument, if not of the entire book:

> An absolute can only be given in an intuition, while all the rest has to do with analysis. We call intuition here the sympathy by which one is transported into the interior of an object in order to coincide with what there is unique and consequently inexpressible in it. Analysis, on the contrary, is the operation which reduces the object to elements already known.[32]

Somehow – and this "somehow" will be the topic of our whole investigation – there exists a form of consciousness capable of placing itself at "the interior of an object." Two things are important here. First, this consciousness concerns the interior, making it at once part of our sectional fabric that cuts through things. Second, it concerns an object and considers sympathy to be not exclusively reserved for a relationality between people or between people and things but also occurring between things, or, just as easily, between animals and plants. Sympathy, as the etymology of the word indicates, is more of a feeling than a thought. Unlike love or hate, however, it is a feeling that is unspecified, "an instinct that has become disinterested."[33] Since life pervades all matter, sympathy goes with it in all directions:

> On the page it has chosen from the great book of the world, intuition seeks to recapture, to get back the movement and rhythm of the composition, to live again creative evolution by being one with it in sympathy.[34]

James's threads of feeling now start to penetrate all things, every object, every being, leading us into them through an ongoing attention, making up the tempo and timing of life. In an admirable example that has been discussed over and over – and usually ridiculed[35] – Bergson introduces the notion of sympathy in a most unexpected way. Drawing on the notebooks of Jean-Henri Fabre, the preeminent entomologist of his day, he discusses extensively the way the Ammophila wasp paralyzes a caterpillar without killing it. With nine successive stings to the caterpillar's nine nerve centers, it paralyzes the caterpillar completely, drags it to its nest and lay its eggs on top of it, so that when the eggs hatch the larvae will have fresh food. The offspring can live on the involuntary host for weeks.

We can be fairly sure that, although the Ammophila acts with precision on the nerve centers under the neck and in the thorax and the abdomen, it acts without intelligence, at least in the sense in which we understand the term; that is, it does not act with the help of symbols and schemata. On the other hand, says Bergson, we cannot presuppose any form of reflexive instinct either, and here we find his most powerful criticism of Darwinian thought. He does not oppose the fact that Darwinian evolution comes up with brilliant solutions but simply defines it as sloppy philosophy, since evolution doesn't "come up" with solutions, in the absence of a located intelligence. He accuses scientists of continuing to use concepts they say they want to leave behind, e.g., when they say a species "adapts." Often Darwinians turn out to be closet Lamarckians: if the tree doesn't stretch the giraffe's neck, then surely natural selection does. To explain the Ammophila's behavior simply by replacing divinely created intelligence with evolved automatic instinct will not do, since the victim moves in space, varies in size, has behavior that changes over time, and cannot simply be mapped by a set of instinctive actions. Something new always happens, even on the side of the wasp, the stings sometimes do not work or need to be redone, or the wasp accidentally kills the caterpillar or does not completely paralyze it. In short, the Ammophila knows *something*; at least, its instinct is slightly *elastic*, so that simple inborn instructions can be stretched and broadened by experimentation, though not generalized into pure symbols. The variability of outcomes and conditions cannot be handled by simple instinct but requires a form of knowledge between intelligence and instinct, between pure abstraction and pure bodily response. Bergson defines this in-between as intuition or sympathy:

> But there is no need for such a view if we suppose a sympathy (in the etymological sense of the word) between the Ammophila and its victim, which teaches it from within, so to say, concerning the vulnerability of the caterpillar.[36]

The sympathy "teaches it from within,"[37] that is, through a form of internal copying, the wasp feels the other's external bodily movements internally, in its own body, giving it an immediate knowledge. This is the same kind of knowledge we see in the actor who starts to come up with his or her own lines while rehearsing scenes from a play or movie. As the actor practices, plays the character day in and day out, new lines pop into his or her head, often ones the playwright deems better or more fitting. Likewise, the wasp acts simultaneously with the caterpillar, since it cannot be a second too late:

> The Ammophila, no doubt, discerns but a very little of that force, just what concerns itself; but at least it discerns it from within, quite otherwise than by a process of knowledge – by an intuition (*lived* rather than *represented*), which is probably like what we call divining sympathy.[38]

We tend to associate sympathy with gentility, with tenderness or help; rather than calling the Ammophila's behavior sympathetic, we would normally qualify it as cruel, or at least cold and calculating, but this is why it is such an illuminating example. There is no cruelty or aggression at work here, just as there is no cruelty in a leopard's killing of a young antelope; on the contrary, one can observe how precisely she does her work. Her attention is extreme but unstrained; the act takes place in a sphere of care and precision – and of a certain calm, in spite of the speed with which it is executed. Similarly, there is no disappointment when the hunt fails to bring the desired prize. We tend to psychologize sympathy, make it part of a personality, or of some subjectivity, but this is a grave mistake we should learn never to make.

What takes place in each case is that a mobile, transforming, behaving creature synchronizes its own behavior with that of another. This is not just an "inner mirroring," the term used by most commentators in discussing empathy and sympathy, which is too dependent on dualistic notions. If we mentally disconnect the act from the final result for a moment and look at what actually happens, we have no choice but to call this sympathy, exactly as it occurs between two people dancing, or two stars orbiting around each other, or when one person nods constantly while another speaks. We should resist what we have supposedly learned about sympathy in our own age, which has made it into a weak notion of identification and located it completely in the domain of psychology. Unfortunately, the word has lost much of the meaning of what James Frazer called "sympathetic magic,"[39] and the meaning it had for the ancient Greeks, who adhered to a less magical form. According to the Stoics, the universe was held together by a "cosmic sympathy,"[40] *sympatheia* (συμπάθεια), a form of all-out accordance and affinity, and human psychology was equated fully with the physicality of things.

Instead of acting by knowledge, by reading from an internal manual or schema, the Ammophila acts intuitively; that is, it incorporates the movements of another creature, mapping them back to a few crucial, nodal points it can act upon. Of course, finding nerve centers is not as easy to imagine as pinpointing joints, for instance, which would be a purely visual form of mapping and would not need to be internalized. However, the process of sympathy is internal, but "*felt* rather than *thought*."[41] In this way, feeling becomes an "abstract," interiorized form of motion, a preparing and tensing of muscles, and the integration of such tensing provides orientation. It is as networked as the brain, though it is not located there but sited in the whole body, with all its points and nodes, not as a preexisting map but as an experiential fabric. It certainly adds up to an awareness and readiness. It does not map the other as an image or as a form but as a rhythm of behavior over time that it acquires immediately and can relate back to as a form, or, as we have said before, a pattern. In a way, Bergson came to the same conclusion as his older contemporary Étienne-Jules Marey did when he placed successive chronophotographs of a running horse on top of each other in the hope of finally seeing movement, only to see the image dissolve into a blurry cloud. Only after concentrating on the changing placement of the horse's joints over time and tracing their movement by drawing the continuous curves through these points was he able to discern a pattern of change.[42] What he saw was not a form moving or changing but the reverse, he suddenly saw change itself, *the form of change*. And he saw that that form – a graph – was different for each animal, each person, for every specific act. And, though it was abstract in a sense, it was particular and unique to each being, more a *temporary* abstraction than a generalized one. Bergson called such a pattern duration, and he called the special knowledge we have of such patterns intuition. Now, the Ammophila does not have an internal eye with which to study such a pattern (we would lapse into fatal dualities if we postulated such an eye); rather, it must be *lived*, lived *sectionally*, which means in you as much as in the other. Though its duration becomes the duration of the other, in a way we can no longer tell who is the other – if we can even still speak of an other, or, more disturbingly, of a self.

Étienne-Jules Marey. Chronomatography of a running horse (1885).

In a sense, it is not enough to speak about "being transported *into* the interior of an object," since that object is constantly "in the making" and deploys a pattern of behavior, a whole set of interrelated movements, and therefore one must also move *with* the object, after having moved into it. And after you move with the object, you must *adjust* your own speed; you must be careful and attentive and time your actions, because along with synchronizing, you must also act upon your sympathies. Sympathy necessarily carries a certain risk. To return to the example of dancing for a second, dancing always starts with the mere mirroring or complementing of the other's moves; one subsequently starts to vary the moves, expand on them, make countermoves, insert extra steps, i.e., *act within the act of sympathy*. This is exactly what the method of intuition is: an extension of sympathy through a floating and modulating of attention, a specific effort of gradation.

All things exist elastically; they are part of a stretch of gradations, as in Bergson's famous example of how we perceive a dissolving lump of sugar ("I must wait until the sugar dissolves"[43]). Even perceived without the hot tea, a sugar cube is potentially sweet, just as a vase implies a table and flowers even when not in use. All things are situated in time as much as in space.

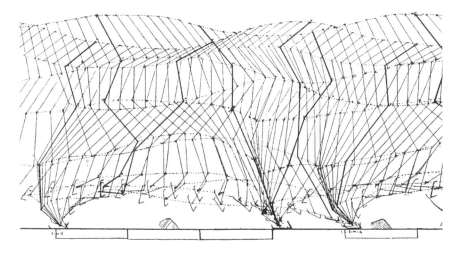

Étienne-Jules Marey. Analysis according to the "graphic method" of the
chronomatography of a running horse (1885).

When the vase stands on an actual table, but close to the edge, the vase implies its falling as much as its holding of flowers. As William James would
say, the vase is enveloped by a withness and a nextness. Sympathy guides us
into things, into their existence, which is one of gradations. We are constantly filled with the duration of things. We encounter such words in Bergson time and time again; for him, sympathy is not at all the vague,
"disorderly" feeling of "lived identification" that Deleuze makes of it[44] – it
is a feeling that is anything but disorderly, and intuition as a method completely relies on the procedural steps of sympathy. It is probably the only
feeling that, unlike others such as love and hate, draws you into a movement
at the start, then drags you along with it, and then allows you to live with
the other – that is, adjust your life so you can live with the other, and then
step out when you change your sympathies. I would say sympathy is the
only feeling that leads to thought by itself (love and hate automatically lead
to fantasy). If I had to distinguish between sympathy and intuition, I would
say sympathy was at the head of the process and intuition at the tail. Remember, we are still weaving, and threads leading into something feel different from threads entangling and making nodes. We enter a process by

feeling, but we cannot exit it without thinking.

Between pure material, reflexive instinct and pure mental, analytical intelligence, Bergson carved out a specific place for a non-discursive, non-analytical intelligence, such as that we know in animals, or artists, or from doing skilled work like carving wood or whipping cream. To take that last example, one should ask oneself: Where am I when I hold the bowl in one hand and the whisk in the other? Where is my consciousness? My feeling stretches all the way through my arm, from elbow to wrist to the top of the whisk, and extends into the cream itself; they all move simultaneously, alert for the moment when the cream starts to stiffen. It is a completely haptic operation; no space separates me from the cream. The longer it takes, the closer attention I pay; one beat too many and the fat will congeal into butter and all my effort will have been in vain. Not only cream but all matter that moves internally is capable of such a self-forming transition, agitated at first, it starts to settle and find a new pattern, all without the use of molds. Such consciousness is an intelligence that is immediate, that acts in matter and finds its way in it, and, as Bergson would say, the life in matter and in me, the cook, are shared; it is one and the same life now, for as long as it takes.

Peeking briefly forward into our study, I do not think it will come as a surprise that the material transitions we are gathering in this chapter, from James's threads turning into a Bornean Dyak's head to the whipped cream a moment ago, are the very same as those in the previous chapter, such as Semper's *Stoffwechsel* and the iron hinge stretching across the wooden door of the cathedral in the Yonne valley. Can we say that the attention the hinge pays to the door, so to speak, through elaboration and ornamentation, is exactly the same as the attention the smith paid to the iron and, more radically, the attention we again pay to the ornament when we look at it? I am sure we can. We do not so much look *at* it as live *with* it. Let us just say that the sympathy between the smith and the iron, and subsequently between the iron and the wood, on a good day in 1185 was the same sympathy I have with it today, more than eight hundred years later. I would not even call it "relived," because the duration and intuition are still the same. This is where we need to go, but first we must clarify the steps and the nature of sympathy in more detail.

Since I am Dutch, I hope you will not mind the following brief examination of my native language. Dutch has three words that can help us understand the ascending intimacy of felt relations (all relations in the Jamesian sense are relations of activities): *invoelen, meevoelen* and *meeleven*. The first, *invoelen*, is very close to the German *Einfühlen* (which we will return to soon) and means "feeling-into"; in English it is mostly translated as "to empathize" or the noun "empathy." The second, *meevoelen*, is the same as the German *Mitfühlen* and literally means "feeling-with"; it is generally translated as "to sympathize" or "sympathy." The third, which is more difficult to explain, as it has neither a German or English equivalent, is *meeleven*, "living-with," and is generally understood to be the most intense variant of "sympathize" used in sentences like "I sympathize with your loss." This "living-with" cannot be used as a noun in the manner of the first two. Again, if we disconnect the terms from day-to-day psychology for a moment, their literal meanings clearly describe the three-step methodology of intuition: feel-into, feel-with and live-with, specifically in that order. Bergson was adamant about intuition being a form of thinking, though one without any processing of symbols. On the one hand, it is immediate and reflexive; on the other, it must be a kind of "warped" or flexible reflection, since one is allowed, invited even, to expand one's acts of affinity. Sympathy as it is usually understood, as a caring, helpful attitude, occurs precisely during the third of the three steps, because it acts within the act of sympathy. Primatologist Frans de Waal gives dozens of examples in his book *The Age of Empathy*,[45] and he argues powerfully and unexpectedly that the mechanisms behind acts like torture are exactly the same as those that drive helpful, caring actions. A torturer needs to find the same points of duration as the one offering help, though the former tries to find them to inflict pain and the latter to provide support. And though morality is not part of our discussion, it should be made clear at this point that the choice for one or the other is separate from initial sympathy. But, if you don't mind, I feel more comfortable with the caring option. In the following example, involving the bonobo Kuni, De Waal shows how much helping is based on this notion of sympathy:

> The event concerns Kuni, who had found a stunned bird that
> had hit the glass wall of her zoo enclosure. Kuni took the bird
> up to the highest point of a tree to set it free. She spread its
> wings as if it were a little airplane, and sent it out into the air,
> thus showing a helping action geared to the needs of a bird.[46]

We immediately appreciate here how the perception of a flying bird, the
experience of that bird crashing into a glass wall, and the intuition of the
wings being the acting part of the now nonfunctioning bird are all rolled
into one act of sympathy, moving the bonobo toward trying to help the bird
regain its flight. This example is fundamentally the same as the Ammophila
stinging its prey to paralyze it. Let us not forget that both the bonobo and
the wasp have acquired an intuitive knowledge of the *motor* functions of the
body in question, and that both sympathies concern the vulnerability of
their objects. Perhaps only one cares about its subject, but certainly both are
careful and attentive, and this attention guides them not only into the other
but extends their sympathy into a behavior that can either support or paralyze the other. There is an incredible form of objectivity at work here, a *felt
objectivity* that is completely distinct from the rationalism we normally associate objectivity with. There is nothing personal about sympathy. It is an
objectivity focused not on inert matter but on matter as part of time, on
matter as something transformable and ever-changing.

It is an attentiveness that Bergson finds to an equal degree in art:

> Our eye perceives the features of the living being, merely as
> assembled, not as mutually organized. The intention of life, the
> simple movement that runs through the lines, that binds them
> together and gives them significance, escapes it. This intention
> is just what the artist tries to regain, in placing himself back
> within the object by a kind of sympathy, by breaking down, by
> an effort of intuition, the barrier that space puts up between
> him and his model.[47]

Today, a hundred years later, it is a bit too obvious for a philosopher dis-

cussing intuition to start investigating aesthetics, and after a century of expressionism, improvisation, process art and action painting, we should perhaps stay away from investigating intuition as a driving mechanism for art,
since we would be slipping over too many truisms. What I find interesting
in this context, however, is not only the use of the word "sympathy," nor the
fact that space seems to completely collapse but that the artist is working
on a portrait ("his model"). Suppose we use Bergson's formula "lived rather
than represented" and apply it to the artist painting a portrait. Since the act
is performed in sympathy, the artist cannot be satisfied with remaining on
the outside of his subject, with the representational image, on the contrary,
he needs to be "transported in," to become the other and then paint a self-
portrait, so to speak. Again, this is not very different from an actor coming
up with new lines that are not his own (he would never say such things) nor
those of the character (because they have not been written by the author)
but something entirely new. After living through a century of abstract art,
we can hardly imagine someone sitting with an easel in front of a landscape
or person any longer, but the act of sympathy, as a method or procedure,
starts with a naturalist attitude[48] – however, it does not end with it. The
episode of sympathy is exclusively an aesthetic one, an immediate seeing-
feeling-thinking relationship with things. It is a relationship of caring. This
does not mean, however, that all our acts and views are suddenly works of
art, or our social relations, or our politics; it simply means that the method
of intuition is one of aesthetics (more than of philosophy, and more than of
religion). When we see, we see-feel. And when we feel, we feel-think.[49] And
when we think, we think-act. We orient ourselves by feeling, either in space
or in time, and as James says, we are with, next to, in, over, against, towards
things. *All relations are felt relations* and therefore relations of sympathy.

As anticipated we have proceeded from perception to experience, and from
experience to intuition and sympathy, to finally enter the field of aesthetics;
this last step is inevitable. Anyone familiar with nineteenth-century aesthetics will immediately have recognized Bergson's phrase "transported into
the interior of an object" as a description of *Einfühlung*. This term, which
has an intense, very well-documented but very brief history, has mostly had

to do with German art theory, starting with Robert Vischer's thesis in 1872, which developed the concept in the most admirable way, not only explaining *Einfühlung* as a form of aesthetic experience but extending it into *Ausfühlung, Zusammenfühlung* and even *Nachfühlung* – respectively feeling-out, feeling-together and feeling-after: all terms that indicate that durations need not be exact synchronizations but can be expanded in more directions.[50] Though the word was in use long before Vischer, he and his father Theodor reintroduced it into aesthetics. It was extremely influential for the next thirty years, until it slowly became psychologized by Theodor Lipps, but still remained part of aesthetic theory and was eventually taken over by the same Wilhelm Worringer whom we met in our discussion of the nature of the Gothic. After Worringer wrote *Abstraktion und Einfühlung* in 1908, the term moved to England via T. E. Hulme, translator of Bergson and advocate of expressionism, and to the United States via Edward Titchener's *Experimental Psychology* (1909), who was the first to translate it as "empathy," a term picked up immediately by Vernon Lee, writer of ghost stories as well as aesthetic theory. Consequently, in the English-speaking world, Worringer's book became known under the title *Abstraction and Empathy*. During World War I, the concept was buried in the trenches and replaced by pure abstractionism. Ever since, empathy and sympathy have been outcasts in the fields of philosophy and aesthetics and become completely adopted by psychology, which inveterately continues to speak of selves and others. Over the years, sympathy has disappeared, and empathy has become a fluffy thing, a weak, timid form of sympathy. Today, one book after another is published on empathy – empathy in animals, in civilization, in business management – which is a significant development and a sign that our times may take a turn for the better, but most of these treatises are a far cry from Bergsonian aesthetics.

As far as I am concerned, contemporary empathy is only a faint echo of classical sympathy, nothing but a psychological residue of what originally lay at the heart of all the relations within the realms of the animate and inanimate. Worse, if we recall the three-step method of intuition, empathy should be considered an *interrupted sympathy*, broken off in a way that has troubled relations among things, among people and things, and subsequently also among people. It has caused human relations to crystallize into a frosted web of globalized media and art to founder in dead abstraction. Every other day, we see a picture of a car crash in the newspaper, or hear of a young person's online suicide announcement, or see footage of a bleeding, thrashing whale – all horrendous images, obviously, but their power never goes beyond that of the shock, precisely because they are images, precisely because media know only the aesthetics of the instantaneous. These images are cold, in the terms of McLuhan's analysis, not because they are abstract but because they lack the abstraction of design. Mediated images are so specific that they cannot possibly be of any concern to us. There is no way we can "live-with" these images, weave them into our lives: the care needed by living beings must go out to things first, things more abstract but also more gentle in a way. Since the day our world completely crystallized, it has been expected that our personal psychology will make up for the loss of sympathy, but the images could not be more crude. Things are capable of generalizing care; images are not. And things truly are part of a web, rather than just dropping out of one; that is, they exist in relation, in entanglement, while the very definition of an image is its detachment (since we need a cave or a camera to produce one.) Do not misunderstand me: I am not saying that an image cannot be elaborated as a material and into a thing – it can – but that is as far removed from mere broadcasting as possible.

Adjusting our politics, being a little kinder in our daily encounters, is all very well, but it is not nearly enough. We have made all our interactions so mediated that all our sympathies now emerge solely from pure, personalized psychology, in a manner similar to the way charity was detached from religion ages ago. But that is only the lowest form of sympathy, one that remains when the relationship between things has been replaced completely by mediation. The highest form is one that relates all things, whether they are human or made of stone. A thing is always a thing made, taken care of and needing to be cared for, as Heidegger elucidated with his notion of "cura,"[51] meaning both concern in the sense of design and care in the sense of maintenance, a coinciding of concepts that is utterly Ruskinian. We must come to recognize that sympathy is not something extra, added on top of our relations with things and with each other; rather, *it lies at the core of those relations*. Sympathy is the very stuff relations are made of, but, as we will see in the second half of this chapter, those relations exist between us and things – all designed things – before playing out between people. Sympathy is the power of things at work, working between all things, and between us as things. Humans are nothing but things among other things. There is no need for mediation between a world supposedly on one side and people on the other; we only need a web of things, corresponding, resonating, synchronizing, existing in sympathy.

My central argument is that the way we live with each other depends on how we furnish our lives. Now, natural things – clouds, trees, rocks, mountains, all the Ruskinian requisites – design each other and are formed in relationship to each other, in full sympathy; therefore, aesthetically, these products are fine as they are. And even if we do not accept the distinction between natural and artificial things – or go so far as to insist that things can only be artificial – the latter category can still be designed *badly*, produced under the wrong conditions, obstructing every possibility of sympathy instead of opening towards it. Now that we have mentioned Heidegger anyway, we might as well identify the former as objects (his notorious *Gegenstand*, or "what stands against") and the latter as things, things we require to be related, not to be signs, images or objects. It is not sufficient for these things to be made; it matters *how* they are made, i.e. designed. The first and most important thing we ought to learn from John Ruskin is that our morality is rooted in these things, and so we should be unforgiving about them; we can negotiate anything except the designing-making of things.

Honestly, I could not care less about most things. Why? Because they do not care about me, or they care only about my money, or my opinion, or my taste, desires, dreams, comfort, whatever. All such accessories cause them to circulate in secondary systems. Things only need to expose their making, in a way that is both delicate and elaborate, making them vulnerable and fragile. Not unlike the caterpillar, they (abstractly) sacrifice themselves before being encountered. In the end, this is what relationality means: things are giving and generous. Ruskin's whole economy is one of sacrifice, whether that of the gratuitous ornament in *Seven Lamps*, whose details the stone carver spends hour after hour getting right, or the selfless extraneous labor in *Unto This Last,* in which the physician spends hours of overtime caring for his patients. Things only start to network when they have exceeded their use value, turning them into acts of pure care.

When we say, as we did in the previous chapter, that every technology ought to be a technology that sympathizes with matter (since we refuse all mediation), acting as much at the inside as on the outside, our statement is, after all, an aesthetic one. It is a doing guided by feeling, not the other way around. We not only require technologies of making and philosophies of technology but, moreover, an aesthetics of technology, a – allow me – *fabricism*. A fibrous fabricism. Without such an aesthetics, making will fall back into the hands of engineers, who persistently confuse making with the assembly of predetermined parts according to predetermined relations, such as that between a bolt and a nut or a post and a beam. While we should help bring things into existence without completely abandoning their indeterminacy or eliminating all redundancy, doing so certainly makes a thing less of a form or an object. This enables things to disengage and start relations with other things. And, as in the case of clouds or mountains, which also lack precise definition, things are felt before they are seen or understood: pure unmediatedness and immediacy.

Whether something becomes a thing or an object is a question of design, not of philosophy. Fragility is an issue of design. There is simply no use in overcoming the subject-object and human-world dualities without realizing the vast consequences for our felt relations and shared consciousness. If one talks about things, one must talk about feelings. In my view, sympathy is first and foremost an aesthetic responsibility before becoming a social, philosophical, religious or political one. If we feel the urge to consider a digital Gothic, a digital return to ornament, and (as we will) a radicalization of the picturesque, we can do so only by reestablishing sympathy as fundamental to aesthetics, an aesthetics between and of all things, in order to create a fabric of those things.

Though it is very tempting at this point, we will have to postpone developing this notion of design into a separate theory – *a theory of entanglement* – and comparing our attempt to other concepts, both historical and contemporary. We will do so later, in the final two chapters, as we are clearing the last remnants of a human or divine designer from design (things design each other: this is what entanglement means). For now, let us stay with our central question: Will we be able to weave a web of sympathy between ourselves with the help of things?

You might wonder whether I am out of my mind, assigning such powers to design – do I really think design can change our lives? (Yes, in fact, I think *only* design can change our lives, since living itself is a question of design, and thus of changing it even more.) But keep in mind that we are surrounded by thousands of designed things every moment of the day. All things are designed, not only staplers, teapots and metro cars but also insurance companies, fruit logistics processes and NGOs, as well as clouds and mountains. So, to immediately follow the first question with a second: Do I really think we need these to be Gothic and fabricist? (Again, yes.) As they are now, things seem no longer to know how sympathy guides a feeling into a thing, that is, via a practical object, and how that structures our life, creates a rhythm, and how that rhythm creates a whole fabric of thing-feelings, akin to our feelings toward friends and acquaintances. Part of my investigation in the rest of this chapter will be geared to finding that fatal moment when art "went abstract," severed itself from things – a moment when, in making art go its own way and allowing it to retreat from daily life, we lost something. Abstraction suddenly became the only way forward, and by nature abstraction knows no moderation, because at every moment there is only one option: to abstract again. Abstraction constantly seeks purification, and if it is not stopped, it will keep on generalizing. I aim not only to locate the point when this happened but also to explain how art and design once, with sympathy, recognized the way we lived our lives. We will see that things can do the same, in different ways, by guiding our attention outward toward all things or inward toward ourselves.

But I shall slow down so as not to get ahead of myself. First, we will note how Lipps, in German, used the word *Sympathie* in his aesthetic theories, and observe that his original concept was much closer to Bergson's notion of sympathy than to what we understand today as empathy. Then we will trace the way Worringer split abstraction and empathy in world art history into two apparently forever separate hemispheres. Unexpectedly, we

will also come to recognize that Worringer was theoretically correct in an-
alyzing art in terms of these two components, though not practically correct
in suggesting that artists must choose one or the other. Just as Bergson's notion of intuitive knowledge is composed of two interpenetrating parts, intelligence and instinct, so do abstraction and empathy form the two halves
of sympathy. *Sympathy is abstraction and empathy unseparated* (like the fat
molecules and air bubbles in whipped cream). We will see that sympathy is
felt abstraction or contemplated immediacy; thus, it does not simply function without abstraction, or even a bit of cruelty, but is a different form of
abstraction altogether from the abstraction we are so used to.

lipps's sympathy and worringer's empathy

There is no denying that sympathy, with such far-reaching roots in aesthetics, especially in its German form of *Einfühlung*, rather than turning aesthetics into something naturalized and psychological turns all our
sympathetic feelings into an inborn, hard-wired aesthetics. We feel toward
each other as we do toward things. If the reverse were the case – if we felt
about things as we do about each other – then we would live in a constant
illusion: things would be shadows of living creatures, representatives accepted in lieu of the real thing, for lack of anything better. The relationship
between things and beings would be discontinuous, and we would live in a
half-world: half our contacts would be real, the other half simply an inter-
lude. Bergson had already denied the human exclusivity of sympathy, using
the Ammophila as his chief example; with Lipps, we enter the fundamental
operational field of sympathy: the making of beautiful things. When things
are in-the-making anyway, certainly the feeling and intuition guiding such
continuous fabrication guides the making-of-things too. The intuited reflection itself now becomes the source of production and creation. And what
was still a relationship between living creatures in Bergson now takes on a
more fundamental form, as a relationship between the animate and the
inanimate, but the relation remains unchanged, though it is reversed, but
only if one holds on to dualisms, because it is still a relation of life. Here is
Lipps in 1905:

> What I empathize into it is quite generally life. And life is en-
> ergy, inner working, striving and accomplishing. In a word, life
> is activity. But activity is that in which I experience an expen-
> diture of energy.[52]

Activity. Life. Force. Energy. Striving. Movement. Lipps invariably uses these words together. Let us try to unravel exactly what is happening here. It is not difficult, since Lipps offers so many examples, from simple lines to columns, from a storm to a dance or a willow tree. Lipps's notion of *Ein-fühlung* is thus immediately differentiated from the other, much better-known ones we find in Vischer and Wölfflin, which generally concern the proportions of forms and spaces, as his is definitely about the relationship between movement and form. Let us start with things that genuinely move.

Why do I feel anger and rage when I experience a storm? Lipps asks himself. One sees the trees shaking violently in the wind, the dark clouds sweeping across the sky, the rain gushing over the windowpanes. One sees all that, and one feels rage. Obviously, he says, the anger does not lie in the storm – Ruskin had already dismissed such artistic notions with the idea of the pathetic fallacy – rather, the felt rage lies in me: it is I who feels it. Yet it is not real rage Lipps feels, he is not angry at the storm or any other object; what he feels is an abstracted, disinterested rage, more of a mood. Nor, ar-gues Lipps, is it pure subjectivity, in which one merely animates an object by projecting one's feelings into it, since the "content" of his empathic feel-ings lies in the object. Beauty can be located neither in the object nor in the subject: it is a felt resonance between the two, and as it resonates, it dissolves the dualism. There must be some kind of correspondence between the storm and the feeling, and it is this correspondence that he defines as *Einfühlung*. Between the nature of the movement, of the actual activity of the storm, and that of one's feelings, there exists an *Einklang*, or accordance. When we see a horse jump a hedge or a performer walk along a tightrope, we often contract the same muscles, even if we are sitting still in a chair. We imme-diately – that is, without reflection – project ourselves into the other, the living (or non-living but moving) thing. Certainly, we should refrain from calling such initial bodily responses feelings. It is only after projecting oneself into the other with this involuntary immediacy that one starts to expand and move with the other, that the muscular tension eases and is replaced by a mood, such as rage or anger. William James developed what is known today as the Lange-James hypothesis to explain how bodily movement precedes emotion. When you see a bear, you run away in fear, as anyone understands. But James argued that the observation should be more precise: we run away *first* and *then* experience fear, not the other way around. Lipps takes this concept out of the domain of pure emotion and neurological response and brings it into that of aesthetics, where the movement of something outside you evokes a feeling within you:

> In a word, I am now with my feeling of activity entirely and wholly in the moving figure. Even spatially, if we can speak of the spatial extent of the ego, I am in its place. I am transported into it. I am, as far as my consciousness is concerned, entirely and wholly identical with it. Thus feeling myself active in the observed figure, I feel also in it free, facile, and proud. This is the aesthetic imitation, and this imitation is at the same time aesthetic *Einfühlung*.[53]

The mirrored movement becomes felt and, in a way, even aesthetic: after the bodily imitation, the psychological feeling follows. Or, more precisely, an extensive movement is extended by an intensive one: they both occur in time, though the former is the movement *of* a body and the latter a movement *in* a body. "Of course," Lipps says, "such motion has nothing to do with space." Rather, it operates between time and matter; space has nothing to do with it, not even with the extensive form of motion.

Now, let us look at things that do not move so obviously. We can read the phrase "moving figure" to mean a figure or person that moves, but also as a figure of movement, not so much an image as an expression of it. An image of movement would be like a photograph and could actually appear to be of something standing still; an expression of movement, on the other hand, would take characteristics of movement, such as change, growth or imbalance, and apply them to the organization of an image or form. Suppose such a moving figure consisted of a simple line, such as a spiral:

> Already when, looking at the spiral, I follow it, and its separate
> proportions successively, I am making this spiral come into ex-
> istence for me or in my perception. This spiral is first wide,
> then narrow; or, reversing the way of looking at it, first narrow,
> then wide. As a consequence the spiral becomes successively
> narrower or wider, it *narrows or widens itself*, and it does this
> in a definite manner. The existence of the spiral is a *becoming*.[54]

The line is not simply there, statically; it is a becoming, a narrowing and
widening: these are verbs and actions. But it is not really moving, is it? It is
indeed, but the very movement we called "intensive" a couple of paragraphs
ago is no longer just in you but also in the object. This motion, like heat,
elasticity or tension, can be felt but not seen. The body does not distinguish
between the experience of real movement of an object and an object that
seems to be a *trace* of a movement, such as one of Ruskin's abstract lines,
discussed in the previous chapter. Why is this? Any real motion occurs along
a path, like the flight of a bird or a walk along a tightrope, and as one experiences and sympathizes with it, one extends the present moment into a
possible future. Path and trace, future and past. Clearly, the path of a bird is
not as predictable as the trajectory of a football on its way to the goal, but
for now it is enough to acknowledge that they are both examples of a phenomenon that requires its own particular form of perception. Keep in mind
that, according to James and Bergson, we don't "see" the movement of a bird
– that is, we don't take a snapshot and remove it from time; rather, we see
in time as much as in space, and this seeing includes the dark fringes of the
unforeseen. Motion requires something more than perception, it needs to
be experienced, as James would say, or intuited, as Bergson would. Seeing
must be enhanced by feeling – and this feeling is automatically one of sympathy. Here is Lipps again:

> I *sympathize* with the manner the column behaves or testifies
> to an inner liveliness, because I recognize therein a natural

mode of behavior of my own that gives me happiness. Thus,
all pleasure produced by spatial forms and, we can add, any
kind of aesthetic pleasure, is a feeling of sympathy that makes
us happy.[55]

Is the column not as active as the bird in flight? This is what Lipps implicitly
asks us. And of course it is, because as much as the flight of the bird is the
result of effort and activity, so is the standing of the column. Lipps simply
makes no qualitative distinction between movement and posture:

> The self-raising of the column is its 'proper activity.' Thereby,
> the term activity is meant in its full sense: exertion, effort, use
> of force; a use of force that achieves something.[56]

With a column, we see the movement, the "force," at the same time as we
see its trace, the column itself. How is a column different from the trace of
Newton's apple falling? What is it other than a path for future forces to
glide over? A column is a rail or a road. Structure is infrastructure, always,
be it Greek or Gothic. The only difference between a Doric column and a
Gothic specimen is that the first serves a downward motion and the second
an upward rising. Both are beautiful (if I may ignore my own anticlassical
stance for a moment), because both are active. In itself, a column or a line
is not beautiful at all, and though the object of my aesthetic enjoyment is
the column, the experience of beauty is in me. Again, this does not mean
the whole operation is something subjective or solipsistic. If I am saddened
by the view of a willow tree, Lipps argues, that does not mean there is no
activity on the tree's part. The willow "hangs" and "sways"; obviously we
would not feel anything if it were a white cube or a black box. The sympathy
is the accordance of the activity of the one with that of the other – an extensive movement answered by another extensive one, or an extensive one
answered by an intensive one, or an intensive movement answered by another intensive one. All these are possible, though not the same. Nothing
moves without undergoing that movement internally, not even a planet. In
its rotation around the sun, the earth is not dragged by an invisible cord

(there are no invisible cords): gravity permeates the planet. The gravity that makes the planet spherical is the same gravity that makes it rotate around the star. A person dancing with another "feels" as much as he or she "does" – that is, the movement is as much intensive as extensive, as much of the body as in the body. Force exceeds all form. Life exceeds all form. That is why the activity of the column becomes your activity, and the being-in-the-making becomes your making: "the form is always the being-formed-by-me; it is my activity," says Lipps. In fact, it is not mine alone but shared.

Lipps seems to readily switch between objective notions (the column has its "proper activity") and subjective ones ("it is my activity"), which is quite logical, since he translated Hume's 1739 *Treatise on Human Nature*, which was the beginning of the subjectivist stance on aesthetics. In fact, there is no contradiction here, because we make the activity ours since there is activity already, it *resonates*, not only among us, as Hume presumes when he describes humans as "strings,"[57] but among objects as well, and between objects and us. Of course, this is the step that Hume does not take, while James does, and Lipps adds an extra step. Beauty, of course, is not just perception, nor just perception becoming activity, nor even what we today call interactivity, which is merely reciprocal; rather, it is *attuned activity*, which Ruskin would call work, or help, or collaboration. Beauty is a goal, an agreed goal, and one agreed on by all – two or more – of the involved terms. And, yes, these agreements are local abstractions, merely points between acting parts, postural points, not an overall abstract system agreed on by all the members at a boardroom meeting and resulting in a system of dashed lines that "harmonically" orders all the parts in position. Beauty is what the parts do, not what the whole is. The activity between the parts involves any "onlooker," who in his or her turn becomes a part, or better, becomes part of it. We are not recipients but participants. Lipps's column is sculpted by its relations, and these relations are felt relations, and those feelings between the columns and the beams and the pedestals are directly shared with us. We simply become part of the relational, resonating network of sympathies. So, yes, it is objective, but the objectivity is a *felt* one. The tree feels the wind, and as the tree feels, it takes on form, and as the tree takes on form, we start to feel it too – not physical wind but rage – and then we take on form by adjusting our position or posture. If I were to map out such relations in a diagram, with dots indicating forms and arrows indicating forces and feelings, we would not even be able to see the difference between animate and inanimate things. Of course, the storm is not angry, nor is the willow sad, and though Lipps is not fully clear at every point about the antidualist nature of *Einfühlung*, often enough, he is:

> *Einfühlung* is the fact … that the opposition between myself
> and the object disappears …[58]

And this is simply essential to sympathy. Subjectivity is fully objectified, and vice versa – nothing is left behind. There is just no use in holding onto the dualism of subject and object and then building bridges of feeling between them, while keeping little bits of consciousness behind, as we see in phenomenology. More precisely, sympathy only appears when the dualism disappears, at the point where things become feelings and feelings things. As we argued before, the subject and object share an abstract, sectional plane of life, but what is shared is not shared as the same thing or in the same way. The contracting of forces is done differently by each body or form. The paralyzed caterpillar certainly feels things differently from the stinging Ammophila, but they still share these "Marey points" – points not of agreement, perhaps, but at least of sufficient correspondence.

When we see the bird moving, we feel its motion; with the column, we see it standing still but also feel its motion and activity. The bird lives in an aesthetic relation with the air, as the column lives-with its adjacent partners; a difference only occurs at the point where aesthetics becomes a profession: the making of beautiful things. In short, aesthetics is something that existed long before humans did, exchanged between objects, but we use it to make those objects. When we see-feel a bird in flight, the aesthetics originates in the intensification of an extensive motion, but when we design a column, to make it aesthetic we must draw it in the realm of correspondence, and therefore as a product of motion. Mind you, we do not design the column *as if* it were moving – again, that would make it a mere image of movement, such as we see in the Baroque and streamlining – rather, we use movement to make the column for us. In Jamesian terms, this means we need to draw it *in relation*: the seen object penetrated by the felt transition. Things interpenetrate because they are connected by feeling – fringy, frayed, *Gothic things*. Don't start with Dyaks' heads and then interconnect them; start with threads and feathers and tighten them into nodes, weave and entangle them into surfaces or braid them into sticks. Take James's thinking, but execute it the way Morris would.

Anyone who takes the time to analyze a carpet design by Morris & Co. (for example, Bullerswood or Holland Park) will quickly notice how their notion of the entangled fabric (not the actual fabric but the fabric of the design) exceeds the complexity of, say, a network or a web. In the latter, the nodes consist of zero-dimensional points (connected by one-dimensional lines), while in Morris's carpets, the linear twigs overlap and interlock, sometimes loosely and sometimes extremely tightly, but always in a way that the nodes become zones of exchange. They are zones of exchange of speed and force, again: stations. Sometimes the twigs simply bounce off each other, or, conversely, the interlocking multiplies and starts to form a local braid, or, in two directions, starts plaiting a local patch of surface but then unravels again and divides up in separate strands or ribbons that end in spirals. This is clearly not the kind of design one can schematize in a single network of black lines interconnected by black dots, or, as Bruno Latour calls them, "black boxes."[59] Never fully relations, never fully nodes, never really soft, never really rigid, these entanglements constantly negotiate between extensive things and intensive feelings in all gradations.

To feel sympathy we need to see form and being-formed simultaneously; we need to see-feel form and force at the same time. If we only get one or the other, there can be no correspondence. As we saw previously, only in the transition do objects take on pattern. When we design or draw just the force, we immediately blur the object, exactly like Marey when he stopped being able to see the running horse. In this case, we are unable to *empathize*: we see the inside, but we have missed the point of entry – there is more a seeing-through than a feeling-into. However, when we design or draw only the form, we can see Marey's horse but not its proper activity, not Marey's blur. Then we are unable to *sympathize*: we have found the point of

J. H. Dearle and William Morris for Morris & Co. *Bullerswood* carpet (1889).

entry but miss the inner motion to move with and feel-with.

As Worringer's main thesis states, the first realm is that of abstraction, the second that of naturalism: these are the two poles of art. And the poles are precisely that: peaks in a continuous field, like mountains in a landscape – it is not a case of a choice between two territories with a rigid border between them but of a necessary double orientation. When we say sympathy starts with naturalism, we can take that quite literally as the start of a methodology, but if we stop with naturalism we will only have depicted the outer form, and we will end up with a sensuous work of art, certainly, but we will have created only an image of life and not life itself – recalling the opposition between Ruskin's naturalist outline and his abstract centerline discussed in the chapter on ornament. So far, we have learned that a design cannot make us "see" life itself but only make us feel it, through sympathy. And to feel life, we must go further than the outer form, into the object and into the realm of forces, but if we go too far, we will end up with pure abstraction and pure force, pure action and pure change – in short, right in the middle of the sublime. The experience will become one of pure, lofty contemplation, of a body frozen in awe of the excess of force.

This is exactly why Ruskin could not agree with, or even befriend, Viollet-le-Duc. Comparing Ruskin's watercolors of the Matterhorn, which show a pattern that manages the lower-scale courses as well as the large-scale mass, with Viollet's drawings of Mont Blanc, which turn the mountain into a mega-crystal, into pure structure, one can see what Ruskin so emphatically disagreed with. Viollet-le-Duc turns Mont Blanc[60] into an object of mere engineering. We can observe a similar attitude in his design for a concert hall in *Entretiens*,[61] in which he cleared out all the Gothic indeterminism of the ribbed vaults and compound piers, turning them into determined, structurally defined elements of either tension or

Eugène Viollet-le-Duc. *Salle Voutée, fer et maçonnerie.* Plate 18 from the twelfth lecture in *Entretiens sur l'architecture* (1864).

compression, into a crystalline steel-and-stone classicism. He *shows* all the forces; this is exactly the problem – *he doesn't make us feel them*. He shows them to us like a materialized X-ray, which is the way pure abstraction sees things, as diagrams and exploded views.

Lipps, as a psychologist, never felt the need to unravel the constituent parts of aesthetics, since for him storms, willows, dance performances and columns all served the same illustrative purpose; for Worringer, an art historian, that would have been unthinkable. And Lipps was not the only source Worringer drew on in *Abstraction and Empathy*;[62] Riegl influenced him at least as much, especially the Riegl who discussed the "crystallizations" of primitive art in his *Stilfragen*. The young expressionists of *Die Brücke*

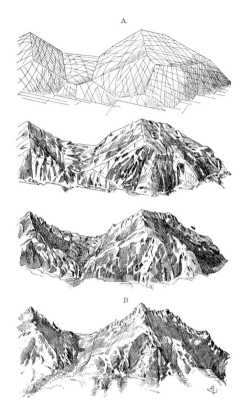

Eugène Viollet-le-Duc. *Modifications apportées à un sommet*. Fig. 36*bis* from *Le Massif du Mont Blanc* (1876).

loved *Abstraction and Empathy*. In it, Worringer implicitly indicated that empathy had had its day, since it was so closely connected to nineteenth-century naturalism and abstraction was to be the new direction. Finally, thought the young artists, a formal art historian understands what we are striving for in art today. And when Worringer published *Formprobleme der Gotik* just three years later, he made the Gothic into an early form of expressionism, furthering an idea already present in *Abstraction and Empathy*, namely that the Gothic occupies a zone between the two poles. Still, when reading Worringer, one gets the strong impression that his notion of *Einfühlung* differs fundamentally from Lipps's and is much closer to the later, more psychologized notion of empathy. Lipps often used the word *Sympa-*

thie as a synonym for *Einfühlung*, which in his case covers a much broader scope and includes as much of Worringer's abstraction as of his empathy. I do not think Worringer would have viewed sympathy as something in between abstraction and empathy, like the Gothic; on the contrary, he would have viewed it as an even more naturalist, if not sentimentalist, version of empathy. In short, Lipps's notion of *Einfühlung* is the more accurate one, but only when understood in Worringer's terms, i.e., as a mixture of abstraction and empathy.

Worringer's best amendment of Lipps's work is clearly his replacement of the latter's distinction between the beautiful and the ugly with that between empathy and abstraction. Worringer was on the right track, since the ugly is not an aesthetic category in itself but merely *failed* beauty. For Lipps, when *Einfühlung* fails to deliver in an artwork, the effect is one of ugliness, which is thus a negative concept. Seen in terms of sympathy, the question of beauty versus ugliness is not really relevant, since moving-with and moving-against are both forms of living-with. Worringer's stance is much more complex: yes, he says, beauty is a form of pleasure and joy, but its reverse is not the ugly but the abstract, which is based not on the "happy pantheistic relationship" with the cosmos we find in the aesthetics of the beautiful but on "dread." An abstract work of art – which for Worringer means a primitive or tribal work full of zigzags, stripes and nonrepresentational markings – is not ugly; on the contrary, it is beautiful, but it is based on a reversed relationship with the world, one of fear and not joy:

> Whereas the precondition for the urge to empathy is a happy pantheistic relationship of confidence between man and the phenomena of the external world, the urge to abstraction is the outcome of a greater unrest inspired in man by such phenomena. We might describe this state as an immense spiritual dread of space.[63]

Of course, abstract art does not result in "dreadful" works, in things failed and ugly, though it remains unclear throughout the book how such art is experienced – if that is still the right word, since we have entered a world of pure time, which, as we argued before, takes the form of a sheet, a flat plane. One of the major problems is that Worringer does not discuss any actual examples of "primitive art" (a form we can no longer mention nowadays without quotation marks), certainly not in the way Owen Jones did. Do we feel-into the work but experience fear? Yes. And do we then feel-with fear? No – this is why we recoil and stand back in contemplation. Just think of Caspar David Friedrich's *Rückenbilder*. The forces we are exposed to are simply too large to deal with. Now, we have learned from Lipps that sympathy at all times involves forces, and there must always be a *risk* of sympathy in art. You cannot have beauty without fear – or, in Ruskin's words, tenderness without cruelty – since there can be no feeling-with or living-with unless you surrender to a shared force, but that force is by definition scaled to your size, since you and the other both act in it. You are not over-powered into a position of pure passivity, though the use of force (*Kraft*) does result in power (*Macht*), but a local, temporary, small form of it. Remember that when you experience sympathy, points of your body are corresponding with those of another body, points connected via an abstract plane, points you can no longer call your own. In the realm of pure abstraction, however, you are cast in a world where life exceeds form, which means you are immediately overwhelmed in pure awe. Awe is not a feeling but a shock. Oddly enough, Worringer never refers to the English aesthetic categories of beauty and the sublime, a couple based on exactly the same opposition of form and force, of joy and dread, which we will return to later, in the chapter on the picturesque.

We must move on and more precisely unravel Worringer's position vis-à-vis those of Bergson and Lipps, since the first accepts the word "abstraction" where the second seems to use "life," and the third "force."

> Just as the urge to empathy as the pre-assumption of aesthetic experience finds its gratification in the beauty of the organic, so the urge to abstraction finds its beauty in the life-denying inorganic, in the crystalline, or, in general terms, in all abstract law and necessity.[64]

Life-denying? Surely Worringer is here following Riegl in his view of abstraction as "the exclusion of life at the most primitive cultural level."[65] For page after page, Worringer assumes a fright in primitive man, a fundamental disquiet that is calmed by regular, generalized abstraction. He even uses Owen Jones's term "repose."[66] If Worringer had explored more of Lipps and his concept of life, he would have noticed there is no implicit distinction to be made between the straight, crystalline frame that guides the forces and the organic form that undergoes them, especially while Lipps continually discusses forms of posture and action. All his examples are ones of force as much as form, as the two are fused from the outset: the storm, the rising column, the tightrope walker, a hemispherical dome, the willow tree, the dance on stage; he never speaks of reclining, organic, sensual bodies but without exception of postures and action. For Lipps, organic forms behave mechanically, while mechanic forces behave organically and seem fully animate. As I have said, it would be much better to understand Lipps's *Einfühlung* as sympathy and Worringer's as empathy. With Lipps, *Einfühlung* is implicitly a mixture of naturalism and abstraction, while for Worringer it is naturalism only. The difference is merely that Lipps does not arrive at this terminology. In this sense, Worringer's analysis is correct: sifting abstraction out of sympathy results in empathy, and all contemplation implicit to sympathy transforms into either pure knowledge in abstraction or pure psychology in empathy. It is like cream turning to butter and water, like separating Bergson's intuition into intelligence and instinct or knowledge and psychology – a division of things that really should not be distinct. James regularly warns us not to distance concepts from percepts. Abstract forces of life should be contained by form to enable sympathy. When one removes the form by allocating it to pure naturalism, as Worringer did, dread and fear must remain for the domain of force, since the forces are immediately too great. And though Worringer is right to assume art as a profession makes such choices, it is completely incorrect to call "primitive art" regular and necessary, as if tribal artists were natural-born Kantians.

The problem with abstraction is that the generalized state is often confused with the local, temporary state of what we should call *specified abstraction*. Such abstraction appears to be a paradox, because abstraction is habitually viewed as the loss of specific traits, but it is precisely the inverse that happens. Generalized abstraction is stored in the a priori world of the mind, of archetype, of order, while specified abstraction occurs in actual encounters, and is what makes actuality proliferate and makes for constant change. When the Ammophila matches the caterpillar, he doesn't abstract it into an average of all caterpillars or an archetypical or eidetic caterpillar, on the contrary, he finds that unique one, but he can find it only via a few points, a few nerve centers, not its whole body. The lived schema is not fixed like the Kantian one but flexible. The points are moveable in an elastic, topological system; if such a set of points were geometrically fixed, one body would never fit with another, and sympathy would be precluded. How else could one sympathize with a column at one moment and a flying bird the next? Is it not all posture? How could I sit in a chair one day, on a rock the next, and on a table the day after that? It is my feeling of fatigue that guides me, leads me to mobilize only the few points of my body necessary to relieve it, not the formal knowledge of my whole body.[67] Local abstraction is a *subtraction* unique to something or someone: it is still specific, and different every time. It does not exist beforehand; it only occurs through the act of sympathy. One moment it carries relief, the next hunger, desire or strength; it doesn't matter, because the specification, the matching, makes it abstract. Of course, life is larger than form, but it does pass through specific points. In this sense, a concept is a piece of fabric: threads of feeling interwoven in crossings that can be grasped or matched. It never leaves the experience. Sympathy is felt abstraction, not known, symbolized or judged. Or perhaps a better formulation would be: Sympathy is abstracting feeling. We tend to call a concept a form of knowledge, but it is merely an interweaving of experiences and felt transitions. Generalized abstraction, on the other hand, is the absolute opposite: it has *retracted* itself from all form. When the Jews were killed in the Nazi gas chambers, they died as abstracted Jews, nothing more. The machine of terror produced identical victims and made them perish as clones. True cruelty lies in retracted abstraction, wherever it occurs, whether it removes life by killing or by understanding things as dead and the same.

Things have to be understood as different, this is what Bergson teaches us. But he does not resort to straightforward pluriformity (if you will permit me to introduce a new word, akin to James's "pluriverse"). The marvel of his metaphysics, of course, is its combination of continuity and heterogeneity. This is why the ongoing criticism of Bergson's "élan vital" is so unjust (I remember Dennett sneering, and of course Russell). It is invariably described as making the invisible hand of God simply immanent, as if time were directing things toward form. But that is not at all what Bergson is proposing: he acknowledges free movement, and therefore the unpredictability of the result of that movement, arguing merely that it is structured by the heterogeneity of matter, that is, things aren't so unpredictable that anything can happen. There are what he calls *tendencies*. Twentieth-century evolutionary biology was stuck between pure necessity and teleology on the one hand and pure chance and contingency on the other. The arrow indicated either one point or all of them. Bergson sensibly swapped this for a *range* of points, a divergence, representing precisely the indeterminacy we have already referred to. Bergson looked at the beginning of the arrow instead of its end, because life simply occurs in matter, and time moves away from form. All contemporary evolutionary thinking vindicates him, especially with respect to concepts like *biased* variation.[68] Time continually fabricates new things – it cannot be said any more paradoxically. Things can only be different. If things were the same, there would be no time, which is of course the Platonic ideal state. The problem of generalized abstraction is that such continuity is understood spatially, not temporally. The rationalists of the "block universe," as James constantly denounces it, reverse space and time, get them the wrong way around. This is why in that mode of thinking things are always archetypal and timeless: a wall is a wall, a vase is a vase, and a rose is a rose is a rose, as Gertrude Stein said.

This is not at all the same abstraction we know from "primitive art." It is not the flatness and the dread of space that is off the mark in Worringer's analysis but the fact that he makes abstraction into a sheet of regularity and sameness. You need only take one look at the painted barkcloths of the Mbuti Pygmy tribes, the lime containers of the Iatmul people of Papua New Guinea, or the raffia cloths of the Shoowa Kuba in Congo to see that there is never any regularity operative at all,[69] not even organic symmetry, and

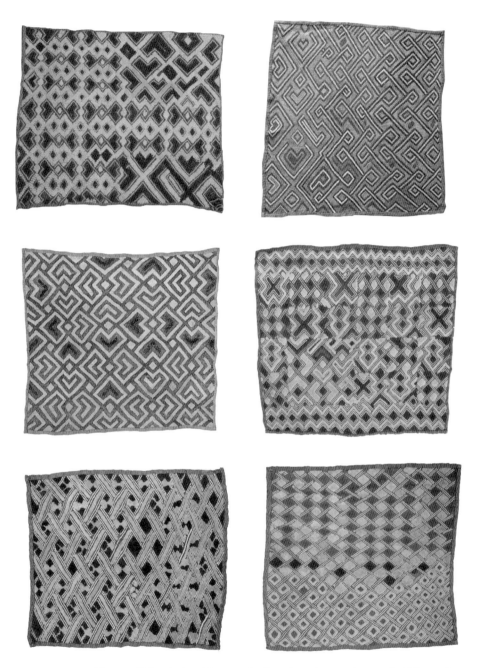

Shoowa Kuba cloths with examples from loop (top row), woot (middle row)
and cross (bottom row) patterns (twentieth century).

certainly no necessity or repose. Yes, the patterns are mostly crystalline, angular and geometric, but this does not mean they are frozen down to absolute zero. Their nonorganic lack of symmetry is crucial, the motifs sweep over the field in a serial, iterative and rhythmic motion. And with each occurrence they vary inexactly, and this variation sometimes leads to sudden shifts, large-scale cracks between groups of motifs on the smaller scale: loops (a crossing closing on one side in an angular manner), woots (double crossings, like two X-figures connecting) and crossings (like a single X-figure) that vary through widening and spacing,[70] in a technique similar to that of Maori *ta moko*. Like ripples in a pond, the spaced offsets manage the relations between the motifs, without any clear distinction between what is motif and what is an elaboration. In short, the three main figures – loop, woot and crossing – are allowed to *deform*, until a certain point at which a whole set suddenly *transforms* along a single cut or shift, and from there another combination of figures begins to develop. No two cloths are ever the same, nor even two loops in a single cloth, nor two woots or crossings.

The Kuba men make the blank, woven canvases (not much larger than twenty inches square), and the Shoowa women create the patterns by embroidering short threads (cut-loop pile) through the fabric, making deliberate "mistakes," with a savageness Ruskin could only have dreamed of. And this is not meant in any metaphorical way, the Shoowa have truly elevated the making of mistakes to a high art. These range from tiny, subtle effects that are gradually enlarged until the pattern as a whole cannot absorb it anymore to extreme, sudden shifts in the pattern to a set of wholly new figures. Every cloth features small gradual changes and sudden jumps. The women start with a black thin-threaded sketch of an initial pattern on the canvas and then elaborate on it, widening the lines by offsetting, creating effects that all have to interrelate, since the whole field must be filled and no two lines are allowed to intersect. They use only two or three of the following colors: an off-white, a long-threaded black, and the light brown of the undyed raffia. It is a truly a pity that Worringer – again, by following Riegl and his subjectivist, axiomatic *Kunstwollen* – refutes Semper so strongly in his discussion of "primitive art," because understanding the state of abstraction would have helped him enormously. For Semper, matter is in transition and is capable of coming up with its own abstractions, i.e., patterns. For Worringer, on the other hand, matter seems to have fully surrendered to a psychology of artist and onlooker. The Shoowa patterns are partially based on the ribbon technique of interlacing; they are closely related to the craft of weaving with real fibers and strips but transferred to a different scale and material. The large, visible pattern of weaving and braiding is actually embroidered on a finely woven canvas. Such a shift towards abstraction allows the embroiderers to use both "real" techniques of braiding fibers under and over each other and "abstract" techniques of cutting them as they please without destroying the coherence of the configuration. Then, between the lines, the often triangular open patches can be filled either by more offsets or with a single color. The Shoowa constantly switch between ribbon and tessellation patterning, making the discontinuous continuous and vice versa. All their patterns are truly in-the-making, the figures are stretchable and flexible, and when the system can no longer resolve the differences within the range of given figures (differences in degree, which correspond to Ruskinian changefulness), they jump, crack and shift to bring about transformations in the field, creating differences in kind (in correspondence to Ruskin's savageness). The Shoowa-Kuba cloths display a thoroughly Gothic form of "vitalized geometry." A certain number of figures is mobilized, but they cannot go everywhere or do whatever they want: all is guided by strict rules of variation. All variation is limited by a threshold, beyond which the whole starts to crack and change into another serial motif. I know twentieth-century art claimed to have brought abstraction to full maturity, but none of it even came close to this level of complexity; it fell back either on pure chance or to pure order and never understood the interdependence of the two as the Shoowa do: chance plus order makes change (either gradual or incremental).

All "primitive art" is an art of tenderness – to use Ruskin's term (which would not please him one bit in this case) – exactly because it is *applied*, decorative art. It cares about things, takes care of things. It makes the canoe, the paddle, the bowl, the basket or the knife into a thing-in-the-making, so it becomes an art of transitional pattern, not of images on canvases or screens. It makes design, which removes things from time and places them into space, an art of putting things back into time – at least partially. In Jamesian terms, design is about giving *whats* enough *that*. However, with the Shoowa cloths the reverse seems to take place. The sudden shifts and gradual variations in the patterns, which we would normally only grasp if they were guiding the making of a handle, edge or window, direct our attention, but not towards a real, practical object or function. It is like a decoration that has removed itself from a skin, a wall, or any given thing, or even like a canvas without a frame – it is *generalized decoration*, not generalized abstraction. There is a generalized sympathy, yes, but also a momentary, unique and specified abstraction. Art seldom reaches this level. This is a pattern that frees itself from a specific object without losing its specificity. The Shoowa people have found a way to peel the pattern from a thing and make it a potential decoration for all things, in a manner similar to that of Dresser's mental art, though the latter leads to general order and structure and the former to general ornament. It is a decoration that is first applied and then taken off. This is exactly what art strives to be: decoration that has loosened itself from the wall to direct sympathy towards all possible things,

Titian. *Venus of Urbino* (1538).

as pure contemplation. If we recall our decorated, sectional James-Morris plane – call it the earth veil, if you will – and remember that we can only access that plane via decorated day-to-day objects, we can imagine that accessing it without a practical need would require a special occasion (though not a museum). One would bring a cloth decorated in such a manner only to special ceremonies, such as rites of passage, burials or weddings. These are the moments when people celebrate that they themselves are in transition. It is no longer the object that is in the making but you yourself, or one of your relatives or fellow tribe members. One's attention first goes outward to all possible things and then back to oneself. It directs all thought, as does all decoration, though it guides it not into sympathy with an object but with oneself. Such art creates self-sympathy. And all great art evokes such a moment when the onlooker's gaze is turned away from the work inward. (No, this is not the gaze into Rothko's abyss, because with his paintings one looks directly into the void; there is no attention to begin with.)

In which forms might a future art of sympathy appear? Let us explore this problem a bit more with the help of Worringer's poles. In a typical naturalist painting, such as Titian's *Venus* of 1538, we can obviously empathize with the subject, but since the painting only offers a representation of life and not life itself, there can be no sympathy: there is nothing to feel-with. She is reclining and passive – sensuous as a *grande horizontale*, fleshy, but certainly not sympathetic, which is always a movement of the spirit, not the body. So let us do a curious experiment. Let us take Titian's model, literally dip her in paint and let her roll around on a canvas. We imme-

Yves Klein. Photo of a performance on June 5, 1958, that was a precursor to the series titled *Antropométries*.

197

diately recognize this as the way Yves Klein created his *Anthropométries* (which had a lot in common with Marey's blur) in 1960. Now we certainly do obtain a view of life and activity, but we can no longer empathize, since we have lost the figure to contract the forces onto; the forces move outward and simply leak away over the canvas.

To create a zone of sympathy, we of course need some kind of mixture, an emulsion, which we can achieve by keeping an eye on both Worringer's poles. Creating this would be not unlike cooking, in which one can opt for various mixing techniques – slicing and shaking, slow stirring, hard beating or even fast blending. Moving from one pole toward the other, either reasoning from abstraction toward empathy or from empathy toward abstraction, however, may not get us to a common middle point. Things works out differently for each procedure, and the consequences for how the achieved form of sympathy finds its way through life will be different too. If you preferred to work from a model, you would start as Titian and work in the direction of Klein. You would start with form and proceed to work in the direction of activity, but without reaching the point of total blurring, since to evoke sympathy the forces still need to configure and contract into form. The process would be similar to the way Cézanne shook the canvas, slicing the image of the mountain into a mosaic. On the other hand, if you preferred to work from the pole of abstraction, you would start with a general pattern, like one of Owen Jones's diapers, or a limited set of abstract figures and have these move together like the curves in Gothic tracery, working toward specificity via deformations and transformations. This is exactly what the Shoowa women do.

The contemplation accompanying the work works in reverse mode as well. With art of the first type, the one transiting from Titian to Klein, from empathy toward abstraction, your eye would start focused and then detach halfway through to begin flowing along with life. *One moves from a specific object to life in general.* With art of the second type, transiting from abstraction to empathy, as in a Shoowa cloth, one starts with an open mind, looking to single out one object among all the possible ones, with flowing attention, and then one's attention focuses and turns 180 degrees, is directed towards a specific person, usually oneself, to reconnect with one's own duration. *One moves from a general object to a specific life.* The first type of art follows the route of decoration, and, in all honesty, I think it would be a major improvement if art today were to try to return to this original problem and work to improve our white walls, empty town squares (more and more of which are becoming parking lots) and smooth, polished objects by making them sympathetic and acceptable for daily use – hence making it possible to live-with them. We are now confronted with both unbearably shiny black boxes in our homes and unbearably mystical black-box art in our museums (art that hangs on the wall or stands on the floor but wants nothing to do with either.) We will slowly become as estranged from our museums as we have from our churches. It is only in special cases, I think, that art is capable of substantiating the second type (in which structure becomes ornament and machines come alive), but this is necessarily an art of installation, of performance or a certain interactivity, rather than the kind that passively hangs on a wall or stands in a courtyard. Since art is not expected to be periodic, like religion, weaving its object into the rhythm of your personal life, it would have to do so explicitly. The decoration would have to function as a script, as the Shoowa cloth is used in rituals: it would start as generally structured, then engage a number of people who have gathered, and finally focus on one of them through transformation. It is certainly an art of the group.

Both art forms can work, but never in their pure states. Naturalism must be desentimentalized and take on some cruelty. Abstractionism must focus and find its object of tenderness. We seem to have arrived at an important distinction between two forms of art – though both, because of their respective strategies, are now safely positioned in the domain of sympathy, being neither pure naturalism nor pure abstractionism. The art which works from empathy to abstraction expands in all lives indiscriminately. This is why it needs to nestle in our bedrooms, our living rooms, our streets, subways, highways and public buildings: it needs to connect daily things to life's abstraction, and this can be accomplished only via decoration. Here art loses its monetary value almost completely. This is the path that William Morris followed. The other form, which works from abstraction to empathy, expands in a specific person's life. It is an abstraction made for you. This is why, in the church, it was first incorporated by rituals and ceremonies, and it must now find another place, not the museum, but perhaps the Web, hidden somewhere in the machines. In this option, art becomes pure exchange value, which is why some Shoowa cloths are used as currency. You could only wish to take a Damien Hirst from its frame, roll it up and put it in a drawer, and wait for the right ceremony for it to be worn or offered.

We are increasingly seeing art dissolving into advertising, not only in the way artists make and sell their work but also, inversely, in the way advertising uses imagery and techniques from art. We find one artwork after the other being quoted and used to sell a car, a piece of furniture, a cell phone. We see automobile companies setting up "experience centers," at which famous artists create installations or even paint vehicles. These interactive showrooms are slowly beginning to replace museums, and their budgets are higher, too. We can only imagine what William James would have said about this. As soon as Dewey took James's notion of pure experience and reworked it for art as "having an experience," something shifted dangerously. Instead of pure experience being understood as building long-lasting relationships between us and things, it potentially became a short-term affair. Publicity and media are on the verge of replacing the web of sympathy. Nowadays, you can be sure that every time you start to care about something, every time your feelings are stirred, the moment will come when you will have to pay for it. We are seeing a devastating reversal of Ruskin's statement "There is no wealth but life."[71] Inanimate wealth seems almost completely to have replaced life, in a phenomenon Ruskin characterized as "illth."[72] In political economy, shortage is understood as the driving mechanism behind value, and today, after a century of mass production and generic sameness, artists are hired as designers to return products to a state of scarcity. Even huge companies like Ikea hire artist-designers to make "limited editions," but of course, the costs are recovered through the unlimited editions discharged daily from their unstoppable machines – how different from Morris & Co., a group of artists who started their own company, making wallpaper one day, a book the next, then a rug or a poem. These artists worked for the group. Morris's designs expressly tried to move art in the direction of design; in our age, things are reversed. Design is moving toward art: all specificity originates from atomic, "signature" individuals working for other atomic individuals. How different this situation is from the Shoowa-Kuba system of gifts and exchange.

the veil is the anti-eidos

Let us return to Worringer. His analysis of the Gothic is, thank goodness, much more accurate than his treatment of "primitive art." This is probably because decoration is a given in art while structure is a given in architecture, so its design proceeds in the Shoowa manner from the outset. Or, as Bergson would say, it moves from matter to life. In this sense, it is the reverse of art, because it is supposed to concern daily life and habits. Architecture is clearly an art of the group. The only pressing question for architecture is: How can structure become felt? As we saw two chapters ago, Gothic architecture found a specific answer, not by covering structure with ornament in the Greco-Roman manner but by *transforming* structure into ornament and vice versa. And though Worringer does not qualify the Gothic as an architecture of sympathy, he observes something that clearly has properties of both his poles:

> … this seeking has no organic life that draws us gently into its movement; but there is life there, a vigorous urgent life, that compels us joylessly to follow its movements. Thus, on an in-organic fundament, there is heightened movement, heightened expression.[73]

Of course, architecture is an art that must remain unaccompanied by joy, since it must be lived in from day to day, but not by retracting into pure structure. Later in *Abstraction and Empathy*, we can already recognize the Worringer of *Form in Gothic* three years on:

> … the Gothic cathedral is a strong appeal to our capacity for empathy, and yet we shall hesitate to describe its inner constitution as organic … In the Gothic cathedral matter lives solely

on its mechanical laws, but these laws, despite their fundamentally abstract character, have become living, i.e. they have acquired expression.[74]

He could as easily be describing Shoowa-Kuba cloths: structural but not regular, joyless but beautiful, abstract but alive. Abstract *and* alive, more precisely: I think Worringer himself recognizes here that life is lived in between, in the transition. To quote Bergson once more:

> ... the role of life is to insert some indetermination into matter.[75]

And this is a quality not just of life but specifically of Gothic design, since it thrives on indeterminacy, with columns changing into vaults in such a way that one cannot say where one ends and the other begins. Life is in between the elements, in the relations between them. The Gothic operates between objects as much as in them, constantly entangling and disentangling, braiding and weaving, knotting and knitting. It is as if we never arrive at the final Dyak's-head terminus, since design is only a managing of speeds and interactions between the nodes. The Gothic is constantly guiding *that* into *whats*, and whats into that. Finally, we can view structure not as some given property of matter but as an activity, a form of standing, of leaning and partially of hanging – that is, as a posture, something Ruskin describes very well in his discussion of rigidity. Greek temples do recline, lethargically lying on the ground like Titian's Venus on her bed, but not these cathedrals, in which structure is a form of life, something to do. Why would life be exclusive to the organic when clearly it can as easily shift into the inorganic? The above quotes show clearly how Worringer was working towards a middle position for art and architecture ("design") that would have been neither pure empathy nor abstraction, would have been joyless but also fearless, and would have led to a pure awareness. In the Gothic, abstraction is informed by empathy from the outset. We obtain a sort of vibrating, double view: the moment we see it configuring (or finding structure), we notice its figures moving, and the moment we see the figures moving, we notice them coming together. Or, as the anthropologist Alfred Gell would have put it, it is the agency that creates animacy – that is, when reasoned from the side of the stone tracery; reasoning from our point of view, one would say it is the animacy that creates agency.

In *Art and Agency*, Gell[76] moves beyond Worringer's opposition of life and structure, since for him all art strives to become alive, to engage with life and become part of it and its organization. Whether art is abstract and decorated or naturalist and representational, being absorbed by ways of living is its goal. The complex, "animated" patterns of decoration and the lively depiction of the face of an idol both have the goal of negotiating life, though the abstract pattern on an Iatmul lime container marks a personal possession while an idol directs attention toward a collective god. In a way, Gell arrives at a distinction similar to mine: abstract, decorative art leads from a general object to a specific life, and imitative, representational art leads from a specific object to life in general. In the latter case, the difference is that if the art cannot lead you through the image into the duration, religion will. Of course, a religious idol does not need Yves Klein to bring its representational image closer to life; rituals and ceremonies do that. As I have said, this is the whole difference between a church and a museum. As an anthropologist, Gell naturally encounters spirits, gods, demons, icons, sorcery and idolatry on an everyday basis, since they form such an inextricable part of primitive (I am getting tired of putting it in quotation marks) cultures, but also our own. This is what is so interesting about his book, he discusses all the usual anthropological material and shifts easily to Duchamp and then back to Maori meeting houses. Art connects you to a spirit, which is of course another way of saying that it relates time to consciousness, indetermination to form and awareness to decoration. If we can in fact share consciousness through sympathy, then clearly it is larger than ourselves, and is at least distributed among a number of us. We do not need to know any more than that. We do not need to postulate a world-mind like Fechner;[77] such a thing we can only *believe* in (and belief is nothing but a form of intuition, though often it works by excluding too much intelligence). It is enough to *know* that consciousness is larger than us. Such knowing, plus the fact that all truth is invention, led William James, the Harvard philosophy professor, to visit mediums and attend séances (I would give anything to have seen him at one). He was serious about ghosts, as were his brother Henry[78] and, by the way, Vernon Lee and Bergson's sister, the amazing Moina Mathers, a member of the Hermetic Order of the Golden Dawn.

Weird? Of course, but at least they succeed in explaining an aesthetic problem – the felt relationship between things – in aesthetic terms. Ectoplasm, magnetism, spiritualism, phlogiston, pneuma, aether – if you ask me, it's all Marey's or Klein's blur; it's all art. What I find especially pleasing about the notion of spirits is that not everything is connected by some monotheistic or monistic ocean flushing through it all but that each thing contributes its own bit of ooze. Each thing is accompanied by a spirit, carrying it not inside, like a soul or *eidos*, but on the outside, like a satellite or a cloak. As Marey's ghostly blur, the notion of *eidos*, especially Husserl's, can be constructed through superimposing images, not in order to see movement or change but in order to find an ideal, unmoving average, as has so often been done with faces. For instance, we could find the ideal woman by putting hundreds of portrait photos of various women from all over the world on top of each other, all semi-transparent, and a "vague essence" of Miss World would emerge. Unlike Marey's images, such an "eidetic reduction" would be sequenced in space, not in time, and would shake off more and more variable, accidental features as we added more images to approach the ideal type. Our satellite-spirit is neither ideal nor timeless and presents itself only *in the interior* of another being during an encounter and can only be felt, not seen or even imagined. And such an encounter can never be repeated.

The other never affects us as an object, image, thing, or sensual appearance; it affects us as something felt. This is the strange topology of feeling: you see the other, but you feel its existence inside you, not as weight, not as image, but as a force that moves you. Because the feeling of being-you momentarily subsides, you can never be sure, while standing in front of the heavily shaking tree like Lipps, whether it is you that feels or the tree. The feeling rises within you as if it is being born, not alien but new, and fills you completely. It is merely when such feelings begin to be absorbed by the senses and the mind that thoughts and images develop, images we sometimes call ghosts, or fairies or demons. Fear not: I do not expect you to tell me you believe in ghosts – in fact, it does not matter whether you do or not. What is important is not so much our philosophies or our beliefs but how we lead our lives, and how we furnish them, punctuate them with things. In a nutshell: we need not believe in spirits, but *our designs should* – which is another way of saying that it is okay to believe in spirits, but never as separate beings, only as part of things. Design means adding spirits to things, or, in James's terms, giving them fringes, or in Ruskin's words, cloaking and veiling them. The veil is the anti-eidos; it uses the minutest possible amount of abstraction to create the most unique thing, like a species containing only a single individual.

Gell's argument is truly a sound one, because once we have accepted Bergson's notion of duration and life being the subjects of sympathy and subsequently understood such sympathy as a fundamental aesthetic, then it makes complete sense to look at how art and design actually involve the lives of people, either as individuals or as groups. If art and design are ways of reconnecting things with the unforeseen, then their objects provide ways of living with it. Design's purpose is not to "make visible" the unforeseen or the invisible, as is often stated, but to make us feel it. Design makes things radiate feelings, to which we and other things can tune in. Sympathy is not *a* feeling or a specific mood but feeling in general, in the form it takes when operating via objects. This is why it is felt as much between us and things and between things by themselves as it is between us. To paraphrase Bergson, the role of design is to sympathize with the indetermination of life. Its role is to connect the personal to the impersonal, whether that means Gell's spirits, De Waal's animals, Worringer's primitives, Lipps's columns, or life itself.

> A disreputable man, a rogue, held in contempt by everyone, is found as he lies dying. Suddenly, those taking care of him manifest an eagerness, respect, even love, for his slightest sign of life. Everybody bustles about to save him, to the point where, in his deepest coma, this wicked man himself senses something soft and sweet penetrating him. But to the degree

that he comes back to life, his saviors turn colder, and he becomes once again mean and crude. Between his life and his death, there is a moment that is only that of a life playing with death.[79]

This is Deleuze, in his final essay, "Immanence: A Life …," discussing Charles Dickens's *Our Mutual Friend*. Since Deleuze's lines have been quoted more than often enough, we do not need to add anything more at this point except to say that though the French philosopher does not define the feeling itself in so many words, he is unmistakably talking about sympathy. More importantly, the feeling erupts at the moment when the person loses his identity and nears abstraction and disappears again as soon as he returns and is overtaken by subjectivity. Sympathy is direct contact with the "immediate flux of life" that, as James says, is given only to "new-born babes, or men in semi-coma from sleep, drugs, illnesses, or blows,"[80] who "may be assumed to have an experience pure in the literal sense of a *that* which is not yet any definite *what*,"[81] in short, things or thing-beings.

In a way, life is primitive (without the quotation marks, finally). Or, as Ruskin would say, savage.

chapter four

the radical picturesque

What is it that appeals to us so intensely about a bookcase that is full of books that are mostly neatly ordered, tightly filling up the whole length of the shelf, but nevertheless strikes us as slightly out of control? A few lie on top, slightly askew, with pieces of paper sticking out, and some shelves even have whole stacks among the upright books – years ago you left one lying about and the others just seem to have followed. And as we look more closely, we see that quite a few are missing, probably in use or mislaid somewhere, making the others on the shelf lean diagonally against each other, pointing left or right, sometimes alone, sometimes in pairs, and sometimes a whole row leaning over. It's a fine mess. Actually, such a bookcase is highly organized, but in a smart way. Or picture a scene from a Saturday morning market. There is the man selling spices from open bags; typically he has hundreds of tagines stacked in front of his stall, most of them forming shaky towers, each a different height. This morning he has sold fewer than usual, and the stacks are bending dangerously, though fortunately against each other, so that they do not fall over. The ornately decorated conical tops are stacked separately, mixed in with the other stacks. Very nice indeed, with all the colors – let's take a picture.

This, in short, is the picturesque: a form of loose order, in which things loosely fit together, more packed than stacked, still full of movement, with things entering the pack and leaving it. The elements barely come together, just enough to make the whole assembly cohere. What actually defines this "smart mess"? In this chapter, we will see that the rules of picturesque composition are much more complex than those of either tightly ordered necessity or of blindly ordered chance – the two only options left after the twentieth century. Mies or Pollock. With the tagines, we notice that simplistic stacking according to exact alignment is replaced by a much richer set of rules that allows elements to actively rotate, shift and aggregate; each part is allowed a certain amount of freedom, on the condition that they all collaborate, lean on each other, and form subgroups, which in turn act as single parts, in a manner no Miesian skyscraper could fathom. The result looks very appealing and very much alive.

But at the same time, this let's-take-a-picture aspect is what threatens the picturesque, as we know all too well. Nowadays, when we see images of the picturesque, we see them in lifestyle books, cookbooks and 1960s movies, used as a way to temper modernism or battle the ironies of postmodernism. A little French harbor is added here, a little Moroccan market there, in often ambiguous images ("You have money, but you visit the slums for fun?"); the complex aesthetics are fully overtaken by the snapshot. The picturesque has consistently been weakened by its imagery, as Ruskin so perceptively stated back in the 1840s. Of course, being a vitalist, he was strongly attracted to the principles behind looseness and imperfection, but he was the first to see how quickly the picturesque became ambiguous, and how often it turned sentimental or cruel. The picturesque needs constant updating if we are to save it from the clean, purified image and restore it to its original unfinishedness. This is what I will define as the radical picturesque: concentrating on the aspect that resists the image, and returning it to things.

As corny as the picturesque may seem, with its pretty landscapes, cute little cottages and villages, one cannot deny that it is actually a radical state of existence. Things can hardly be in a stranger state than that of picturesqueness, in which they are at once present and hidden. The picturesque is the art of things that are under way, that is, on the way in or on the way out, being either assembled or disassembled. It is the art of the object being overwhelmed by time, and it is this vulnerability, this fragility, that so immediately gains our sympathy. This is how an object drags us into its life and offers to share it with us. Together with the silken tracery of the Gothic and the delicate weavings of diaper ornament, the picturesque stands out as an art of fragility.

Again, just as sympathy consists of two originally unseparated ingredients, empathy and abstraction, we will examine the picturesque in relation to the two components that comprise it: the better known and more respected concepts of beauty and the sublime. It is not unusual to map aesthetics as a spectrum, and one will never find two points further apart than these. We will observe that the picturesque constantly positions itself between the two poles, attempting to create an active, productive relationship between them. We will briefly investigate some of its origins, returning to John Ruskin, who will introduce us to what he called vital beauty and the parasitical sublime, and we will take his concepts to William Robinson's wild garden and then, surprisingly, to Martin Heidegger, who constantly switched between theorizing the sublime and the picturesque without ever using either term. In search of some illuminating examples, we'll consider Van Gogh's shoes and Heidegger's famous jug, imagine another jug Ruskin never designed, compare the last two to Bruno Latour's can of Coke, look at an exploded view of a Volkswagen Beetle, and bring in our own stone-washed jeans to conclude the argument. In short, we will look at many *things*.

Until now, we have been cheerfully proclaiming the primacy of aesthetics, but we have only touched on the issue of what is called ontology. How do things exist? Does existence presuppose things? Every now and then, I have taken the opportunity to speculate on a Gothic ontology, and I have sometimes differentiated this from its Baroque and Greek counterparts, but it is badly in need of closer examination – especially because I am arguing that things cannot come into being or exist without style. And I want to make this claim in the most radical sense: every ontology *is* a style, it doesn't just *have* one. Strictly speaking, it is the styles that *are*, and *being* is the verb. Aesthetics, I argue, is ontology. Things are as they are *aesthetically*, or, as some would say, because they have an effect; or, as others would say, because they affect each other – but that is far too mechanical for me, because sympathy means things act in relation ("sym-") and such relations are felt ("-pathy"). An effect issues from just one term; affect occurs between

209

at least two terms, but merely as an exchange of feelings; and sympathy is a resonance, an attunement of feelings, forming a true connection or bond. We will also look more deeply into things, and also into nothings, and even *unthings*; into *eudaimonia* – things going well – and *ergon* – things serving us well. We will even look into *bad things* and demons – things that possess you – categories that cover a great many of today's technological things, sublime things, which sounds like a favorable term to most people, but not to me.

Eventually, the main question will emerge: Can we, by acknowledging technology as the main source of the contemporary sublime, turn the tide? Having arrived at that point, we will collect all the attributes of the picturesque, such as wildness and freedom, and endeavor to radically apply them to technology. I am convinced that this is the only way to retrieve a world of things, i.e., a world of beauty, which I equate with a world of feelings: to move not away from technology but through it. I believe questions raised by art and artisanship should be appropriated by technology – not a technology of purposiveness, instrumentality and mediation, however, but one of variation and flourishing. If the picturesque, as John Ruskin defined it, is something that parasitizes the sublime, then that is what we need to do today. We will try to mobilize some of the concepts we find at the heart of German *Naturphilosophie* – studying the relationship between *Unbedingt*, *Bedingung* and *Ding* – to begin laying out the program for a technological picturesque of what we will by then be calling *wild things*.

Now, let us see if we can locate the two poles of aesthetics a bit more clearly before we start our journey into the picturesque and the wild.

forms and forces

On one side, we find Beauty: still, ideal, *a world of forms*. On the other, we find the Sublime: moving, vast, chaotic, *a world of forces*. We can name many other concepts – the Ugly, the Novel, the Monstrous, the Cute, the Cool, the Elegant – but these turn out to be subcategories of the other two rather than alternatives. Aesthetic issues remain in the hands of these two: beauty, far superior but utterly abandoned by everyone, and the sublime, totally overrated and basically the only category of art that has survived the twentieth century. Honestly, we could not be worse off.

Beauty, though we all probably use the word dozens of times a day, is the more mysterious of the two. Nowadays, you would have to travel the planet to find a single artist claiming to be trying to create something beautiful, and probably that artist would lack talent or be extremely religious, and more than probably, when you finally got to see his or her paintings, you wouldn't agree they were beautiful. Beauty passed art by a century ago. The word describes a world of perfect forms, proportion, harmony, even order, a world of what Alberti called *concinnitas*, transcendent, even divine laws that made things luminous. In contrast to sublime things, perfect forms are in a state of bliss: they seem to have been directly touched and blessed. The more one thinks about it, the more one realizes how few things are truly beautiful. I would not dare name one here. I have declared things beautiful thousands of times, but I would only agree with a handful of those statements now, because either I have changed or the objects have. And where I do still agree with myself, others definitely would not. Perfect situations are not perfect objects. Of course, when you find yourself a thousand miles north of Bangkok and spot a tiger in the jungle, taking its incredibly graceful steps, or an orchid, with its unimaginably delicate open-air roots, what you see is completely beautiful, and ten years later it is even more so, but that fact doesn't help art one bit, because a painting of a beautiful thing doesn't equal a beautiful painting. There is more in the tiger and the orchid than we are allowed to depict, really, something that resists being painted. The more beautiful we think they are, the more seems to be hidden from us. And to make matters worse, both creatures already look as if they have been painted. So art has wisely given up, and subsequently so has religion, because artists are no longer willing to add beauty to the walls of the church. And the ones who are willing to try are no longer of the caliber of Pontormo or Tiepolo.

Most contemporary forms of beauty are found either in films (though increasingly less often, since the movie star is disappearing) or on magazine covers. The world of beauty is certainly one of radiance, and the use of the word "star" is not merely a happy coincidence, nor is the fact that magazines are printed on paper as glossy as their cover girls' lipstick. Those images seem to exist beyond that form of agreement that is generally taken to be the foundation of beauty. Few things are as strange as being in an airport and scanning the hundreds of covers arranged in rows and columns, bathed in fluorescent light, with their hundreds of faces staring, not at us but rather *beyond* us. Though many are smiling, nothing here seems to want to please us. Of course, the contemporary notion of cool is related to a kind of indifference, quite appropriately for a mass medium, as McLuhan stated. Beauty is never meant for us; like the sublime, it contains nothing subjective at all, permits no judgment. Such radiant beauty has been an impossible goal for the fine arts to achieve. It is not something one can sculpt, paint or evoke in words; it is much more technological than that. Cover photos are not beautiful shots by great photographers, nor are they of especially beautiful women, rather, they appear to be utterly constructed things. A coolness is produced by the combination of model, lighting, camera, and even computer, if you count the Photoshop treatment afterward. There is something going on between these objects that makes it work, this closed loop that excludes us, the photographer, and even the model her- or himself. Something inhuman is operating here. According to Kant, beauty was supposed to be the embodiment of our pleasure being disinterested, but the truth is that beauty is disinterested in us and seems to hide from judgment. I think that every now and then, when we say something or somebody is beautiful, we mean not to agree but to confirm that the object transcends judgment and is untouched by subjectivity.

All this is fine; this is exactly what beauty is – idealized. But when we marry such a concept with technology, it becomes a mere product. To be cool is to act like a product. This is the final upgrade of the *flaneur*, who, strolling among commodities, began to behave indifferently, moving around with the gaze of Poe's "The Man of the Crowd," a man of the masses. But that was an act of a subject confronted with objects; here in the land of covers, we are all objects. Suddenly, idealization is not some mythical artistic enterprise for stilling time and freezing all forms but an actual technical option. In a vast, calm ocean of media, we find spectral landmarks we have come to call *icons*: technological objects of inexplicable beauty that stand alone, completely isolated to become the ultimate obstacles, like contemporary versions of Ganesh, the luminous elephant god (I think Alfred Gell would have liked that comparison).

The world of the sublime doesn't even seem to contain forms, just vast, enormous forces. We look straight into nothingness. It is not a black and static nothingness, though, like that which we see at the end of a movie. It moves, is even turbulent, atmospheric; at certain moments, things seem to form and assume shapes – but no, we are mistaken. The sublime is not the world of the ugly, of slimy monsters disproportionately shaped, tentacled, drooling and oozing. Though amorphous, monsters still have shapes; it is only because those shapes are anything but beautiful that we qualify them as ugly. To call something or someone ugly is as intimate as calling them beautiful, without a doubt. Indeed, ugliness is not opposed to beauty at all, since both are qualities of forms, they must be continuous and originate from the same source. Rather, it is all that is invisible that constitutes the sublime: invisible forces that, since they are not contained by forms, are no longer associated with pleasant feelings but evoke a feeling of awe, because forces are always larger than objects and seem unable to gather or focus. Forces come and go, from and in all directions. As Kant said, we cannot qualify anything as sublime, since it is a category outside the domain of things; this has been a problem for all the artists of the sublime, some in the eighteenth and nineteenth centuries and all those in the twentieth. If one wishes to depict forces, one unavoidably has to do so in the form of a depiction, e.g., a poem or a painting, and paintings are tiny in comparison with the universe of forces. So when you stand in front of one of Caspar David Friedrich's paintings, though it is awkward at first, since the figure in it stands with his back toward you, making you look with him into the abyss of the horizon or the depths of the Harz mountains, you still experience properties of the beautiful, since the picture is the size of a painting, not a mountain. And of course Friedrich knew one could not paint the sublime itself – he shared this awareness with Turner – nor the relationship between the viewer and the sublime, only the relationship between the painting's subject and the sublime.

Once again, technology was able to solve that little problem. Observe what happened to the size and format of paintings and how they were adopted by the movies. First, we see the emergence of the panorama, in which the painted image lost at least part of its frame in the creation of a circular, 360-degree image, and which partially returned in fine art in the form of the *color field*, which signified a resurgence of the sublime in modernism, initially with Rothko and later with Barnett Newman. Then, more technically, the panorama transformed into the Sensurround movies of the 1970s, followed by the IMAX theaters of the 1990s and the mainstream 3D movies we go to see today. The sublime has been completely technologized: we no longer properly see such images; we fall through them. The experience is not like that of technological beauty, where everything comes to a standstill; here there is movement, but it is a continuous falling. It is no coincidence, by the way, that the world of beauty seems to reach its climax in the portrait, while the world of the technological sublime originates in landscape art. Spaghetti westerns managed to combine the two, alternating between close-ups of sweaty faces and horizontal, widescreen views of Monument Valley. It is no accident, either, that so many IMAX movies deal with landscapes, and more often the whole universe and the Big Bang, replacing even the old planetarium. Kant still had to refer to volcanoes and hurricanes to illustrate the powers of the sublime; we have adjusted the type of imagery to the type of attribute by making images that exceed themselves and have lost every notion of the frame.

It seems as if everything ends here – but don't worry, it doesn't. Beauty and the sublime are categories, nothing more, and art will probably be saved now that both have been delegated to other realms. They are the extremes and have been so for ages; beauty is too perfect and the sublime too dangerous to even consider living with. They are all right when they occur in an artistic context, since art so clearly must fail in its mission, but with both categories so completely absorbed by media, it is time we started thinking about a real alternative.

It has often been argued that the picturesque occupies a middle ground. Uvedale Price, one of its main theoreticians, conceived of it as "a station between beauty and sublimity"[1] – maybe not precisely in between, but certainly oscillating around that virtual midpoint. In fact, it wouldn't make sense for the picturesque to prefer forms over forces or vice versa, rather, they have to be thought of as existing in a productive relationship of contraction and expansion rather than as opposites. You can try to hold on to one or the other, but in the end you will never find perfect beauty, and you will find that the sublime needs a face. Early on, the Romantics substituted the concept of form with that of formation, i.e., *Bildung*, which went hand in hand with *Trieb*, the vectorized movement of forces.[2] For who would favor a world of pure forces and time when we can so easily point out objects in space, and who would favor pure objects when we can as easily point out that they change over time? The separation of sympathy into the two distinct aspects of abstraction and naturalism proved a useless and even dangerous enterprise; likewise, we should consider the picturesque not as a latter-day temperance of two initial extreme positions but as the original position par excellence, which was later broken in two. This reasoning makes the picturesque radical from the outset, that is, existing at the *radix*, the root of the making of art and design. The middle is always more radical than the extremes.

We should at all times consider forms and forces simultaneously, as existing in full interdependence. As an aesthetic category, the picturesque has offered two versions of this reciprocal relationship: the forces are in the process of either (1) *entering* the thing or (2) *exiting* it. In the former, the forces help to create the object: they are constructive, or *constitutive*. In the latter, they should be considered *erosive*: the object was already structured, and now the forces are helping to make it disappear. In both cases, things are imperfect and unfinished, and if one were to hold them up to the light, so to speak, they would show the same irregular contours. They are two forms of unfinishedness, with the same frayed, serrated profile: things are unfinished either because they are still under construction or because they were finished but are now undergoing a process of erosion, of wear and tear. In short, *young* things and *old* things – or, in German, *Dinge im Aufbau und im Abbau*, just to prepare you for our upcoming discussion of Heidegger. They respectively exhibit spontaneity and character, two very romantic inventions.

The first category aesthetically fits the theories of William Hogarth, who, as Ronald Paulson points out,[3] was already explicitly using the term "picturesque" in *The Analysis of Beauty* of 1753, associating it with young women wearing their hair loosely to display its "wanton ringlets."[4] It also fits in with the notions of *Bildung* and growth in more general terms, and with gardening, and especially the wild type of garden we will discuss in this chapter. If you insist, we can still place this form of the picturesque on the ribboned, vegetal, beautiful end of the spectrum, the empathetic end. The second category is closer to the sublime and is situated at the more angular, tessellated, mineral end of the picturesque, forming a world of harder things, a world of ruins but also of wear and tear. The young picturesque is delicate and curvy, and on the side of Ruskin's changefulness, while the old picturesque, being rough and jagged, sides with savageness. We shouldn't drag this double existence of the picturesque into a new state of opposition, however, it is still a single "veil of strange intermediate being," merely one that contains soft green bits along with the hard gray ones. It is still a world without humans, one of things only, things both mineral and vegetal, nearly alive and nearly dead. Our Gothic ontology has never aspired to distinguish strictly between the two: stones act like plants, and plants act as strange and still as rocks.

The picturesque is part of the broader notion of sympathy, or, better, the aesthetics of sympathy. Along with webbed Gothic ornamentation, such as tracery and illumination, the picturesque has offered a specific way of guiding our feelings into objects, into their existence. All things exist in time, though many try to hide the coming in and out of time with a persistence, a stability of form, as if form, when it perishes, needs to be doubled by a more persistent, timeless archetype, the form of a form. The picturesque shows a deep suspicion toward any such metaform, and it has always appreciated and acknowledged the temporality of things. Naturally, it is almost impossible to say when a thing comes into existence or when it departs again, since its materials and parts live on in one way or another, in other things. Therefore, we can never say exactly when something is born or when it dies; flows of organization pass through the thing, which is nothing but that word we have continually been using, quasi-innocently, "life." Life exceeds form, but for a thing in itself, that might not matter much, since the thing has its own sphere of existence in which it functions and acts. For the following discussion, this ontological dispute need not particularly bother us, we have more important matters to concentrate on.

Contemplating such temporality, we might distinguish between four different, successive "times" of things: the time of its design, its construction, its existence, and its demise. Now, before you prematurely throw this book into a corner, please let me stress the artificiality of this division into four times right away. It is not meant as an ontological order – the four seasons – but as a set of aesthetic requirements or aspects; they are not necessarily actual phases or periods. Every object undeniably is patterned and config-ured ("designed"); it is undeniably made of something; it undeniably spends time in existence, and it undeniably perishes. Obviously, this does not mean the four times have to stay distinctly separate. The time of design can coin-cide entirely with that of construction; as we have seen with ice crystals and mountains, there are no advance plans for the production of such objects, however, in my view, this does not mean we can simply skip design. We have designated this phenomenon as constructivism or configurationalism on several occasions in this book. The time of existence can also be the time of perishing, as no doctor will cease to remind us. And, slightly more ex-tremely – and I have made this my own stance on the matter – we could just as well say everything is design, from conception through construction, existence and demise, since the fact that things are patterned and decorated makes them work. Or we could say it is all existence, and things are just things, and whether they age or not doesn't alter that fact; every time they change they become different things.

The picturesque as an aesthetics of youth emphasizes the first and sec-ond categories, design and construction, sometimes in such a way that no room seems left for existence, so fresh and frail are these objects. We see delicate curves – "serpentine lines," in Hogarth's words[5] – and we see them trying to gather, but they have not yet fully succeeded. In the old picturesque, by contrast, we see the third and fourth category merging, existence and de-mise; we see time gnawing at the thing, taking out rough chunks, yet it per-sists. Time overwhelms the object; things either have not yet settled or are wearing down, are either in the process of forming or of falling apart. Picturesque objects are never mature or middle-aged; they are either young or old, either in the making or moving out of it. But, mind you, in the picturesque all is presented to us as things, and this is the beautifully solved paradox here: things are not amorphous blurs or *informes* – as Rosalind Krauss calls them, following Bataille – that is, modernist objects that have surrendered to the sublime. There is not a shred of deconstruction in the picturesque.[6] Things in turn seem to overwhelm time, and to encapsulate it – and that, again, is why the picturesque is ultimately a project of beauty. Time is abstracted by the object. The picturesque, then, is the *objectified age of a thing*. Aesthetics doesn't care whether the time or the thing is more real, nor does the picturesque care if a cottage or ruin was designed by the passing eons or last year by an architect. The fact that there is design suffices to make sympathy function.

Before we get any deeper into the philosophy of the aesthetics of the picturesque, I should provide a little more historical background. It is not my intention to add to the vast number of comprehensive books on that subject[7] – my project is primarily theoretical, not historical – but clearly we must acquaint ourselves with the most important protagonists and concepts. In brief, I believe the picturesque is the influence of landscape aesthetics on all other design, be it landscaping itself, landscape painting, poetry or the design of objects such as buildings. Others would say it was purely landscape painting, such as Claude Lorrain's (and his famous Claude glass), that drove the picturesque, and there are good reasons for that as well, but I will stick with a broader notion of aesthetics. It fits more logically with the objectification of time: more than most arts, landscaping deals with the temporalities of both growth and decay, and transferring such notions to poetry and architecture necessitates objectification. The laying out of a landscape garden, walking around in it, the depiction of it, the changes over time, its maintenance – it is all part of the driving influence behind the picturesque. The picturesque is not simply "pictorial," though certainly the tendency toward snapshots and scenery formed the basis for later travel writing and tourism. One of its major theoreticians, William Gilpin, actually began producing travel writing out of an interest in the picturesque, authoring guidebooks that instructed travelers exactly where to stand for the best views. For instance, Wordsworth's *Guide to the Lakes* was a direct descendant of Gilpin's *Observations on the River Wye*, published some thirty years earlier, in 1782. Conversely, the reader should know, for instance, that landscape designers like Capability Brown painted scenery first before doing the actual planning; that is, Brown sketched views and perspectives before drawing a plan in top view. This would be the normal way to proceed for a stage designer, whose audience sits in fixed positions, but it is a radical technique in landscape design, where the viewer must move and hence change his or her perspective. Now, we cannot simply understand the picturesque landscape as a sequence of intentionally manufactured views, because the question of what happens between those views immediately arises, since we cannot close our eyes in between standpoints. But then how do a bunch of unstaged and accidental views make up the substance of a landscape?

One of the answers of the landscape painters and designers of Brown's day was to disconnect the planning of walkways from that of views.[8] This might seem simple to accomplish, but it isn't at all. In the formal gardens of the previous age, the eyes would look in the direction the feet were going, based on a proper Cartesian notion of the homunculus. Not so in the picturesque garden; there, one might look at an object diagonally across the field while walking a sinuous path in another direction, or the object might suddenly become hidden; views would be obstructed by other elements as often as they became visible again. Sometimes you would seem to lose your way, only to discover you were surprisingly close to the stand of trees, folly or lake you had spotted earlier from a distance. In short, the "picture" was never balanced or finished, subtly provoking you to take another step. The picturesque has little to do with picture postcards, they are merely a derivative of it. The main notion was that the image provided an impulse for movement and travel – not the reverse, in which travel precedes the image, as in tourism. One would either see one's path but lack a landmark or see a carefully designed object but not the way leading to it – *there was always something missing*. The picturesque typically relies on movement and feeling to cope with this gap; if it were up to the eye and the mind alone (as in classical aesthetics), the gap would simply remain. Therefore, the resulting plan cannot be organized as a sequence of finished perspectives on the ground but only as a mosaic of views that are necessarily fractured.

Of course, mentioning fractures immediately calls to mind the preeminent romantic object, the ruin, but they have just as much to do with another, the cottage. The ruin arrived on the scene somewhat earlier and should be viewed more as an icon of the sublime, in the sense that it offers a countermodel of beauty, which is why we find it more in classicism, such as that of Schinkel, who gave us finished white temples alternating with dark, decaying ruins. However, the ruin never became a positive act in itself, and most ruins therefore ended up as follies and never reached the status of exemplary models for creating other architecture, such as city buildings. Things were completely different with the cottage, which was a model of construction, but one in which the previously mentioned time of design merged with the time of making. The cottage, of course, has a broken form, but not a broken structure like the ruin's. The original picturesque model of the cottage is one that accumulates on its own, without an architect interfering, "more grown than erected," as Wordsworth said.[9] During the 1830s, a vast number of publications, especially *The Architectural Magazine*, which published John Ruskin's first series of articles ("The Poetry of Architecture"[10]), and the *Encyclopaedia of Cottage, Farm, and Villa Architecture*, both edited by John Loudon, treated the cottage and the English farm as aesthetic subjects with a characteristically irregular, asymmetrical, heterogenous form. As an architectural example, the picturesque cottage was highly influential, most town halls, hotels and city villas were modeled on the concept in the nineteenth century. Manchester's city hall, for instance, can only be described as a *megacottage*, an assemblage of loosely organized parts producing an irregular contour, with hundreds of turrets, bow windows and gables creating an architecture that wrests itself away from urbanist constraints.

The cottage became the main architectural model of formation and *Bildung*, an object that literally grew over time, through addition: rooms were attached as required, with no specific attention paid to the design or composition of the whole. A cottage would aggregate pieces, like rooms, shops or stables, which would be added and sometimes removed later, so that it never became a finished object. The time of the cottage's making, in fact, coincides with that of its existence. The parts (rooms, turrets, balconies, chimneys, porches, etc.) were often symmetrical, but the whole was not. On the other hand, a cottage as a whole was not simply an asymmetrical, aggregated clump; the connections between the volumetric parts still followed rules, and sometimes even made them align on one side, or merge back into a single volume containing multiple rooms, but just as often, they would move away from each other, barely touching. In general, we can speak of *local* rules of assembly, i.e., ones operative in individual parts and connections, rather than global laws applying to the formation of a preconceived whole; such laws are often axial and proportional, like those we find in Palladio's famous Tuscan villas, which are based on harmonic subdivision, not picturesque addition. The rules for making a picturesque building are closer to those governing the positioning of water droplets on a table: when two get close enough together, they reorganize into a single drop, but if they barely touch, each drop keeps most of its original contour. Of course, a picturesque house has no such rounded contours, but the comparison indicates the flexibility of interaction between the house's parts, even though they mostly possess angular and crystalline features. Sometimes a part yields to another and they merge into a new, larger part; sometimes it resists and merely connects to the other. And this method of formation stays active throughout the house's existence.

We tend to think of such compositions merely as images of aggregating and growing systems, but this is only our typical late-twentieth-century critics' minds taking everything as a sign of something else. Recalling our discussion of James and Bergson for a moment, we can begin to understand how radical such a notion of design actually is. We never actually get to see the object in full, something stays occluded and hidden. The picturesque object is continuously growing and changing, an occurrence as much as a thing, making us intuitively act to try to grasp what is going on.

I hope you won't mind if we don't go into all the details of picturesque composition, which were heavily debated by the likes of Richard Payne Knight[11] and Uvedale Price; again, I would like instead to concentrate on the radicalism of its position. The fact that the picturesque did not remain

a way of looking at existing landscapes and rural buildings but instead developed into a way of designing new ones is particularly amazing when you
think about it. It is like believing it is possible to design a worn rug. If we
cannot tell whether something is new or old, unfinished in one direction or
in the other, it is truly objective and radical. Splitting the time of making
and that of design once more does not change the nature of the picturesque
thing at all. But we need to keep in mind that objectified age is also what
threatens it. The middle position of the picturesque generally starts out as
radical, but it proves extremely difficult to maintain this central position.
And there is more going on at this point than merely an avant-garde becoming vulgar and mainstream. Moderation necessarily haunts the picturesque: cottages become suburban houses, travel becomes tourism, tourism
becomes slumming, and the broken image of sympathy becomes a repaired
image of sentiment. I do not think anyone understood this better than John
Ruskin, who observed how quickly the picturesque could revert to superficial imagery and become sentimental, even cruel. The picturesque must be
radicalized over and over again to find its subject, life – even in our time.

ruskin: the parasitical sublime

If we wish to summarize his position on aesthetics in a few words, we could
say Ruskin made two major adjustments, amending the ideas of both beauty
and the sublime, logically moving them both toward the middle by adding
life and excess to beauty and moderation to the sublime. Ruskin observed
that "typical" forms of beauty tended to become clichés and needed to be
replaced by "vital" beauty; for the sublime, he offered an alternative he called
the "parasitical sublime."[12] In short, he proposed a warmer, livelier form of
beauty and a smaller, more manageable form of the sublime, with the two
categories coming so close together that they could almost touch, and in
some cases actually did.

Let us start with the first concept. Why is beauty persistently explained
with categories beyond itself? Utility, truth, imagination, and formal aspects
such as order and proportion are just that, and none of them has been able

to locate beauty where it occurs: between things, and between us and things, in encounters. Beauty happens in life itself, and it would not be particularly problematic to fully extend this idea to all of existence, which Whitehead tried as hard as Ruskin to do. Both men would agree that there is a happy teleology in the world – not a purposiveness that is automatically beautiful, but beauty *itself* as a purpose. Life enjoys itself. Vital beauty certainly occurs where form opens itself more to the realm of forces, yet never as deformation but rather as formation: forces help the form come into existence. Ruskin's vital beauty coincides with our young picturesque. However, this statement is not much help if you are an artist and beauty is supposed to be your area of expertise, because you need to make things of beauty, forms themselves, be they poems, paintings or buildings. As a realm of forms, beauty is inherently threatened by Platonism, by formalism and typology, which represent a point at which forms seem to retreat from life and become casts of themselves. At first, it seems an easy thing to do to add life to a painting. Since "life is activity," as we have learned from Lipps, we merely have to paint our subjects in a more active way, going about their daily business, moving around, walking down the street, getting out of a chair. Or one can go further and change one's subject matter from people and trees to animals, as Delacroix did, depicting ferocious tigers and noble horses. But things are not that easy. One would have plenty of life, plenty of movement, but in a painting that was framed and hanging motionless on a wall. Changing the subject matter would provide a mere image of movement and would in fact detach us onlookers more from life rather than attach us to it. The problem the artist has to solve becomes, in a way, Gothic again; he or she should not follow the Baroque option of building or capturing movement but must make stability and stillness into an activity (like Lipps's notion of posture); at that moment, the activity of the subject can converge with the stillness of the art object. The stillness must be pure and accidental and at the same time seem to last forever. If one paints only the eternal, one ends up with Ingres's dead two-dimensional statues, and if one sculpts the moment, one ends up with Bernini's marble photographs – neither is an example of the vital beauty Ruskin was looking for.

Ruskin likes things to stand still; for him, the strange intermediate

being is more than half made of stone. He likes rugged towers, and wind-
mills, and old men with tanned skin, and women getting up from their seats,
like Millais's *Mariana*. These are not very special things, nothing that would
get anybody excited today. Here is Ruskin in *Modern Painters* (Vol. IV):

> For instance, I cannot find words to express the intense pleas-
> ure I have always in first finding myself, after some prolonged
> stay in England, at the foot of the old tower of Calais church.
> The large neglect, the noble unsightliness of it; the record of
> its years written so visibly, yet without sign of weakness or
> decay; its stern wasteness and gloom, eaten away by the Chan-
> nel winds, and overgrown with the bitter sea grasses; its slates
> and tiles all shaken and rent, and yet not falling; its desert of
> brickwork full of bolts, and holes, and ugly fissures, and yet
> strong, like a bare brown rock; its carelessness of what any one
> thinks or feels about it, putting forth no claim, having no
> beauty or desirableness, pride, nor grace; yet neither asking for
> pity; not, as ruins are, useless and piteous, feebly or fondly gar-
> rulous of better days; but useful still, going through its own
> daily work, – as some old fisherman beaten grey by storm, yet
> drawing his daily nets: so it stands, with no complaint about
> its past youth, in blanched and meagre massiveness and ser-
> viceableness, gathering human souls together underneath it;
> the sound of its bells for prayer still rolling through its rents;
> and the grey peak of it seen far across the sea, principal of the
> three that rise above the waste of surfy sand and hillocked
> shore, – the lighthouse for life, and the belfry for labour, and
> this for patience and praise.[13]

How can one ever cut a Ruskin quote short? (His sentences are themselves
like illuminated knotwork, tightening into a braided patch and then suddenly letting go and loosening, moving away via tendrils and sometimes returning via a long loop.[14]) We seem to have moved from vital beauty to an
older picturesque, meanwhile – though it is no less vital. It is a form of the

picturesque that borders on decay but subsists and asks "for no pity." Time and time again, Ruskin warns us against finding pleasure in decay, in suspended activity, since that pushes us into the sublime, or at least into a form of the picturesque that he disqualifies as "low" and superficial. The other form is the higher, noble form, the one we see in Turner. A few pages further on, he writes:

> And, as we think farther over the matter, we shall see that this is indeed the eminent cause of the difference between the lower picturesque and the higher. For, in a certain sense, the lower picturesque ideal is eminently a *heartless* one; the lover of it seems to go forth into the world in a temper as merciless as its rocks. All other men feel some regret at the sight of disorder and ruin. He alone delights in both; it matters not of what. Fallen cottage – desolate villa – deserted village – blasted heath – mouldering castle – to him, so that they do but show jagged angles of stone and timber, all are sights equally joyful. Poverty, and darkness, and guilt, bring in their several contributions to his treasury of pleasant thoughts.[15]

We have already discussed cruelty in relation to Ruskin in previous chapters, with reference to the forces of abstraction, direct relatives of the forces of the sublime. Accepting the fact that objects or people are worn out and even about to die does not mean one is heartless and cruel; *it is the enormity of the forces that is cruel*, not the acknowledgment of them. This is actually a caring position, such as we find in the description of the Calais church tower. The low, superficial picturesque is heartless because it enjoys depicting objects that have expired, fallen ill or been abandoned; the high, noble picturesque is caring because it shows the traces and accidents *within existence* and therefore its quiet persistence and perseverance – again, wholly fitting with the objectification of time. The picturesque is necessarily touched and affected by the sublime but not overwhelmed by it. A painting of a windmill, or of an old man, or an old cottage or a dirty street, certainly depicts objects that border on the sublime, but it does not relinquish them to it, and thus actual sympathy is at work in it.

Let us try to understand this more clearly. Ruskin is obviously worried when he discusses the low picturesque, but he is worried about the *reality of the painting*, not the so-called reality behind it. He is not making a representational comment; he is not referring to the actual old man (who might be dead by now) or the cottage (which might have burned down) but to the painting itself. That is, he continuously questions the sympathies of the painter, and whether they are genuine or whether they have been overcome by sentiment or pity. Sentiment is the *sympathetic fallacy*. Since the reality of the painting is not the actual old man or cottage but the sympathy the painter has for them, *that* sympathy has a life of its own, and it subsequently detaches itself from the artist to begin the independent life of an art object, which will survive us by hundreds of years. Ultimately, this is what legitimizes art: when sympathy is based on encounters, art is capable of sieving out the sympathy and allowing it to create fresh encounters.

Therefore, Ruskin would never oppose the idea of building a *new* picturesque cottage in the countryside; he would only object if it were designed and built as fake-old, if the house were to lead us into a life that was not its own, offering only an image of decay. Indeed, if you wanted to go and build a cottage, he would advise you to make it out of a combination of rough-hewn stones and precisely carved Gothic ornament, with irregular features, but not to make it *look as if* it were hundreds of years old. In a similar manner, Ruskin wants us to paint a tree completely correctly, as absolutely unique and real, full of growth, taking nourishment from the elements around it: not the image of a real tree but a presentation of one, without the "re." For John Ruskin, a painting is real. Most art critics forget to mention that an artwork itself is always real – all analysis should start from there: what does the work actually do? How does it realize itself? A painting is constructed, woven like a carpet. In the fourth volume of *Modern Painters*, Ruskin draws a diagram of a tree that looks exactly like Aristid Lindenmayer's L-systems of a hundred and twenty years later, with all the systemic bifurcations and recursive iterations correctly organized, as in an algorithmic script.[16] We should not forget that the exact structure of a tree that has grown over decades can be generated in a millisecond through calculations. A tree is an expression, not just of energy or striving but of code. In short, things do not meet without a veil between them; this is not a mediation but the actual taking on of a pattern during an encounter. In the case of the iron hinge, the final tendrilized, ornate form does not prevent the hinge from meeting the door; on the contrary, it actually makes it touch it and plug into it. That is why I never use the term "realism": for things to encounter each other sympathetically, they need that abstract veil of life, and for the same reason we will never find any metaphysical divide between a tree and a painting of it. Nothing is mimicked or simulated; neither the hinge nor the painting acts "as if" it is alive; they are simply life forms extending onto screens, doors and canvases. Because of its abstraction, life flourishes in all directions.

As George Landow has pointed out in his book on Ruskin's aesthetics, published forty years ago, sympathy is the major driving force behind both his vital beauty and his "noble" or high picturesque. I think this is an observation of major importance, since Ruskin was not overtly clear or consistent in his use of the term. Sympathy was so strongly embedded in English (and Scottish) aesthetics and moral philosophy that he must have felt he hardly needed to elaborate. However, I have deviated from the direct lineage, because I think Ruskin made some serious alterations to the older form. Surely, it would only be correct for a historian to perform a comparative analysis of Ruskin's sympathy and that of his predecessors or contemporaries. But for a more theoretical account, I do not think that the typical British form of fellow-feeling, the sympathy of David Hume, Francis Hutcheson, James Beattie and Adam Smith, is sufficient for helping us to understand Ruskin's version – which is why I left Ruskin out of the previous chapter, even though his concept of sympathy takes a central place in this book. His sympathy is more advanced, since it distributes itself among all things, organic and nonorganic, since they are all equally saturated with life and force. Ruskin pays most attention to this topic in the chapter of *Modern Painters* entitled "Of the Turnerian Picturesque," written in 1856:

> But if these same outward characters be sought for in subordination to the inner character of the object, every source of pleasurableness being refused which is incompatible with that,

while perfect sympathy is felt at the same time with the object as to all that it tells of itself in those sorrowful by-words, we have the school of true or noble picturesque; still distinguished from the school of pure beauty and sublimity, because, in its subjects, the pathos and sublimity are all *by the way*, as in Calais old spire, – not inherent, as in a lovely tree or mountain; while it is distinguished still more from the schools of the lower picturesque by its tender sympathy, and its refusal of all sources of pleasure inconsistent with the perfect nature of the thing to be studied.[17]

Such a relationship can never be categorized as mental contiguity or association, as Hume presumed; that would imply a detour via the mind. Ruskin's sympathy is felt immediacy, and of a far more objective kind than Hume's aesthetics. It is the relation itself that is experienced. The life of the old spire is directly part of his. Ruskin's notion of sympathy shows considerably more similarity to Lipps's and Bergson's than to Hume's, in large part because of his vitalism. When things encounter each other, they share each other's lives, according to the rule of Jamesian intimacy. We should constantly keep in mind that the actuality of the relation with which James radicalizes Hume's empiricism is that of feeling, not of the mind. Things encounter each other in the manner of Lipps meeting the shaking tree, or the Doric column, or Bergson's Ammophila meeting the caterpillar, or the Gothic iron hinge meeting the wooden door: they all act in a relation of sympathy. Ruskin's sympathy is an ethereal, indeed *asensual*, aesthetics that offers no pleasure whatsoever in sharing appearances or tastes but only in sharing each other's life and actions. Wordsworth wrote almost sixty years earlier, in a very similar, "mineralist" vein,[18] of a picturesque encounter on the banks of the River Wye:

> While with an eye made quiet by the power
> Of harmony, and the deep power of joy,
> We see into the life of things.[19]

For Ruskin, likewise, art is not an appearance but an act: it is what a thing does, how it leads its life and shares it. And every act is an encounter and therefore an act of sympathy. Nobody and nothing acts in empty space; everyone and everything acts in relation, by resonating, by synchronizing, in encounters that are not sensual but spiritual. How could the encounter between us and an old spire ever be sensual? That would be impossible. The encounter is spiritual but not conceptual, immediate but not physical. It is a realism without materiality and an idealism without mind. Of course, when Ruskin starts writing about the spire in his typical meandering, explorative style, his mind and its imaginative powers come into play, but it does not intervene between him and the spire but rather helps him to proceed and to sympathize more *after* the encounter, and to pass his sympathy on to us. The sympathetic connection immediately dissolves the notion of the Other – Ruskin's must be the most unsentimental ethics ever. He never turns into a humanist but remains a persistent and consistent vitalist. Life is what connects things (or, if you prefer, the connection of things is what we call life.) To Ruskin, a painting is not a *sign* of sympathy between us and some tree or old house; it is itself that sympathy, yes, between us and the tree, between us and the painting, between the painter and the tree, and between the painting and the tree, but removed from all the betweens to lead the separate, independent life of an artwork. It is as if the artist takes the veil between things and transforms it into a canvas. Art is never an unveiling, a manifestation of something latent or an expression of something hidden, it is purely veiling. Art is the original method of multiplying sympathy, the privileged form of distributing it among as many of us as possible. But aesthetics doubtless existed long before we humans did. Life on earth has always been artificial and still is artificial; it did not suddenly become natural because humans came on the scene.

Let us return to our discussion of the picturesque. While being touched by the sublime is inevitable, because life is a world of forces as much as of forms, clearly at this point those forces are increasing beyond the world of vital beauty and, of course, beyond that of a young picturesque into that of the older, more savage, more jagged, more rugged form. There is no disgust here, no horror, no rotting, none of the things that have so obsessed us for the last hundred years; no deconstruction. This aesthetics is what Ruskin called the "parasitical sublime," and it constitutes his formula for the picturesque:

> This sublimity, belonging in a parasitical manner to the building, renders it, in the usual sense of the word, "picturesque."[20]

Ruskin had previously developed this idea more broadly, in *The Seven Lamps of Architecture*,[21] but what a fitting term: "parasitical." Something has been attached to the sublime and is *symbiotic* with it, though it is smaller, living on and from it. The picturesque cannot live by itself. The jaggedness, the ruggedness, the angular, crystalline lines (think of Riegl and Worringer) – all this belongs to the sublime; the picturesque merely borrows it, or, better, feeds itself, taking the smallest bites possible. In short, the picturesque already lives in sympathy, plugging into the sublime immediately and directly, free of interpretation and mediation. The picturesque is exactly what we worked out in the previous chapter, when we argued that the relation between abstraction – the world of forces, diagram, the sublime – and empathy – a world of forms, naturalism and beauty – must be one of transformation and production. The picturesque cannot exist as a stable middle point, as a search for excess when viewed from the angle of beauty or as a search for moderation seen from the angle of the sublime. It should always be viewed as a movement, a transition. Moving from empathy to abstraction means vitalizing beauty; moving from abstraction to empathy means parasitizing the sublime. Life comes to form, and form comes to life, one more mineral, the other more vegetal, but the two constantly intertwine, enmeshing and entangling in a world we can only call *wild* – a world that is home to tigers, butterflies and orchids but not to our domesticated selves (which is why we retrieve chocolate, coffee, tobacco, sugar and mescaline from the jungle).

Having categorized Ruskin's as the first radicalization of the picturesque, following Gilpin, Knight and Price's original concept, we should now slowly proceed to the second radicalization, that of William Robinson's wild gardens. The wild we find in Robinson is quite different from Henry David Thoreau's wilderness,[22] or Walt Whitman's. Both American men spoke often of sympathy, especially Whitman, so often that it bothered D. H. Lawrence, who spoke of Whitman's sympathy as being too confused with love, not a feeling-with but a feeling-for.[23] What struck the Europeans about the Americans, when the latter encountered the Rockies or Yosemite Valley, in reality or in poetry, was that they didn't experience the typical fear of the sublime, though they had every reason to, since their mountains were higher and more rugged, their canyons more desolate and prehistoric, and their sequoia trees five times as big as anything in Europe. They were immediately at ease with the wild, and Thoreau, of course, literally lived in it, building a cabin and catching fish on the very first day – he had no time for awe. But let us return to Robinson's mini-wilderness.

The first thing we should acknowledge is that there is nothing natural about the wild – in fact, the wild is *the home of decoration*. It contains painted animals, painted flowers, painted mountains – birds, frogs, fish: all painted. The wild is the realm where makeup was invented. Nothing is bare there, or naked, or true, or authentic – an insight the neopagans, among many others practicing earth religions, have yet to arrive at. Above all, the wild is excess – not the postmodern, Mae West form of maximalism, oozing with irony and camp, since in the wild there is nothing to distance oneself from, but the place where things bloom and flourish. These vegetal terms are no accident. The wild is a place more than a state of mind, but it is *a place without space*, not merely full but overgrown. Ornament is the art of overgrowth, a movement *in situ*. In the wild, there is no space between things; everything rubs against everything else, according to James's rule of intimacy.

The wild is the end of Deleuzian smooth space. Firstly, it contains no space – it is absolute density and intensity – and secondly, there is nothing smooth about it. Everything is territory, everything is marked, everything designed, interrupted by flowers and connected by plants, fibrous and floral. Ruskin is the most vegetalist of all the vitalists (though he perhaps shares that position with Gustav Fechner, author of *Nanna, oder, Über das Seelen-Leben der Pflanzen*); he is an exception, because most of them are animalists and animists. To John Ruskin, all things are plants, be they houses, women, carpets, city halls, church spires, paintings, countries or anything else –

everything is immobile and flourishing at once. An impenetrable, dense realm such as we find, for instance, in Edward Burne-Jones's *The Legend of Briar Rose* paintings – a world without views, without depth, of pure en-tanglement – is what we could perhaps call the wet, vegetal sublime, as an alternative to the dry, mineral one we have been acquainted with for the last two hundred years. It is not the sublime of the vast, open, smooth spaces of the desert, the sky or the ocean but the one of the jungle and the forest, with their billions of niches – if we can justly call it a sublime, since it has so many properties of beauty as well. But the model is clear: here, beauty grows directly on the sublime, and it overgrows it. Every time Ruskin draws a rock, a plant grows from it somewhere, since for him it would be unimag-inable without one.[24] Nor could he ever imagine the Alps as uninhabited, not because of any misguided Victorian theology holding that nature was ultimately destined to serve mankind but because to portray the sublime as without inhabitants would be to mistake it for a source of decay and death rather than one of flourishing and of life. The wild should not be confused with Ruskin's savageness: it is the point at which changefulness, with its graceful, delicate curves of vital beauty, is directly grafted onto the angular, savage crystals of the parasitical sublime. The wild forms a new, second-generation middle, a new form of vitalized geometry.

When plants bloom, they grow ornaments – flowers – but when people bloom, they "fulfill their potential." This term simultaneously points at a teleological notion, since fulfillment is complete, and a notion of freedom, since "potential" signals a broader range of options than just one; this ful-fillment is different than, say, filling a can. It is more of an overflowing, a radiant, divergent blossoming, a form of happiness. We can easily quote Ruskin a thousand times on happiness; his words never imply the hedonis-tic, Epicurean notion of pleasure or sensuality but the Aristotelian sense of *eudaimonia*[25] (εὐδαιμονία), of well-being and flourishing, of being guided by good spirits (not just by an inner life or striving). In *The Seven Lamps of Architecture*, he writes:

> I believe the right question to ask, respecting all ornament, is simply this: Was it done with enjoyment – was the carver happy while he was about it?[26]

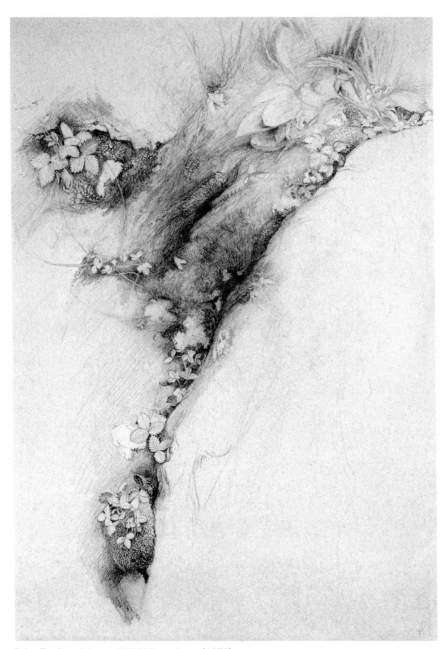

John Ruskin. *Moss and Wild Strawberry* (1873).

This is probably the all-time favorite Ruskin quote, and I only want to bring it in now, against the ethics-over-aesthetics argument and not in favor of it, though the quote is usually misunderstood that way. Surely Ruskin is not introducing into aesthetics the notion of amateurism, the idea that as long as one is happy the result is fine; rather, he is talking about the independence of the professional. Intuition is not granted to those who lack skill but to experts who can do things with their eyes shut. We might find Ruskin's words utterly paternalistic at best and neo-liberal at worst, or vice versa, unless we absorbed his opinion that a hand laborer performed his work exactly as a physician or any other specialist did: independently, as a service we should simply accept and pay for, whose provider we should not order about or try to control. Ruskin would not have viewed the craftsman as a *free man*, since he was strongly bound to his task, but as having a *free hand* in executing that task and as doing more than necessary by nature, since the joy lay in exploring that freedom. Additionally, when we realize that the same book opens with the statement that ornament is useless, it begins to dawn on us what a radical, wild economy Ruskin had in mind: "That country is the richest which nourishes the greatest number of noble and happy human beings."[27] The more uselessness, i.e., life, accumulated in a nation, the wealthier it was.

At the same time, we realize how counterintuitive and uncomfortable the world of the wild must seem to the 1968 generation. Since it is not accompanied by space, freedom here is not the expected nomadic, vehicular, born-to-be-wild sense of open extensiveness. Freedom of movement has been completely replaced by a freedom of flourishing. There is a trade-off: ambulant action becomes action in contemplation.[28] Either you are born with movement so you can visit things or you bloom and things visit you – in Victorian terms, you are either the knight or the maiden (I am immediately reminded of yet another series of paintings by Burne-Jones – the stunning *Perseus Cycle* – showing the maiden chained to a rock). Of the two, our contemporary culture has only managed to retain the armored, polished steel body, be it male or female.[29] The knight has a different relation to the sublime than the maiden, who is fixed to it, while he is a free man and allowed to move about in the sublime, but only at the cost of turning himself into a sublime object, cast in iron, excluding all that is delicate and fragile.[30] It is not that beauty does not pay a price as well. In Ruskin's world of strange intermediate being, vegetal flourishing necessarily goes together with the mineral and architectural sense of fixation. We have encountered this over and over again, in the active rigidity of the Gothic, in entangled ribbon ornament, in the still figures of the Pre-Raphaelites, in Lipps's postures; it always amounts to the same thing: action becomes structure, structure becomes action. All plants are rooted; they are allowed to move only a tiny bit (in the wind, and when they grow), yet instead they exude the most divine fragrances and dress in the most incredible colors. Their passivity is nothing but an illusion, *decoration is pure action*.

Ruskin was deeply disturbed by Darwin's concept of decoration in animals and plants as the basis for sexual selection, and he worked for years on a response countering its mechanics and utilitarianism, which he published eventually as *Love's Meinie* (on birds) and *Proserpina* (on flowers). Though we will return to this obscured conflict in the last chapter, for now, let us focus on the wild.

The title *The Wild Garden* (1870) sounds like the most paradoxical of all possible titles, but to its author, William Robinson, it was not.[31] Like the picturesque, the wild garden is a style of design, not something we find in the wild, wherever that may be – it is an aesthetic qualification, not a naturalistic one. The wild garden is not a "natural garden," a term flawed for hundreds of reasons (there is no nature, and even if there was, you could not make a garden out of it, nor could you make a garden that looked like unspoiled nature, because if you did, you would end up with two trees, lots of weeds and two types of flowers, and you would also be ignoring the fact that nature, whatever it is, designs itself). Though Robinson often calls certain effects "pictorial," it would be incorrect to call the wild garden a mere resurgence of the picturesque, especially since the latter is a form of landscape gardening, specifically intended for large parks and vast estates. In fact, Robinson's form of the picturesque should be viewed as a relatively

Alfred Parsons. *Colonies of Poet's Narcissus and Broad-Leaved Saxifrage.*
Ill. on p. 93 from William Robinson, *The Wild Garden* (1870).

small one, even as a kind of microgardening. In the book, which was so popular that it came out in dozens of editions, as Robinson kept improving it over the years, he did not concentrate on the top view plan at all, probably out of the same aversion to the plan expressed by the first picturesque designers, such as Brown and Loudon. Here, as in his later book *The English Flower Garden* (1883), we find no plans, only views, which we can hardly call "perspectives"; they are close-ups, though zoomed out far enough to show more than just single plants. Such plants

> will look infinitely better than they ever did in formal beds, in consequence of fine-leaved plant, fern, and flower, and climber, grass and trailing shrub, relieving each other in delightful ways.[32]

Relieving is the central word here. The plants relieve one another; that is, they nest together or form groups in an unforced way, though tightly, not spatially. The wild garden is not spatial in any way; it is a *textural garden*, more a form of drapery than of living architecture. All wild gardeners are obsessed with plants, and Robinson offers endless lists of them. Gertrude Jekyll (1843–1932), for instance, knew about every possible plant by heart but never elaborated on design and layout, and my Dutch contemporary Piet Oudolf prefers to call himself a horticulturalist instead of a designer; both work very much in Robinson's tradition. They create gardens that are closer to mosaics in William James's sense, than to actual spaces. Clearly, the picturesque is fed by an empiricism that prefers the parts to the whole every time, but wild gardening is most related to its radicalized version, where it is not only the parts that count but also how they nest and pack together. Like James, Robinson repudiates any type of bedding, James when he challenges Kantian apriority and accepts only "uncemented stones" and Robinson when he rejects the Victorian manner of "bedding out" gardens, with hard, geometric edges keeping the flower beds in order. They are both fighting the same schematism. Again and again, Robinson stresses the parasitical nature of his wild gardening technique in the book, advocating the use of hidden ditches, shady lanes, broken walls and rocks, and including various places where nothing is planned, such as groves and the edges of existing parks. It is almost like a strategy, a bit similar to that of today's guerrilla gardeners. We see deteriorating walls with flowers sprouting from the broken joints (Robinson was an avid reader of Ruskin), ivy crawling up the walls of a cottage, a wild rose climbing an ash tree, bushy groupings everywhere with blurry edges, surely this is the wild notion of an overgrowth that strategically probes certain spots, dark edges, hidden stones:

> In the gardens at Great Tew, the charming Balearic Sandwort, which usually roots over the moist surfaces of stones, planted itself high up on a wall in a small recess, where half a brick had been displaced.[33]

Alfred Parsons. *Cheddar Pink, Saxifrage, And Ferns, on cottage wall at Mells, Somerset.* Ill. on p. 115 from William Robinson, *The Wild Garden* (1870).

It planted itself! Nothing would have pleased Ruskin more than such a reversal of decay into life. Plants seem to become probes or scouts sent out to explore, turning into design agents of a sort, little active parts that find their places among all the other things. To use our earlier terminology, here it seems that the time of making is far more important than the time of design; the design is only half done, sketchy, in the typical *malerisch* style[34] of clumps and swaths, with plants that seem scattered rather than placed in any precise way, all indefinite, with irregular edges. The most striking "designs" are the flower fields on forest floors; the endless narcissi and daffodils drifting among the birch trees of Gravetye, Robinson's lifelong project, and the tiger lilies popping out of the grass wherever possible. Of course, no mowing, "no manicure," was allowed, so that the grass in Robinson's gardens resembled a living canvas that regulated all communication between parts. The grass, which occupies such a prominent place in Oudolf's designs,[35] seems even wilder here than the blooming flowers, resembling Hogarth's young women with their loose hair – six-foot-high Malepartus grass and broad sweeps of purple pennisetum, all "in a wild profusion." To Robinson, design is more like beginning a process, initiating something. And though he minimizes the time of design, it does not have to be compensated for by the time of existence, i.e., maintenance – no, wildness means something else:

> … this term is especially applied to the placing of exotic plants in places, and under conditions, where they will become established and take care of themselves … it does not necessarily mean the picturesque garden, for a garden may be highly picturesque and yet in every part be the result of ceaseless care.[36]

Of course, such a notion of care starts with the choice of plants. Robinson hated to use delicate annuals that did not survive the transition to winter and preferred rowdy perennials and hardy exotics, not necessarily native plants, placing them in such a way that they would "flourish without further care."[37] On critical examination, we see that this could not have been com-

Alfred Parsons. *Tiger Lilies in Wild Garden at Great Tew.* Ill. on p. 135 from William Robinson, *The Wild Garden* (1870).

pletely true, because even the wildest garden needs some kind of maintenance – weeding, fertilizing, though nothing extensive. This is a different
kind of care than the constant patrolling and manicuring a formal garden
needs; it is a more supportive kind of care that helps the plants and the garden grow without making the process predictable. Wild gardening is a *eu-
daimonic* design technique, in which things help each other to grow but also
make each other stop growing. Note that the wild garden does not "run
wild," since the plants check each other; though there is a tendency toward
overgrowth, and it often occurs, the plants limit and tame each other simply
through their adjacent and neighboring positions.

But let us not fool ourselves, it is specifically a *design* technique, not a
way of piling up accidents; there is the continuous substance of the garden.
I think it is of the utmost importance to state this, because removing humans from the design process (which I applaud) does not mean getting rid
of design. Actually, I think we would all agree that it is a way to improve
design, and that wild gardens are exceptionally beautiful. Today, if you went
to visit Gravetye Manor,[38] you would end up shaking your head in the presence of so much beauty. If I may step ahead of my own argument for a second, I think we can observe a model here that we should apply to all design
– and, since design is a technical act, to all technology. All picturesque interventions work best when they veer away from naturalism and spread into
other fields of design, but for that, we need to invent a *technological wild*.

Of all the design professions, gardening and cooking are the most sympathetic, because they are not merely techniques of putting parts together;
instead, the parts form and develop as they participate in the process, each
at its own rate of change, its own pace. A great gardener or chef not only
sees the state of things but senses where they are going. Commentators
often speak far too lightly of a "process," probably thinking the word merely
indicates the time it takes for the parts to come together, but that thought
originates in the same mistake William Paley made, which we discussed in
the chapter on the nature of the Gothic. One of Bruno Latour's favorite
artworks, for instance, Damián Ortega's *Cosmic Thing*,[39] consists of a Volkswagen Beetle taken apart and hung from the ceiling in a real-life exploded
view. It is an engineer's dream, Viollet-le-Duc's dream, and fundamentally

no different from Paley's watch found on a heath.[40] The work implies things are just assemblies of parts encased in transparent necessity, and time is merely a moment. In fact, parts transform as they interact, and as I said before, *that* is their action, and this action takes place in two directions: that of the part itself – what it feels – and that of the other part – what we call

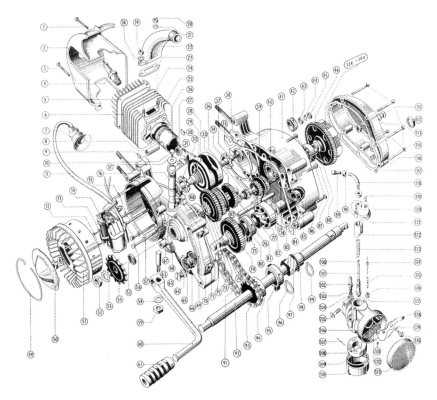

Exploded view of a 1970s one-cylinder moped engine.

a relation. In a Gothic ontology, you can try very hard to separate things from their relations, but you won't quite succeed. Yes, you can disentangle them, but they will change back beyond recognition, back to indeterminacy – no less real, but less defined. For instance, taking a Volkswagen apart in a reverse-engineering design process would result in a large number of loose parts that would stay predetermined, such as bolts and pistons, but others, like the car's body, would, in disentangling, unfold back into flat sheets of metal, which nobody would ever call "parts." In this sense, the monocoque frame is much more part of a Baroque ontology, since it is folded from an as yet underdefined substance (the sheet of metal), a half-product more than a product. An exploded view is never a diagram of making and design, since time is an inherent part of the component itself. And such diagrams are never generative, because parts take on form in relation to each other; separate them and they will lose their form accordingly. The exploded view of a cooked dish – if one were able to draw one – would in no way resemble the ingredients readied for cooking, all sliced and diced, prepared for participation in a process. For a salad, it might work, but not for a cooked dish. Such a clean unravelling is possible only in a Greek ontology, in which all parts are put together in the same way as they can be taken apart: the columns, the friezes, the pedestals all lie there waiting to be used, as if in a storage rack in a workshop (the exploded view is that of the mechanic, not the designer), waiting to be put together to form a temple without transforming.

Gothic things exist *only* in relation. If one were to imagine William Morris's carpets literally grown or generated on a computer screen, run as a digital script (named *Tangle Carpet*©) with variable parametric figures interacting according to rules of configuration, one would see the twigs growing in four directions from the middle of the screen outward (since it has biaxial symmetry); they would bend and start to bifurcate, and then some twigs would spiral inward in order to stop growing, while others moved on and continue to bifurcate, as leaves sprouted, and at the ends, flowers would pop out. All Morris's carpets would behave in exactly the same way, the figures would change and interact as they grew, and the result would be dependent only on the preset rules of the system, i.e., the amounts of bifurcating, tendriling, entangling and sprouting allowed. For instance, if you set the entanglement slider at zero, the result would be Carbrook; at halfway, you would get Holland Park; and with the slider on maximum, Bullerswood.

A gardener or a chef has to initiate multiple processes, all running in parallel, each with its own characteristics that he or she must feel-into and live-with in order to arrive at the final composition. Clearly, this is not something one "controls" in any way, but one can ensure it by attention and timing. At a certain moment, one would understand that stepping back and letting go would constitute giving care as much as nourishing or helping would. We have discussed Gothic configuration (and now Morris's carpets as well) as a procedure of interaction between mobile digital parts or figures, in what we have called thing-actions, but we should endorse gardening and cooking as the fundamental models for all art and design. There is nothing like the designing of a living thing.

sublime things

Before we move to the realm of the technological wild, we need to probe more deeply into the nature of things. Many will undoubtedly raise their eyebrows when they see Martin Heidegger and John Ruskin make an appearance in the same argument. They have a lot in common, the notion of care and craft is very important to each of them, as is a devastating (but inconsequential) critique of technology. When we investigate more precisely, though, we will see how much they differ, and where else besides on the matter of aesthetics. Soon enough, we will find the pervasive opposition between the Greek and the Gothic respectively fully embodied in these antagonists. Since Ruskin's topic is aesthetics, the notion of the thing is implied, because aesthetics specializes in the making of things, but still, as a concept, if we can call it that, the *thing* is purely Heidegger's, and it is a marvelous invention, powerful enough to emancipate things and liberate them from human interference, as Harman recently showed.[41] If anyone in philosophy has been able to grasp the importance of furnishing our lives, it was Heidegger. For him, things are continuously haunted by their own absence, either through dissolving in a network of actions or in the way they are "open" to the "world." He quickly discovered that artists were experts in speculating on the nature of things. Like Kant, he found that artworks could consciously move away from the formal state of beauty in the direction of the sublime. And if it works for that class of things, it should apply to all of them. As we proceed, we will allow a dialogue every now and then between the two men; neither was very polite by nature, and we will therefore have to moderate heavily and be careful about when we allow each to speak and the other to intervene.

Let us start with Heidegger's description in *The Origin of the Work of Art* of a painting by Vincent van Gogh:

> From the dark opening of the worn insides of the shoes the toilsome tread of the worker stares forth. In the stiffly rugged heaviness of the shoes there is the accumulated tenacity of her slow trudge through the far-spreading and ever-uniform furrows of the field swept by raw wind. On the leather lie the dampness and richness of the soil. Under the soles slides the loneliness of the field-path as evening falls.[42]

It may come as a shock to most Heideggerians, but this description of Van Gogh's painting, as we can now see, is a model of picturesque rhetoric. It could easily have been written by Ruskin, with the same sense of wandering and exploration. The painting itself, 1886's *A Pair of Shoes*, is obviously picturesque in all its particular attributes: the worn leather, the agrarian connotations, the dirt, the implied poverty, the proud perseverance. We should first establish how capably Van Gogh walks the thin line between sentiment and sympathy here – Dickensian sentiment for the land laborer and Ruskinian sympathy for the network of things that have made the shoes as they are. The shoes are an object of encounter,

Vincent van Gogh. *A Pair of Shoes* (1886).

they have rubbed against other things; time has inscribed all possible relations into their surface. Van Gogh's painting seems to consist only of such traces; the brushstrokes all seem to slightly resist the paint's liquidity and are busy constructing something. The shoelaces seem to be made out of steel wire, as do the highlighted edges of the leather and even the background. One should at all times keep in mind the constructive nature of the picturesque: the parts collaborate, though not necessarily willingly. But Heidegger is not merely echoing a picturesque that is already present; the next line indicates that he has selected the work for other reasons:

In the shoes vibrates the silent call of the earth …[43]

Oops. Actual things, a farmer's shoes, that have rubbed against other actual things and then been painted sympathetically, so that we are led into the life of those things, are reversed by Heidegger into a silence. It is a literal reversal of perspective. Any art historian's description would immediately put the viewer in the position of the other things the shoes encountered, in an attempt by the painter to involve us in the same web of sympathy. This would be the correct analysis. But Heidegger projects the empty shadows caught in the shoe, casting them back into space. He fatally mistakes the picturesque for the sublime; he believes the painting expresses it rather than parasitizing on it, as a chant or call, even. Turning a space of feeling into one of thought, a thought that does not progress, does not lead us into things' lives – the sublime brings only awe. In Heidegger's view, we are filled with the same numb silence as the shoes. Contrary to what Heidegger thinks, things are not open to the world; they are open to relations with other things and allow those things to inscribe themselves on their skin. It is, again, a matter of sacrifice, the shoes offer themselves vulnerably and sympathetically – but not to the "world." The world is nothing, or, if we give in to the obligatory hyphen, no-thing. In the sublime, all things are haunted by nothingness, which is an object merely of language, not of existence. The shoes are open to and long for possible other engagements, but not specific ones. Certainly, this is a longing without content yet, but it does not amount to a *Welt* of any sort. For the shoes, the world does not exist. Every time the discourse shifts to the design of a world or environment, we automatically become part of the sublime, if not "thrown into" a sublime. To view this emptiness as structured has been the main project of modernism, especially the modernist project of space. The picturesque saves us from the silent call of the sublime and reminds us not to mistake our longing for space itself. I think the picturesque is implicated in quite a different project: understanding continuous relations without a prestructured and preconditioned space, pointing at what we could call *an ecology without environment* – but that is a discussion we will save for the last chapter. The picturesque does not oppose the sublime, easing our minds with fair-haired girls running in flowered meadows, but makes the sublime inhabitable. It tells us that we must cope with fear and chance in order to live, but to a reasonable degree, neither too much nor too little, as an act of moderation. The picturesque is a positive act of accepting chaos: in order to live, we must attach ourselves to something that is too large – a form of excess and instability not great enough to blow us off our feet but sufficient to make us act.

Further on in *The Origin of the Work of Art*, Heidegger expands Van Gogh's farmer's shoes and transforms them into a Greek temple on a mountainside, in an attempt to transform the soles into a solid temple foundation "holding its ground" and the shoes' dark openings into the temple's roof, which shelters us from the "raging storm above"[44] in the sky. This is Heidegger's conception of art and dwelling: existence can happen only in *stasis*, with the feet stuck firmly in the mud, "fixed in place,"[45] protecting us from the sky, and simultaneously opening up to it in *ek-stasis*. Let us now look at Ruskin's answer to this very same problem; at first sight, it seems similar to the fixity of his rooted plants and flowers.

In one of Ruskin's most astounding diagrams, again in the fourth volume of *Modern Painters*,[46] we see a mountain range, drawn with as much meticulous precision as if it were one of Mandelbrot's fractals, and clearly conscious of the fractal's nested hierarchy of large-scale peaks alternating with a larger number of smaller peaks, interspaced in turn with even more smaller peaks, creating the complex line of the ridge. For added clarity, Ruskin repeats the fractalized contour at the top of the diagram, marked with letters that refer to points in the text. Below the mountain range, we

see a cottage, nicely drawn from a
low angle, and though we do not
notice it at first, suddenly we grasp
that the contour of the roof is *exactly the same* as that of the mountain range! What an excellent
mind the man had: the same jaggedness, the same roughness, the
same algorithm are shared by the
mountain and the cottage. This is
why Ruskin called the picturesque
parasitical: by taking the site of
the mountain and displacing it
("para-") onto the contours of a
house, the picturesque manages
and mitigates the huge forces of
the sublime, tapping into the same
set of forces that sculpts moun-

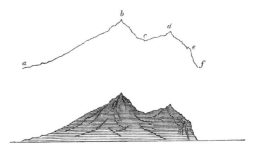

John Ruskin. Mountain-cottage diagram. Fig. 30
from *Modern Painters*, Vol. IV, Part V:
Of Mountain Beauty (1856).

tains and using them to create a home. Let us take the fact that Ruskin has
drawn a cottage as seriously as possible, at least as seriously as we do
Thoreau's and Heidegger's cabins, and let us treat the diagram not as a small
jest but as a design proposal. To live, we do not need to root in the earth
and stay fearful of what is to come; rather, we must displace ourselves, not
by nomadically trekking about but by finding a counter-place, a para-site,
not as a shelter or as a clever place to hide but as a way to cope and negotiate
with accident. Strictly speaking, with Ruskin, things are not rooted but
grafted. At first sight, his and Heidegger's concepts seem very similar, because they are based on fixity, but Ruskin's moves – "grows" – away from the
sublime, while Heidegger's moves – "opens" – toward it. There is a vast
metaphysical divide between the open flower and the open shoe. Ruskin's
picturesque does not resist the forces of the sublime but rather uses those
forces to build our lives and homes. The act of dwelling amounts to simply
sucking enough blood out of the sublime to live, taking in enough – and a
little bit more – of the excess. For Ruskin, in the end, the sky and the earth

do not stand in opposition, as they do for Heidegger; rather, they create each other, they mediate precisely on that single abstract line of design, structuring the rock as it develops both downward under the influence of water, wind and ice from the sky and upward under the influence of vast geological forces. It is precisely on this indexical line that we find our homes – or, more accurately, build them, since we are speaking of an act of construction and technology.

To compare the two acts of construction, Heidegger's and Ruskin's, let us move to an area where they seem at first to overlap. Ruskin constantly speaks of care and keeping, of tenderness and sympathy as the driving mechanisms behind the act of art or design. But though he uses these words in every other essay on the picturesque, on great art, on old buildings, he never elaborates on the terminology. Things are different with Heidegger, who spells it out exactly:

> Once when Care ("Cura") was crossing a river, she saw some clay; she thoughtfully took up a piece and began to shape it. While she was meditating on what she had made, Jupiter came by. Care asked him to give it spirit, and this he gladly granted. But when she wanted her name to be bestowed upon it, Jupiter forbade this, and demanded that it be given his name instead. While Care and Jupiter were disputing, Earth ("Tellus") arose and desired that her own name be conferred on the creature, since she had furnished it with part of her body. They asked Saturn to be their arbiter, and he made the following decision, which seemed a just one: "Since you, Jupiter, have given its spirit, you shall receive that spirit at its death; and since you, Earth, have given its body, you shall receive its body. But since Care first shaped this creature, she shall possesses it as long as it lives. And because there is now a dispute among you as to its name, let it be called *homo*, for it is made out of *humus*."[47]

According to most commentators, this fable shows two sides of sympathy or care, which we have hesitated to discuss properly until now, except briefly in the previous chapter, when we observed that *Cura* means both concern (*Sorge*) in the sense of design and care (*Fürsorge*) in the sense of maintenance. It signifies both simultaneously and is thus a relation active in two directions, like any proper relation, though it is often read as two separate arrows moving in opposite directions. This amounts to a reversal of experiential order, which I am convinced Ruskin would not approve of, but we find it in Heidegger and some of it in Whitehead. When the object precedes sympathy, the feeling must take on the form of joy, because we take pleasure in such an encounter, transported into the life of another being. We feel lightened, carried and supported by the life of the other, exactly as Lipps points out, again and again ("aesthetic enjoyment is objectified self-enjoyment"[48]). As we quoted before:

> I sympathize with the manner the column behaves or testifies to an inner liveliness, because I recognize therein a natural mode of behavior of my own that gives me happiness. Thus, all pleasure produced by spatial forms and, we can add, any kind of aesthetic pleasure, is a feeling of sympathy that makes us happy.[49]

We experience such meetings between us and things as literally uplifting. But when there is no object yet to sympathize with, our *Cura* switches to concern – imagine the worried frown of the designer, or, if a group or team is involved, the extensive discussions and deliberations. The human act of design and planning weighs us down, though not in an unpleasurable manner: we must now initiate the thing, carry the project through, since we are the ones who have launched it – as Heidegger would put it, it is our "throw," our pro-ject or *Ent-wurf*. These are grave matters, acts against gravity, and implicitly acts of a collective, a group, a project team. Though it is the same force, it is joyful when one is carried by it, and when one bears it – as a human being taking on responsibility for matters that normally happen by fact – it becomes worrisome and a burden.

For Ruskin, however, the *eudaimonia* never fades. It is not heavy labor at first, followed by the receipt of a gift from the Gods, but happily offered from the start. For Heidegger, all things are little Greek temples; for Ruskin, all things are little Gothic cathedrals (or plants). The temples are made of what Morris calls a "lintel architecture,"[50] a carpentered, post-and-beam structure resisting earthly forces, while the cathedrals grow by themselves, their parts changing as they interact. Remember, *eudaimonia* does not strictly mean you as a person are particularly happy, it is more of an impersonal qualification of how things are going, as in "things are going well," with you and things yielding to each other, sharing each other's spirit. We merely happily collaborate with them, as the stonecarver happily collaborates with the stone by making his perfect mistakes, or the blacksmith happily collaborates with the hot iron. All work, whether performed by columns or people, flower stems or physicians, is sacrifice, is something *extra*, since it is work *with* things, not against them. Gothic ontology is that of collaboration, redundancy and active rigidity. Heidegger's Greek ontology is that of a passive grounding; everything adds up, with no redundancy, and must stand up by itself, while the sacrifice enters from the sky, *too late*, after all the work has been done. The Greek gods are your typical lazy lot, always recalcitrant, unwilling, and lacking in concentration. The Gothic spirits, meanwhile, enter from the mud and get their hands dirty, like Oscar Wilde during the week he spent laboring on Hinksey Road, which at the end of his life he remembered as his best. With Heidegger, you have to take root, protect yourself against the sublime, but it immediately turns into an act of fear. Dasein is closely related to the continuous struggle with existence of Kierkegaard (*Fear and Trembling*), who, after long deliberation, also voted against aesthetics. So, to refute the contemporary paradigm of my countryman,[51] design is *not* Dasein; that would turn everything into a continuous battle with the Big Nothing. There is no other side, no *Welt*, no *Dasein*, no Other; there is only the sympathetic entanglement of things, in a word, design.

If you were to push me toward a preliminary conclusion, however, I think it would be safe to say that for Heidegger, *Cura* comes down to concern, an attitude more of engineers or builders than of gardeners, while with

Ruskin, it seems to be care in all its stages – care as a form of designing as well as keeping. Initially, Heidegger and Ruskin seem to share much more than just a disagreement about care, in particular a favorable opinion of craft over industry, where the first controls the making of things and the second merely produces objects.

> When we fill the jug, the pouring that fills it flows into the empty jug. The emptiness, the void, is what does the vessel's holding. The empty space, this nothing of the jug, is what the jug is as the holding vessel … But if the holding is done by the jug's void, then the potter who forms sides and bottom on his wheel does not, strictly speaking, make the jug. He only shapes the clay. No – he shapes the void … The vessel's thingness does not lie at all in the material of which it consists, but in the void that holds.[52]

To understand their differences, we must first see the point on which Heidegger and Ruskin agree: they both abhor instrumentality and utility. For them, the fact that something like a jug is *used* is completely irrelevant to understanding its reality, and the concept of a sacrifice or gift is directive. In opposition to what Heidegger denounces in an object, namely its full form and its materiality, the thing – again, like a little temple – is a gathering place, a void that holds, and that gives by pouring. The thing itself *qua* object is absent, an empty vessel. It invisibly steps forward when it has to pour; the thing is a thing-act or thing-occasion. All things in the world add to the dimensionality of the world, not through extension but through adding more relations, more nodes in the network. Heidegger's things are hardly visible, because they slip in and out of working relations; they "conceal"[53] themselves. For Ruskin, the gift does not lie in what the jug does *qua* jug, because it does so habitually, but in how it is made, and how it is to be made precious and delicate, namely by being cloaked in something useless. This is the powerful thought guiding architectural design in "The Lamp of Sacrifice" (the first of the seven lamps): building has to do with material presence and necessity, while architecture has to do with that which has no use whatsoever. The very first sentence of the first chapter warns against confusing architecture with building.[54] For Ruskin, the thing is present, but in a strange, contorted way; it can only present itself as useless, and this is only possible when design and making have done *more* than was necessary, the portion that constitutes the gift. In the case of a jug, I guess – Ruskin never discussed such an object – that this would have meant applying ornament. Now, it would not be Albertian ornament, which treats the structure of the object as a given merely to be covered by beautiful, organic additions. Ruskin's ornament would be Gothic, following the principles of "strong decoration," it would manage the fact that the jug stands by guiding the bulge of the jug's body toward the bottom edge, and it would manage the transition from the handle to the volume of the jug. Something would probably begin growing in opposite directions from the middle of the handle and then crawl over the jug's surface, as if to construct the connection between them. Gothic design always amounts to the reversal of classical order. In the Gothic, ornament precedes structure; a collective of living linear figures builds a thing, with its stability and rigidity emerging *a posteriori*, not existing *a priori*. The form of the object itself, not just its functioning, can be considered a collective act. The linear figures do not simply move to find each other (that would still fit the Greek ontological paradigm), but they change while moving toward each other. The pattern does not have to be excessive; simply acting constructively suffices, and in so doing, the pattern animates and supports the connection between hand and beer (the jug's likely contents). For Ruskin, all design is a form of help, and composition follows even what he calls the "Law of Help." The design of the pattern as a form of construction, leading to the making of the jug by the potter, who preferably does it in a state of happiness and adds some traits of his own, imperfect or not, would then carry through into the life of the jug and the pouring from it. We can now draw our first conclusion: both men seek to get form out of the way, Ruskin by making it fabricist and constructivist, Heidegger by deconstructing it into a void.

The point where the two meet is the point where they start to differ. Heidegger would certainly reject the ornamentation of Ruskin's jug, since in his mind it would make it more present, more of an obstacle, preventing it from opening to the void. Ruskin, in turn, would look at the Bavarian jug and ridicule its boorish, minimalist design, declaring that its bare form actually changed it into an object of mere extensity – in short, an obstacle – since holding a void would mean taking in space.

"Maybe it disappears for the one who pours, but not for everyone else," Ruskin would say. "For them, the thing turns into obtrusive, unsympathetic form." And he would add that the jug turns usefulness into pure servitude, making the thing wait behind a curtain to do its work, like a waiter:

"How can the jug be viewed as an offering when it serves you, and worse, when it does nothing but serve you? That is not what gods do; that is what slaves do. Gods are supposed to offer help."

The crucial difference lies in the fact that one jug does its work passively and the other actively – if that doesn't sound too strange. The acts of designing and making the jug do not become part of the jug itself in Heidegger's view, because they may only shape the void, while for Ruskin, these acts participate. My second conclusion: both overcome the subject-object discrepancy – Heidegger because the object becomes a thing in absence, a thing withdrawn, and Ruskin because feelings of sympathy lead one directly into the thing, collapsing the space between.

Nevertheless, the poor jug is staring straight into the abyss, like Van Gogh's shoes. The sublime itself has become a mold (what Germans call *Form*), a negative shape, or the shape of negation.

"With the mold as the form, minimalism becomes a *formal fallacy*, a form that is allegedly not there, while the whole world sees that it is," Ruskin tells Heidegger, who shouts back an accusation:

"You are merely adopting your own *pathetic fallacy*[55] as a design principle, trying to animate the object!"

"…"

Slowly, it becomes clear that for Heidegger, the sublime transforms into the modernist concept of space, a space that is too large, too vast, and *absolute*. Even when anchored to a place, it always leaks away into the "open." The act of making and the act of building together transform into a counter-act, one of destruction, of *Abbau*, while for Ruskin, they are completely positive and constructive acts. For him, it is the thing, not the space, that taps into the sublime, because it uses the notion of forces to construct the transition from handle to container. Heidegger's thing does not protect us from the sublime; rather, it hands us over to it through what he calls unveiling. Hence our third and final conclusion: Ruskin believes design is a veiling, a mere constructing, while Heidegger sees it as an unveiling, a constructing of the void.

Heidegger's unobstructed world leads us to one where the void is accessible, a world of infrastructure, roads and bridges (examples he often uses), but also highways and airports – an accessible sublime, a world of built no-things. It is one of pure service, if not excessive comfort. This absence of things is the primary dream of all ubiquitous computing, all ergonomics (though nowadays they believe an air-conditioning system that creates a bit of a draft, or a chair that stimulates motility, is better than mere service), and all engineering. Did Heidegger initiate the slave-master reversal of technological objects, in which things work perfectly and seem to take care of everything, cushioning and comforting us into blissful sleep? The horror house of ergon … Certainly, *eudaimonia* is not *ergon*, things serving us well. Beware of perfect butlers![56] Before you know it, things will simply be talking to each other all the time and will have forgotten all about us. Before you know it, things will be gathering among themselves. It might just be that Heidegger, in closing the door to beautiful objects, opened it for sublime things. Latour unwittingly comes to the same conclusion:

> Needless to say, although he develops this etymology at length, this is not the path that Heidegger has taken. On the contrary, all his writing aims to make as sharp a distinction as possible between, on the one hand, objects, *Gegenstand*, and, on the other, the celebrated Thing. The handmade jug can be a thing, while the industrially made can of Coke remains an object. While the latter is abandoned to the empty mastery of science and technology, only the former, cradled in the respectful idiom of art, craftsmanship, and poetry, could deploy and gather its rich set of connections.[57]

For Latour, all things are sociological entities, what he calls societies (borrowing Whitehead's terminology), pure gatherings, whether they are crafted by hand in a workshop or produced by the millions in a factory. Latour repeatedly reminds us of Heidegger's etymological connection between the thing and the Thing, a Nordic form of assembly or gathering, "specifically a gathering to deliberate on a matter under discussion, a contested matter."[58] Of course, the conclusions that Latour draws from Heidegger's position are perfectly justifiable. When the world functions, it is not because a special class of things are assembled but because all of them are.

System thinkers, political economists and sociologists look at things from so far away that they resemble tiny black dots (or, as Latour calls them, "black boxes," or even more atomistically, "punctualizations"[59]) that move about. Firstly, we should praise without reserve the conceptual shift from static object to acting thing, allowing for the mergence of a thing's object state ("Where are my things?") with its active state ("He is doing his own thing"). Secondly, however, if we move a bit closer to things than the system view allows, we will not just notice things act but do not possess such agency because they are dressed in black and shaped like a box; they can only act and can be acted upon *because they exist aesthetically*, and that goes for Heidegger's ceramic jugs as much as Latour's metal cans and metro cars. To reclassify all objects *en masse* as things and thing-actions is vital for restoring them to their pre-Kantian status, but we must grasp that all things are not just made but also patterned and articulated. Clouds, Volkswagens, Reims cathedral, the Lindisfarne Gospels: they are all designed, that is, made with care and concern, and at least as much care as concern. Things are not made at boardroom tables where matters are endlessly discussed and faxable diagrams coughed up; they are made through meticulous drawing and redrawing, extensive discussions on the factory floor and in workshops, and the making of dozens of models and prototypes. And then, later, they get scratched, dented and worn. With luck, at some point, they will get patched up too. This kind of craftsmanlike care goes into the making of a car or a can of Coke as much as that of a cloud or a cathedral; it is just that with twentieth-century metal objects such care is completely overwhelmed by concern, and with cathedrals care supersedes concern, and in the production of clouds mere care suffices. And we should keep in mind that a great many more things are designed than have names, many things go through the world without names. These we cannot even list.

Things are simply part of the interaction that shapes them. What does this mean – that they are of human origin? No. Of divine origin? No. That it all signifies something? No. That we can be critical of them? No. Deconstruct them? No. It means that the relations with and among them are of an aesthetic nature: *all relations between things are felt relations* – and, I must add, not sensed relations. Things feel each other, and we feel for them before we know them. This also means we feel more for them if they have been designed better, more meticulously, more delicately, with more care. This is what *eudaimonia* means: things going well, or being carried by the spirit of things. When Lipps is exalted by seeing the storm pass through the tree, he feels what the tree feels. The beauty he experiences is neither objective in the sense that the tree transfers it to him nor subjective in the sense that Lipps is the only one who experiences it. It is a congruence, a shared matching. And between all things at all moments, this matching is different, that is what thing-actions are. All thing-actions are encounters. The tree is internally structured to process the wind's forces; in short, it feels, and then it acts by bending and swaying, which can be seen. This seeing immediately leads Lipps into feeling the wind as well, not by bending as much as the tree but through exaltation. This feeling, however, does not entail what he sees, it is not the image that gives him pleasure (as the common view of aesthetics has it) but what he does not see. Feeling takes over where seeing stops, as a seeing-feeling; the seen part leads one into the felt, invisible part, which is not an essence that exists at the core but a veil at the fringes. A dark, concealed essence is by nature something that separates us from things, because we can only speculate on it (in philosophers' dreams and fantasies); the frayed, dark fringes, on the other hand, are to be felt, intuited and sympathized with. Essences are by definition inaccessible because they must be wrapped in a sensual appearance and therefore uphold all possible dichotomies, while fringes offer a way of feeling-into, feeling-with and living-with, a way as accessible to humans as to nonhumans. Essences are concepts of things as autistic, as withdrawn, while fringes understand things as generous and outgoing. This is all the more reason why we need to devote ourselves to ornament, the picturesque and the Gothic: they present us with fractal and frayed things, taking James's notion of the fringe out of the world of metaphor and making it real and constructive, making the transitive substantive.

Latour denies such feelings of care a proper place within the *Cura* spectrum, filing them under a story of "immediacy and intuition that is too sad to retell,"[60] which is a truly terrible thing to say. He probably mistakes immediacy and intuition for aspects of existentialist Dasein, human struggling outside the domain of things. If I had to choose, I would reject concern in favor of care every time for exactly the same reasons: concern places consciousness and feeling on the wrong side of the object, on the outside of it. Immediacy and intuition are ways things live with each other; the wind blowing across the Matterhorn is as caring as the blacksmith's hammer. When Latour buys a can of Coke from a vending machine, it is not merely because he is thirsty, or that the can secretly pops up in his hand like Heidegger's magic equipment. If we take Ruskin's view, nothing in the whole universe ever functions without sympathy; hence there must be some kind of sympathetic relationship between him and the can, or else neither he nor we would ever buy it. Things, like us, are fully involved in each other. That is what the veil of strange intermediate being requires: transcendental care. Beauty is a form of care, of keeping things alive and making them flourish. Even in the case of the Bavarian jug, which, like Van Gogh's shoes, is not staring into the abyss at all (let's forget about that) but is highly picturesque, carrying the innumerable traces of crafting – the irregularities of heating the furnace, the cracking of the glaze – and the traces of permanent use, with chips broken off and wear at the edges. Its rustically understated, *wabi-sabi* design is not sufficient, but it improves with wear and tear. If this were not the case, its minimalist features would need to be accompanied by a whole set of graceful acts of preparing and pouring, in the style of *The Book of Tea*, but that would be a bit much to ask for during Oktoberfest, since we cannot expect any slow and thoughtful pouring there. As we have seen in previous chapters, ornament is strong decoration, but the weak version – texture – can be strengthened by a web of actions enveloping the object. Or, to put it differently, an insufficient time of making can be compensated for by the time of existence, as long as we find sufficient life in the object. Clearly, a can of Coke does not wear either type of cloak of sympathy, but again, according to Ruskin, it must have one. In itself, a can of Coke is what I would call *een onding* in Dutch, or more fittingly, *ein Unding* in German – an unthing; we would not even consider drinking from it. This is precisely where the media enter the scene.

As we concluded earlier, the more abstract things become, the more our own psychology must compensate for sympathy (in the form of empathy). The aforementioned skin, the veil of the jug, now needs to be delivered separately, through mediation, i.e., advertising. This is how we should view the split model of decoration: machines producing abstract, cylindrical, metal cans draped *in distans* by advertised imagery, which has to be naturalistic, since it needs to evoke empathy. In its advertising, Coca-Cola has been particularly good at showing worlds of friends sharing drinks on happy occasions, thus enveloping the products in an atmosphere of sympathy. I know, dear reader, that you are sitting there cringing, but bear with me. From the viewpoint of an ecology of design and entanglement through sympathetic relations, we cannot take the actual content of these ads seriously enough. We often think far too lightly about the so-called lure of advertising. All the emotional attachment among the actors in the ad, the overt sense of brotherhood, the state of bliss, the singing and dancing in the street, the youthfulness of the actors – all these are spot on for evoking empathy, and aesthetically they could hardly be improved. A complete sphere of feeling is produced, though one's feelings do not lead us into the life of the can or a shared life with the group but only to the purchase of the can. Advertising is the weakest form of decoration possible (but a form of decoration nonetheless).

We can take this quite literally: we have a cold, abstract can in one hand and a set of warm, naturalistic images in the other, and when we bring them together, i.e., bring concern and care together, at the point where they are very close, the naturalism of the imagery transforms into a sheet of delicate, necessarily more abstract ornament that transfers itself to the can, wraps around it, and adapts to its features, such as ridges and edges. The pattern now treats the can as a thing, and of course at this point we can no longer separate the worlds of abstraction and empathy, because they have reunited to become sympathy. Alas, we can also imagine the process working the other way around, the movie playing backwards, as it were, and returning us to where we are today, in a double world where the original realm of sympathy has been bisected, with sublime objects floating about in one hemisphere and naturalist imagery in the other.

As the abstraction of the industrial product and the psychological imagery are as separate as two brain halves irreversibly severed after surgery, the process never makes it back to unified sympathy, in which the product and the group are one. I would call this indirect or redirected sympathy, or, perhaps better, *mediated sympathy*, to distinguish it more clearly from the *immediate sympathy* we discussed in the previous chapter, in which we directly plunge into the object and become part of its life. The process only works, i.e., leads you to the vending machine, because you yourself have made up for the gap in attention and awareness. These immaculate things – armored, polished vessels and black boxes – are constantly draped by imagery *in exile*. Objective sympathy is compensated for by subjective psychology; forgive me, but that is what I call bad design, though there has surely been plenty of concern and gathering around tables on the part of the forces of production. Actually, I shall not hesitate to call it a *bad thing*, too, because by now we have come to inhabit a double world of pristine things on the one hand and detached imagery, circulating in a separate domain (magazines, television, websites – what is called "visual culture"), on the other, and all there is left for us to do is to deliver the images at the doorstep of objects, trying to quasi-repair it all by projecting the implanted memory of a happy life onto a thing. It is now we who have become the messengers, not the media. We live in a world where more things than ever surround us, but when we look at them, we see only ourselves, as in polished, reflective objects. It is a world of bad things and demons, of *daimons* that refuse to escort us and force us to carry their images around instead. Such agency is nothing less than possession. We do not live among Ruskin's veiled things but among unthings we are conditioned to see as veiled. This is why I argue that art and design should move away from images and return to things.

To conclude our Ruskinian rebuttal: the problem with a great many industrial objects is that all those boardroom meetings have split the original *Cura* of care and concern in two. First, there is the concern of design and production, and second, the care or maintenance involved in guiding them through existence, which the board would call marketing. With Ruskin, we come to understand that the two should coexist, that design should be about care as much as concern. Could that group of happy young people ever be considered the designers and producers of the can of Coke? That would be Ruskin's simple question. It is a question that inverts everything. I certainly think it is technically possible (not just socially necessary), but it would mean an enormous shift to another kind of technology, one that does not produce purified finalities but impure, wild things, with the productivity of technology exceeding the products themselves.

Let us move slowly. After considering Heidegger's jug and Latour's can of Coke, we should bring in a few other objects to balance the argument. Why not consider contemporary objects that we could call "technologically picturesque"? What about, for instance, stonewashed jeans, or a much smaller item, the rough-cut sugar cube? Each product shows us how technology can relate to our earlier idea of objectified age, and the two have similar qualities, namely total dependency on the picturesque on the one hand and industrial production techniques on the other. Let us concentrate on the jeans, since the rough-cut lump of sugar is of the same type. Jeans that become worn naturally, through use by students or carpenters, are produced as clean denim trousers and then subjected to processes of wear and tear, in perpetual interaction with lecture hall seats or through heavy labor. Mechanically worn jeans, by contrast, are a wholly industrial product. In the first stage of the process, they are produced like any other pants, pristine and clean, but they are then placed by the hundreds in huge drums filled with water and pumice stones. Pumice is especially suited to the accelerated wearing effect because it floats and thus does not immediately destroy the fabric. Companies can manufacture stonewashed jeans in every gradation, from those with only slight markings around the thighs and buttocks to those that are excessively torn in every imaginable place.

Customers can buy such a battered pair of jeans for a price double that of normal jeans, since all the time spent wearing them out through human use is now concentrated in the period of machine use. Evidently, we here encounter a theoretical reversal of delicate ornament and rough wear and tear: the patterns of abrasion that normally occur after decoration are now used in the production process to actually create it. Stonewashing should definitely be understood as ornament, which is, as we explained a chapter ago, fabricist by nature and elaborates the process of making through, for example, filigree or tracery. By contrast, in this case, the end stage of the making of the thing amounts to the actual weakening of its fiber structure, which seems paradoxical but is not. Both the naturally worn and the artificially worn jeans do exactly what aesthetic objects should do to gain our sympathy: expose their vulnerability and exist in fragility. Think back for a moment to the bird saved by Kuni the bonobo, the Ammophila's caterpillar, the hyperfibrous Gloucester Cathedral, Morris's no less entangled carpets, the Gothic bird's nest, the Insular illuminated pages – all things of extreme delicacy.

the technological wild

Our little example shows that it is not technology *qua* machinery preventing objects from becoming things; thus, we can move beyond merely discussing shoes, jugs, cars, cans of Coke and stonewashed jeans, leave them be and concentrate on the making of things. It has been shown that the picturesque, whether in its young or old form, is something we can produce. We can draw it, we can grow it, we can manufacture it, but it must be radicalized over and over again in each era. If the main task of the picturesque is to make the sublime inhabitable, we must follow the sublime in its course through time. A major question results directly from this, not only because of instrumentality (*how* do we actually make a picturesque thing nowadays?) but because the sublime has become the house style of technology. A vast portion of twentieth-century art – Malevich's black square, Picasso's fractured cubes, Mondrian's grids of primary colors, Rothko's *amor vacui*, Judd's repetitive installations, the Zero group's whiteness – created the kinds of images machines used to dream of. That enormous continent of abstraction left no room for sympathy or empathy, the only options left – Schwitters's Merz, Duchamp's conceptualism, Warhol's irony, Dali's psychoplasm, Beuys's psychofat – were immediately part of the same world, but secluded, as in a nature reserve for the human interior.

When today we pose the question of the picturesque and of wildness in the sphere of machines, it adds up not merely to the instrumental issue but to something more important: *Can we make technology itself go wild?* If the realm of machines is as angular and crystalline as that of uninhabited mountains, how can we grow something there, make it blossom? Or, to re-phrase: would it be legitimate to direct all the questions we had concerning nature in the early 1800s – about freedom, variation, spontaneity, develop-ment, epigenesis, etc. – at technology? Maybe if the questions were some-how answerable, it would be, though I admit that this viewpoint takes a technological perspective. At some point, technology and nature have switched positions. If nature was for centuries our inexhaustible source of savageness and wilderness, we have slowly come to doubt it with the years and begun to ask ourselves what exactly is natural in nature. We never lived "in nature" anyway; we lived among fish, trees, birds and berries. No one ever found nature, certainly not any of the people who actually looked for it, like Henry Thoreau. And conversely, while technology at first seemed to be a clear-cut nightmare of discipline and abstraction, we now doubt this view as much as we do our ancient relationship with nature – and some of us actually feel more alive than ever when we are scrolling through our iPods, sending text messages and driving our cars. No one today feels particularly disciplined by technology, certainly not in the way Mumford and Ellul did; rather, we experience its effect as an unleashing, as a connection to some-thing unpredictable. Every technical object seems to have the power to ex-pose us, to make us vulnerable, because it immediately turns into an occasion or event that links us to others. Jacques Tati was able to ironically reverse technologies like conveyor belts and traffic jams, but that would be unthink-able today. Watching the television traffic report at 8 a.m. is like watching the weather report with its fronts and depressions: you can do nothing about it. And our cars will start talking to us, suggesting alternative routes, and there is nothing funny about a talking car, either.

Mumford and Ellul told us how technology was changing from a set of means into an end in itself, a continuous, overwhelming presence undergoing out-of-control development from something presumed useful into a phenomenon referring only to itself. But this critique was vacuous from the outset, since the notion of mediation and instrumentality, with its fundamental separation of human beings on one side and the world on the other, prevented us from living more than what we experience today – one was always living on the wrong side of things. The problem has never been things but the supposed world behind them, and we find this in Heidegger as much as in any Giedion or Mumford. Thank goodness technology's goals have never been usability and purposiveness! Things have never given us any access to the world; they have given us access only to … well, things themselves and the scripts they embody. We have ever tried to find life *in* and *with* things, never behind them or through them. Behind things, there exist other things, not a world. The true problem is not that we have been forced to live with a technology that epitomizes the end in itself, but that its aesthetic has been that of the sublime. Machines are dedicated to the production of sameness in huge quantities – mountains of butter, lakes of milk and wine, monocultures, white bread, refined sugar, frozen fish; the list is endless. Heidegger may not have been right about the "uprooting of man"[61] and all the other evils he saw in technology, except with respect to the notion of *Bestand*: storage or stock. It is like the *Doppelgänger* of that other modernist concept, space. All that global access used to require vast amounts of storage space, with all products averaged out into one, which was copied millions of times. All of modernist technology relied on homogeneity, pure abstraction and purification. But half a century later, things have changed slightly. Today, when we eat organic food, soft cheese from a specific region, or fish from a particular coastal area, we can do so only because digital technology allows tiny businesses to run as smoothly and agilely as only large companies relying on vast amounts of storage could fifty years ago. Storage is over and done with. No one wants to store anything any more; we go directly from production to distribution. Mumford's "female" technology of basketry and bowls, Heidegger's worries over *Bestand*

and *Gestell*[62] – all that passive accumulation of technology has been completely replaced by neoliberal flow. The open, free seas of Hugo Grotius's *Mare Liberum* have transformed into today's open networks.

We have survived or, better, *seem* to have survived the twentieth century, which we can now start to look back on as our true Dark Ages (instead of one of whiteness and transparency) – our darkest age of all. As a species, we have somehow survived Auschwitz (a terrible thing to say); we have abandoned Apollo; Concorde has abandoned itself; our nuclear weapons seem to have buried themselves in underground stations where the lights have gone out; we have even gotten rid of the World Trade Center, by far the two worst buildings ever built anywhere on the planet. Baudrillard was right on that point: who in his right mind would build two identical buildings next to each other? And then we even survived semiotics and deconstruction. And criticality, too. One way or another, we have slowly gotten rid of the worst of the sublime. Technology is still the main source of the sublime and of excess, but it provides it in moderate, personalized portions. Things are, in a way, starting to clear – with the emphasis on "starting," undoubtedly.

For the last twenty or thirty years, there has been increasing interest in German Romantic philosophy, or *Naturphilosophie*.[63] Instead of reading early Romanticism as a simplified precursor to complexity theory, contemporary thought has planted a much more disconcerting idea at the heart of nature: that a special form of technology is at work there, a technology whose full meaning terms like "mechanism" and "organicism" fail to convey. Expanding on these ideas, I am convinced that today we can start asking the very questions *Naturphilosophen* like Schelling and Kielmayer used to ask, but directed at technology, mainly because we can now feed machines information that is itself variable, can adapt and change in a millisecond and does not act according to vast preset quantities to be distributed over a world populated by the masses, who are nothing but preset quantities themselves. If there is one model of storage that has vanished, it is the masses. Nature never stored things (except raw materials like ice at the North Pole, heat at the earth's core, and water in the oceans), and today, technology no longer does either. We just want to make things, construct them continuously, as nature does. One of Schelling's main concepts of nature was twofold: we encounter products – things – but for these to exist, we also need productivity:

> As the thing is never unconditioned (*unbedingt*) then something per se non-objective must be posited in nature; this absolutely non-objective postulate is precisely the original productivity of nature.[64]

A philosopher of nature must explain two things: why are things produced, and why are they all different, or, in other words, why are they individuals? Since the former is explained by productivity, that is, by the entry of the unconditioned into the conditioning process (*Bedingung*), that must lead to an answer to the second question. For the passage from *Bedingung* to a unique thing (*Ding*), freedom is needed. A thing that is not different cannot be free. So instead of liberating people, we might as well start liberating things, every last one of them. They will then be *wild things*. But we cannot understand this process unless we open our eyes to the fact that a massive technology resides in nature, generating production and copying in vast quantities, whether it is of fields of daffodils, clouds, or waves in the water. Each day, 500 million cells are copied in your body. It is only because this productivity does not result in exact copies that we refrain from calling it technological, but we should. The making of individuals is coupled to enormous production figures, and we must understand these as codependent. In aesthetic terms, the production process moves from the sublime to the beautiful during a generative process of individuation, not through blindly choosing between two poles nor blindly positioning a thing somewhere in between but through a process that starts with the sublimely unconditioned and sees it taking on form, step by step, to teleologically end with a beautiful thing/individual. The means transform into an end, and the ends reorganize themselves into means to produce other ends. In other words, there are no factories isolated from products: the interaction – the sympathy – between products constitutes the factory.

Now we can begin to think about what a *Naturphilosophische* technology would entail: a technology as its own means and end. It has persistently created its own development, but only recently has it achieved a level of variation that is fundamentally changing its aesthetics. Technology itself is evolving from the realm of the sublime to that of the beautiful. Every thing is a new thing. Going directly from productivity to product has been shown not to be sufficient: this would lead straight to either unfree determinism – pure, engineered necessity – or blind chance. From the bland, omnidirectional spherical range of the unconditioned, we must progress from its center outward in the direction of the single thing, but stepwise, or, if you insist, algorithmically, or, as Schelling – and, in a way, Ruskin – has it, geologically, converging onto subsequently smaller ranges of conditioning, and finally arriving at a single individual thing that can claim its freedom at the surface of the sphere. As in Ruskin's flourishing, it grows away from the sublime into beauty. For this to occur successfully, this production must be spontaneous; it must take on its *own* direction at a certain point, as we described in the chapter on the nature of the Gothic, in which things interact and halfway trade their freedom for that of a single thing becoming. If the parts have not lost their freedom somewhere, i.e., their being-unconditioned, the final thing cannot be conditioned and cannot be free itself. The switch from free, unconditioned movement in all directions to a coordinated conditioning is achieved through sympathy, since it is a resonating, synchronizing event. In Romantic terms, a thing would need to be produced *epigenetically*, or, in more general terms, it would have to be *grown*, but if you find that too organismically charged, then I hope we can agree on *generated*. The time of design can include the time of making only under these conditions; we know this already from our discussion of the young picturesque, but it works just as well for webbed ornament, as we remember from the second chapter ("abstract making"), and for Gothic ontology, as we remember from the first ("craft as design"). We have given some brief examples along the way – Ruskinian trees produced with an L-system, Morrisian *Tangle Carpet*© software – but this model should be radically applied to all things.

Can we have a liberated technology, one that, like nature, is capable of producing all things differently? Just as every lake and every mountain is different, no two the same, and just as all the leaves on a particular tree are different, and the leaves of all the trees in a forest, and of all the trees spread across the whole planet, and even through the ages – can we have difference like that? Infinite numbers of identities, of free individuals – can we produce such wild things?

The answer will not be an easy shift from a hylomorphic, fixed-mold technology to a morphogenetic, variable-mold technology; that would merely take us from a Greek ontology to a Baroque one. As the *Tangle Carpet*© shows, we will need a digitally Gothic, configurational ontology that allows for things as much as continuity. Let us imagine a website equipped with the aforementioned sliders for (1) entangling, (2) tendriling, (3) bifurcating and (4) sprouting, perhaps extended with a color generator based on Morris's natural dyes. One would be able to set the object size, generate several patterns, make a reservation, perhaps print one pattern out in order to get used to it and see if the carpet suits the room, and then purchase it. With the purchase, the software's settings would become yours alone; no one would be able to reproduce your carpet. It would take a while to produce, but it would not be impossible, since the Jacquard loom of the early 1800s, with its punched cards, was one of the first computed systems. The carpet would be "printed" in wool and then sent to the buyer. Since the software would be based on the expertise of William Morris and his office, it would absorb the existing, historical carpets as instances in a much larger number of virtual carpets. Though the design system would be open to accident and amateurs, the result would never be either accidental or amateurish, since the potential buyer would be able to manipulate a single parameter at will, but one or more of the other three would immediately adjust their positions to make it a Morris & Co. product. Each carpet would be grown, or generated – we could even say bred – parented by four main attributes, to become a singularly unique individual.

Let us consider one other example, one as romantic as I can imagine. It is simply unbearable that the world is unable to offer, say, 500 million *unique and individual* cans of Coke, every day. All the cans all over the world should be different. This product would probably be called *iCoke*©. Let us recall Ruskin's question to Latour here: Could that group of happy youngsters ever be considered the designers and producers of the can of Coke? Well, not in the sense of a neo-Morrisian workshop (probably more of a sweat-shop) artistically producing each can, hand-painting it and selling it for $0.0001 to Coca-Cola, which would then fill it with the produce. Let us envisage an *iCoke*© website instead, not too different from today's car websites that show all the dozens of variations in color, type and accessories, but slightly more radical. One would start by mixing one's own flavor of Coke first, adding ingredients and changing their amounts, and then move on to the design of the can. One would probably start with a generic can and generate it from there, step by step, going from genus to species to individual can – gloriously colored, embossed with ornament, of the desired size and material – then "add to basket," with the extra charges indicated in the bottom left corner, and press "place order now," and a day later the crate will be delivered on your doorstep. Or you could buy it in a store from us, a merry band of technoromanticists known as the Digital Guild of St. George, who would specialize in certain design characteristics we could sell to our fans and families. I can imagine thousands of such groups emerging all over the world, each specializing in its own style, selling it all over the world, not necessarily locally. The brand would slowly move into the background, though it would continue to produce billions of liters of Coca-Cola per day.

We definitely would have no more need for advertising, with its imagery stuck in our brains for the next several decades.

chapter five

the ecology of design

Any vitalist argument must work in two directions. If we say, after Ruskin, that the Gothic can be considered as structure coming to life; that ornament and the picturesque can be considered the respective coming to life of surface and form; and that these three must inherently be related – and, on top of that, we claim there is nothing metaphorical in these statements, then the reverse must also be true: living creatures are objects of design. And while the first set of arguments is often accepted, or at least tolerated, the second usually is not, at least not outside theology. Anyone who advocates aesthetics as a fundamental form of existence, and even of the production of all things, from clouds to Hadron Colliders, inevitably needs to respond to the notorious "argument from design."[1] Generally, this argument is not developed strictly as one concerning design but as one concerning circumstantial evidence for the existence of an absent designer, or, as William Paley wrote in 1802: "Contrivance must have had a contriver, design a designer."[2] Until far into the nineteenth century, human beings proclaimed things beautiful because they had been designed and fabricated by God and then copied by us in his natural style, making beauty a form of natural theology. Since I am not a theist or deist and, as you know, do not even believe John Ruskin ever confused his Christianity with aesthetics, for me one of the most urgent questions today is how, *after God*,[3] one can proclaim a thing beautiful. Of all the questions that can be raised, that of beauty is so fundamentally lacking in our thoughts and decisions that I can hardly imagine it possible that we will survive another century.

In the two hundred years since Paley, we have slowly surrendered ourselves to the opposite aesthetics, that of the sublime, which became the sole norm in the twentieth century. After taking God out of the equation, we seemed occupied more with the void he had left behind than with things. In fact, we adhered to Paley's argument by refusing beauty, since we believed that now had we lost God we had lost beauty too. My claim in the course of this book has been that the sublime, from the earliest modernist notions of it, which took forms such as Cubism, to its latest release in the form of deconstruction, has brought us nothing but cultural devastation. Things have been left to themselves. Though I prefer not to use generalizing words like "culture," in hindsight it seems as if a massive, coordinated enterprise changed our aesthetics to a taste for the gap, the fracture and the hiatus, while we would have done better to try to explain beauty as existing in itself, without transcendence. One of my goals in this chapter is to finally work out a valid argument from design and, more explicitly, an argument from beauty – necessarily, after what we have learned from the previous chapter, a radical beauty, of the kind we argued existed between Ruskin's vital beauty and his parasitical picturesque. Hence, the vitality of the former can be produced only by the sublimity of the latter.

As is well known, the vitalists we have persistently quoted, Lipps and Bergson, have been accused of merely substituting a transcendent god with an immanent life force, and the allegation has not been without good reason. How often do we find Bergson describing matter as inert, as if forces are not anchored and merely continue through objects, as if the force field has an existence of its own? As we made clear in our discussion of beauty and sublime as the respective worlds of forms and forces, we should understand movement as part of matter, as we have known since Diderot.[4] In this sense, movement and life are qualities inherent in inanimate things at first, because intensity precedes extensity. Of course, "life" is far more accurate a concept than "God," who is sadly condemned to remain on the outside of things, while the former explicitly embraces movement as an organizing quality – extensive bodily movement as well as intensive and internal occurrences. Hence, we could conceive of things and feelings as looped without adding life as a ground. Life is a byproduct of interaction between thing-feelings.

Internal feelings *transform* into external movements, or actions, and external movements, for their part, transform into internal ones; that is, uncoordinated vectors begin to become coordinated through an abstraction that does not lie ahead of the process but develops as things substantiate. The abstraction is itself part of the movement but encapsulates and internalizes it; in short, it feels. It is a feeling abstraction. As far as I am concerned, the only thing we can be completely sure of is that everything feels to some degree, and that the feelings we have towards the object are of the same nature as the ones that have made it or are still making it. To simply replace the notion of design with a term such as "self-assemblage" or "self-design" would be vacuous, because no self exists prior to the process. How can something assemble itself when there is no self yet? Impossible. The problem of teleology hereby becomes even more urgent. I have become the most radical advocate of the design argument: I believe in design without a designer. Paley's argument was that things were beautiful because God made them that way.[5] To repeat that sentence now and simply leave God out – "Things are beautiful because they are made" – is not terribly convincing; that much is clear.

Through Ruskin, I have found a curious alternative answer: things are beautiful because they are made beautifully. Beauty is produced by the agency of beauty. Granted, this sounds like high-school philosophy, based on seemingly tautological argumentation, but I find it more and more convincing by the day. Of course, it is another way of saying that beauty is "intrinsic" and that it cannot emerge *ex nihilo* or be applied. It exists from the start or else it does not exist at all. The argument of aesthetics is that the forces stay present and active even after the thing is finished, if it ever is, since nothing ever comes to rest. Construction is persistent activity, first as parts coming together, then as parts staying together. Thing-feelings need no other grounding; they themselves form a ground. When Darwin states at the end of *The Origin of Species* that "endless forms most beautiful and most wonderful have been, and are being, evolved,"[6] the central issue is not merely evolution but beauty as well. And – we should add, following Ruskin – beauty first and foremost. Or, following Whitehead: "The teleology of the universe is directed to the production of beauty."[7] We cannot content

ourselves with merely some kind of "evolution-plus," in which natural selection would operate with all its finely tuned mechanisms and we would
experience its products as beautiful afterwards, since this would only serve
to pass on the problem, making the mystery of beauty the mystery of evolution. No, beauty itself works. Throughout this book, we have never defended our radical aesthetics as one of leisure, as *l'art pour l'art* of Wilde,
Pater and Art Nouveau, as a beauty that comes after work. In the end, aestheticism necessarily turns against itself; an art that considers itself isolated
and must be enjoyed in splendid isolation will eventually assume a numb,
bored, anesthetic state. Ruskin's aesthetics, and ours, is one of configurational
work, of attunement. My hypothesis is that the feelings one experiences
when seeing a beautiful thing are the same – to a degree – as those that actually create it. Not the same as in the sense of a repetition or even a continuous extension, but the same in the sense of resonating or sympathizing.
The issue of design is more relevant than ever – but, again, only our self-
referential kind of design, one without extra grounding or, perhaps better,
one that forms its own ground. There is nothing behind things, or behind
you. If they are internally coordinated, the process must rely on a constant
redefinition of composite parts, an entangling and disentangling, making it
impossible for things to come out clean and pure. For human aesthetics, we
have proposed a specific class of objects that accept and incorporate such a
notion of redundancy: the frayed, fragile things of the webbed Gothic; the
rough picturesque; things covered with delicate filigree ornament; even
those purely improved by wear and tear, made delicate by time and touch –
or any combination of these four. Let us look again at what makes our
frayed, Gothic things so significant.

As we have seen, a frayed object has two aspects: (a) an elaborate, patterned skin that makes it exist in the visual domain as an object of delicacy
and (b) an occluded part that relates it to time in two directions: one to the
time of making, the other to the time of unmaking. This is a generalized,
averaged pair of aspects; no individual entity possesses both aspects in the
same amount. This double, visual-unvisual existence makes objects relate to
other objects and people in a specific and particularly strong manner.
Though the first aspect makes them as visible as any other thing, the second

makes them felt, and felt immediately. This double existence, or a single but extended existence, occupies a unique position in the discourse of aesthetics. Generally, every time the word "veil" is used in this context, it is meant in the spatial sense, as a surface hiding another, deeper, more essential existence, such as structure. Yes, Ruskin's veil does provide such an act of concealment, but only to protect us, because such relations, if unveiled, would become those of bodies, of mechanics and effects. A world in which objects communicate merely by connecting their inner workings to each other would simply turn all agency into operationality and functionality, without any feeling. Ruskin's veil is different, its act is not one of hiding, it merely needs the act of spatial hiding to "show" something in the realm of time. Such "seeing" in time is called feeling, and such feeling fills up and orients a whole perceiving object, enabling it to act. The veil leads into an existence in time, a proper fragility. It does not lead us into the specific strengths of existence, such as structure, but to its frailty. Then how do the two sides of existence, which are so deeply interdependent, relate to each other? We have used the word "veil" for both aspects, but it would not be correct to call them the same. If, for a moment, we imagine ourselves standing in front of a frail object, a skin rises up between us, a *vertical veil*, which is the one we know as that delicate skin, the one of ornament or wearing. It is a surface, a cloak, dress – we have employed many names for it; it is the face of visibility. But the fragile objects – there are always a minimum of two, like the hinge and the door, a cloud and a mountain, a viewer and a painting – intersect directly with the *horizontal veil* (the "sectional plane" in our discussion of James's fringed mosaic tiles) connecting the objects in the encounter: a landscape of feeling, which is invisible and extends things in time. It is not a landscape that precedes the objects; it is momentary and occasional, but it is fully perpendicular to spatial objects.

Following Ruskin's cosmology, we can term these two types of veil the *wall veil* and the *earth veil*. Generally, two opposite and mutually exclusive philosophies each deal separately with these. Obviously, pluralism – siding with the wall veils – would emphasize the distribution of objects and use spatial metaphors, while monism – siding with the earth veil – would emphasize the horizontal field and favor notions of time. Used separately, both

273

have a problem of grounding: pluralism needs space to preexist (with time being local), and monism time (with space as a byproduct). They embody the mineral tiles of being and the vegetal, growing fibers of becoming. I do not believe we have to choose, as long as we roll one into the other. In philosophy, it would be unimaginable to mix these two ontologies as if they were pepper and salt, but since I believe aesthetics is primary to all thought, I think it is wiser to consider the matter as one of ornament. The world – we and things – is clothed with ornament, and there we find ribbon ornament fully entangled but still existing in the dashed territories of the tile.

We can be perfectly pluralist as long as we replace all things with encounters: that is, a minimum of two things connected by that strong, now local field, not like a whole carpet but more like a piece of fabric. It is a strange mosaicism indeed: the basic unit is a chunk, but a chunk of fabric, without hard edges, fringed. Yes, I am a fabricist, but not of the organismic kind, for whom the morphogenetic or epigenetic field weaves itself uninterruptedly through everything. Or at least I do not believe it does so as a "whole," since it is being made in as many places as it is being torn and shredded. On the other hand, areas which are not felt are not part of the fabric. Unrelated things do not exist. Do not think I am slipping now into overall harmony and *Einklang*, a pure organicist holism and pure interiority like Teilhard's noosphere or Fechner's *Weltseele*. Certainly everything does not have a relationship with everything else, nor does it maintain relations at all times with the same number of others. There is no one thread that runs through all the way; there are only ends tied together and others hanging loose, waiting to be tied in. Also, no two threads are of the same thickness and strength; some can easily be broken, others never can. It is a polymonism (sic) that acknowledges both the mosaicist pluralism[8] of discrete things and a fabricist continuity, yet a monism that is local and does not extend towards the ends of the universe nor far outside the confines of the thing itself.

I admit that some awkward things are going on here, with multiple aspects adding up to a single thing. This strangeness, however, makes it impossible for us to relapse into a purely spatial state of pluralism, since the reciprocity does not occur between two upright veils facing each other in space; they might exist in space and do all sorts of things – have sensual encounters, exchange messages – but the relationship is one of felt involvement, not between bodies but between fringes entangling. Though the concept of entanglement is often used as a metaphor, such a metaphor would fall hopelessly short of explaining the type of relation that develops, which is more precisely a knotwork in which actions come out of a thing, feelings go into it, and the two overlap, in such a way that it becomes impossible to tell from which end each originates.

With Manuel DeLanda's *A New Philosophy of Society*, attention has been drawn anew to Deleuze's notion of the "relations of exteriority,"[9] which constitute assemblages. With this concept, Deleuze largely followed Hume, and in an interview with Claire Parnet, the French philosopher illustrated this with a simple example – "'The glass is on the table': relation is neither internal to one of the terms … nor to two together"[10] – emphasizing that the glass could stand anywhere and the table hold any object. But precisely how exterior is such a relation? We can only answer this question properly if we first ask ourselves whether such a relation plays a role in the making or design of both objects; otherwise, there would be neither a continuity of becoming nor from becoming to being. Did the table cut the bottom of the glass flat, or did the glass slide over the wood so long that it smoothed out into a table, in a reciprocal act of two exteriors touching and shaping each other? No, exteriority can never explain their respective shapes; for something to be formative it must be internal, and when one object becomes internal to another, the relation is one of sympathy. The glass and the table have come to *share* flatness, and they have both *internalized* flatness and taken it as directive of their respective formations, since both forms sprout from that flatness. And "internalized" means "felt," and "internalized flatness" means a "felt abstraction." Even when I hold the glass in my hand, it longs for the table. How else would I put it back there? Would I, by taking conscious action, help the two back together again? I hope not; this would mean all things need either an exterior mind to relate them to each other or mind-independent accident, and I do not know which would be worse. Whether I place a glass – barely stably – on an irregular rock in the garden or fit it into a cup holder in my car that is exactly the right size, the abstract points making up the plane of flatness are equally present and felt. I am afraid we can never explain any whole or thing, however loose and shaky or even broken and torn, without reference to the interiority of feeling, because it is feeling that makes things act, i.e., take on or change shape, in accordance with others. Every relation is a modulation of interiority, hovering somewhere between a loose fit and a tight one, and every thing is a multiple interiorization, since every thing has multiple relations. Things simply do not aggregate without sufficient correspondence, or resonance, which is more than can be explained by Deleuzian affects: affect relates things, to be sure, but it does not hold them together, since it lacks the notion of fitting. Things are shaped by mutual agreement, by that thin sheet of felt abstraction.

Things have affairs, too. If we consider the ties between a table and a glass, newspaper or vase as "stable" relationships, varying roughly between true brotherhood and mere acquaintanceship, then the table can as easily develop deeply intimate relationships with other things, such as a chainsaw or a fire – relationships that are clearly not stable yet are as intimate and internal as the others. Affectivity lacks the ability to abstract, because it does not experience the other as a force but as a sensible sign; it simply misses the constructive quality of sympathy. As I argued at the beginning of the previous chapter, affectivity is a mere exchange of affects, going from one sign to another affect, of which a sign affects another reciprocally, but these affects might "have nothing to do with each other,"[11] as in Deleuze's famous example of the orchid and the wasp (quoted from Rémy Chauvin). Surely, as in the case of Bergson's Ammophila and the caterpillar, the affects, i.e., the *content* of the feelings, need not correspond at all. They constitute the subjective end of the felt relation, its local coloring, *not its orientation*. Sympathy is always oriented. The very basis of the relation is sympathy, which is the feeling proper, the resonance and correspondence itself. Sympathy occurs first; all other feelings are modulations and derivations of it. Even a killing cannot succeed without initial sympathy. A doctor would be incapable of treating us if he or she were unable to sympathize with the disease, with its pace and personality.

Now, to clarify: Deleuze does discuss sympathy briefly in the same context[12] – borrowing the notion from D. H. Lawrence, not Bergson – but he locates it within the realm of the interactive, never the constructive. Affects pass each other in the night, and when two forms connect it is purely by accident, or, as DeLanda calls it, "contingently obligatory,"[13] which means "accidentally necessary," a dual concept even less effective than either term considered separately. When DeLanda explains affect, he does so by framing it in the realm of virtual capacities that have a broader range than actual properties. For instance, a knife has the property of sharpness thanks to the capacity "to cut," but that affect can only be reciprocated by the capacity of another object, such as bread, "to be cut."[14] But how they come to share the abstract line of the incision remains a mystery without one affect attuning itself to the other, as occurs with sympathy. Yes, affect is relational like sympathy, but it consists of two separate arrows, while sympathy consists of feelings matching and interpenetrating each other. With affect, things accidentally connect back to back; with sympathy, they connect face to face (veil to veil). There is a necessity here, to be sure, though not one of logic but rather a *felt necessity*, which means a thing acts in relation with others on a temporary basis, whether it is a person catching a ball, a glass standing on a table, a knife cutting a loaf of bread, or even a Gothic hinge holding a door, spanning eight hundred years of temporariness. Form cannot be distinguished from the action itself, and such action sprouts from feeling.

All things and all beings require this abstract matching, this coordination of posture and action. In sympathy, the feelings themselves resonate – not their actual content but the "feeling of feeling," to use Whitehead's expression, which Charles Hartshorne frequently quotes.[15] Neither of the participants needs to feel particularly sympathetic, although I think lack of sympathy is the exception rather than the rule. I wholeheartedly attribute feelings, and perhaps even minds, to plants, rocks and insects, but certainly not psychology or consciousness. When we realize that our feelings can abstractly focus to match others, we cannot deny that this mechanism has aspects of a mind though not a brain. The brain is simply an organ for processing and reprocessing feelings and mixing them with images, symbols and other emotions. The brain claims to be the seat of feelings only because it has the ability to speak. Yet feelings are not made of gray matter. Consequently, the nature of feeling must remain primal, or even primitive, and such basic feeling at all times amounts to sympathy. In Whitehead's words again, now particularly close to Bergson:

> The primitive form of physical experience is emotional – blind emotion – received as felt elsewhere in another occasion and conformally appropriated as a subjective passion. In the language appropriate to the higher stages of experience, the primitive element is *sympathy*, that is feeling the feeling *in* another and feeling conformally *with* another.[16]

Surely the sympathy between a rock and a plant is not more primitive than that between a bonobo and a bird, or between two people; sympathy is wild and primitive of itself. Later on in this chapter, we will compare notions of battle and help as we find them in Darwin and Ruskin respectively, but I can let you know in advance that we will find a lot more of the latter than the former, since it is closer to the primary orientation of sympathy. I do not think either the orchid or the wasp can disappear without the other perishing as well; they help each other (surely without "knowing," but cognition is irrelevant in relations) and have evolved cooperatively (without any moral intentions). That the orchid copies the shape of the wasp is a feat of pure felt abstraction. What happens between the plant and the insect is no different than what happens between the iron hinge and the wooden door, to use the example that we have returned to again and again in this book. To build something, two or more entities must bond, momentarily or for a longer time, either through a simple, short-lived act or a long-term genetic change, and nothing accomplishes this better than sympathy. In short, affectivity can be used to explain relations between things, but things must thus precede affects; feeling can actually make things and precede them.

Until now, in speaking of veils, I have not always made it clear whether I was referring to the vertical veil of ornament or the horizontal veil of feeling; perhaps it was not necessary to do so, since both consist of the same entangled structure, the same variation of intertwinements, some strong, others weak. But in our discussion of the ecology of design, the notion of a double veil will prove useful and important. Perhaps we can clarify the re-

lationship between the two, which is unbreakable, by invoking the most famous artificer of all time, Daedalus, the mythical Greek inventor, artist,
builder and strategist. He remains known chiefly as the maker of artificial
wings (which caused his son Icarus to be killed), the labyrinth at King
Minos's Cretan palace, and statues that seemed so alive they scared the day-
lights out of viewers. In ancient Greek, however, the related verb *daidallein*
– δαιδάλλω – has a double meaning: "to elaborate skillfully" but also "to
decorate," or, in other translations, "to work cunningly" and "to embellish."
In some of his letters, John Ruskin mentions the same double meaning.[17]
At first, the presence of such seemingly disparate connotations may seem
accidental, with one aspect referring to the inner mechanics of machinery,
of pulleys and cogs, and the other to the outer appearance of delicate ornament. However, both can be described in reciprocal terms: ornament as the
product of elaborate work and skill and machinery as cunning and complex.
For Daedalus, the decorated object is not an especially pleasant form of
wrapping but a potential trap, an intricate – in Hogarth's sense of the word
– construction no different from the horizontal layout of a labyrinth, with
its characteristically spiraling progression. When things are decorated by a
mass of entangled curves, our relationship with them follows the same
curves and entanglements. This is quite a reversal: things work because of
an aesthetic interaction *between* them, not of a mechanics hidden *in* them.
Between us and a decorated thing, or, more generally, between things, there
exists not an extensive, neutralized Cartesian space but a curved, charged
space, the space of involvement and felt intensity.[18] Involvement makes
space collapse and itself takes on the form of a spiral, of a thread slowly
curling itself up,[19] dissolving the opposition of James's tile and fringe.

From the vertical veil, tendrils sprout, twisting and spiraling horizontally to entangle with each other halfway, preventing things from making a
direct, spatial connection. But we can just as well describe it the other way
around and say that working forces of feeling start to entangle and create
veils and patterns. Ontologically, I cannot see any reason to favor one over
the other, or to put one before the other, since they form an inextricable
unit. We can as easily imagine larger horizontal fields with multiple veils
emerging from them, or series, or strands, or irregularly shaped islands. Or,

in a similar vein, we could imagine an entangled field with upright veils sprouting more veils and more entanglement. I do not believe that even time runs through them all, since each patch has its own time of operation, but certainly the relations can never be spatialized either. This chapter will explore the inseparable relationship between the two veils of entanglement.

We will see that Charles Darwin, who acknowledges decoration and sympathy, stresses the mechanics of contraptions (his favorite word to replace the much older term "contrivance," used by Boyle and Paley), and that John Ruskin, who inversely does not deny the existence of agency, stresses the aesthetics of decoration.

ruskin: beauty is the end

Although the two gentlemen were polite and friendly to each other – Darwin visited Ruskin at his Brantwood home in England's Lake District, where they took long walks together and admired the vegetation as much as the Turner drawings in Ruskin's possession[20] – they are the proponents of two completely opposite views of existence and aesthetics. We know Ruskin was an expert on plants and birds, but one is likewise amazed to see how many references Darwin makes to beauty and aesthetics in both *The Origin of Species* and *The Descent of Man*. At first, there is the more obvious version of beauty, a high-minded wonder at nature's endless variation, which we have already cited, a sort of primary beauty that for Darwin is the product of natural selection. Secondly, such aesthetic experience can be derived from a lower, more instinctive notion of beauty, that which passes between animals themselves. Darwin plays with this idea in *Origin*, and it comes to full fruition twelve years later in *Descent*, when he posits a secondary form of aesthetics driven by sexual selection. Males compete for the attention of females by attracting them with extensive song, repeated dance, the construction of elaborately decorated nests, or the "finery" of their own plumage.

What makes the study of the relationship between Darwin's aesthetics and Ruskin's natural history particularly problematic is that aesthetics and science are even more non-overlapping magisteria than religion and science.

Religion can battle endlessly with science about any truth, but aesthetics is purely about categories of beauty, including the ugly, the monstrous, the sublime, and never the truthful or right. When Ruskin decided in the early 1870s to write a thinly veiled response to Darwin's *Descent*, he did so in the guise of art education. The book, with an obscure title in obscure old English that advocates birds as symbols of love, *Love's Meinie*[21], became his answer to *The Descent of Man*, especially the second volume, which deals with sexual selection. Another book by Ruskin, *Proserpina*[22] (1873–85), a study on plants in the same vein, was meant more as an answer to Darwin's works on botany, such as *Orchids* and *The Power of Movement in Plants*. Despite Ruskin's strong objections to Darwinism, he clearly states that he has no scientific ambitions[23] and is not writing a treatise on botany; his interests are solely aesthetic. For Ruskin, studying the aesthetics of plants and birds means looking at them as living creatures, not lying dissected on the anatomist's table or drawn in exploded or sectional diagrams exposing their internal structure, including the reproductive organs. Several authors have stressed Ruskin's disapproval of sexual selection as a manifestation of his own supposedly twisted sexuality (of which we know nothing); not, however, Jonathan Smith, who attempts a more neutral stance in his book *Darwin and Victorian Visual Culture*,[24] but even when he brings Darwin onto the specifically Ruskinian turf of aesthetics, Ruskin still comes across as rather awkward, if not backward. True, it is difficult to understand Ruskin's arguments, especially those that do not concern noted aesthetic categories, such as the picturesque, the Gothic and ornament, but rather matters of biology. On top of that, the two men, though contemporaries, seem to move at a different pace. Darwin is an example of a late-career success who, awakened by Alfred Russel Wallace, finished *Origin* at the age of fifty; Ruskin, ten years younger, published the first volume of *Modern Painters* at the age of twenty-four. One seems to be moving into and the other out of the center of public attention, which should not distract us from a difference of much greater importance. Darwin, when he mentions aesthetics, bases his opinions on those of Hume and Kant – in short, on an aesthetics of pure subjectivity widely accepted at the time – while Ruskin is ahead of his time, not only because he is inclined to vitalism in the manner of Bergson but because he relates vitalism directly to aesthetics.

I think to reject vitalism as bad science would be the biggest mistake we could make. My claim, rather, is that vitalism is aesthetic theory, i.e., a theory of composition by feeling, despite the fact that it does not consider works of art as its primary subject. Evidently, a theory of composition implies an ontology, which would not only be applicable to works of art but to animate creatures as well, simply because both are equally composed. In vitalism, something seems to happen to things and beings that is beyond the scope of pure biology or sociology and generally falls more into the category of art. For instance, Henri Bergson worked mainly with fundamentally artistic notions such as intuition, creativity and spontaneity but only occasionally touched upon the subject of art, and others like Hans Driesch would not for a moment have considered their work to be aesthetics. Maybe Ruskin is closest to the later "American" Whitehead, who likewise turned ethics into a function of beauty, though he never committed himself to vitalism. Now, before proceeding, I think we must first make an amendment to vitalism, though it is not in itself the topic of this book and therefore can hardly be satisfactorily discussed. I think vitalism has a tendency to overgeneralize aesthetics: the sympathetic, resonating relations between two or more entities are mistaken for the sharing of a single force. I prefer aesthetic ontology over vitalism. Certainly, beauty animates us because it coordinates disparate feelings, but that is not the same as the disparate experience of the same feeling. Hence, vitalism is the *wrong* conclusion to the *correct* assumption that relations are felt and aesthetic. I do not think there is a directive force, but I do think forces tend to calibrate and coordinate with each other and therefore to have a single direction as an outcome, not as a resultant but as an agreement. This puts sympathy closer to animism than vitalism, since it is not the case that life goes through things but that life is shared between things, as an anima not contained in an object but felt by the other during the aesthetic encounter, the anima-satellite of the previous chapter. As stated before, it gives radically different things the chance to share feelings, to feel the same while not being the same.[25] It is shared as beauty, and it is as capable of shaping things as of being experienced by things. Beauty is both the productive and the product. For Ruskin, beauty is not what remains when science has left the scene to clear things up; for him, aesthetics exists at the very core of those things.

On the other hand, to proceed with our earlier discussion, I think Darwin's appreciation of beauty has been underestimated or at least undervalued by his neo-Darwinist followers. Many evolutionary biologists occasionally make use of the term "beauty," but its usage is the most frequent in a special branch of biology that emerged with Goethe (needless to say, he was an artist and argued aesthetically) some two centuries ago: the study of morphology.

> Morphology rests on the conviction that everything that exists must express and indicate itself. The inorganic, the vegetative, the animal, the human – each expresses itself; each appears as that which it is to our outer sense and to our inner sense. Form is a moving, a becoming, a passing thing. The doctrine of forms is the doctrine of transformation. The doctrine of metamorphosis is the key to all signs of nature.[26]

For Goethe, such morphological change was precisely articulated and structured. For instance, he intended his famous example of the *Urpflanze* as neither a once-living historical creature nor a simple Kantian schema but as the principle of generating the form of a plant and explaining the variations between them. For Goethe, every part of a plant stemmed from a leaf – "*Alles ist Blatt*" – stalks, petals, they were all modulations of the leaf form. Not unexpectedly, this concept already follows the aesthetic paradigm – variation amidst uniformity – not allowing the parts to be understood as heterogeneous nor even homogeneous but at least as homologous. Darwin's concept of variation, especially in the form of gradualism, heavily relied on that of homology. Nature, in its construction of forms, displays a consistency of production techniques that is even more wondrous than their functionality. Thus, in morphological discourse, the word "form" is not used in the sense in which we understand it today, to denote an actual physical form, but rather to indicate organization, supported not by a geometric shape but a topological structure. Scientists like Ernst Haeckel, D'Arcy Thompson,

William Bateson and, in our era, Brian Goodwin have written book after book on this structure of variation, and we sometimes find bits of it in Stephen Gould. Sean Carroll, one of the proponents of the latest and more intermediate branch of morphology, evo-devo, puts it as follows: "many large animals were constructed of repeated parts, and many body parts themselves were constructed of repeated units."[27]

I will not follow the trail of morphology all the way through, since my subjects are aesthetics and beauty, but it will show up at specific points, because it plays an important role in the relation between aesthetics and teleology. At this point in our discussion, what is important is merely the relationship of what a form is and what it does, its function. In the classic concept of teleology, the former is fully subordinated to the latter; in morphology the reverse is the case. For adaptationists, form can never exceed the notion of function, since it would be selected away. They must therefore believe variation is random and blind (but then they also believe genes are selfish) and natural selection is like a perforated blanket that smothers all misfits and tames the divergent force of variation, gives it direction, but only afterward, by filtering out the fittest. First of all, this is simply not true; a lot of form is undefined, or at least underdefined, while other forms are overdetermined. Not every object is like the curved bill of the hummingbird hawk moth fitting perfectly inside the curved flower of the dianthus so that it is able to drink the nectar. Fit, in the sense of a singular utility, hardly ever occurs, and when it does, we can still debate the concept of utility itself, for nothing is constantly in use, and when it is in use it partakes in whole variety of actions that can hardly be defined as utilitarian. Secondly, and far more importantly, the end should not be confused with the cause, and the Aristotelian parallel between causality and teleology has deeply troubled evolutionary theory.

Even our teeth, Aristotle's favorite example[28] in his argument for the final cause of teleology, organize in double arched rows before they specialize into cutting and grinding. There is a patterned or, if you prefer, rhythmic repetition to parts that allows them to vary and take on specific functions, though some never do because they occur between others and never reach the moment of clean determinacy. Patterned regularity should be understood more as a theme than a schema, or, as Brady argues in the case of Goethe,[29] as seriality, a pace in time more than mere repetition in space. Such patterns are unexplained by natural selection and are much more on the side of Darwin's co-founding concept of variation, part of a triumvirate with selection and inheritance. In this sense, morphology implies a surplus of direction in evolution, a proto-teleology that explains the forms of things in a way that it would be impossible to account for merely with the *destructive* concept of natural selection. Purely because of their subject, morphologists are by nature closer to the classic aspects of vitalism, such as creativity and drive, than are neo-Darwinian adaptationists. The productive and *constructive* forces of evolution contribute a certain directionality, while its selective forces should be considered much less judgmental. Morphological variation is viewed nowadays by biologists like Marc Kirschner as *biased* instead of randomized,[30] not only because it is itself structured but moreover because it understands mutations on beings that are already highly structured, guided on the one hand by a genetics that does not allow great variation (most mutations on genes are lethal) and on the other by a physical environment saturated with forces that guide all production of form. For instance, the reason cells are often spherical, like soap bubbles, is that they grow in a liquid environment of equal pressure, not because of genetic instructions.

Morphology precedes teleology: things need to organize before they can specialize. The feathers on the body of the pheasant Darwin discusses[31] are highly articulated, yet not all are functional. Of course, the feathers that thin out the shape of the wing are as necessary as the flaps on an airplane wing (except the pheasant doesn't fly), though the breast and back could as easily be covered with fur. Of course, a bird with fur in one place and feathers in another would be impossible and ugly, but that is the point: form precedes function. The pheasant's body is completely covered with a pattern of feathers, some of which take on more determination and others less. Morphologically, it makes no difference if a feather grows into part of the flying mechanism or takes on a specific color pattern; they are all part of the same structured, mosaic canvas. I think this is the beauty Darwin is talking about in his famous closing line about forms being "endless," and such variation is very close to the concept of changefulness Ruskin proposed in his discussion of the Gothic, with the same emphasis on "perpetual novelty." This is a notion of beauty that connects Ruskin, Darwin and Goethe more than most evolutionists would admit. When we take the notion of our moving Gothic figures meeting up in structural configurations, we come even closer to Goethe's "animated totality."[32] Nobody in his right mind would explain the beauty of rose windows as a result of their purposiveness as windows. As I said in the chapter on the nature of the Gothic, the fact that the windows are transparent is secondary to the configurational fact of form, since the closed walls are decorated and configured by the same patterns of tracery.

Morphology takes a creative view of variation, endless in time but limited in space, and I think Darwin recognized this by using the word "beauty" dozens of times in *Origin* and even more frequently in *Descent*, though he swings between objective notions of order and subjective notions of beauty being in the eye of the beholder. As we know, Darwin never developed this first, morphological notion of beauty; he merely used the term occasionally in wonder. But a second notion of beauty, one that occurs not between man and animal but between animals and between animals and plants, became his main subject in *The Descent of Man*. The book consists of two substantial volumes totaling almost a thousand pages, more than three-quarters of which do not deal with the descent of man at all but with beauty and how it makes up part of animal relations, in the form of various types of dance, song, antics and particularly the development of ornamental plumage and coats: "the most brilliant tints, combs and wattles, beautiful plumes, elongated feathers, top-knots, and so forth."[33] Whereas *Origin* deals mostly with natural selection – the constantly testing of species' fitness by the environment – *Descent* deals with what Darwin termed sexual selection: the way living creatures make use of beauty in courtship. As Darwin puts it:

> This depends, not on a struggle for existence in relation to other organic beings or to external conditions, but on a struggle between the individuals of one sex, generally the males, for the possession of the females; the result is not death to the unsuc-

cessful competitor, but few or no offspring. Sexual selection is, therefore, less rigorous than natural selection.[34]

This means that a form of beauty becomes tied to an actual judgment of beauty, since the females now select the males that are most attractive. So, while in natural evolution beauty can either be described as accidental or teleological – beauty as an end in itself – in sexual selection the purpose of the latter type is not beauty itself but procreation. Though morphological beauty can still be dismissed as metaphorically teleological – a Kantian form of judgment that remains fully within the domain of the human subject and its consciousness – the beauty experienced between animals is an actual judgment, often made by the female in choosing her male partner for mating. Let us first go back to Kant's teleology of nature for a moment:

> Suffice it that there are objects whose one and only explanation is on natural laws that we are unable to conceive otherwise than by adopting the idea of ends as principle, objects which, in their intrinsic form, and with nothing more in view than their internal relations, are cognizable in this way alone. It is true that in teleology we speak of nature as if its purposiveness were a thing of design.[35]

Whatever we make of it, any form of selection is a form of judgment, and this makes Darwin's evolutionary biology immediately teleological. Of course, one should never confuse the agency of a thing *afterward* with the agency that constructs that thing *beforehand*. That is what Spinoza dismissed as the reversal of cause and effect. Those ends that in Darwin's mind are selected by nature are generally confused with the intent of a planning and designing mind operating beforehand. Even if Darwin does not believe in a creator, he still explains living things "as-if designed." Hence, when nature does the selecting, teleology can be explained only by such a Kantian *as if*, but with sexual selection this changes, since the end actually does become an intervention of a mind afterwards, not the designing mind of a maker but the selecting "mind" of a female bird. Though it is not an overseeing designer's mind, there is a choosing mind nonetheless. Darwin's conclusion was that when a female bird did the selecting, a less conscious – if not unconscious and instinctive, certainly a more bodily or physiological – form of aesthetic judgment had to occur.

The two types of beauty must be related, however, and while Darwin does not explicitly discuss this, it will be important for us. Since morphology structures variation, and variation is the engine of ornamental pattern, a creature's skin pattern, as well as its skeletal structures and organs, is immediately a morphological issue. The colors of a fish's scales depend on their structure, as do the gradual shading and patterning of feathers, the coloration of a flower's petals, the stripes on tigers and zebras, a butterfly's wings – they are all mosaic and variegated. The two types of beauty inform each other. We must keep in mind that neither natural nor sexual selection contributes to the actual making of something, rather, it participates in a process of unmaking, by eliminating the less fit and less beautiful. Selection is often described as a painstakingly slow process of sculpting or painting, but those practices start with an empty canvas or a block of marble; here, the metaphor would have to be extended to that of a painting filling itself with color or marble growing like a clay model, adding piece after piece, followed by critical interventions that take some bits back out. But a critical audience's reasons for taking things out are not the same as the artist's reasons for putting things in; in this sense, the way morphology varies is not at all the same as the way selection eliminates things. This worries even Darwin, who states that the result of sexual selection is

> … as incredible, as that one of Raphael's Madonnas should have been formed by the selection of chance daubs of paint made by a long succession of young artists, not one of whom intended at first to draw the human figure.[36]

It is surely incredible, especially given that there is no Goethean rhythm to the picking of colors, the size of the stroke, the organization of the work, the size of the canvas, the variation of contrasts, and so on and so on. And these are only aspects operating beforehand; we have not even mentioned the quality of the critics needed to do the meticulous selection afterward. Neither form of selection constructs or does actual work, it merely undoes, since it is judgmental and critical. But aesthetics – and we will return to this later – needs another explanation, since it is about what is constructed, about what is made, and therefore beauty itself remains purely uncritical. Of course, it was the second, physical form of beauty in particular that made Ruskin so angry, because it brought to aesthetics a physiological, if not sexual, component that he deeply abhorred. And, probably worse, it suggested an inverse relationship between the first and second forms of beauty, namely that all aesthetics was derived from the second kind, evolving from a "proto-aesthetic feeling" between animals to our more developed version. That concept of an animal proto-aesthetics was developed by Grant Allen in *Aesthetic Evolution in Man*,[37] and it came as no surprise, since he had quoted the Darwin of 1871 on the first page of his *Physiological Aesthetics* a few years earlier:

> No doubt the perceptive powers of man and the lower animals are so constituted that brilliant colours and certain forms, as well as harmonious and rhythmical sounds, give pleasure and are called beautiful; but why this should be so, we know no more than why certain bodily sensations are agreeable and others disagreeable.[38]

But in the sixth edition of *Origin*, published in 1872, Darwin seems a bit more careful:

> How the sense of beauty in its simplest form – that is, the reception of a peculiar kind of pleasure from certain colours, forms, and sounds – was first developed in the mind of man and of the lower animals, is a very obscure subject.[39]

While the Darwin of *Origin* believed the first kind of beauty, that of morphology, was more important than the second, the beauty of finery, the Darwin working on *Descent* slowly came to think the reverse: the first beauty

Robert Kretschmer and Alfred Brehm. *Paradisea rubra, male.* Fig. 47 from Charles Darwin, *The Descent of Man, and Selection in Relation to Sex.* Vol. 2. (1871).

was actually a derivative of the second. In other words, instead of explaining the beauty that animals experience as varying in degree from that of morphology, from coordination and composition, he saw the sensual experience between animals as the explanation for the first. Since the experience of that type of beauty is related to sexuality, hunger and all other types of physiological desire, suddenly such emotions became the foundation of all aesthetics. In the same way as Thomas Henry Huxley became Darwin's bulldog, defending the evolution of species, Grant Allen became his defendant on the matter of "evolutionary aesthetics," though not as successfully. The notion of evolutionary aesthetics is hardly taken seriously today, though there continue to be outposts in adaptationism where the idea is held onto. To refute it is not as simple as it seems, mainly because the concept is not based on the premises of aesthetics but on those of evolution, i.e., its argumentation lies outside of the realm of aesthetics, which is exactly the reason why no artist, critic or art historian would ever make use of the concept. We see the same in evolutionary sociology ("sociobiology"), evolutionary psychology (which so angered Stephen Gould), evolutionary linguistics, and every other evolutionary epistemology – they do not explain in the proper sense, since they make no use of concepts; evolutionary history merely provides advantages and benefits that make it so. In Kant, aesthetics were never allowed to become interested, to focus on the agreeable itself, since obviously we were not going to eat a painting depicting a roast and bread on a table; we would not even feel hunger or physiological desire. Kant would allow us to enjoy only the orderliness and unity of the composition without the actual bodily sensation.

To complicate matters somewhat, I strongly believe a bodily sensation goes along with looking at a composition, but this is because I do not believe "looking" is the right word for describing what occurs in aesthetic relations. Rather, we sympathize, i.e., the unity is not the result of some general law of proportion or of color harmony but is situated and real, with real parts connecting into a structure that holds together because of felt relations between those parts. When I am interested in the unity of composition, it is because the constructivist *activity* of the parts matters, not the resulting "order." Nothing could be more erroneous than conceiving of beauty as a "sense of order," as Gombrich did. The recognition or cognition of a pattern, a *Gestalt* or any other type of informational entity is completely irrelevant, we merely feel-with; the parts' activity resonates with our own, often postural activity, in a synchronization of feelings that is immediate. Posture really is at the intersection of force and form. Some type of response should always be detectable, and many of the theoreticians interested in *Einfühlung* tried all types of measurement, even Fechner and Lipps but also Vernon Lee. When you place a small blue square beside a red one and your wired-up experimental subject shows more response in the visual cortex than when he or she sees a green square next to a red square, does it mean anything? No. Detecting a neurological pulse of any sort does not mean that what is measured discerns the aesthetic relation, you are merely measuring the presence of a response. It is not even isomorphic. I need not explain here how deeply disturbed Ruskin was by such sensualization of beauty – again, not because of any presumed twisted relationship with sensuality but because the effect, pleasure, could not be the cause. Of course, art and beauty give, and are made with, pleasure, sometimes great amounts of it and sometimes none at all, but the last thing we would want is for an artist to be pleasing.

Let us examine this idea step by step. First, we must banish from our minds the idea that Ruskin opposes Darwin merely out of a Victorian discomfort with sexuality, even if it would be supported by his own complicated psychology. In *Proserpina* Ruskin does not even really oppose Darwin's theory of sexual selection as a physical mechanism:

> I observe, among the speculations of modern science, several, lately, not uningenious, and highly industrious, on the subject of the relation of colour in flowers, to insects – to selective development, etc., etc. There *are* such relations, of course.[40]

It is not a wholehearted endorsement, nor is it a theoretical one, but clearly Ruskin does not deny the physicality of relations, nor that such physicality can be instrumental in the development of species. But he proceeds:

> So also, the blush of a girl, when she first perceives the faltering in her lover's step as he draws near, is related essentially to the existing state of her stomach; and to the state of it through all the years of her previous existence. Nevertheless, neither love, chastity, nor blushing, are merely exponents of digestion.[41]

This makes things a bit clearer. The blood is rushing through her body, reddening her cheeks, surely, but she is not blushing because her blood pressure has been elevated but because she is in love. Of course, this is only the beginning of Ruskin's response, since Darwin and Allen do not discuss blushing girls but red strawberries and raspberries that attract birds or insects; the elaborate feathers of the Argus pheasant,[42] which led to Darwin's remark about Raphael's Madonnas I quoted earlier; and the blue cheeks of male mandrills[43] that attract females. In particular, Darwin's observation that "[w]hen the animal is excited all the naked parts become much more vividly tinted,"[44] which associates coloring with sexual arousal, disturbs Ruskin so much that he refers to it as "unclean stupidity," which seems exceedingly prudish to us, but again, he does not disagree with the explanation of the functioning of pleasure but objects to the confusion of aesthetics and physical pleasure. In Ruskin's vein, we could as easily reverse the whole line of reasoning: if hedonistic pleasure was the goal – we are discussing teleological issues here – of a plant, why would it not directly expose its seeds and its reproductive organs? Why, if pleasure is the goal, do we not find a great excess of pornography in the natural world, with male and female animals exposing their genitals directly? Why do the males not simply force the females into submission? If you want sex, why not go get it? If you want food or nectar, why not go get it? Yet we encounter no such behavior. On the contrary, the question is: Why does a mandrill, a bower bird or any animal with a patterned coat make use of such elaborate rituals, extensive formalities and delicate indirectnesses? For a Ruskinian, the question could not be easier to answer: aesthetics is primary. For the world to work, it must rely on aesthetics. Relations cannot simply be utilitarian and functionalist, like plumbing, and physically, physiologically or mechanically direct. Everything must take a detour.

We could as easily argue – even more closely approaching Baudrillard[45] – that animals hardly have what we would call sexuality; they restrict their sexuality to prescribed periods, they have no libidos, no sexual capital, not even desires or fantasies to "express"; they merely dress up and dance. Instead of an unconscious, animals have territories and ornament, Baudrillard wrote almost thirty years ago – and it still rings completely true.[46] Nothing is as dedicated to artificiality as animals. Why is everything so excessively dressed up? The Darwinian answer – so the dress can be taken off – is a complete reversal of the facts. The much bigger question, of course, is: Why on earth is there so much beauty? Ruskin goes on in his rant against Darwin:

> Peacocks' tails, hc thinks, are the result of the admiration of blue
> tails in the minds of well-bred peahens, – and similarly, man-
> drills' noses the result of the admiration of blue noses in well-

bred baboons. But it never occurs to him to ask why the admiration of blue noses is healthy in baboons, so that it develops their race properly, while similar maidenly admiration either of blue noses or red noses in men would be improper …[47]

Ruskin is not in denial, since he confirms the effect on the baboons; he merely raises the issue of why the noses are blue, and why they are blue for mandrills but not for us. And blue noses are not just proper for mandrills but healthy as well. The subject of health moves the abstract Darwinian subject of survival (of the fittest) onto another, more everyday level of life and living. We should also keep in mind that most animals keep their coats all year, not just during the mating season, so their aesthetics cannot be derivative of sexuality but rather the other way around. Color must play a broader role, one that helps the baboon to organize its life, as an individual and as part of the group. A few pages later, Ruskin returns to the word "proper":

> When therefore I said that Mr. Darwin, and his school, had no conception of the real meaning of the word "proper," I meant that they conceived the qualities of things only as their "properties," but not as their "becomingnesses"; and seeing that dirt is proper to a swine, malice to a monkey, poison to a nettle, and folly to a fool, they called a nettle *but* a nettle, and the faults of fools but folly; and never saw the difference between ugliness and beauty absolute, decency, and indecency absolute, glory or shame absolute, and folly or sense absolute.[48]

Though it sounds quaintly puritanical, the notion of "propriety" as a "becoming" was an everyday question for a designer in an era when everything was so obviously decorated, an era, unlike our own, without nudity. If one was designing a bank building, for instance, one of the main questions would be what kind of ornament would be proper. Which ornament should one choose for a museum, a city hall, a house? For us, it would be unthinkable to design the most important judicial buildings in the country completely in Gothic style, like the Law Courts on the Strand in London – the architect George Edmund Street's most beautiful work ever. Or consider the Gothic St. Pancras railway station, George Gilbert Scott's best design ever, which immerses travelers in the most radical feeling of suspension of a nation's past and its future: we can go forward only if we go backward. Postmodernists would leap to speculations on communication, language and semiotics, but ornament is not meant to express any meaning. Since each of these objects is pervaded with a vast variety of actions and formalities, its decoration must supply the proper feeling and mood to guide those actions. This is not a question of space and appearance but of atmosphere.

A color or a colored pattern fills us with a certain mood, generating a persistence of feeling that exceeds brief moments of exchange and enables us to perform actions within the same sphere. Neither we nor mandrills or pheasants could ever live without such elasticity of feeling; we would stumble from instant to instant. It is feeling that prevents things from falling to pieces. How could we have a conversation in a room without decoration? The colors, the patterns, the furniture, all drench us with feeling, filling the gaps between sentences, glances and gestures.[49] Feeling creates stretches of time in which we can act. Hence, proper means suited – which suit to wear? – and by that, Ruskin means which suit to wear to which occasion. A mandrill or peacock has its own life to lead, and we all live forward (Kierkegaard); living is its own aim and is not even close to synonymous with survival. Furthermore, the question of ornament is inherently related to a specific body; the striping of a tiger is proper to its volume and its size, as is the Voronoi pattern on a giraffe, the striping of a zebra's coat or the spots on a leopard, as we learned from Turing in the chapter on ornament.

A bit further on, Ruskin actually calls it "ευπρεπεια– *well*-becomingness,"[50] relating color and pattern not merely to what is proper and suited but to what suits a specific creature particularly well. We could actually extend the wordplay from suitability to fittingness and conceive of ornament as a dress code, but one in which the social model is reversed into an individual one. Ruskin's concept of fitting does not follow the environmental model of Spencer's "fittest" but concerns the animal itself in its own group. The blue nose fits the mandrill, and *only* the mandrill, and it fits him *well*.

This, again, brings Ruskin's notion of ornament close to Aristotle's teleology of the final cause, which, especially in the case of animals, is never related to how it fits into its environment but to what the animal is, to how it lives its life, and to whether it does so well: *eudaimonia*, well-being. In Ruskin's own terms, *euprepeia*, well-becoming, is a form of health. Healthy life is lived forward, openly and inclusively, without any obstacles or struggle. Life makes its own suits:

> The flower exists for its own sake, – not for the fruit's sake. The production of the fruit is an added honour to it – is a granted consolation to us for its death. But the flower is the end of the seed, – not the seed of the flower. You are fond of cherries, perhaps; and think that the use of cherry blossom is to produce cherries. Not at all. The use of cherries is to produce cherry blossom; just as the use of bulbs is to produce hyacinths, – not of hyacinths to produce bulbs. Nay, that the flower can multiply by bulb, or root, or slip, as well as by seed, may show you at once how immaterial the seed-forming function is to the flower's existence. A flower is to the vegetable substance what a crystal is to the mineral.[51]

Before we delve deeper into Ruskin's argument, we should first look at the oft-used term "for the sake of," since it brings the whole argument back into the domain of teleology: something exists for the sake of something else. Now, the word "sake" is etymologically related to the German *Sache* – meaning "thing" in its broader context – just as "cause" is related to the French *chose*, which also means "thing."[52] Such linguistic reference merely indicates that an end is not some indeterminate nonentity but a potential connection to real entities. The hummingbird's bill is curved "for the sake of" drinking nectar from ornithophilous flowers. To merely call it a function or an end would be misleading; there is a real connection to real things. Generally, this relationship with things is indicated by the term "external teleology," and it is often limited to artificial objects, notably by Aristotle in his *Physics*. A natural object like a hummingbird or a tiger would only display an internal teleology. In Aristotle's conception, a tiger would not live to devour weakened and unfit prey, as it would in Darwinism, or to survive its own less fit peers, but merely to be a "good" tiger, i.e., to tear up small animals for nourishment. Such goodness, or well-being, would be the tiger's final cause. This idea has been criticized millions of times in the 2,350 years since, but at least Aristotle relates the final cause to growth, to the cub or young tiger's development into a mature animal; in short, to its lifestyle and well-being. Kant, when he criticizes the concept of the final cause, does so because he argues that a natural object, or organic object, in his words, does not proceed in a straight line from causes that precede its existence to the object's becoming a cause of other things itself after it has been made, since that, in short, is the teleological hypothesis: what a thing does is the intent of its design.

In a fabulous display of reasoning, Kant relates this same notion of growth to an end that is excluded from the organism before it is fully grown.[53] The tree cannot be said to be mechanically composed of functioning pieces, since some pieces cause the existence of other pieces, i.e., the branches make the leaves grow and the leaves in turn feed the branches, hinting at a form of nonlinear causality. Nature constantly switches between means and end,[54] Kant says; therefore, it cannot be designed or have final causes. A demiurge going through a nonlinear design process would not be worth his title; instead, he is obliged to work with straightforward causality and have the parts ready next to the drawing board before starting. In this sense, a tree, like our example of the dish in the previous chapter, cannot be said to be made of parts, since we would have to hide the leaves in the branches beforehand, in an impossible form of apriority. One cannot explode a tree into a mechanical diagram like a Volkswagen Beetle (which I think is already ontologically a mistake in the case of the car). Things *transform*; they change as they grow; they do not merely "size up" through deformation. The only problem with Kant's conclusion is that in his epistemology, human intelligence fails so utterly at understanding the workings of organic complexity that we need to resort to explaining it *as if* it were acting mechanically.[55]

Instead of preserving Aristotle's development toward well-being and taking out the designer, Kant metaphorically left the designer in and re-moved well-being. What was internal for Aristotle, because it had to be lived by an individual, became external again in Kant. Well-being and being well-suited perfectly coincide with design, but not with a designer. Since the designer has already left the scene by the time a thing starts living its life in all its unpredictability, how can that designer be part of well-being? He cannot. What a pity that Kant repaired Aristotle the wrong way around: the notion of means becoming ends and ends becoming means leads to a sort of *U-turn teleology*, a curved, looping arrow similar to the sinuous paths of entanglement we discussed with reference to Daedalus' labyrinth. Kantian as-if teleology is ultimately very close to Darwin's and turns out to be the weakest point in all evolutionary thinking. Terms like "natural selection" and, worse, "adaptation" are wholly fake teleology, though the former casts the environment as more of a sieve and the latter as a mold. Certainly, force is as powerful a metaphor in physics as natural selection is in evolutionary biology, but it may be more acceptable to us because we experience it so clearly ourselves. In the whole realm of physicality and genetics, how can there be room for an "as if"? No, natural things can only differ in degree from artificial ones; it is just that ages ago such a remark led to the notion of a Designer, and I think we can now get by with design alone.

It might seem surprising to make a distinction between design and a designer, since they are so inextricably bound up with each other in every theory that deals with the "argument from design." One camp sees design and jumps to the conclusion that there must be a designer; and the other camp, equally thoughtlessly, cannot locate a designer and thus promptly dismisses design as well. Both clearly miss the point that things are perfectly capable of designing each other, without intent of purpose, merely through a coordination that is fundamentally aesthetic, since it proceeds by felt relations. Now, one might believe that this excludes intent altogether, but when relations are of an aesthetic nature and the resulting products are as aesthetic in their relations, a consistency appears that must be viewed as intentional. I would accept at any time the proposition that things feel (termed "panexperientialism" by David Ray Griffin), and a bit less quickly to the idea that things think ("panpsychism"[56]), as long as aesthetic intent is not viewed as a conscious plan concocted by the participating terms but as a shared direction that has all the qualities of abstract thought, since the attentional effort becomes formative. The intent is the power of abstraction of feeling itself, since it selects what we earlier called points of agreement, for instance, shared points over which to bend both the hummingbird's bill and the flower's petals. Both, though made with very different materials and morphological structures, must find exactly the same curvature – a match so close that the hummingbird must beat its wings 70 times per second to hover immobile in the air, as still as the plant. Certainly, the bill and the flower share no *intent of purpose*, since they act completely differently in the relationship, but they do share an *intent of beauty*, which makes them follow the same resultant curve. This conclusion means, however, that beauty overrides purpose, order, desire and all the other aspects associated with beauty over the course of history.

Beauty does not need purpose – parts can be indeterminate, like the obstinate vestigial organs or the hair on your head – or order, since the active parts never surrender to static space, or perfection, because a system based on variation can by its nature never be perfect. So beauty is the end, but *there is no straight path that leads to it*. It is not that aesthetics is against purpose, but it is against viewing lived action as utilitarian, as mere labor, as something external to beauty. The hummingbird drinks the nectar enveloped by the full redness of the flower, a redness that does not go away when it starts to drink and will stay with it for a while after it finishes drinking. Beauty shakes off all ulterior motives, because it adopts pure feeling as the source of action.

I think we must accept teleology to the full: things are not artifact-like, they are artifacts. As I have said, this does not mean natural objects are the product of a designer's hand and mind, nor that they are full of gears and bolts, as in Paley's *Natural Theology* or Raoul Francé's *Die Pflanze als Erfinder* of 1920, since that would imply an intent of purpose and linear causality, which is merely a chain of efficient causes. No, they are artifacts in the sense that they are fully composed by aesthetic relations, by final causes only, out of the reach of any human or divine designer. Astonishingly, if we push this argument even further, I believe it means that human design *could also do without designers*, just like nature, as was alluded to in the previous chapter in reference to a *Naturphilosophie* for machines. What if we allowed not just flowers and birds but also machines to be understood outside the domain of purpose and utility, within the wider sphere of felt relations, radically postulating the concept that things can act only by feeling, through felt connection? This theory would explain all misuses of tools and alternative uses of software and machines. What if you get in the car just to drive around? What if you pick up a hammer in anger? What if a chimpanzee picks up a stick to extract ants from their nest? It is feelings that make things work, not tools. We reach out in feeling first, placing ourselves into other things, collapsing the space between us. Tools are usually understood as mediators, as in-between instruments, as if the goal already exists, as if the end has already been reached. But what machine has a single end? Which machine controls its purpose? Not one: they are all connected in lived aesthetics. I think the more machines shake off single and multiple purposes and simply try to engage in spheres of action, the more they will be able to free us from designers. I long for the day when I encounter a beautiful new thing and nobody can tell me who it is by. Finally – a thing without a signature! Are we anxious to know which individual made the rose window at Saint-Chapelle or an iridescent early-1900s vase from the Lötz glassworks? No, we are not: they are pure matter abstracting itself, either through style or through procedure. When Darwin first uses Paley's term "contrivance" and then later opts to use "contraption," he is certainly hinting at such felt relations. Things are traps because we cannot see what they are with our senses; they are merely determined in a sphere of feeling, an immediacy without any betweens. I think this is why *daidallein* necessarily implies both agency and embellishment. But it is a crooked way of working; nothing reaches its end, not even a machine; all things are bent. That is what an aesthetic teleology would amount to – beauty not as a means but as an end – and that is what Ruskin argues for.

As we slowly move toward addressing Ruskin's quote about the seed and the flower, we should first list all possible rejoinders to religious teleology, according to which a transcendent power – God, logos, idea – guides each being into purposeful existence. We now know this model is indefensible, because the parts cannot be generative, and one cannot foresee un-predictable effects. The creativity in the world is radical; something always stays occluded. Things seem to be directed but take a turn somewhere, which can bend the trajectory slightly or even make it loop. And such novelty occurs at the level of an individual being, not of a species, making creativity a function of freedom.

The first response was Aristotle's immanent teleology, or entelechy, similar to the vitalist, driving forces of *Bildungstrieb*. We will leave this concept on the burner for a moment and let it simmer, since he seems to have agreed with both the initial direction and the eventual unpredictability of development. The second response, the as-if teleology of Kant and Darwin, is highly problematic, if not untenable; if transcendence is impossible, how can we have an illusory version of it? A third response could be the complete denial of design and the assertion that it is pure accident that leads to substance – also an untenable position, since there is so obviously development and growth. A fourth would be a certain morphoteleology, which we know in two versions, linear and nonlinear. The former (4a) would be that all efficient causes necessarily lead to beautiful forms, since the process follows laws of formation, such as phyllotaxis or the golden ratio – also untenable, such laws do not exist and belong to the first category of transcendent causes. In Aristotle's terms, the efficient causes would have to merge with the formal causes, and things would have to mold themselves during the process. The latter, non-linear version (4b) would be such a morphogenetic teleology, which at first seems blindly emergent but of course follows the lead of an attractor in phase space, which does not push the process forward but pulls it from the future into a stable state. The spherical cell, like a soap bubble, follows such a route of minimal energy expenditure – an interesting alternative, surely, but an optimized soap bubble seems light-years away from excessive pheasant tail feathers, to say the least. Morphogenesis generally stresses uniformity more than variation and resorts to a fully baroque, unfolding monism. It stresses formal development, not well-being. And on top of that, both morphoteleological concepts are forms of *order*, be it statically imposed or dynamically emergent, and therefore the accompanying sense of beauty remains one of cognition.

Yes, ornament is a question of form, and yes, patterns arise out of morphological expressivity, but ornament exceeds every notion of *Gestalt*, order or information. It is as if all the initial indeterminacy returns at the end of the process of formation, and not necessarily by losing form. Often, ornament is a literal excrescence out of a formal arrangement, like the spiraling horns of an antelope, the branching antlers of a deer, or the tendril- and even pendant-like feathers that we often see in tropical birds. These last types of ornament, in particular, similarly to human jewelry like bracelets and earrings, add movement to specific parts of the body, and bring form into the actuality of well-being. Or better: ornament takes form beyond itself into a flourishing. *A form can never be felt; it needs decoration.* It needs decoration or else it can never have relations. If we squint, we can see that the Argus pheasant has a strikingly similar profile to the dried Dyak's head, William James's exemplary model we discussed in the third chapter: a fringed thing with feelings leading *into and out of* its substance. In this sense, ornament follows a double path, as the picturesque does, a path that runs parallel to the distinction between ribboning and tessellation; it can work *toward* form, with delicate figures that configure but remain patterned and fragile, or *away* from form, extending and exceeding it, though guided by the same notion of fragility. Either way, forms always come out as veiled; to understand the production of things as an unveiling, as Heidegger does, is to get ontology the wrong way around. It might be that a process starts as purely morphological, but it cannot end there: things will take on color and pattern as soon as they begin to join life.

Ruskin's teleology is closest to Aristotle's entelechy, certainly, though taken not as a formal becoming but as flourishing being, full of activity and relations. Beauty is not only a product at the end of a process but itself in turn part of a process. While for Darwin the flower is a mere way station, a means to pollination and procreation (or, as Samuel Butler ironically said, "A hen is only an egg's way of making another egg"[57]), with Ruskin the trajectory follows a curved path, a reversal of means and ends: it all ends with the flower. Development needs well-being, and only taken together are they sufficiently formative. When Ruskin writes, "But the flower is the end of the seed, – not the seed of the flower," it is not the opinion of a Victorian

Robert Kretschmer and Alfred Brehm. *Spathura underwoodi, male and female.* Fig. 49 from Charles Darwin, *The Descent of Man, and Selection in Relation to Sex.* Vol. 2. (1871).

dinosaur refusing to step into the glorious world of modernism; it is a radical reversal of means and ends. Beauty is not an epiphenomenon of a deeper mechanical purposiveness; the purpose itself is beauty, and all agency is that of beauty. The aim of life is to flourish, not to survive. Life is not lived against the odds of natural selection but lived forward. Self-formation is the activity that stabilizes, the movement that is formative. From the first chapter of this book to this last one, it amounts to the same transformation: movement becoming structure, whether it is the interlacing of our Gothic ribs, the iron hinge crawling over the door, Morris's tangled webs, Lipps's postures or Ruskin's ornamental veils. It is certainly a form of health, of persistence, but it is explicitly not one of strength; it is the health of frail things. Only in fragility can we be relational.

In the transition from one dimension to the other, the object takes on pattern, which is form as much as decoration. Force-form or thing-action always emerges patterned and clothed. In commentaries, entelechy is usually described as Aristotle's formal cause merging with the final cause, but this is still too hylomorphic, as if life casts its own form; rather, it is felt from the inside, like Ruskin's girl's blush. It is a blooming of form. When Ruskin writes that "[t]he flower exists for its own sake, – not for the fruit's sake," it may sound a lot like "art for art's sake," as if we are leaving all the mechanisms to work behind the scenes and merely proclaim art as primary, with all the efficient causes remaining safely secondary. But – as we argued in the case of the Gothic ("a beauty that works"), ornament ("strong decoration") and the picturesque ("objectified age") – to do this would be a fatal mistake. When he advocates ornament as useless, he is not merely veiling a world of utility, rather, he is emphatically acknowledging all the possible action enveloping things, yet not as utility but as life, as involvement. The workings are between things, not behind or hidden in them. Useless art, useless ornament, supports all action, lightens it, takes out the intent, so an insect does not need to fly over to a flower by its own little Cartesian self, crossing that vast extensive space between A and B. The insect is entangled with an aesthetic source in B; it becomes involved, is helped, guided, carried by sympathy. Pure *eudaimonia*. Our makeup, our beautiful shoes, skirts and shirts, our curled hair and our patterned coats take us where we need to go;

they carry us. It is not that we want to be "attractive" but that we want to feel well, with cheeks and lips redder than red, eyes darker than dark, nose bluer than blue. Yes, all this makes us attractive, but it is sympathy that is at work, not sexuality or desire. Aesthetics brings relief, *a radical relief*: we do not have to drag ourselves over, weighed down by our desires, needs or psychology; things carry us.

All this sounds very objective, but note that it is a *felt objectivity*, not one of reason. Classic notions of objective beauty involve inherent laws of perception or form, such as harmony and proportion, an order we must extract using our cognitive abilities; objective, yes, but of the mind. On the other hand, classical notions of subjective beauty, such as David Hume's ("Beauty is no quality in things themselves: it exists merely in the mind which contemplates them; and each mind perceives a different beauty"[58]) or Freeman Dyson's ("Why should nature care about our feelings of beauty?"[59]) do acknowledge feelings, but they wrongly anchor them in the perceiving subject. Sympathy posits a felt objectivity that states that all things feel and all things engage in aesthetic relations by sharing those feelings and coordinating them. Nature *only* cares about our feelings of beauty; humans, with all their consciousness, are only part of the plot insofar as they increase the number of designed things. Natural objects, as well as artificial objects, have feelings of beauty, and when we encounter them, we are not elevated to the status of judging subjects; we merely sympathize in varying degrees, share in adding more objective feelings. If anything is subjective, it is reason. No mind interferes at any point in aesthetic resonance, no cognition, no desire, no imagination – all that comes afterward. We have full access to objects, but *only aesthetically*, not in any other way. Darwin's concept of beauty, we should always remember, completely relies on Hume ("beauty obviously depends on the nature of the mind, irrespective of any real quality in the admired object"[60]), and this means that ultimately it can only work through mental association: a beautiful thing attracts the subject because it sensually evokes *other* emotions in him or her, those of sexuality, hunger or taste – every time we say "beautiful" we mean something different.

I believe Ruskin had every reason to be upset with Darwinism.

a veil of strange intermediate being

> The face of Nature may be compared to a yielding surface, with
> ten thousand sharp wedges packed close together and driven
> inwards by incessant blows, sometimes one wedge being struck,
> and then another with greater force.[61]

It is one of Darwin's darkest, most Malthusian images of the struggle for existence, and in his notebooks, "driven inwards by incessant blows" was first accompanied by "forcing out others," but in all editions of *Origin*, these sharper words are cautiously left out. More than a metaphor or a comparative image, it is something like a diagram, one that is organizational, not visual, a model that is almost the opposite of what today we would call an adaptive landscape, one made up not of peaks but of teeth or wedges. Each tooth represents a species, a closed entity, which is quite at odds with Darwin's own notion of variation. First, we should note that, in our terms, Darwin's yielding surface fits the mosaic model, a tightly packed system of polygonal (triangular) tiles, and second, it is dynamic: massive forces make some tiles sink deeper, while others are pushed out (though it would be more fitting for them to shrink and expand.) It would not be difficult to contrast this model with Ruskin's, mentioned in the chapter on the nature of the Gothic, in which the girls hold hands to build crystals, acting as a model of an interconnected system, a fabric, but one as dynamic as Darwin's mosaic. I do not think it will be particularly helpful to keep constantly opposing mosaic and fabric, though I think an important distinction emerges when we look at how Ruskin and Darwin respectively consider aesthetics as actually lived in everyday encounters. In one chapter in the second volume of *Descent*, Darwin cites the "law of battle," this time referring not to the reliance of male finery on sexual selection by females but to the way males fight among themselves (during mating season) for the right to reproduce. Interestingly enough, a few years earlier, Ruskin had entitled his chapter on aesthetic composition in the fifth volume of *Modern Painters* "The Law of Help."[62] Let us not allow this distinction to slip into morality and the long-running debate over selfishness (at the level of the genotype) and altruism (at the level of the phenotype), honestly, I do not believe either actually exists or at any rate is of special importance. The concept of selfish genes is so utterly ridiculous ("We are survival machines – robot vehicles blindly programmed to preserve the selfish molecules known as genes," Richard Dawkins wrote[63]) that we should not expend another thought on it, while altruism is the mere humanization and subjectification of something that is fully objective, namely, sympathy.

During the century and a half since Darwin, many amendments have been made to his Spencerian utilitarianism, in which the individual organism elbowed its way up against the stream of natural selection. One of the most famous was made by Peter Kropotkin, who argued in his 1902 book *Mutual Aid* that a world of pure selfishness and competition could never lead to any form of progressive evolution. For him, aid was at least as beneficial to a species, if not the norm, since it supported the organization of the group and therefore helped individuals survive.[64] The same argument, combined with a knowledge of genetics, was put forward by Wynne-Edwards in the 1960s, who referred to what he called group selection,[65] in which certain individuals reject the quest for immediate benefits in favor of the "good of the community," something Darwin himself mentioned in the third chapter of *The Descent of Man*.[66] Darwin uses the term "sympathy" dozens of times, especially in the third chapter, usually as derived from Adam Smith or Alexander Bain, but in an argument similar to that of Wynne-Edwards, who states that group selection can sometimes override the natural selection of single individuals. Another form is Joan Roughgarden's social selection, a postulation of an even broader notion of cooperation than that which we find in groups.[67] These few examples merely serve to correct the idea of competition as it occurs at the level of daily life and its presupposed struggle for existence; many others have adapted the concept of competition into cooperation at the level of species as well, not only with special cases such as the coevolution that exists between the hummingbird and the nectar-carrying flower but with the idea of symbiogenesis, developed mainly by Lynn Margulis.[68] She argues that evolution, especially half a billion years ago, when organisms and their genes were almost the same size, occurred through physical rather than genetic mergence, like that between bacteria and cells. This caused the evolutionary tree to contain many shortcuts, branches linking branches, creating detours in the standard history of bifurcation.

However, all these amendments to the idea of natural selection are still evolutionary theories based on the larger, teleological notion of selection and progression, and most of the time the discovered altruism of the individual is checked by the selfishness of a larger entity of the group. The problem I have with all forms of selection is that they are acts of elimination, not of construction. It should be made clear, though, that in the aforementioned theories of Wynne-Edwards and Margulis an increasingly large contribution is made by construction rather than competition. Our goal in this chapter is not to map out the different types of evolutionary theory – we are concerned with well-being and aesthetics – we need to keep in mind that some serious doubts have been and are being cast on the core concept of competition between individuals or genes. Looking at cooperation from my own perspective, I do not believe that altruistic behavior, even in primates or humans, is a moral layer located on top of deeper, more selfish instincts. My claim is that aesthetics and therefore configuration or composition are primary, primordial even, not just operative between living things – plants, animals and human beings – but between atoms, rocks and clouds as well. If one thing can explain the forward movement of life and the progression of evolution, it is composition, since things that are built become parts for building new things, simply by following the notion that things sympathize, no matter what. Things are put together out of whatever is available. I believe that aesthetics supersedes ethics, and not just by a little bit: often, what we call ethics (whether of the selfish or altruistic kind) is an aesthetics that is lived in the present instead of hanging on the wall or confined in a book. I am simply stating that what we take for the moral decision of altruism, with a subject rising above its own interests, is actually pure aesthetics: it does not concern individuals and their morals but pairs and groups and their encounters. And, aesthetics specifically involves "a theory of composition through feeling," as I stated at the beginning of this chapter. Here again is Ruskin, in "The Law of Help":

Composition may be best defined as the help of everything in
the picture by everything else.[69]

So we are either ascribing ethical considerations to color patches or aesthetic
feelings to humans and other animals beyond the world of art. I choose the
latter, partly because we have shown sympathy to be a noncognitive and immediate response to another thing-action. Things help each other, and they
take part in the collective act of composition, in an aesthetics that can in no
way be distinguished from acts of caring between humans or animals. I will
say it yet again: Ruskin's ethics is often explained as a social form of Christianity, but for him, help and care are constructive acts, acts whose intent is
beauty. To Ruskin, all acts are Gothic. And here, we should immediately
cite Whitehead:

> … Actuality is in its essence composition. Power is the com-
> pulsion of composition. Every other type of composition is a
> halfway stage in the attainment of actuality. The final actuality
> has the unity of power. The essence of power is the drive to-
> wards aesthetic worth for its own sake. All power is a derivative
> from this fact of composition attaining worth for itself. There
> is no other fact. Power and Importance are aspects of this fact.
> It constitutes the drive of the universe. It is efficient cause,
> maintaining its power of survival. It is final cause, maintaining
> in the creature its appetition for creation.[70]

Whitehead puts it in explicitly evolutionary terms ("survival," "creation"),
and while he is not an expert on aesthetics like Ruskin, "for its own sake"
makes clear that both men see a flower as flourishing not in a vacuum but
in a world of composition and relations. The term "composition" does contrast wonderfully with Darwin's idea of competition – which is why I have
been using it in this chapter instead of the previously introduced "configuration" or "construction," though in this book they are completely inter-
changeable. I do not think we should now oppose "competition" to "composition" everywhere, but I do think we should reverse their order. Instead

of thinking of a thin layer of aesthetics wrapped around a harsh utilitarian world, we should place beauty at the core, surrounded by a wide range of diverse emotions and behaviors. Obviously, there is much conflict between animals – though it is highly ritualized, if not aestheticized, mostly in the form of rivalry – and there is struggle, though not necessarily in opposition with *eudaimonia*. Life being lived forward does not mean we get things for free; Ruskin would be the first to acknowledge that. The sole point I will make throughout the remainder of this chapter will be that composition is primary and competition or battle is secondary, directly following from the primary cause. Aesthetics is primarily about building, about construction, not only in the more general sense but in the specific sense of patterns of living. Moreover, aesthetics builds not to internally connect things together against the outer forces of the sublime that threaten it; rather, it builds delicately away from the sublime, creating fragile webs that immediately include others when they encounter them – it is a construction of frailty, not strength. To understand such everyday aesthetics, we must look more specifically at two kinds of construction: the aforementioned *building of groups*, such as flocks, herds and packs, and the actual *building of territories*, which include elements such as paths, trails and burrows but also nests and mechanisms such as spider webs and mimicry.

Animals are not only designed; they likewise design their own lives and habitats as well. Let us see whether we can create a consistently aesthetic argument. If our hypothesis is that aesthetics makes everything function, it would be unacceptable to slip halfway through the argument into the domain of the social or ethical to explain the existence of groups and territories.

Until now, we have discussed sympathy and aesthetics as formative but hardly touched on how they create entities larger than pairs, in what we have called encounters. Only in the cases of Morris & Co., the Shoowa-Kuba tribes and the happy young Coca-Cola drinkers have we touched upon the notion of groups. Of course, this is not sufficient, since when people or things sympathize, they often form groups larger than two. Sympathy works in multiple directions and has the capacity to form larger groups;

oddly, however, at a certain point the group has formed and requires no new members to join it. If feelings are intensive, and if feelings have the capacity to build extensive things, why is the amount of extensity limited? Things seem to concentrate at first only on the act of composition, the gathering, the building of a group, but then, once the group is built, they begin to act within that group and to maintain it. As we discussed in the chapter on sympathy, every approach to another starts with a feeling-into, followed by a living-with. One's relational act has to contribute to one's own well-being, though it does require one to adapt and vary one's actions. What makes swans live in pairs, wolves in packs and wildebeests in herds? And what makes ants live in colonies and termites in highly elaborate structures more complex than any conference center built by man? One answer is that in forming groups we begin to design our lives and our environment, instead of waiting for circumstances to batter us. The other answer, since our theory is based on a notion of things, is that parts collaborate and attract others to collaborate likewise until the group starts to become a thing itself and to maintain its *own relations* and develop its *own feelings*. In short, the group-thing, in turn, should be able to act and abstract, i.e., adapt its shape to conditions of sympathy.

Though this sounds a lot like old-school organicism, I would assert that it differs at some crucial points. In an organicist theory, participants would sympathize not only with other participants but with the larger group as well, and that certainly does not occur here. The parts sympathize with each other, it is true, but never with the whole. Contrary to earlier concepts of sympathy, which equate it with harmony and conceive of it as a feeling radiating in all directions in equal amounts, my view is that it is variable and directed. Sympathy is not between all and all, and therefore things are not as seamless and smooth as in an organic whole, and hence the well-being of the group never exceeds that of the parts. The well-being of the parts is exactly as great as that of the group, if one starts to exceed the other, we will see either the part or the group perish. The intent of beauty implies an act of composition, not an intent towards a specific finalized form for the group. Nobody lives-with the group *qua* group; we live, and things live, among things, and our actions and feelings are always local. On the other hand, contrary to the theory of assemblages, things do intend to be *part* of a group; they do not work back to back, with the whole suddenly popping up without anyone expecting it. In assemblage theory, the emergent property of a group completely escapes the parts, and we should ask ourselves: if the parts collaborate, to what end do they do so?

Things like to make friends and form groups. They are not withdrawn; on the contrary, they are outgoing and generous, if not jovial. Things do better in a group, eudaimonically speaking, but only if they coordinate their actions or, in Ruskin's words, help each other. However, this does not mean the participants in any way control the shape of the group; their intentions focus on the grouping itself, not to what the group is for. To return to one of Ruskin's weirdest examples, the little girls holding hands in a crystal formation: they do want to hold hands (by the way, to form a crystal, the girls would need a minimum of four hands each instead of two) – that is intentional – but the shape of the final outcome, the crystal, is not. Does that make the shape of a crystal "emergent"? Not really. For instance, a starling in a huge swarm has no control over the whole of the swarm, but it is wholly participating. The shape of a swarm seems to be emergent when generated on a computer screen, where all the cyberstarlings (or "boids"[71]) act by following the four simple but flexible rules of flocking – separation, alignment, avoidance and cohesion – but a real starling in action *feels* all these conditions and responds to them with feeling, flapping its wings accordingly. I am not denying that a swarm is computable, merely that computation cannot explain what occurs in reality, since a bird does not compute its next position and then fly over. So if the swarm acts "as a whole," it is precisely that: an act. Perhaps there is no whole, and if there is, I am not sure I can see it. I think anyone who marvels at the beauty of thousands of starlings (there can be more than 50,000) flying over a field marvels not at some sort of "emergent order" but purely at the gracefully coordinated effort. One simply takes part in the act of construction. The problem with DeLanda's assemblage theory is that, since the parts refuse to help each other, they must be forced into a group shape by the "immanent patterns of being,"[72] the minimum-expenditure forms that lie waiting ahead (as an attractor in what is called "phase space") of all interactions. Subsequently, the felt interaction has nothing to do with the formation. Strictly speaking, it separates the efficient causes from a final cause again by hiding it in the future: small efficient causes are attracted by one single but hidden end. In contrast to assemblage theory, our Gothic ontology proposes that things do have sympathetic, interior relations, but, in contrast to organicism, that they do not have such felt relations with anything larger than themselves.[73]

If we take up Deleuze's example of the glass again for a moment, we should imagine the glass as not only entangled with the table because of shared flatness but equally entangled with a hand because of shared roundness and with a bottle because of shared hollowness. It forms groups with many things simultaneously, maintaining multiple relations, as if caught in elastic bands stretching from one thing to another. We should not forget that in proper aesthetics – the aesthetics of relief – you do not have to put the glass on the table yourself; your hand is brought over to the table by the glass (or to the bottle, for that matter.) This is exactly what Ruskin's help and care entail. Things do half the work. However, such things are not substantiated all the time by *actual encounters* – with a particular table, hand or bottle – though they are supported by *actual feelings*, feelings on the lookout (the "spirits" of the previous chapters), which will immediately animate any hand, table or bottle when it gets close enough. The hand, bottle or table will need to meet the glass by fitting its roundness, hollowness or flatness to create an encounter and to finish the work collaboratively.

There is nothing virtual about feelings; things stretch out continuously, creating a *surplus of action*. There is absolute generosity, always exceeding use. Feeling is what makes a thing take shape, it is directional, intentional and active. Feeling is formative, and it therefore precedes form. How could my hand fit around the glass if it had not felt its roundness beforehand? How would the glass take on a round shape if it had not internalized the abstract points on my hand? Even if the feelings are continuous, the sympathy is still in the encounter. In contrast to what assemblage theory would say – being based on the distinction between virtual capacities and actual properties – feelings are always actual and present, i.e., each feeling is an act – a jovial, generous, affluent, even sacrificial act, a pure gift – but this does not mean the act is reciprocated automatically. The glass *acts all the time*, in

several ways – round, flat and hollow – it is just that its actions are not necessarily registered by a hand or table or bottle, since these objects have their
own matters to care of. If unreciprocated, the initial act of feeling – left over
from previous encounters that shaped it, with an internal structure that actively maintains it – never develops or dissipates; it remains constant until
the moment of encounter, when new feelings become involved and create
an event of sympathy. When something happens, it is not an actualization
of a virtual state but an intensification and strengthening of the actual, an
actual-plus, an empowerment. In the end, this is what aesthetics is: being-
well with the help of things. Therapy, for example, especially the kind that
concerns the way one lives (or does not live), should be aesthetic therapy
that restores the way one deals with things – how one wears one's clothes,
feels the chair one is sitting on, drives one's car, combs one's hair. A whole
sphere of feelings radiates from things, feelings that are factually there, and
at any moment a certain portion is reciprocated, making it live-with many
others, involving them aesthetically, but a certain portion not, and these
feelings – more a *longing* than actual sympathy or empathy – are unchanging. I see things as Morrisian rugs, but with irregular, fringed contours, full
of arabesques, imbroglio and labyrinthic paths, but we cannot all walk on
all the paths at the same time. Think of Deleuze's glass again, but this time
sitting alone in the dark in the cupboard. Only the flatness is shared (with
the shelf) and not the roundness or hollowness, but the glass still stretches
out, and the better designed it is, the further it stretches out. Such abstract
feelings are not mere archived memories of previous encounters; they are
active longings, a *constant activity*, unchanging. Change only occurs during
encounters of sympathy. Things never drop back into a state of anesthesia
or, worse, apathy; they always feel, stretching out in many directions, but
only some of those directions are taken up and developed. Nothing is virtual,
or held back, on the contrary, things overflow. We see nothing but a constant
shifting and intensifying of reciprocities, since only so many events fit into
the real. In assemblage theory it is the virtual that is larger than the real,
and the real is equated with the actual, in our case, however, it is the actual
that is larger than the real, not the other way around, since the real is what
happens and the actual is what is felt.

When we return to our original question about group formation, we can see not only how things internalize their relations but also how they vary sympathies to produce a specific type of group. Seen in this way, not even billiard balls are externally related, since the force has to be processed internally to overcome its inertia in order to respond. Even linear causality is a form of *actio in distans*, even when two billiard balls have an abstract sheet consisting of only a single point between them. If we take Ruskin's group of four-armed girls again as an example and, in contrast to the homogeneous crystal, begin to vary their ages and sizes, we will see that even if they want to hold hands, some will not be able to. For instance, if a small group or alignment of taller girls suddenly occurs, internally lengthening the subgroup to such an extent that it can no longer coordinate with shorter girls, a mismatch will occur – or they might be able to rearrange themselves and partially fit together again, enough so that the taller girls will not break away into a separate group, but we would still see an internal gap or fracture. This often happens in metal alloys. We hardly ever get to see atoms packed neatly into hexagonal formations; we tend to observe complex forms of cracking, obviously because subgroups that have organized themselves in directional patterns are unable to fit with others in other directions. Such gaps, or cracks, are not sudden occurrences of external relations ("back to back") within a system made up of internal relations ("face to face") but mere loosenings of the latter. Thus, even the disjunctive is a form of the conjunctive. In animals, feelings are much more elastic, however.

If we imagine each girl's four arms made out of rubber (this is as weird as it gets, I promise), so that each can double or triple in length, we can immediately picture a type of group movement that is more gradual and variable, such as that seen in the aforementioned flocking of birds, or schooling of fish. Generally, all such group forms are explained by emergence or self-organization, clearly a term that has been developed in a stance against transcendence and in favor of an idea of order being leaderless and out of control, which is fine. But self-organization is a highly paradoxical term and therefore unsatisfactory to say the least, if not completely unusable. Do we find linear causality at the local level transforming into the nonlinear version at the global level? Or, if that seems inconsistent, do we see mini-selves adding up into a mega-self? No; this is not a very satisfactory model either.[74] If for a moment we forget order (whether or not on the edge of chaos) and merely look at beauty, it becomes so much easier to accept that its participants do strive aesthetically, but only aesthetically. All things live forward, grouping jovially. The parts may be dumb, but *they are not insensitive*; i.e., the intelligence may be distributed, but the intuition is fully coordinated. Feeling is fully congruent with formation, while the mind can only admit being baffled and term it "emergent." Every member orients itself, and all orientation is supported by feeling, and all feelings are mutual. The fact that the participants in the formation have no control over its final shape does not mean all is blind, automatic and instinctive at their level of existence. So we cannot qualify a swarm as a superorganism of any sort nor as a lucky occurrence, not as an emergent mega-mind nor as a mindless emergence, but as a group of mini-minds in temporary agreement. Clearly, all such agents can vary their behavior, measure out their sympathy, and have *some* control over their local formation. If coordination consists of agreeing on an abstract set of points between terms, these points can vary in number and alignment. Such variation can be guided only by sympathy, by an elasticity of instinct itself, and not by conscious decision. Regardless of how deep down into the micro-universe of matter one goes, one will always find variation.

On this point, Ruskin is even more radical than Whitehead, since for Ruskin, whether we speak of life or death, organic or inorganic, is merely a matter of degree: "Things are not either wholly alive, or wholly dead. They are less or more alive" – the best description of what, in a different context, he calls "the veil of strange intermediate being."[75] While Whitehead acknowledges that there is "no absolute gap between living and non-living societies,"[76] he does make a distinction between mere aggregates (similar to Deleuze's assemblages) and what he calls societies: the former are extrinsic unities and the latter intrinsic and organic.[77] Ruskin rejects such distinctions. Why impose such a new division after all things had finally been placed on the equal footing of feeling by what Whitehead himself so marvelously calls "the critique of pure feeling"?[78] If all things are exceeded by feeling, it follows directly that relations can only be intrinsic, in a rock as much as in a dancing couple, but they will never lead to a smooth universe, to a so-called "fabric of things." The veil of strange intermediate being – which I think is the most beautiful term ever – ranges from gray to green, oscillating violently between the crystalline and the arabesque; green petrifies to become gray and gray comes to life, but all is fundamentally entangled. Sympathy does not form a perfect sphere around things so they might include all other things; rather, it is a strange, fluctuating, pointed, asymmetrical zone of feeling, larger than the thing itself, yes, and more often than not stretching into other things, but not always and everywhere. In the end, that is exactly what entanglement means: the occurrence of a thing as felt in another thing. Entanglement is the network of sympathy, a network that not only includes things and actions but also feelings. Certainly, gaps and tears appear, but simply as internal edges, which have their own abstract points to coordinate with new things that might correspond. To keep opposing mechanism and organicism will not do. To be sure, assemblage theory tries to transcend that opposition as well, but as an upgrade of the former, by broadening the scope of causality. Meanwhile, in what we should perhaps call *entanglement theory* (though I prefer Gothic ontology), we depart from the opposite starting point, saying there are always feelings, and feelings are always felt relations and therefore internalized, but limited in their range and scope, exactly as sympathy is supposed to be: a "feeling with, not a feeling for," as D. H. Lawrence put it. In that sense, entanglement theory is an upgrade of organicism (turning it less holistic), while assemblage theory is an upgrade of mechanism (turning it less linear). Things cannot be entangled without relations of interiority.

The term "entanglement" or even "entanglement theory" (or "tangle theory") has its origins in Erwin Schrödinger's elaborations on quantum theory, in which the observer is entangled with the reality he or she observes,[79] but it has found its way into contemporary social theory, in particular through the writings of Latour and Callon, who have used the term in a similar fashion to explain the relations between intricately interwoven human and nonhumans – often technologies – in which one takes decisions for the other in a process in which we cannot distinguish who contributes what. What is even more interesting is that Latour, in *Pandora's Hope*, specifically argues that such entanglements consist not of means leading straight to ends but of *displaced ends*:[80] machines change the ends of humans, and humans those of machines. As an illustration, Latour cites the curved path of Daedalus' labyrinth, which could not be more apropos, though, again, he makes displacement an issue of concern, while Ruskin adds to it the second meaning of embellishment. In Latour's assemblies or "societies," things do not simply have functions but exist within networks of actions. It goes without saying that this comprises a fully ecological notion of the entanglement of humans and nonhumans, which he has been advocating since 1993's *We Have Never Been Modern*.

But there is more to ecology than things and actions. We must add feeling to the system, or else we cannot explain the Daedalian detouring. When an object is used in a different way than intended (what Latour calls a "translation"[81]), such a shift can occur only because the object's range of feeling is larger than its program of uses. Calling this a translation and a matter of concern implies that alternative usage is part of the manual as well, as a mere extension of the program, instead of a shift toward feelings that follow the bent paths of involvement. When a bridge carefully designed by a well-meaning engineer to take us from side A to side B suddenly becomes the focus of local bungee jumpers, such a development can only be the result of a surplus of feeling radiating from the bridge itself. As with the chimpanzee's stick, there is nothing prescribed in the bridge to allow for people to jump off it while attached to elastic cords; on the other hand, neither is it a purely human invention. The bridge, like any other object, spills out many invisible abstractions that can only be met by the feelings of others. Such generosity we cannot term a performance – a subject's enacting of an object's activity – and perhaps not even an affordance[82] – an object's enabling of a subject's activity. It is closer to an offering, a spending, or what Marcel Mauss calls a prestation.[83] An object is not mere activity; it is initiative and has an aim. Even in the most utilitarian object, there is something of a gift that, as Mauss insisted,[84] needs to be reciprocated, needs to be met, not because of social conventions or the fact that the gift passes between subjects but first and foremost because a thing is itself a gift. The stick offers itself, but the chimp in turn must become "stick-like" to be able to retrieve ants from the nest.

So, yes, as Latour says, such translation amounts to an act of composition,[85] though not merely because it is a society of agency and agents but rather because it is felt, and the aim of feeling is beauty and composition. The fact that tools disappear in our hands is due to the gracefulness of action, of the shared action, not because of a Heideggerian subservience of the tool. Yet "disappearance" or "concealment" is really the wrong term. His famous hammer[86] participates in a composition of the most fluid and skillful gestures; it does not disappear because of its submissive nature. This is only logical, because things want to go well. It is often breathtaking to see how delicately cranes and power shovels handle the heaviest loads. All aesthetic relations are postural correspondences between matched sets of points, such as, in the case of the bridge, the point of jumping and the point of tying the cord as much as the body's center of gravity. And such aestheticization of use has direct effects on the organization of human beings. An arbitrary collection of bridge users will never form a group, not even if they see each other every day in the 5:30 traffic jam, but bungee jumpers, by contrast, immediately form close-knit groups, exchanging favorable bridge locations to jump from and organizing collective jumps. To call such clusters of relations networks hardly conveys what occurs: things feel-into us, and we feel-into things. We are definitely entangled, but the concept of entanglement must add more than mere metaphor to the complexity of a network, because however complex it is, Latour's actor-network is still made up of simple black dots ("boxes") interconnected by simple black lines, and if we want to include notions of feeling such as Ruskin's sympathy, James's intimacy and Bergson's interpenetration, this model will be insufficient. The only question is: How do we draw this entanglement?

Generally, to depict an ecosystem as a network of black dots and lines is sufficient, and we find networks illustrated in many books on ecology, often in the shape of what are called food chains or food webs. Each of the agents represents a species, such as "shark," "tuna," or "plankton," and the lines between them represent actions, which do not have to be continuous. The lines are often drawn as arrows, each pointing in a single direction, since sharks eat tuna but not vice versa. Such networks are mostly called complex, not because of their intricacy but because it is impossible to see in such a diagram how the frequency of actions and the actual number of individuals belonging to the species affect one another. To add affect – as would be necessary in assemblage theory – each line would have to be split, because each relation consists of two affects, to eat and to be eaten, like the "cut" and "to be cut" of the knife and the bread.[87] However, in both ways of depicting relations – Latour's assembly network and DeLanda's assemblage meshwork – we still find things related only externally. If things actually have feelings that are both constant ("longing") and variable ("sympathy"), it would mean their feelings were not only experienced by them but by their possible partners as well – in whatever form. Hence, their intensities can link up before their extensities do. *Einfühlung* means one feels what the other feels; one has encountered his or her sphere of feeling and created a sympathetic connection. The fact that one feels the other, as James does when he walks to Memorial Hall, and that things are present outside themselves are what makes the relationship entangled, not merely spatial. The fringes of the table grow into the glass, i.e., the table feels the glass, and the glass feels the table, and the glass longs for the hand to pick it up, but the hand is not there yet; the table longs indeterminately for all kinds of things that are not yet there but are expected. The whole picture is filled with actual elastic feelings. If we wish to draw a diagram of such an interior scene according to entanglement theory, we will need to leave out the black dots for a moment. We can draw a line from the glass zone – a zone that would have to be drawn as dashed, since we are leaving out the representations of objects – into the table zone, loop it back and let the line tie into the glass zone again, entwining with other lines, and then project out and loop back again. And so on. We can draw numerous lines made of only curves of variable curvature – a whole system of relations in which we can hardly tell which line belongs to which zone; to add color would do little to clarify the picture, because colors would disregard the spatial distinctions as well. Again, this does not mean there would be only one single line, as in knitting; rather, there would be dozens of separate threads, some proceeding through many zones, others remaining short and others remaining loose ends.

Funnily enough, if we were to print out our diagram and hang it on the wall, from a distance it would look like one of Latour's actor-networks; we would see dots and lines. If we came a few steps closer, it would start to look like DeLanda's assemblage diagram: we would see dots, but the lines in between would suddenly reveal themselves to be multiple, indicating bidirectional affect as well as unidirectional action. When we came very close, we would see that our diagram was an entangled system of sympathies and longings, with no dots whatsoever, just lines, all curving, shooting in and out of knot stations consisting of all kinds of textile art: braids, knots of every type, loops, crossings and interlacings – a wholly Gothic art of linkages between interiors.

In the terms used at the beginning of this chapter, however, such a diagram captures only the horizontal veil, the labyrinthic structure as merely a cunning machinery, not a collection of embellishments. It is a diagram that visualizes the topology of relations, not the geometry of bodies. Now, such bodies, be they the skins of individuals, the surfaces of their homes or the defensive measures taken by groups or the shapes of a territory, are not all materialized in the same manner, though they are without exception aesthetic. The stripes or colors on an animal's coat, the interwoven blades of grass in a hanging nest, the territorial markings of wolves, birdsong in its infinite variety (about which Charles Hartshorne wrote a wonderful book[88]), the waggle dances of honeybees; all of them exist to evoke feelings in those whom they encounter. To understand these aesthetics, we have to study them as they related to each other, as a cluster or even a knot of elastic feelings all involved with each other. The aesthetics are often described as signs or information, making the waggle dance a mere language (*"Tanzsprache,"* Von Frisch calls it[89]) for the bee's hivemates to decode. But the dance is made of movement and feeling, and the response is one of movement and feeling; it could not be more direct and postural, so why squeeze information and cognition in between? Even animals have been forced to take part in the linguistic turn.

Animals' coat patterns, their grouping styles, their various types of accommodation – they all relate additively to the shape of the animals' territories and how these are marked and defended. In this sense, an animal builds a fully integrated atmosphere in which feelings and space cannot be distinguished: colors, smells, shapes, actions, all patterned together, make up a complex canvas, a three-dimensional installation of pure mood. If pressed to discuss evolution in terms of survival techniques, I would – in a similar vein to Gregory Bateson, who stated (in *Steps to an Ecology of Mind*) that the evolutionary unit should be considered as the "organism plus environment"[90] (not the gene, individual, group or species) – prefer to consider such aesthetic units as the primary candidates: entangled knots of mutual feeling and action, or, in short, units of design. All ecologies are ecologies of design. Such an aesthetic entity relies completely on the strong ties – and weak links – of sympathy and can in itself be considered a design entity, an ambient group made up of smells, colors, songs, animals of every type, vegetation and light, a group completely closed, like an interior, but closed in an organizational sense, not materially by walls and windows.

If we recall the tiled wallpaper of William Morris or the fringed mosaics of William James this is all quite logical, since wholes tend to break up into tiles and parts tend to connect via fabric. Fabricism leads to mosaicism, and mosaics leads to fringes that proceed from one into the other. That is what polymonism entails. We tend to believe that if the environment were only homogeneous and smooth, the brotherhood between things would likewise be continuous, but this is not the case. Everything breaks up *because* it builds relations. For instance, we tend to believe that countries exist only because of the topography of a variegated landscape. Of course, the cracking mechanism is affected by topography and edge conditions, such as the presence of water, but even if it were a smooth Deleuzian desert, we would see a vast pattern of cracks emerge, exactly as in the tessellated structure of dried mud. And why did the mud break up? Because it started out as a whole, as a surface first, a smooth pond of liquid. There is nothing so fascinating as the shapes of countries, and the question of why some are small and others large, or why some are irregularly tessellated while others have smooth, straight borders. We tend to believe that things break up into groups, species and territories because of external conditions, because of the environment, but this is not the case: things break up of their own accord. Countries take tessellated shapes *because* they are connected, because they have relations and exchanges, because they have roads, rivers and railways going from one to the other. Paths, trails, always occur first; animals and humans create lines, create a fabric, and even if those lines cross each other and the crossings grow into villages and the villages into cities, it does not matter: even if the crossings do not substantiate into sedentary nodes, the territories still break up, and the breaks are *perpendicular* to the threads of the fabric. And I would add that the more nodes are connected, the more fracturing we will observe.

For example, when we look at the territories of ants living on the forest floor, as studied by Eldridge Adams,[91] we observe the very same Voronoi patterns of dried mud, the same tessellated structure, but with lines that are dashed and invisible, not materialized in the form of fences or property lines. And such tessellation is not necessarily limited to two-dimensional cracking patterns, either: for instance, the distribution of species of cichlids in Lake Victoria consists of a three-dimensional tessellated structure, more akin to foam than to cracked mud, but again, without visible borders. Only the stripes and colors of the fish are visible, only the furnishing, the *interior decoration* of the territory. Today there are cichlid populations that are pure blue and pure red[92] – what an amazing idea to have all the forces of evolution directed towards a fully aesthetic end. Of course, we humans are hardly capable of distinguishing the fishes' hundreds of shades of red; we can only guess at such incredible ambient richness. Aesthetics always strives at a world of pure nuance. The design of a territory is a direct alternative to the design of a group and the sharing of its colored patterns; it replaces the organization of a group with all types of markers, mostly olfactory; but each kind of territorial design adds up to a single atmosphere – a word that, as we learn from the prolific German philosopher Peter Sloterdijk, contains "sphere" for good reason. If spheres are nested in a three-dimensional space – not unlike oranges packed in a box at the greengrocer's – they do indeed add up into a nested system, like foam, consisting of a four-legged nodal structure.[93] Viewed two-dimensionally, however, the spheres act as circles that, not unlike a group of coins on a table, when packed together take on the tessellated, three-legged nodal structure of a Voronoi pattern. It seems that we can only find interiors rubbing against each other, never exteriors.

Somehow, we habitually conceive of "the environment" as an analogue to the architectural concept of the exterior, similarly to how Heidegger's

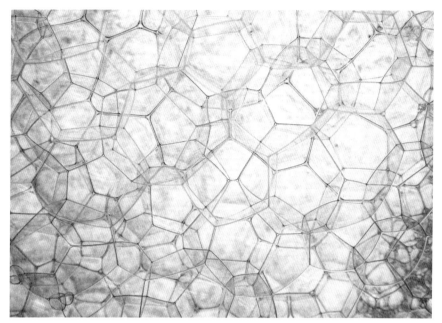

Example of a foam structure.

Welt equates to the "open," which I classified as the final form of the sublime in the previous chapter. But there is no such thing as an environment. Territory has nothing to do with Dasein; the whole crux is that being – as designed and felt – excludes all forms of "there." We, and things, exist in interiors, and these interiors are finite. Jakob von Uexküll's term *Umwelt*[94] ("surrounding world") replaces Heidegger's indistinct sense of the open with a finite set of markers. However, he treats his closed entity mostly as functional, not territorial, and therefore bases it on meaning and signs, far removed from any feeling or correspondence. Only when he studies animals that actively design their environments, such as spiders, does Uexküll switch from semiotics to a compositional concept – quite literally, in fact, by using a vocabulary borrowed from music, with words like "motif," "counterpoint" and "melody," to explain correspondence. For instance, a spider building a web must become "fly-like," a mimetic concept very close to sympathizing, since the spider must feel-into the fly's size and movements to build a successful trap.[95] He describes how the spider "has taken up certain motifs of the fly melody in its bodily composition." The choice of words seems merely metaphorical, if not lyrical, at first, but the spider uses the rhythm of the fly's movements to plot the threads of its web (again, in a direct transfer of movement to structure) – this is nothing like naturalist mimesis but more of an animist metempsychosis.

In its literal meaning, *Umwelt* contrasts directly with the French word *milieu* ("mid-place"), whereas the former emphasizes the environment's circumference, the latter emphasizes its center and interior state, though in Uexküll's terminology they seem much closer. The father of physiology, Claude Bernard, conceptualized a stable state as a *milieu intérieur*, and Georges Canguilhem stated that a milieu was necessary to sustain life, which was "an ensemble of functions that resist death,"[96] a completely Ruskinian concept. Biologist Scott Turner, who considers himself a pupil of Bernard, explains in his important book *The Extended Organism* how many structures built by animals can be viewed as physiological extensions, and often even as external organs. Termite mounds, for instance, function as external lungs, ventilating the underground nest.[97] However, I think we should push the notion of atmosphere beyond one of merely breathing and nourishment into one of feeling, which involves all aspects of the territory, not only its material structures and cunning mechanisms. We should keep in mind that territories are *open interiors*. Not all built structures fit such specific physiological functions. A milieu is never a vague set of circumstances but rather a fully designed system, in which individuals, group formations, and their architectural arrangements, ranging from trails to nests, are wholly interrelated. Yes, "extension" is the correct word, meaning a web of felt relations, not necessarily an externalized physiology. It is the interior milieu that shapes things, not the environment; things are shaped by the felt relations they maintain, not by ones they do not have. Now, to clarify, milieus or atmospheres are built in turn by things, from the inside out, by aggregation, by gathering, not very differently from the interior of a house; but spatially, they are open, with no fixed borders; their atmosphere is sustained purely by decorated things and actions occurring in felt relations. I think we should view ecosystems as architectural interiors, as designed entities of feelings and space, furthermore, we should frame such a concept within Gothic ontology: is the interior capable of sustaining and structuring itself?

Let us go back to our Victorian examples for a moment. When we take a careful look at how Owen Jones created partitions in the Crystal Palace for the Great Exhibition of 1851 by literally hanging carpets bought from every corner of the Empire, recalling exactly Semper's dreamed-of origins of architecture, we can already see an important reversal taking place: hanging carpets replace standing walls. We have to keep in mind, of course, that the Crystal Palace was not a typical architectural interior but more of a construct of the interior of the whole Empire, i.e., the territory. As Sloterdijk explains so well,[98] it is a model of globalism. There is an inherent danger in prestructuring territories, since it severs relations of beauty from relations of construction. When we look at the rise of the Parisian arcades from the same perspective, we find two almost opposite desires being materialized. One is that of the labyrinth: dark *shortcuts* created between Haussmann's sunlit streets of control. At the same time, we see glass roofs suspended between buildings, creating *interior streets*, making the exterior into a conditioned interior, where we observe a similar phenomenon to what occurred in the Crystal Palace: things become pure fragrance and color. In short, when we preconstruct the interior, objects immediately turn into a psychological substance, things in a dream world. Historically, we can observe a direct genealogical line originating at the Crystal Palace, with its massive five-volume catalogue of objects; proceeding to the arcades, inhabited by almost-amorphous Art Nouveau objects, decorated with flowing water plants and drenched in the most exotic fragrances; to the oneiricism of Odilon Redon, the expert of indistinction; to Dalí's surreal objects, modeled from psychoplasm; and to 1960s psychedelia, which painted the bodies of Volkswagen Beetles with flowered Art Nouveau patterns, and the liquid light shows of Pink Floyd concerts. This is the shape things take when they have lost the responsibility for collaborating and structuring the house themselves.

According to Sloterdijk, Walter Benjamin made a crucial error in conceiving of the arcades as more fundamental to modernity than the Crystal Palace.[99] On the one hand, this may be true, not only because the vast Victorian glass building encapsulated the exterior with structure but also because of the way the enclosed objects turned spineless, degenerating back to the unpetrified textile of Semper's origin myth. On the other hand, the arcade embodied the labyrinthic *détournement*, while the Crystal Palace took on the role of the glorious, radiating center of the universe. The French covered street was an urbanism for sleepwalkers saturated with glowing objects far more radical than any World's Fair could ever hope to be. The medieval city had taken its revenge on Baron Haussmann. The message of the Crystal Palace is unambiguous, but that of the arcades is not: there, we still find a world of the gift as much as that of the commodity, of the labyrinth as much as the dome, the Gothic as much as the modern.

Recall Edgar Allan Poe's *The Philosophy of Furniture*, which contains a complete interior description, with the protagonist lying asleep on a sofa, or all the interior descriptions of the Guermantes house by Proust (who deeply admired and even translated Ruskin), so fittingly discussed by Mario Praz[100] – a pure individual memoryscape made up of cabinets, vases, drapes and wallpaper. Art Nouveau shared many sensibilities with the Gothic – it was the final spasm of the neo-Gothic – but, alas, it occurred after the great divide had taken place, after the Joneses and the Morrises had parted ways à la Worringer, one going in the direction of abstract structure and the other going for naturalist empathy. It was a Gothic that had dropped structure in favor of mere ornament. If you cut the ribs of a Gothic cathedral at the top of the vault, they would recoil irregularly, like elastic bands, taking on the shapes of Art Nouveau's whiplashes. A vast transformation has taken place; a whole world of stone has been swapped for the vegetal decoration of the steel and glass house. I have made this argument before,[101] but it is important to do so again here, because the Crystal Palace should be denominated as the anti-cathedral, the anti-mountain: *it leaves things without anything to do*, drifting about in a glass world like tropical fish in an aquarium. In the end, all the aspirations of the arcade are completely buried in the contemporary shopping mall, that vacuum-sealed world without doors in which one moves about without being woken up, guarded by security officers and their German shepherds, surrounded by vast parking lots like tarmac lakes, with shoppers strolling along like latter-day flaneurs who, as Koolhaas has so acutely observed,[102] encounter no obstacles, not even when they change floors, thanks to the invention of the escalator.

Our main question now becomes: Is this our inescapable destiny? One major sign of the times is the fact that environmentalism has so utterly failed in its political mission. When planet earth is turned into a spaceship, as Buckminster Fuller said,[103] into a technical project – which implicitly means a project of the sublime – all the systemic relations between us and every tree in the Amazon identified and mapped, documented daily with live imagery, but not furnished as a collective interior, not as a territory of shared feelings. Why are we no longer capable of building such collective interiors? The problem is a fundamental lack of aesthetics, of a constructed knot of objects acting as stations for feelings. Feelings cannot be mediated; you cannot put them on television. Feelings can only be used to make things. Buildings, vases, cars, cupboards, wallpaper, tables – all our furnishings are things. Images on television do not seem to qualify as things because the fact that they have been fabricated is hidden under such a thick cloak of actuality that they become impossible to live-with. They simply pass by, perishing continuously (in what must be our best model of hell to date.) Advertising is the last resort of artificiality on television, the last remnant of ornament. Regardless of what I have said about Art Nouveau, it did absorb Darwin's peacocks, Haeckel's radiolaria, and Fechner's lilies and dragonflies into its aesthetic – my criticism is merely that it did so only in order to add more gems to the glowing, psychotropic cloth wrapping the interiors of Northern Europe. In contrast to Art Nouveau's velvet drapes, Gottfried Semper's petrified textiles and John Ruskin's silken tracery made use of weaving to construct houses and cities, not just to drape the glass houses the engineers made for us. Art Nouveau had the same problem we do: feelings were no longer allowed to construct things. Construction began to be the exclusive vocation of engineers and politicians, the men of concern. At least the Art Nouveau designers made a serious effort; a hundred years later, we seem completely lost.

Sloterdijk's claim, made in his monumental three-volume work *Sphären*,[104] that limiting Heidegger's *Welt* of the sublime to a manageable size comes down to a question of design, of how we design our lives and bodies (an act he calls *Anthropotechnik*) as well as our interiors, can only be applauded. The phenomenological delusion that we are subjects thrown into the world requires all things that surround us to be mere mediators of an outside no one ever encounters. Sloterdijk is very close to McLuhan on this matter: things do not mediate; they configure the real themselves, creating a reality in which fact and value cannot be distinguished. I could not agree more; it is the direct consequence of saying all things are artifacts. It is only that in spherology facts get overrated compared to values, that it understands the extended interior as a purely technical act, not as an interrelated set of feelings but as a set of supplies and services. As with Latour,[105] for Sloterdijk fabrication does not lead to the aesthetics of fabricism – the Gothic – but only to an excess of engineered facts, of things calculable, and we must re-alize that engineered facts are inherently a question of values: fabrication needs fabricism or else it is either merely a pack of lies (from the viewpoint of facts) or a belief system (from the viewpoint of construction) – and values are by nature aesthetic. It remains conceived from the outside on, the con-struction of an exterior shell, the *domus* as a dome. The sphere is more of a conditioning of design by space than the reverse, and that still means build-ing the sublime, since it is set up as a structure that provides for interiors, a structure of the void that can one day be filled, a world *in vitro*, air-condi-tioned and well-tempered. The great danger is that what starts out as a spherological project turns out immunological, and worse, *turns out to be fully anesthetic* – not only do objects fall into a coma, but we do as well. The sublime as a biospherical glass house is not the answer, even when it is scaled down to the size of an apartment or capsule, because it celebrates the *closed interior* in opposition to that of the territory, which is fundamentally a non-spatial, open interior, with things existing in an open state of conditioning. Not unexpectedly, we find ourselves in a paradoxical situation in which the closed interior of the capsule is oriented to the sublime and the Open, while the open territory of things and animals is closed and merely oriented to itself, which is why it is a project of beauty. Admitted, Sloterdijk's froth of foam is a picturesque volume, on the verge of being amorphous, consisting of a full expression of each unique part. But, that said, it remains within the modernist project of space, of living in the sky, suspended in steel crystals and breathing conditioned air. In this sense, it varies only in degree from Corbusier's *bulle de savon* and Uexküll's *Seifenblase*.

Ruskin's earth veil demonstrates a far deeper insight than Buckminster Fuller's Spaceship Earth. It does not take the biosphere as a mere technical, systemic whole but makes it a system of feelings and sympathies. The veil of strange intermediate being accepts mineral crystals as well as vegetal ribbons, structure as well as ornament, technology as well as art. We should refute technology as a mere *dispositif* of contrivances; we need embellishment as much as cunning. Or, to word it more strongly, Ruskin's veil accepts things only when entwined; feelings create entangled webs, and webs can only emerge through felt relations. And because things – buildings, clouds, teapots, trees in the Amazon – are things of beauty, they have absolute value. Absolute, intrinsic value: this is the consequence of fabricism, because beauty is the end (it is made of what it is). A "politics of nature" will never suffice: if we want to find a way to live (and to survive) we need a wholesale construction of nature, not merely on technical and physiological grounds but on aesthetic grounds. I fully accept the fact that nature and technology have become entangled categories, but that should not simply lead to a technologization of nature. Of course, we cannot rely on the mere naturalization of technology (biomimetics, biotechnics, sustainability) either – I accept that as readily – but the reverse is as dangerous, because if we can only come to terms with nature as part of our technical, systemic interior, it will end up fully domesticated.

If we were to travel back to the days before monotheism, with its pure, pristine and paradisaical nature, we would encounter various forms of animism,[106] a pre-spherological religion (though it would be more correct to call it a religious practice). At least animism makes no distinction between things of culture and things of nature, since all the organic and inorganic is to some degree alive and capable of sympathy. Ruskin, who is not an animist, but something close, a vitalist, is not afraid to introduce a self-referential value system in *Unto This Last*:

> *Valor*, from *valere*, to be well or strong (ὑγιαίνω); – strong, *in*

life (if a man), or valiant; strong, *for* life (if a thing), or valuable. To be "valuable," therefore, is to "avail towards life." A truly valuable or availing thing is that which leads to life with its whole strength. In proportion as it does not lead to life, or as its strength is broken, it is less valuable; in proportion as it leads away from life, it is unvaluable or malignant.[107]

When we read these words a century and a half later, they offer us a concept that actually allows us not to simply accept the entanglement of nature and technology as a matter of concern, i.e., an engineering problem, but to see it as a matter of life (and death), and in Ruskin's cosmology, this immediately means a matter of care and beauty. In vitalism, life is larger than technology, culture or nature, separately or together. Only when a thing – being either natural or cultural, or any hybrid mixture of both – is "life-availing" does it have such unmarketable value: "an intrinsic value developed by a vital power" as Ruskin states in *Munera Pulveris*.[108] As stipulated earlier, I do not think Ruskin is a vitalist in the sense of Hans Driesch or Caspar Wolff, but he tries to develop an aesthetic philosophy of life, one closer to those of Lipps and Whitehead, that consists of finite, spiritual encounters that do not tap into a vast life force but merely into the other's life. Only beautiful things have intrinsic value; it is an aesthetic, constructivist power, not primarily moral or religious. We do not need to disentangle anything; on the contrary, the earth veil is all about entangling. All we have to concentrate on is what the hybrid contributes to life. So, for example, when Monsanto promotes the spread of monocultures,[109] it should be fought relentlessly. But when a state environmental department decides to remove all the fir trees from a forest because they are not indigenous, it should be fought just as hard. Life is not something stored in biological creatures; hybrids or bastards can be more alive than the purified versions, naturally, because they are imperfect, wild and radically picturesque.

The roles have reversed, however: nature, that old source of the sublime, now seems overwhelmed by technology, our new reservoir of forces seemingly untamable and savage. As I said in the previous chapter, we absolutely need the sublime, the crystallized world of forces, though not to structure things but as a datum, as a grounding for productivity. We need *the sublime as the ground, not as the sky* – not as what things should strive for but as what they should parasitically plug into and grow away from, as we discussed in relation to William Robinson's wild gardens and Ruskin's cottage with a mountain's profile. But we have been uprooted forever, displaced and scattered; nothing can change that. So, if we cannot go home again and refuse to live in the sky with the other outcasts, we need a new wilderness where things can flourish. We need to reconfigure the ground and our territories – as always. The horizontality between things has to be constructed over and over.

I think that ultimately this is what technology is: since we create our own nature, we human beings need to be able to harvest beautiful things from a ground, i.e., from technological fields. We construct out of what we *can* construct. That is why in nature it is a complicated matter to give networks an ontological status, but in the case of us humans, networks have to be built. Technology is not simply the means to the made, it is the construction of a vast horizontal plane of making. Without going so far as to declare the Internet as our new ground, it is the first attempt to create such a ground without anyone being able to claim ownership. In nature, the earth veil and the wall veil, i.e., productivity and products, form a cyclical, reciprocal system, in which we can never separate the sublime from beauty or structure from ornament; we humans are obliged to create a separate field of productivity. That is why that operation has proven to be so dangerous, because the actual ecology of things, when it is dislocated, can end up being realized at the expense of other things. Iron Age attempts to squeeze metal from the earth seem more akin to our contemporary situation than the vast machine parks of the nineteenth century, which were inherently based on scarcity and competition, not affluence and generosity.

I do not think the Internet is particularly modern, or in any way related to space, I think it is a deeply Gothic project – not because the Web is about veins and fibers and the Gothic loves fibrous systems but because *it interrelates work and aesthetics.* In contrast to television, the Web is there to make things. Today it still acts chiefly as though it is part of media culture, or worse, visual culture – still part of that separation between talking about things and making things – but there is nothing inherent in its structure to make it do so; it is mere habit. On the contrary, when all mediation has evaporated, it could emerge as a distributed, generalized factory, like Schelling's nature, a platform of productivity – pure abstraction that strives to produce real things. The Internet is not going to change space or the layout of cities much, nor "turn urbanism irrelevant," as McLuhan said,[110] but things will come into being differently, via a kind of electronic medievalism. I will not repeat my earlier examples of the *Tangle Carpet*© and *iCoke*© here – I am sure a hundred better ones could be thought of – but the shift from craft to design, turning design into the new craft, will, like fabrication, take place more and more on the Web, though for now design as the new craft lacks any notion of style or expertise and is still flooded with images, news and opinion, the three worst things it could have inherited from television culture. The Web does not yet grasp its own Gothic heritage.

I long for the day when we can see objects forming, like pools of mud, flowers on a wall or clouds in the sky, as pure products in a context of pure productivity, without any intermediaries. There will be no desires, no opinions, no critics, no designers, just pure flourishing.

acknowledgments

Parts of this book began developing more than five years ago, when I started my program at Georgia Tech and was given the opportunity to organize symposia and publish books on what I call Research & Design. The first symposium, in 2007, brought me back into contact with Manuel DeLanda, whom I had first met years before in Amsterdam when he gave a five-hour lecture, pacing back and forth across the stage without stopping. Since then, he has delivered many more lectures at V2_ in Rotterdam, and I, like many, have learned a lot from him. The same goes for Brian Massumi, who slept in my *Vision Machine* installation in Nantes, France, and got me to read William James and Charles Sanders Peirce. Through the organizing of another symposium at V2_ called *The Ecology of Design* – which became the title of this book's final chapter – I met Caroline van Eck, whose *Organicism in Nineteenth-Century Architecture* had put me on the track of John Ruskin. Another speaker there was Henk Oosterling, elaborating on his famous idea of "Dasein as design" – something that took me two years to figure out.

The librarians and assistants at various collections provided me with all possible help, especially some at private organizations that must remain anonymous. I would like to thank George Landow, who read an early draft of Chapter One and kindly commented on it. At Georgia Tech, I had the good fortune to discuss this book almost page by page with Stuart Romm, who added many valuable insights. And I extend special thanks to the people at V2_, who have been an enormous support throughout the years – first of all, Joke Brouwer, who not only designed this book but also read every draft, adding comments, asking questions, and relentlessly removing my quirky and often testy remarks. If any remain, it is my fault, not hers. My gratitude also goes out to Arjen Mulder, author of many books on media art and interactivity, who read several versions and commented extensively. Finally, I would like to thank my copy editor Laura Martz, who had the superhuman task of correcting an English that is only spoken high above the Atlantic, since I fly back and forth between the United States and the Netherlands with such frequency that neither my English nor my Dutch can be called fully comprehensible.

list of illustrations

p. 6   John Ruskin. *Entrance to the South Transept of Rouen Cathedral*, 1854. Graphite, black chalk, pen and ink and wash, with some white on paper, laid down. 49.3 x 32 cm. ©The Fitzwilliam Museum, Cambridge.

p. 15   John Ruskin. *Ornaments from Rouen, St. Lô, and Venice*. Plate I from *The Seven Lamps of Architecture*, 1880 edition (engraving by R. P. Cuff), orig. 1849. 30 x 44.2 cm. *Works*, VIII: f.p.52, r. Birmingham Museums and Art Gallery, Birmingham.

p. 23   Robert W. Billings. Three examples of rose windows with their corresponding geometrical diagrams. Plates III, XXXVII, XLIII from *The Power of Form* (London: Blackwood and Sons, 1851).

p. 27   John Ruskin. *Plans of Piers*. Plate II from *The Stones of Venice*, Vol. 1: Foundations, 1851 (engraving by R. P. Cuff). *Works*, IX: f.p.130, r.

p. 28   W. A. Bentley and W. J. Humphreys. Example from *Snow Crystals* (New York: Dover Publications, 1962, orig. 1931).

p. 37   Second initial page of the Gospel of Matthew, or the *Chi Rho* page from the Lindisfarne Gospels (680–720 AD), folio 29. The British Library, London.

p. 39   John Ruskin. *South-West Porch of St. Wulfran, Abbeville*, 1848. Graphite on paper. 32.5 x 15 cm. Private Collection.

p. 43   John Everett Millais. *Design for a Gothic window*, 1853. Charcoal, gouache and watercolor on paper. 213 x 277 cm. Private Collection.

p. 46   Eugène Viollet-le-Duc. *Maçonnerie*. Plate 22 from the twelfth lecture in *Entretiens sur l'architecture* (Paris, 1864).

p. 47   Gloucester Cathedral, view of the south cloisters (1351). Photo by the author.

p. 64   Plans of Bourges (top) and Salisbury cathedral (bottom).

p. 73   Claude Monet. *Rouen Cathedral (The Portal, Morning Fog)*, 1894. Oil on canvas. 101 x 66 cm. Museum Folkwang, Essen.

p. 79   John Ruskin. *The Cervin, from the East, and North-East*. Plate 38 from *Modern Painters*, Vol. IV, Part V: Of Mountain Beauty (engraving by J. C. Armytage), 1856.

p. 84   John Everett Millais. *Mariana*, 1851. Oil on wood. 59.7 x 49.5 cm. Tate Gallery, London.

p. 88   Owen Jones. *Female Head from New Zealand, in the Museum, Chester*. Ill. on p. 14 from *The Grammar of Ornament* (London: Day and Son, 1856).

p. 100   Example of cracked mud pattern. Digitally reworked photo by the author.

p. 104   Owen Jones. *Persian Nº 2*. Plate XLV from *The Grammar of Ornament* (London: Day and Son, 1856).

p. 105   Owen Jones. *Celtic Nº 1*. Plate LXIII from *The Grammar of Ornament* (London: Day and Son, 1856).

p. 108   Owen Jones. *Savage Tribes Nº 3*. Plate III from *The Grammar of Ornament* (London: Day and Son, 1856).

p. 109   Owen Jones. *Moresque Nº 5*. Plate XLIII from *The Grammar of Ornament* (London: Day and Son, 1856).

p. 112   Example of Penrose tiling, quasi-crystal structure made up of kites and darts. Digitally reworked image.

p. 115   John Ruskin. *Abstract Lines*. Plate VII from *The Stones of Venice*, Vol. 1: Foundations, 1851. *Works*, IX: f.p.268, r.

p. 116   John Starkie Gardner. *Hingework at Montréal, Yonne*. Fig. 26 from *Ironwork*, Part I (London: Chapman and Hall, 1893).

p. 118   Detail of Gothic hingework at Salisbury Cathedral (mid-13th century). Photo by the author.

p. 121   J. H. Dearle for Morris & Co. *Design for the Golden Lily wallpaper*, 1897. Watercolor, graphite and ink on paper. 34.3 x 27.3 cm. The Huntington Library, Art Collections, and Botanical Gardens, San Marino, CA.

p. 124   William Morris for Morris & Co. *Pimpernel* wallpaper (1876). Digitally reworked image from Victoria and Albert Museum, London.

p. 125   William Morris for Morris & Co. *Acanthus* wallpaper (1875). Digitally reworked image from Victoria and Albert Museum, London.

p. 127   George Bain. Example of a method of construction for the Book of Kells. Plate R from *Celtic Art: The Methods of Construction* (1945). By kind permission of Stuart Titles Ltd.

p. 153   Gallery of a Dyak-chief's house, decorated with headhunter's trophies. North-east Borneo. Photo: J. Jongejans (date unknown, probably mid 1920s). Collectie Tropenmuseum, Amsterdam.

p. 154   Drystone wall, Cotswolds, United Kingdom (1980s). Digitally reworked photo by the author.

p. 166   Étienne-Jules Marey. Chronomatography of a running horse (1885). Collège de France, Paris.

p. 167   Étienne-Jules Marey. Analysis according to the "graphic method" of the chronomatography of a running horse (1885). Collège de France, Paris.

p. 185   J. H. Dearle and William Morris for Morris & Co. *Bullerswood* carpet, 1889. Hand-knotted with woolen pile on a cotton warp. Victoria and Albert Museum, given by J. Sanderson.

p. 186   Eugène Viollet-le-Duc. *Salle Voutée, fer et maçonnerie*. Plate 18 from the twelfth lecture in *Entretiens sur l'architecture* (Paris, 1864).

p. 187   Eugène Viollet-le-Duc. *Modifications apportées à un sommet*. Fig 36*bis* from *Le Massif du Mont Blanc* (Paris: Baudry, 1876).

p. 193   Shoowa Kuba cloths with examples from loop (top row), woot (middle row) and cross (bottom row) patterns (20th century). Approx. 53 x 53 cm. Cut-pile embroidered raffia, natural dyes. Photos by the author.

p. 196   Titian. *Venus of Urbino*, 1538. Oil on canvas. 119 x 165 cm. Uffizi Museum, Florence.

p. 197   Yves Klein. Photo of a performance June 5, 1958 in the apartment of Robert Godet in Paris. In March 1960 this experiment became the series at the Galerie Internationale d'Art Contemporaine titled *Antropométries*.

p. 233   John Ruskin. *Moss and Wild Strawberry*, 1873. Graphite and traces of bodycolor on gray-blue paper. 54.1 x 37.6 cm. The Ashmolean Museum, Oxford.

p. 236   Alfred Parsons. *Colonies of Poet's Narcissus and Broad-Leaved Saxifrage*. Illustration on p. 93 from William Robinson, *The Wild Garden* (London: John Murray, 1870).

p. 238   Alfred Parsons. *Cheddar Pink, Saxifrage, And Ferns, on cottage wall at Mells, Somerset*. Illustration on p. 115 from William Robinson, *The Wild Garden* (London: John Murray, 1870).

p. 239   Alfred Parsons. *Tiger Lilies in Wild Garden at Great Tew*. Illustration on p. 135 from William Robinson, *The Wild Garden* (London: John Murray, 1870).

p. 241   Exploded view of a 1970s one-cylinder moped engine.

p. 244   Vincent van Gogh. *A Pair of Shoes*, 1886. Oil on Canvas. 37.5 x 45 cm. Van Gogh Museum, Amsterdam (Vincent van Gogh Stichting).

p. 247   John Ruskin. Mountain-cottage diagram. Fig. 30 from *Modern Painters*, Vol. IV, Part V: Of Mountain Beauty, 1856. *Works*, XI: 223.

p. 290   Robert Kretschmer and Alfred Brehm. *Paradisea rubra, male*. Fig. 47 from Charles Darwin, *The Descent of Man, and Selection in Relation to Sex*, Vol. 2. (London: John Murray, 1871).

p. 303   Robert Kretschmer and Alfred Brehm. *Spathura underwoodi, male and female*. Fig. 49 from Charles Darwin, *The Descent of Man, and Selection in Relation to Sex*, Vol. 2. (London: John Murray, 1871).

p. 324   Example of a foam structure. Digitally reworked photo.

notes

1. the digital nature of gothic

1. Where possible, I will reference the titles of John Ruskin's original books in the text, but when quoting I will use the standard edition, *The Works of John Ruskin*, Library Edition, eds. E. T. Cook and Alexander Wedderburn, 39 vols. (London: George Allen, 1903–12), abbreviated in the endnotes as *Works,* with reference to the volume and pages. The three volumes of *The Stones of Venice* correspond to volumes IX, X and XI of the library edition. The essay "The Nature of Gothic" is the sixth chapter of the second volume of *Stones* (X: 180–269). The Ruskin Foundation in Brantwood has issued a CD-ROM version of *The Works of John Ruskin.*

2. John Ruskin, *The Nature of Gothic: A Chapter of The Stones of Venice* (printed at the Kelmscott Press, Hammersmith and published by G. Allen, London, 1892).

3. Augustus Welby Northmore Pugin, *Contrasts or a parallel between the noble edifices of the fourteenth and fifteenth centuries, and similar buildings of the present day; shewing the present decay of taste; Accompanied by appropriate Text* (Salisbury, 1836).

4. Wilhelm Worringer, *Formprobleme der Gotik* (München: R. Piper & Co., 1912). Translated in English as *Form in Gothic* for G. P. Putnam (1927), later revised and introduced by Herbert Read (New York: Schocken Books, 1957).

5. For instance, in: Gilles Deleuze, *Francis Bacon: The Logic of Sensation* (London: Continuum, 2003), 108, 129–30, and Gilles Deleuze and Félix Guattari, *A Thousand Plateaus,* trans. Brian Massumi (London: Athlone Press, 1987), 495–99.

6. Henri Focillon, *The Art of the West,* Volume Two: *Gothic Art* (London: Phaidon, 1963).

7. Hans Jantzen, *Die Gotik des Abendlandes* (Köln: DuMont, 1962).

8. Paul Frankl, *The Gothic: Literary Sources and Interpretation through Eight Centuries* (Princeton: Princeton University Press, 1960), 557–62.

9. For an extensive discussion of the differences between Jones and Ruskin, see the next chapter.

10. Ruskin, *Works,* X: 203.

11. Not many Ruskin scholars have made this assumption, and I would have to write a separate chapter to make the hypothesis more convincing. One would first need to figure out how often Ruskin makes use of the word "vital" (though he never mentions "vitalism" or the "vitalist"), compare the different occurrences – vital beauty in aesthetics, vital power in plants, vital energy in the Gothic, vital force in organisms, and the vitality of a body or of a nation, etc. – and then reconstruct his broader concept of life, which would lead from aesthetics to political economy, explaining how this vitalism inherently connects ethics and aesthetics. And then finally one would need to trace the typical teleological view of life as a creative driving force producing animate as well as inanimate form. I will follow these three steps throughout this book, but in a distributed and fragmented fashion. One of the outstanding books arguing for a relationship between Ruskin's thought and vitalism is Wolfgang Kemp's *The Desire of My Eyes: The Life and Work of John Ruskin* (New York: Noonday Press, 1992), 354 and passim.

12. Ruskin, *Works*, XI: 227.
13. Ibid., X: 214.
14. Ibid., X: 260.
15. The most famous such argument among Ruskin scholars is John Unrau's "Ruskin, the Workman and the Savageness of the Gothic," in: Robert Hewison, *New Approaches to Ruskin* (London: Routledge & Kegan Paul, 1981), 33–50.
16. Quoted from: Alain Erlande-Brandenburg, *The Cathedral Builders of the Middle Ages* (London: Thames and Hudson, 1995), 61.
17. Ibid., 78–80. "In the south transept of Reims Cathedral, on the east wall of the triforium is a drawing of the inner side of the central west portal as executed." Tracings and incisions in stone also remain in the floor of the mason's loft at York Minster; see: Philip Ball, *Universe of Stone: A Biography of Chartres Cathedral* (New York: HarperCollins, 2008), 186.
18. Villard de Honnecourt, *The Sketchbook of Villard de Honnecourt*, ed. Theodore Bowie (Westport: Greenwood Press, 1982).
19. William Hogarth, *The Analysis of Beauty*, introduced by Ronald Paulson (New Haven: Yale University Press, 1997); see, for instance, p. 28: "I mean here … a composed variety; for variety uncomposed, and without design, is confusion and deformity." See also note 45, Chapter Two, and, more extensively, notes 3, 4 and 5, Chapter Four.
20. Ruskin, *Works*, X: 208.
21. Frankl devotes much attention to the emergence of the rib in *Gothic Architecture*, explaining it as a feature that arose during the groin vault's development into the ribbed vault. He does not, however, address its position between structural and ornamental, and about how its suspended status can function as a tool of variety. See: *Gothic Architecture* (London: Penguin, 1962, republished by Yale University Press, 2000), 41–50.
22. Such as we find, for instance, in: Robert William Billings, *The Power of Form* (Edinburgh: William Blackwood and Sons, 1851).
23. With these names, we should again mention Paul Frankl, who, in *The Gothic: Literary Sources and Interpretation through Eight Centuries*, dedicates some positive words to Worringer's ideas (pp. 669–80), and, in *Gothic Architecture*, frequently makes use of the notion of empathy. Rudolf Arnheim devotes a chapter to Worringer in *New Essays on the Psychology of Art* (Berkeley: University of California Press, 1986), 50–62. Likewise, Carl-Gustav Jung discusses Worringer's ideas in *Psychological Types* (Princeton: Princeton University Press, 1976), 289–99.
24. Wilhelm Worringer, *Form in Gothic* (New York: Schocken Books, 1957), 40.
25. Karl Lamprecht, *Initial-Ornamentik des VIII. bis XIII. Jahrhunderts* (Leipzig: Alphons Dürr Verlag, 1882).
26. Wilhelm Worringer, *Form in Gothic* (New York: Schocken Books, 1957), 41. As is well known, Gilles Deleuze often made use of Worringer's "vitalized geometry" and "Gothic line," for instance, as noted earlier, in: *Francis Bacon: The Logic of Sensation* and *A Thousand Plateaus*.
27. Ibid., 41.
28. See: David Channell, *The Vital Machine* (New York: Oxford University Press, 1991). A similar argument has been made more recently, and more powerfully, by John Johnston in his *The Allure of Machinic Life* (Cambridge, Mass.: MIT Press, 2008).
29. W. A. Bentley and W. J. Humphreys, *Snow Crystals* (New York, Dover Publications, 1962, orig. 1931).

30. Ruskin, *Works*, X: 178–79.
31. Ernst Gombrich, *The Sense of Order: A Study in the Psychology of Decorative Art* (London: Phaidon, 2006), 42. A few pages later, he relates Ruskin directly to Worringer and empathy (46).
32. As Henri Bergson puts it in *Creative Evolution* (New York: Dover Publications, 1998, orig. English translation 1911), 89.
33. Robert Willis, *Remarks on the Architecture of the Middle Ages, Especially of Italy* (Cambridge: Pitt Press, 1835), as cited by John Ruskin in *The Seven Lamps of Architecture*.
34. Ruskin also compared illuminated books to Gothic cathedrals in his autobiography, *Praeterita*: "For truly a well-illuminated missal is a fairy cathedral full of painted windows, bound together to carry in one's pocket, with the music and the blessing of all its prayers besides" (XXXV: 491).
35. Ruskin, *Works*, XIX: 258–59. We find a slightly similar line of thought in John Hayman's "Towards the Labyrinth: Ruskin's Lectures as Slade Professor of Art" in: Robert Hewison, *New Approaches to Ruskin* (London: Routledge & Kegan Paul, 1981), 111–24. Ruskin's love-hate relationship with the Flamboyant demands extensive study, though in a more historically oriented book. One angle would be to investigate his comparisons to webs and fabric (see note 10, Chapter Two), while the other angle would focus on its supposed relationship to death, which Ruskin assumes in his lecture "The Flamboyant Architecture of the Valley of the Somme" (XIX: 269–77), illustrating it with his drawings of frost-bitten oak leaves and many of Dürer's engravings, which, according to him, exhibit an excess of flames, thorns and curls. For Ruskin both aspects are fundamentally connected, since fabric when it is too flexible shifts from delicacy to weakness, and such weakness easily leads to a taste for death (ibid., 261), as in Holbein's *The Body of the Dead Christ in the Tomb* from 1521 (ibid., 273). Ruskin tries to draw a line between the typical Gothic ossification of vegetal flexibility on the one hand and the insincere (ibid., 262) adaptation of the *image* of textile by stone on the other. However, in making such a clear-cut distinction, he does not distinguish sufficiently between the *structure* and the image of textile. My view is that the Gothic – be it early, middle or late – always concentrates on the structural (and configurational), while the Baroque focuses on the image, on the theater of folds. See also the discussion at the end of this chapter distinguishing between fold and rib.
36. Ruskin, *Works*, XVII: 25–42.
37. The best discussions in a similar vein of Ruskin's views on political economy are: James Clark Sherburne, *John Ruskin, or the Ambiguities of Abundance* (Cambridge, Mass.: Harvard University Press, 1972), and: P. D. Anthony, *John Ruskin's Labour* (Cambridge: Cambridge University Press, 1983).
38. Ruskin compared cusps to thistle leaves. See, for instance, the passage in *Seven Lamps* (VIII: 122) in which he refers to the St. Lô example of a decorated finial (Plate I, "Ornaments from Rouen, St. Lô, and Venice," ill. p. 15), in which four thistle leaves sprout from the circular bottom to distribute the thorny endpoints of each leaf over the body of the finial including delineating its square top. The coordination of the thorns is extraordinary – making the veins in each leaf become continuous with the next leaf – and clearly structures the variable form of the finial. See also note 48, Chapter Two.
39. "[W]hich the knights of Nicopolis had to cut off in order to be able to flee," as Huizinga adds in *The Autumn of the Middle Ages* (University of Chicago Press, 1996, orig. 1919: 302).

40. Henri Focillon, *The Art of the West, Volume Two: Gothic Art* (London: Phaidon, 1963), 139–57.

41. John Everett Millais, in two separate letters to William Holman Hunt and Charles Collins, as quoted from: Mary Lutyens, *Millais and the Ruskins* (New York: Vanguard Press, 1967), 80–82. The months after the trip Millais turned his sketch into a painting of a much larger size, with the intention Ruskin could use it for the Edinburgh lectures in November of that year, but he never did and in *Lectures on Architecture and Painting* (XII: 13–164) we don't find any reference to it. See also: J. Mordaunt Crook, "Ruskinian Gothic," in: *The Ruskin Polygon,* eds. John Dixon Hunt and Faith Holland (Manchester: Manchester University Press), 65–93.

42. William Morris, *Gothic Architecture: A Lecture for the Arts and Crafts Exhibition Society* (Hammersmith: Kelmscott Press, 1893).

43. Ruskin, *Works*, X: 239.

44. Ibid., X: 240.

45. Eugène Emmanuel Viollet-le-Duc, *Discourses on Architecture*, trans. Benjamin Brucknall (New York: Grove Press, 1959), esp. Lecture XII.

46. Pol Abraham, *Viollet-le-Duc et le rationalisme médiéval* (Paris: Vincent, Fréal et Cie., 1934).

47. In his *Believing and Seeing*, Roland Recht even considers Mies van der Rohe a direct descendant of Gothicism (Chicago: University of Chicago Press, 2008), 20–21.

48. Viollet-le-Duc, *Discourses*, again, esp. Lecture XII with its proposals to replace stone buttresses with iron rods and columns in several buildings, such as a 3,000-seat hall.

49. Richard Sennett, *The Craftsman* (New Haven: Yale University Press, 2008).

50. In: *L'échange symbolique et la mort* (Paris: Gallimard, 1976), 187–89.

51. A similar argument is made by Malcolm McCullough in his *Abstracting Craft: The Practical Digital Hand* (Cambridge, Mass.: MIT Press, 1997). Two major concepts explain the affinity of digital manipulation with craft. The first is *dexterity*: anyone watching a 3D modeler at work in architectural or game design (not to mention the film industry) will immediately notice the resemblance to glassblowing and iron forging in the continuous rotation of the object, the continuous zooming and clicking of the left and right mouse buttons with the right hand, the continuous keyboard control with the left hand, the fluent hand-eye coordination, the stepwise progressive techniques of deforming and cutting, and so on. The second is the fact that both work with *flexible rules*; in craft, rules must be flexible because materials are not homogeneous, while in digital design, rules are inherently flexible because of their configurational and parametric nature. Rules are always methodological and never formal, and the final forms result from techniques, not from blueprints. In *The Architecture of Continuity* (V2_Publishing, 2008) I have elaborated on the similarities between digital splines and the wooden splines used in naval architecture design and argued that the oft-made comparison between digital and clay modeling is deeply flawed. There is more interactivity between the artisan-modeler and the object than, for instance, between the artist and the drawing.

52. Wilhelm Worringer, *Form in Gothic* (New York: Schocken Books, 1957), 42.

53. Henry Thomas Colebrooke, "On Presenting the Gold Medal of the Astronomical Society to Charles Babbage," *Memoirs of the Astronomical Society* 1 (1825), 509–10.

54. Ada Lovelace, as quoted in: P. Morrison and E. Morrison, *Charles Babbage and his Calculating Machines* (New York: Dover, 1961). See also: George B. Dyson, *Darwin*

Among the Machines: the Evolution of Global Intelligence (Reading, Mass.: Perseus Books, 1997), 38–43.

55. Charles Babbage, *The Exposition of 1851* (London: John Murray, 1851), 49. See also Joseph Bizup's excellent *Manufacturing Culture: Vindications of Early Victorian Industry* (Charlottesville: University of Virginia Press, 2003).

56. Ibid., 49.

57. Adrian Stokes, *Stones of Rimini* (New York: Schocken Books, 1969), Chapter Four.

58. Comte de Georges-Louis Leclerc Buffon, "Histoire naturelle des animaux," in: *Oeuvres Complètes*, vol. 3 (Paris, 1885), 450.

59. Gilbert Simondon, *L'individu et sa genèse physico-biologique* (Paris: Presses Universitaires de France, 1964), 41–42. Often cited by Gilles Deleuze, as in: *Francis Bacon: The Logic of Sensation* (London: Continuum, 2003), 140n20.

60. Erik Davies, *Techgnosis* (New York: Harmony Books, 1998).

61. Ruskin, *Works*, XVIII: 233–40 and 346.

62. Ibid., VIII: 236.

63. Gottfried Semper, *Style in the Technical and Tectonic Arts; or, Practical Aesthetics,* trans. Harry Mallgrave and Michael Robinson (Los Angeles: Getty Publications, 2004, orig. 1860), 463 n381. A similar quote on page 80 reads: "In just the same way, Gothic architecture was the lapidary transformation of the Scholastic philosophy of the twelfth and thirteenth centuries."

64. Erwin Panofsky, *Gothic Architecture and Scholasticism* (New York: Meridian Books, 1951). Perhaps Panofsky also read Johan Huizinga, the celebrated Dutch historian, who in his *The Autumn of the Middle Ages* (1996: 269. The English translation originates from 1924) makes a statement that is closer to Panofsky's argumentation than Worringer's: "The foundation is furnished in both instances by that architectural idealism which the Scholastics call realism: the need to separate each insight and conceive of it as an individual entity and then to link the entities into hierarchical units and to continuously erect temples and cathedrals with them …" The first part is certainly true, but the act of linking does not necessarily lead to hierarchies.

65. Wilhelm Worringer, *Form in Gothic* (New York: Schocken Books, 1957), 168.

66. Ibid., 169.

67. Alan Turing, "Computing Machinery and Intelligence," *Mind*, 59 (1950), 433–60.

68. See: Martin Tweedale, *Scotus vs. Ockham – A Medieval Dispute over Universals*, 2 vols. (Lewiston: Edwin Mellen Press, 1999), and: John Duns Scotus, *Ordinatio* I, d. 3, p. 3, q. 1, n360.

69. Gilles Deleuze, *The Fold: Leibniz and the Baroque*, trans. Tom Conley (Minneapolis: University of Minnesota Press, 1993).

70. William Paley, *Natural Theology* (London: Faulder et al., 1813, orig. 1802), 1. We will return to this famous allegory at several points in this book.

71. Erwin Panofsky, *Studies in Iconology: Humanistic Themes in the Art of the Renaissance* (New York: Harper & Row, 1967, orig. 1939). Iconology is the application of the content of Neoplatonic and religious Renaissance art to all other art: the artwork is viewed as a carrier of meaning, not as an act of construction or method. The construction of a painting or a cathedral is not even close to being linguistic or following linguistic thinking, and as a result, Panofsky fails to account for the existence of beauty.

72. Alfred Haddon, *Evolution in Art* (London: Walter Scott, 1895), which makes many references to Semper's *Der Stil*.

73. Henri Focillon, *The Life of Forms of Art*, trans. Charles Hogan and George Kubler (New York: Wittenborn, 1948, republished by Zone Books, 1992), 102.
74. As theorized for modernism by Colin Rowe and Robert Slutzky in: "Transparency: Literal and Phenomenal" (*Perspecta*, Vol. 8, 1963), 45–54.
75. Morris writes of "Gothic or organic Architecture" and therefore equates the two. See: *Gothic Architecture: A Lecture for the Arts and Crafts Exhibition Society* (Hammersmith: Kelmscott Press, 1893).

2. the matter of ornament

1. Adolf Loos, *Ornament and Crime, Selected Essays*, ed. Adolf Opel, trans. Michael Mitchell (Riverside: Ariadne Press, 1998).
2. This book would perhaps have been improved if the first chapter had traced the transformation of Ruskin's explorations of geology, including the whole nineteenth-century debate around the topic, rising up from the volcanic center of the Earth to Ruskin's central concept of mountains – his "mountain gloom" – and the Swiss Alps, moving past Bruno Taut's glowing crystals, proceeding slowly down into France and the origins of the Gothic, making brief visits to the dreamt cathedrals of Hugo, Huysmans and Proust, and then crossing the Atlantic to Hugh Ferris's New York and ending with Cyrus Pinkney, the imaginary architect of Gotham City. The second chapter would then have been "The Digital Nature of Gothic," and so on, and we would have ended with the biosphere in the final chapter, "The Ecology of Design." That was not to be, however: instead, much of the geological argument is dispersed throughout the book. As we will see again in this chapter, Ruskin is a radical vitalist; he does not apply vitalism to living creatures, as biologists like Wolff and Driesch did, but first and foremost to stone. Stone is alive; becoming alive deep within the earth, it works its way up to the crust, where it turns into mountains and architecture. We should always keep in mind that the stones of Venice are a geologist's stones, registering forces and accumulating time and memories, which is why Ruskin so fascinated Marcel Proust.
3. Ruskin, *Works*, IX: 85–90.
4. Ibid., VI: 216–319.
5. Ernst Gombrich, *The Sense of Order: A Study in the Psychology of Decorative Art* (London: Phaidon, 2006), 42.
6. Ruskin, *Works*, IX: 86.
7. Ibid., IX: 88.
8. Ibid., IX: 88.
9. Benoit Mandelbrot, *The Fractal Geometry of Nature* (New York: Freeman and Company, 1983), 24: "A Mies van der Rohe is a scalebound throwback to Euclid, while a high period Beaux-Arts building is rich in fractal aspects."
10. Ruskin, *Works*, X: 262 and 264. Ruskin always struggled with the Flamboyant, though at a certain point, in 1868, returning to Abbeville after many years, he played with the idea of writing a *Stones of Abbeville* (XIX: xli). Sometimes he compared the style of the late Gothic to "cobwebs" (VIII: 92), "sapling trees" (XXII: 188) or "sculptured flames" (X: 233). Paul Walton (*Master Drawings by John Ruskin*, 75–80) rightly draws our attention to this ambiguity, calling it "both striking and ironic," since the drawings,

though few in number when compared to those of the Venetian Gothic, are so obviously among Ruskin's best. At a certain point, recalling his visits to the Flamboyant St. Wulfran in Abbeville, Ruskin writes: "One great part of the pleasure, however, depended on an idiosyncrasy which extremely wise people do not share, – my love of all sorts of filigree and embroidery, from hoarfrost to the high clouds. The intricacies of virgin silver, of arborescent gold, the weaving of birds'-nests, the netting of lace, the basket capitals of Byzantium, and most of all the tabernacle work of the French flamboyant school, possessed from the first, and possess still, a charm for me of which the force was entirely unbroken for ten years after the first sight of Rouen; and the fastidious structural knowledge of later time does not always repay the partial loss of it" (XXXV: 157 n3). Like Walton, I am convinced Ruskin has an instinctive liking for the late Gothic but feels it goes too far in its application of flexibility and substantiates his disapproval with quite incorrect structural arguments. Contrary to his own views, Ruskin's examples – bird's nests, ice flowers, lacework, braiding, filigree – are of a wholly structural, i.e., configurational, nature, and completely fit the requirements of his active rigidity and changefulness. In the second chapter of *Seven Lamps*, he notes in aphorism 16 that "[t]racery should never be considered or imagined as flexible," and a few sentences later that it should be viewed as "delicate indeed, but perfectly firm" – meaning tracery should never *mimic* textile. Though made of stone, tracery should still be delicate – the term I will be using in the course of this book. In short, tracery is about the *transformation* of flexible textile into rigid stone, not the application of imagery to an object. See also my treatment of active rigidity in Chapter One.

11. Millais's *Mariana* is based on Tennyson's 1830 poem of the same title. *The Lady of Shalott*, Tennyson's subject in 1833 and 1842, has been painted in many versions, by Holman Hunt as caught in the wires and by Waterhouse as drifting downstream in a boat to certain death. See: *Ladies of Shalott: A Victorian Masterpiece and Its Contexts* (catalogue for the exhibition in Bell Gallery, List Art Center, Providence, R.I., 1985), ed. George Landow.

12. "Surely he hath borne our Griefs, and carried our Sorrows. Yet we did esteem him stricken, smitten of God, and afflicted" (Isaiah 53:4). And: "the Goat shall bear upon him all their iniquities unto a Land not inhabited" (Leviticus 16:22). Several commentators have made it clear that the goat of the Old Testament represents the Savior of the New Testament; that is all very well, but the religious explanation does not answer the question of why the painting succeeds where mere faith might not: the greater the "contrast" between animal and landscape, the more believable it is.

13. This is symbolized by Duchamp's *3 Standard Stoppages*, in which three meter-long strands of yarn dropped from a height of one meter are converted into three wooden, curved rulers, which are later used to create *Network of Stoppages* – hardly a Gothic configuration, let alone a mineralized landscape. Pollock simply kept dropping paint in liquid arabesques until the canvas was full.

14. "And the Lord God took the man, and put him into the garden of Eden to dress it and to keep it" (Genesis 2:15).

15. Ruskin, *Works*, VII: 14–15.

16. Semper fled Germany because of his involvement in the Dresden uprising during the German revolution of 1848–49 and lived in London between 1850 and 1854.

17. Owen Jones, *The Grammar of Ornament* (London: Day and Son, 1856, with 100 folio plates). The later edition with 112 folio plates published by Bernard Quaritch in 1865

is the one I will be referencing (also reprinted by Studio Editions in 1986), 14.

18. Ibid., 13.

19. Gottfried Semper, *Die Vier Elemente der Baukunst* (Braunschweig: Vieweg Verlag, 1851). Translated by Harry Mallgrave and Wolfgang Herrmann as *The Four Elements of Architecture and Other Writings* (Cambridge: Cambridge University Press, 1989), 74–129.

20. Gottfried Semper, *Style in the Technical and Tectonic Arts; or, Practical Aesthetics*, trans. Harry Mallgrave and Michael Robinson (Los Angeles: Getty Publications, 2004), 248.

21. Ibid., 247.

22. Semper, *Four Elements*, 103–4.

23. Ibid., 104.

24. Alfred Haddon, *Evolution in Art* (London: Walter Scott, 1895), 75–117, esp. 101–3, with direct references to Gottfried Semper. The subject deeply fascinated Alois Riegl as well; see: *Problems of Style*, trans. Evelyn Kain (Princeton: Princeton University Press, 1992, orig. 1893), Chapter One, "The Geometric Style," which is also full of references to Semper and does its utmost to detach him from his followers.

25. Semper, *Style*, 250.

26. Ibid., 109.

27. Ibid., 248.

28. Ibid., 80 (on speculative aesthetics) and 106 (on coarse materialism).

29. Semper himself remarked that the German word *Noth* ("necessity") was related to *Knoten* ("knot") and *Naht* ("seam" or "joint"), as Joseph Rykwert has already extensively discussed in *The Necessity of Artifice* (New York: Rizzoli, 1982). This idea was later picked up by Kenneth Frampton (*Studies in Tectonic Culture*, 1995), who reverses the whole argument into one in favor of the expression of joints between industrially made elements such as panels ("cladding"), and therefore against ornamentation. Frampton accepts elaboration and articulation as a "poetics" of structure, as an elaboration of the act of building, not of architecture. For Frampton, it is real making that becomes abstract; for us, abstract making becomes real building.

30. Riegl discusses the case of zigzag lines engraved in reindeer bone (*Problems of Style*, 32–33) as a mere expression of "horror vacui," though it is clear from the accompanying image that the woven pattern of zigzags precisely follows the crease in the marrow spoon and that the carver, as in the case of the Maori head, created a woven pattern as an expression of the whole formation of the object, as if texture and volume had co-emerged. Ornament is a form of making, but necessarily after the fact; it applies a pattern afterward that can only be understood as having emerged simultaneously. In this sense, ornament is always a form of constructivism (what Morris calls "growth"), but obviously a delicate version, not the bold Russian type of the 1920s.

31. For instance: Joan Evans, *Pattern, Vol. I: Middle Ages* and *Vol. 2: Renaissance to 1900* (New York: Da Capo Press, 1976), or: Archibald Christie, *Pattern Design: An Introduction to the Study of Formal Ornament* (New York: Dover Publications, 1969).

32. Gregory Bateson, *Steps to an Ecology of Mind* (Chicago: University of Chicago Press, 2000), 455. Over the last thirty years, one book after another on the topic of pattern has been published. Among the best is Philip Ball's *The Self-Made Tapestry* (Oxford: Oxford University Press, 1999), a title that should interest us for obvious reasons.

33. Jones, *Grammar*, 157.

34. I prefer the word "ribbon" over other possibilities, such as "band" or "arabesque." First,

"ribbon" relates to the rib of the first chapter, and, like Worringer and Ruskin, I think there is a deep relationship between the two: the ornamental ribbon acts structurally and the structural rib acts ornamentally, as both use flexible linear elements to construct larger entities, be they bundled columns or woven surfaces. Also, "ribbon" is as-pecific, unlike "band ornament," which applies specifically to fifteenth-century forms, or "arabesque," a term that has already been used by Riegl. While my distinction be-tween tessellated and ribboned resembles that of crystalline/arabesque or mineral/veg-etal, I prefer a new terminology, since my distinction is based on a more fundamental, broader, material notion of pattern and not on representation or meaning. And the no-tion of mosaic and fabric will play an even more fundamental role in the following chapters. Ribbon ornament covers a wide field that includes Morris's interlacing vines, Mucha's hair (not Bernini's), Pollock's drips, Horta's wrought-iron railings, and, in more stylistic terms, Art Nouveau whiplashes, Celtic knotwork, Gothic tracery, tendrils in ironwork in all kinds of styles, three hundred years of illumination, etc., all of which always form constructions and surfaces, in contradistinction to Riegl's Hellenic bands of arabesques, which are without exception linearly repeated and are not capable of forming configurations. Last but not least, Hogarth uses the very same term in *The Analysis of Beauty* (34).

35. See: Carol Hrvol Flores, *Owen Jones: Design, Ornament, Architecture and Theory in an Age of Transition* (New York: Rizzoli, 2006), 14–29.

36. Jones, *Grammar*, 66–74.

37. See, for instance: *Symmetry Comes of Age: The Role of Patterns in Culture*, eds. Dorothy Washburn and Donald Crowe, esp. Chapter One, 12–15.

38. Jones, *Grammar*, 5.

39. Ernst Gombrich, *The Sense of Order* (London: Phaidon, 2006), 1. This is a wonderful book with hundreds of examples, but it is unnecessarily preoccupied with "order" and not with the transdimensional nature of pattern operating in two opposite directions.

40. Jones, *Grammar*, "Proposition 22," 7.

41. Ruskin, *Works*, V: liv.

42. Ibid., XVI: 265.

43. Ibid., IX: 266–67.

44. Ibid., IX: 268–69.

45. William Hogarth, *The Analysis of Beauty*, introduced by Ronald Paulson (New Haven: Yale University Press, 1997).

46. Ruskin, *Works*, IX: 268.

47. Ernst Gombrich, *The Sense of Order* (London: Phaidon, 2006), 165. The original is from: John Starkie Gardner, *Ironwork, Part I* (London: Chapman and Hall, 1893), 63.

48. Returning for a moment to our brief discussion of Ruskin's Plate I ("Ornaments from Rouen, St. Lô, and Venice") in note 38 of the first chapter, we can apply similar rules. As the finial is symmetrical like the capital of a column it is covered by four thistles (we see only the three at the front), one on each bulging corner. When we study the centerline of the leaves first, we see the veins bifurcating twenty times, producing nine Y-figures on either side of the central vein. Here, as in all leaves, the veins inform the outlines of the leaf, which is strongly toothed. I count about a hundred thorns on each leaf. Together, the four leaves distribute some four hundred points over the body of the finial. In a manner similar to Euclidean geometry, the volume is made of lines and points networked into a system; however, the difference here is that the distribution is

not in any way isomorphic but is generated by a growth algorithm that moves stepwise from four to twenty to four hundred, without any hierarchical subdivision.

49. William Morris, *Some Hints on Pattern-Designing* (printed at the Kelmscott Press, Hammersmith, and published by Longmans & Co., London, 1899), 14. Many of Morris's writings are available on the Internet at marxists.org and openlibrary.org.

50. Ibid., 15.

51. Ibid., 15.

52. Ibid., 36.

53. "Simplest" in the form of the ribbon itself, but certainly not in the configuration of the pattern! Celtic knotwork is clearly the apex of ribbon ornament, as we see in George Bain's indispensable book, *Celtic Art, The Methods of Construction* (London: Constable, 1951). His studies of the Book of Kells, the Lindisfarne Gospels, the Book of Durrow and Pictish ribbon ornament designs surpass the general art-historical research because of his deep understanding of techniques. Late nineteenth-century designs, such as Morris's wallpapers and carpets and Archibald Knox's carpets and caskets, were strongly influenced by the mind-boggling ninth-century examples of knotwork and illumination.

54. Ruskin, *Works*, XVI: 281.

55. And enjoying the honor of pushing "Mr. Ruskin's especial wheelbarrow," as Wilde himself said. See: Richard Ellmann, *Oscar Wilde* (London: Penguin Books, 1988), 48. The Wilde we know as a supreme aesthete and exponent of Walter Pater's idle beauty always strongly defended John Ruskin and "his mighty and majestic prose" ("The Critic as Artist," in: *Complete Works of Oscar Wilde*, London: Book Club Associates, 1976: 1028).

56. Quoted from: David Brett, *On Decoration* (Cambridge: The Lutterworth Press, 1992), 44.

57. Gombrich, *The Sense of Order*, 62.

58. Of course – but not only geometrical abstract art deriving from Jones's and Dresser's notions of repose and order. Gestural abstract art, such as Matisse's and, later, Pollock's and De Kooning's, has its sources in ribboned and vegetal decoration.

59. The teddy bear trend in art started with German artist Haim Steinbach lining up three teddy bears against a wall in 1986, evolved to the point where artists were producing enormous machines inhabited by hundreds of bears (Annette Messager at Documenta XI in 2002) and culminated in Ydessa Hendeles's 2010 "Partners (The Teddy Bear Project)" (Gwangju Biennale), which included more than 3,000 photos of people with their teddy bears. The hugging started with Juan Mann's Free Hugs Campaign in 2006.

60. Ruskin, *Works*, XVI: 307.

61. The distinction between tenderness and cruelty should not be equated with, for instance, that between sensuality and abstraction. Ruskin's notion of tenderness does not work without some abstraction, which is why his sympathy often seems somewhat reserved, and even cold to some. A true sympathetic encounter is one of attunement and coordination, which by implication must be patterned, i.e., abstract, like that between the hinge and the door. In Ruskin's radical vitalism, not only does life pervade lifeless things, but the reverse is true as well. The relationship between vegetal and mineral, and between fabric and mosaic, is always operative in both directions. For Ruskin, direct touching would become sentimental and therefore again what he calls heartless,

since it makes the encounter one between images. This follows his distinction between the noble and low picturesque, which we will study in Chapter Four, and the complex relationship between abstraction and empathy in sympathy, which we will study in Chapter Three.

62. Antonin Artaud, "The Theatre of Cruelty," in: *The Theatre and its Double* (New York: Grove Press, 1958), 99.

63. I am referring to the famous line "This will kill that" in his 1831 *Notre-Dame de Paris* (Book Five, Chapter Two), in which he means the book's power will kill that of architecture.

64. Alan Turing, "The Chemical Basis of Morphogenesis," from: *Philosophical Transactions of the Royal Society of London* (Series B, No.641, Vol. 237, 14 August 1952). An excellent discussion can be found in: Philip Ball, *The Self-Made Tapestry* (Oxford: Oxford University Press, 1999), 77–94.

65. A digital application of Turing's patterning procedure can be found in: Greg Turk, "Generating Textures on Arbitrary Surfaces using Reaction-Diffusion," *Computer Graphics* (SIGGRAPH 91), 25(4), July 1991.

66. Ruskin, *Works*, VIII: 177.

67. Ibid., XIX: 251. "Egyptian building is essentially of porphyry, – Greek of marble, – St. Mark's at Venice of glass and alabaster, – and this is – built of chalk, common chalk – chalk with the flints in it left in, and sticking out here and there. Well, that's the first point to think about. All flamboyant architecture is essentially chalk architecture, – it is built of some light, soft, greasy stone, which you can cut like cheese, which you can drive a furrow into with your chisel an inch deep, as a ploughman furrows his field. Well, of course, with this sort of stuff the workman goes instinctively in for deep cutting; he *can* cut deep, – and he does cut deep; – and he can cut fast, and he does cut fast; – and he can cut fantastically, – and he goes in for fancy." Writers generally relate the Gothic in various ways to wood, and there are strong arguments for that analogy. Such a relationship is embodied in two technical aspects, that of bending wood and that of cutting it. It was, of course, Sir James Hall who, in his *Essay on the Origins, History and Principles of Gothic Architecture* of 1813, famously argued that Gothic architecture had its origins in the bending of trees and branches (see: Simon Schama, *Landscape and Memory*, Chapter Four, par. 4). Ruskin makes a similar observation in *Seven Lamps*, saying tracery should have the firmness of branches (VIII: 92), by which he means it should adopt a type of curvature produced by bending: "flexible … not ductile." Similar comparisons, such as that between the Gothic and the forests of northern Europe, have often been made, with the tree trunks rising upward like piers and the canopies of leaves meshing into vaults. We find another type of relationship with wood carving, especially during the late Gothic of the limewood sculptors in Germany, such as Tilman Riemenschneider who created an extraordinary Flamboyant with curls, hairs and flames. Like Ruskin we could say that this type of sculpture would be unthinkable in marble or granite, but the German limewood communicates uncannily with the limestone of Northern France. Again we see an abstract exchange (since the stone cannot be bent like wood it has to adopt its curvature via the drawing) mixed with real analogies where the cutting of soft stone directly relates to that of wood. Actually, an exchange so abstract it not only enters the world of architecture and sculpture, but that of painting and engraving as well. When we compare Riemenschneider's *St. Mary Magdalene* fully covered in curly hair, Dürer's dog from *Knight, Death and the*

Devil, Hunt's long-haired *Scapegoat*, the hair of Millais's *Bridesmaid* or the grass in his *Blind Girl*, and we simultaneously glance over the multi-mullioned façades of Strasbourg Cathedral or Rouen Cathedral's west front, I think we easily recognize the gothic obsession for fibrous textures.

68. Ibid., XIX: 262.

69. See, for example, the work of Patrick Blanc, who found a final solution for ornament with his "vertical gardens," but at the cost of a radical separation of mineral architecture and vegetal curvature and growth.

70. See: Richard Coyne, *Technoromanticism: Digital Narrative, Holism, and the Romance of the Real* (Cambridge, Mass.: MIT Press, 1999).

3. abstraction and sympathy

1. George Landow, *Elegant Jeremiahs: The Sage from Carlyle to Mailer* (Ithaca: Cornell University Press, 1986), 144–53. In the early 1990s, Landow started the Victorian Web site (victorianweb.org), a vast collection of material on English literature from 1700 onward.

2. George Landow, *The Aesthetic and Critical Theories of John Ruskin* (Princeton: Princeton University Press, 1971), 146–79. We will return to the Ruskinian side of the argument in Chapter Four.

3. Johann Gottfried Herder, *Sculpture: Some Observations on Shape and Form from Pygmalion's Creative Dream* (Chicago and London: Chicago University Press, 2002, orig. 1778), 78. "The more a part of the body signifies what it should signify, the more beautiful it is; inner sympathy alone, feeling and the transposition of our entire human self into the figure we touch, is the true teacher and instrument of beauty."

4. See, for instance, Mallgrave and Ikonomou's book *Empathy, Form, and Space: Problems in German Aesthetics, 1873–1893* (Santa Monica: Getty Center Publications, 1994), in which we find hardly any mention of Lipps or Worringer. Someone who does discuss all these protagonists in one book is the Earl of Listowel (William Hare), in *Modern Aesthetics: An Historical Introduction* (New York: Teachers College Press, 1967), especially Chapter Seven, "The Theory of Einfühlung." Hare was a pupil of Victor Basch, who advocated a symbolist notion of sympathy in *Essai critique sur l'esthétique de Kant* (1896).

5. William James, "A World of Pure Experience," in: *Essays in Radical Empiricism* (Lincoln: University of Nebraska Press, 1996), 55.

6. Ibid., 42.

7. Oliver Sacks, "To See and Not to See," in: *An Anthropologist on Mars* (New York: Knopf, 1996).

8. James, *Pure Experience*, 44–45.

9. Ibid., 59.

10. William James, "Does Consciousness Exist?" in: *Essays in Radical Empiricism* (Lincoln: University of Nebraska Press, 1996), 4.

11. James, *Pure Experience*, 57.

12. William James, *The Principles of Psychology, Vol. I* (New York: Dover Publications, 1950), 25, with two diagrams showing the baby and the flame.

13. James, *Pure Experience*, 56.

14. Ibid., 42.

15. James, *Principles of Psychology I*, 258–59. The notion of the fringe has been intensely discussed ever since in psychology and philosophy and plays an important part in James's broader concept of the stream of consciousness.

16. James, *Pure Experience*, 46.

17. Gilles Deleuze, *Essays Critical and Clinical* (New York: Verso, 1998), 86–87. "Not even a puzzle, whose pieces when fitted together would constitute a whole, but rather a wall of loose, uncemented stones, whose every element has value in itself but also in relation to others …, not a uniform piece of clothing but a Harlequin's coat, even white on white, an infinite patchwork with multiple joinings … the American invention *par excellence*, for the Americans invented patchwork, just as the Swiss are said to have invented the cuckoo clock." It is true that the drystone wall is not a puzzle, since the builder works with a pile of stones, and when he picks one, nine out of ten times, it will fit somewhere on top of the wall he is building (as I was assured when I visited a building site in the English countryside). However, the looseness is only momentary, since the internal relations between the stones quickly make it as stable as any puzzle. And the fact that a puzzle piece only fits in one way, like a metaphor of Kantian apriority, while the stone fits in multiple ways, does not mean the stone does not also share points of agreement with its neighbors that make it exceed its own formal limitations.

18. James, *Pure Experience*, 69.

19. "Terminus" is the word James regularly uses for known entities such as Memorial Hall: "… the result is that their starting point thereby becomes a knower and their terminus an object meant or known." Ibid., 57.

20. A similar argument has been made previously by David Lapoujade, in "From Transcendental Empiricism to Worker Nomadism: William James" (*Pli* 9, 2000), 194. An adapted version appeared as "From Network to Patchwork," in: *The Pragmatist Imagination* (Princeton: Princeton Architectural Press, 2000). In this chapter, I build on both Lapoujade's text and Brian Massumi's essay in the same volume, "The Ether and Your Anger: Towards a Pragmatics of the Useless."

21. William James, "The Thing and Its Relations," in: *Essays in Radical Empiricism* (Lincoln: University of Nebraska Press, 1996), 93.

22. Ibid., 93.

23. Clearly, this goes against the so-called "exteriority of relations" as developed by Hume, Deleuze and DeLanda. For further discussion of this topic, see Chapter Five.

24. James, *Principles of Psychology I*, 297–98.

25. David Ray Griffin, *Whitehead's Radically Different Postmodern Philosophy: An Argument for Its Contemporary Relevance* (New York: SUNY Press, 2007), passim.

26. Henri Bergson, "Introduction to Metaphysics," in: *Creative Mind* (New York: Citadel Press, 1946, orig. 1903), 188. When James discusses Bergson in *A Pluralistic Universe* (Lecture VI), he follows him even more: "… put yourself in the making by a stroke of intuitive sympathy with the thing …"

27. Henri Bergson, *Creative Evolution* (New York: Dover Publications, 1998, orig. English translation 1911), 165.

28. Ibid., 126.

29. Ibid., 23.

30. Gilles Deleuze, *Bergsonism* (New York: Zone Books, 1991), 13–35.

31. Bergson, *Creative Evolution*, 175.
32. Bergson, *Creative Mind*, 161.
33. Bergson, *Creative Evolution*, 176.
34. Bergson, *Creative Mind*, 87.
35. For instance, by Bertrand Russell, in *The Analysis of the Mind* (London: George Allen & Unwin, 1921), 55–57.
36. Bergson, *Creative Evolution*, 174.
37. Ibid., 174.
38. Ibid., 175.
39. James Frazer, *The Golden Bough: A History of Myth and Religion* (London: Chancellor Press, 1994), Chapter Three, 11–48. Sympathetic magic is based on two similar but different principles, the optical Law of Similarity and the haptic Law of Contact; in the former, like produces like, and one inflicts harm on a person by destroying an image of him or her, and the latter is based on the principle that objects that have been in contact continue to act on each other at a distance.
40. See: P. A. Meijer, *Stoic Theology: Proofs of the Existence of the Cosmic God and of the Traditional Gods* (Delft: Eburon, 2007), 86–87. And: Katerina Ierodiakonou, "The Greek Concept of Sympatheia and Its Byzantine Appropriation in Michael Psellos," in: *The Occult Sciences in Byzantium*, eds. Magdalino and Mavroudi (Geneva: La Pomme d'Or, 2006), 97–117.
41. Bergson, *Creative Evolution*, 172.
42. This thought was developed by Dick Raaijmakers, a Dutch electronic music pioneer, in: *CAHIER-M: A Brief Morphology of Electronic Sound* (Leuven: University Press of Leuven, 2000, revised 2005), 107–8. At first, Marey's "plaque fixe" of successive photographs of the running horse superimposed resulted in an unreadable blurry cloud. Marey affixed reflective markers to the horse's joints and photographed it again. The resulting image was what we would now call a diagram, an abstract graph of the horse's movement.
43. Bergson, *Creative Evolution*, 9.
44. Gilles Deleuze, *Bergsonism*, 13 and 115. Later, in *Dialogues II* (41), he momentarily returns to sympathy when discussing D. H. Lawrence's remarks to Whitman. Deleuze is never comfortable with Bergson's sympathy, and he constantly tries to remove the interiority from it and replace it with Spinoza's reciprocal affects.
45. Frans De Waal, *The Age of Empathy: Nature's Lessons for a Kinder Society* (New York: Harmony Books, 2009).
46. Ibid., 91.
47. Bergson, *Creative Evolution*, 177.
48. This is in line with sympathetic magic, which operates with the same notions of mimesis and imitation as Frazer's Law of Similarity and Law of Contact. See also: Michael Taussig, *Mimesis and Alterity* (New York: Routledge, 1993), 44–58. Many have tried to construct a theory of art that progresses from fetishes and effigies to representational art, but things are not that simple. Like the Ammophila wasp (or Uexküll's spider that needs to become "fly-like" to catch a fly, which we will discuss in Chapter Five), one has to imitate the other in sympathy, but my point is precisely that this imitation is not a representational or exact mirroring but, rather, occurs through a temporary abstraction, through the finding of points of mutuality, or of agreement, as I call it throughout the book. Exact looking-like is not necessary for feeling-like, though it is advisable, unlike in Method acting, to start with imitation, as feelings will often follow.

The procedure of sympathy starts with imitation but does not end with it.

49. See: Brian Massumi, "The Thinking-Feeling of What Happens," in: *Interact or Die!*, eds. Joke Brouwer and Arjen Mulder (Rotterdam: V2_Publishing, 2007)

50. See: *Empathy, Form, and Space: Problems in German Aesthetics, 1873–1893*, eds. Harry Francis Mallgrave and Eleftherios Ikonomou (Santa Monica: Getty Center Publications, 1994), 89–123.

51. See note 47, Chapter Four.

52. Theodor Lipps, "Empathy and Aesthetic Pleasure," in: *Aesthetic Theories: Studies in the Philosophy of Art*, eds. Karl Aschenbrenner and Arnold Isenberg (Englewood Cliffs: Prentice-Hall, 1965), 403–4.

53. Theodor Lipps, "Empathy, Inner Imitation, and Sense-Feelings," in: Melvin Rader, *A Modern Book of Esthetics: An Anthology* (New York: Holt, Rhinehart and Winston, 1979), 375.

54. Theodor Lipps, *Raumaesthetik* (Amsterdam: E. J. Bonset, 1966, reprint from 1897), as translated by Vernon Lee in *Beauty and Ugliness* (London: John Lane, 1912), 35.

55. Lipps, *Raumaesthetik*, 7. As translated by Gustav Jahoda in "Theodor Lipps and the Shift from 'Sympathy' to 'Empathy,'" *Journal of the History of the Behavioral Sciences*, Vol. 41(2), 151–63, Spring 2005.

56. Lipps, *Raumaesthetik*, 3. As quoted from Jahoda, 157.

57. David Hume, *Treatise on Human Nature*, III, part 3, section 1, par. 7.

58. Lipps, as quoted from Jahoda, 154–55.

59. Bruno Latour, *Pandora's Hope* (Cambridge, Mass.: Harvard University Press, 1999), 183–85.

60. See: Robin Middleton, "Viollet-le-Duc et les Alpes: la dispute du Mont Blanc," in: *Viollet-le-Duc: Centenaire de la Mort à Lausanne* (cat. Exposition au Musée historique de l'Ancien-Evêché, 1979), 101–10. And: Cynthia Gamble, "John Ruskin, Viollet-le-Duc and the Alps," *Alpine Journal* 104: 348 (1999, 185–96). And also: Simon Schama, *Landscape and Memory* (New York: Alfred A. Knopf, 1995), Chapter Seven.

61. Eugène Viollet-le-Duc, *Entretiens sur l'Architecture*, trans. Benjamin Brucknall as *Discourses on Architecture*, (New York: Grove Press, 1959), esp. Lecture XII.

62. Wilhelm Worringer, *Abstraction and Empathy*, trans. Michael Bullock (Chicago: Elephant Paperbacks, 1997, orig. 1908).

63. Ibid., 15.

64. Ibid., 4.

65. Ibid., 17.

66. Ibid., 36. "In the necessity and irrefragability of geometric abstraction he could find repose."

67. I cannot emphasize enough how important this is for the whole concept of sympathy. As we see in sympathetic magic in general, and more specifically in our examples of the Gothic hinge, an actor playing a part, and Bergson's wasp, sympathy operates through disparate, i.e., externally dissimilar, bodies internally coordinating and literally finding points of agreement. When adapting the posture of my body, i.e., sitting down, I find the necessary points on the rock that it offers me. So there is a kind of imitation at work, but one that is internal, never externally realistic, since a body cannot literally look like a rock, nor a hinge like a door. Sympathy operates through finding points of agreement that are internally felt, not externally seen. In the final chapter, this external difference and internal similarity are aligned with *animism* and posited against

naturalism, which follows the opposite formula of being externally the same and internally dissimilar. In fact, this means animism should be viewed as a form of anti-naturalism, not the supernaturalism it is often mistaken for. This thought is developed in the realm of anthropology by Philippe Descola in *Par-delà nature et culture* (Paris: Gallimard, 2005).

68. See: Marc Kirschner and John Gerhart, *The Plausibility of Life: Resolving Darwin's Dilemma* (New Haven: Yale University Press, 2005).

69. Georges Meurant, *Shoowa Design: African Textiles from the Kingdom of Kuba* (London: Thames and Hudson, 1986). There is a single reference to Shoowa-Kuba textiles, as "pile cloth, Congo," in Franz Boas's *Primitive Art* (1983, 154), but he misses the irregularities, asymmetries and transformations. Generally, his examples of primitive art are of the crystalline, symmetrically ordered type.

70. Meurant, *Shoowa Design*, 158–73. The crossing is explained on pp. 158–59, the loop on pp. 160–65, and the woot (a double crossing) on pp. 166–73. A great many examples are available on the Internet.

71. Ruskin, *Works*, XVII: 105.

72. Ibid., XVII: 89.

73. Worringer, *Abstraction and Empathy*, 77.

74. Ibid., 112–13.

75. Bergson, *Creative Evolution*, 126.

76. Alfred Gell's beautiful book *Art and Agency: An Anthropological Theory* (Oxford: Oxford University Press, 1998) has "animacy" as its central thesis: art's mission is to cross the threshold between organic, living things and inorganic things. The book also contains an extensive discussion of Gombrich, Frazer and Taussig.

77. Gustav Theodor Fechner, *Religion of a Scientist*, trans. W. Lowrie (New York: Pantheon, 1946). William James was very sympathetic to Fechner's ideas; see: *A Pluralistic Universe* (Cambridge, Mass.: Harvard University Press, 1977, orig. 1909), Lecture IV, "Concerning Fechner."

78. See: Martha Banta, *Henry James and the Occult: The Great Extension* (Bloomington: Indiana University Press, 1972). Both Henry James and his brother William were members of the American branch of the Society for Psychical Research – Henry only from 1881 to 1888 but William from 1884 to 1909; he served as its vice-president and president (1895). Also in the list of presidents, we find Henri Bergson (1913) and Hans Driesch (1926). In light of my remark "It's all Marey's or Klein's blur; it's all art," I would like to draw attention to the 1901 book *Thought-Forms*, by Annie Besant (president of the Theosophical Society from 1908 until her death in 1933) and Charles Leadbetter ("celebrated clairvoyant"), which mixes expressionist painting, early abstractionism and scientific research in vibratory patterns that are very close to Marey's movement graphs.

79. Gilles Deleuze, "Immanence: A Life," in: *Pure Immanence* (New York: Zone Books, 2001), 28. It is unclear why the American translators left out the ellipsis, which is so intensely analyzed by Giorgio Agamben in *Potentialities* (Stanford: Stanford University Press, 1999), 220–39.

80. James, *Radical Empiricism*, 93.

81. Ibid., 93.

4. the radical picturesque

1. Sir Uvedale Price, *On the Picturesque* (Otley: Woodstock Books, 2000 facsimile reprint from 1796), 82.

2. For some excellent discussions of *Bildung, Trieb* and *Bildungstrieb*, see: Shirley Roe, *Matter, Life, and Generation* (Cambridge: Cambridge University Press, 1981) and Helmut Müller-Sievers, *Self-Generation: Biology, Philosophy, and Literature Around 1800* (Stanford: Stanford University Press, 1997).

3. Ronald Paulson wrote a very informative introduction to the reprint of William Hogarth's *The Analysis of Beauty* (New Haven: Yale University Press, 1997, orig. 1753), xi–lxii. In it, he states that Hogarth deeply influenced William Gilpin (lii), one of the main inventors of the picturesque. Though Hogarth uses the word "picturesque" every now and then, he means something more like what Ruskin calls "vital beauty," which consists of variable curvatures, not the typical broken and angular variation of the picturesque. See my later discussion in this chapter. Paulson's understanding of Hogarth's aesthetics as one "of the crowd" is lucid, and his reference to Alexander Gerard's 1759 *Essay on Taste* (xlvii), published immediately after Burke's essay on the sublime, as an aesthetics "without limit or termination" and having an anaesthetic effect, deeply influenced my concept of the sublime.

4. Hogarth, *The Analysis of Beauty*, 34. Paulson relates it to Milton's identical lines in *Paradise Lost* (4.304–11). Hogarth's chapter "Of Intricacy" is full of terms such as "entanglement," "braiding," "interlacing," "intertwisted," etc., which inform the first two chapters of this book.

5. Similar to Ruskin's "abstract lines," which we discussed earlier, the serpentine line, or "the line of variety," illustrated by a serpent undulating in a pyramidal glass box in the frontispiece of *The Analysis of Beauty*, is based on differential, i.e., "third-degree," variation. The description of the line of variety as a serpentine line brings it very close to the Mannerist *figura serpentinata*, the curved figure that could guide the drawing of an arm, a whole body or a group of bodies. Looking at Giovanni Bologna's sculpture *The Rape of the Sabine Women* (1580) in Florence, one can see the effect of many serpentine figures nested together: the result is a statue without front, back or sides, and if one tries to stand "in front" of it, one cannot stop moving around it. Hogarth's concepts are similar in the sense that the serpentine figures are always packed together, in what Paulson calls an "aesthetics of the crowd," clearly a configurational concept. I have discussed this before, in *The Architecture of Continuity* (Rotterdam: V2_Publishing, 2008), 249–52.

6. This in contradistinction to John MacArthur's chapter on disgust in: *The Picturesque: Architecture, Disgust and Other Irregularities* (London: Routledge, 2007), esp. 91. Possibly the ruin could be taken as a premonition of "deconstruction," but not the object of the picturesque, which by definition veers away from the sublime. For elaboration, see later in this chapter, when I discuss Ruskin's "parasitical sublime" and concepts of the sublime found in Heidegger.

7. A few of them: Christopher Hussey, *The Picturesque: Studies in a Point of View* (London: G. P. Putnam, 1927), and: Walter John Hipple, *The Beautiful, the Sublime and the Picturesque* (Carbondale: Southern Illinois University Press, 1957), and: John Dixon

Hunt, *Gardens and the Picturesque: Studies in the History of Landscape Architecture* (Cambridge, Mass.: MIT Press, 1994).

8. See: Clemens Steenbergen and Wouter Reh, *Architecture and Landscape* (Bussum: Thoth, 1996), 236–373.

9. As quoted by Ruskin, *Works*, I: 46 n2.

10. Ibid., I: 1–188.

11. See: Andrew Ballantyne, *Architecture, Landscape and Liberty: Richard Payne Knight and the Picturesque* (Cambridge: Cambridge University Press, 1997).

12. In this section, I build on George Landow's influential *The Aesthetic and Critical Theories of John Ruskin* (Princeton: Princeton University Press, 1971), esp. Chapters Two and Three.

13. Ruskin, *Works*, VI: 11.

14. Ruskin, as the inventor of the very long sentence, greatly inspired Proust, as Edmund White writes in his Proust-biography (Penguin, 1999: 78). He often constructed sentences that did not progress linearly but formed little patches or knots. I think what made Ruskin feel so strongly for pre-Renaissance architecture was that he could describe it without at any point having to refer to the architect, so he could feel-wander-recall, as one can with a landscape. This has nothing to do with lyricism, however, which feels but does not construct.

15. Ruskin, *Works*, VI: 19.

16. Ibid., VII: 71 and 82.

17. Ibid., VI: 16.

18. See: Paul Fry, *Wordsworth and the Poetry of What We Are* (New Haven: Yale University Press, 2008), 80. Fry makes a "mineral" and "ontic" argument in favor of Wordsworth and criticizes earlier environmental and vegetal readings of the English poet.

19. William Wordsworth, "Tintern Abbey" (officially: "Lines Written a Few Miles above Tintern Abbey, on Revisiting the Banks of the Wye during a Tour, July 13, 1798"), in: *The Major Works* (Oxford: Oxford's World Classics, 2000), 131–35.

20. Ruskin, *Works*, VI: 15.

21. Ibid., VIII: 236.

22. See: Jane Bennett, *Thoreau's Nature: Ethics, Politics, and the Wild* (Walnut Creek: Altamira Press, 2000), and: Max Oelschlager, *The Idea of Wilderness: From Prehistory to the Age of Ecology* (New Haven: Yale University Press, 1991).

23. D. H. Lawrence, *Studies in Classic American Literature* (Harmondsworth: Penguin Books, 1981), 171–87. Cited by Gilles Deleuze in: *Dialogues*; for a further discussion, see Chapter Five.

24. Such as in his "Moss and Wild Strawberry" of 1873, "Ferns on a Rock" of 1875, "Rocks and Vegetation at Chamoni" of 1854, and the beautiful "Study of Gneiss Rock, Glenfinlas" of 1853, to name but a few.

25. Aristotle, *The Nichomachean Ethics*, trans. David Ross (Oxford: Oxford University Press, 1984).

26. Ruskin, *Works*, VIII: 218.

27. Ibid., XVII: 105.

28. Landow, *Aesthetic Theories*, 164–65.

29. It is a male image (chrome motorcycle, polished car, shining armor), but at the turn of the millennium, after the liquid metal T-1000 robot in *Terminator 2* (1991), it turned out to have a feminine version as well. See my own *HtwoOexpo* of 1997, and Anish

Kapoor's technologically more challenging *Cloud Gate* sculpture in Chicago's Millennium Park (2006). However, both versions, male and female, are polished mirrors and should be categorized as sublime objects.

30. Though in the Burne-Jones cycle, the knight Perseus is very boyish and his armor clearly of a vegetal quality, covered with leaflike details.

31. William Robinson, *The Wild Garden, or the Naturalization and Natural Grouping of Hardy Exotic Plants,* ill. Alfred Parsons (London: John Murray, 1870).

32. Ibid., 7.

33. Ibid., 115.

34. *Malerisch* was the word Heinrich Wölfflin introduced (in *Principles of Art History*) for a picturesque style of painting in regard not to choice of subject matter but to technique. In general, this adjective has to do with keeping the brushstrokes visible, something that reached its apex in twentieth-century abstract expressionist work, such as De Kooning's paintings, and was achieved through the use of ever-wider brushes. It is an effort to show the original wetness of the paint, as opposed to the dryness of the final painting, as if the artist seeks to keep the process as visible as the product. Later, in the 1980s, this resulted in all-too-wet brushstrokes, which began to drip, so that the paintings showed brushwork in all directions as well as vertical drips. A few hours before the opening of an exhibition, I remember seeing a German painter pushing an extremely wet brush saturated with paint against a canvas in order to create more drips. Clearly, creating the effect of process requires very precise labor.

35. See, for instance: Piet Oudolf and Henk Gerritsen, *Planting the Natural Garden* (Portland: Timber Press, 2003).

36. William Robinson, *The English Flower Garden* (Sagaponack: Sagapress, 1984), 103.

37. Robinson, *The Wild Garden*, xix.

38. Gravetye Manor was an estate Robinson bought in 1884 to turn into his lifelong laboratory. See also: Anne Helmreich, "Re-presenting Nature: Ideology, Art, and Science in William Robinson's 'Wild Garden,'" in: *Nature and Ideology: Natural Garden Design in the Twentieth Century*, ed. Joachim Wolschke-Bulmahn (Washington: Dumbarton Oaks, 1997), 81–111.

39. Bruno Latour, "Can We Get Our Materialism Back, Please?" (*Isis* 98, 2007, 138–42). Also available at bruno-latour.fr. This paragraph discusses Latour's view of the artwork, not the artwork itself.

40. See note 70, Chapter One.

41. See note 53.

42. Martin Heidegger, "The Origin of the Work of Art," in: *Poetry, Language, Thought*, trans. Albert Hofstadter (New York: Harper & Row, 1971), 33.

43. Ibid., 33.

44. Ibid., 41.

45. Ibid., 41.

46. Ruskin, *Works*, VI: 223. The diagram is meant to show what we view as a peak of the mountain is in fact a ridge.

47. Gaius Julius Hyginus, *Fabulæ*, ccxx "Cura," ca. 70 B.C., as quoted in Heidegger's *Being and Time*, trans. John Macquarrie and Edward Robinson (New York: Harper and Brothers, 1962), 242.

48. As quoted from Worringer, *Abstraction and Empathy*, trans. Michael Bullock (Chicago: Elephant Paperbacks, 1997, orig. 1908), 7.

49. See note 55, Chapter Three.
50. William Morris, *Gothic Architecture: A Lecture for the Arts and Crafts Exhibition Society* (Hammersmith: Kelmscott Press, 1893).
51. "Dasein is Design: Ontwerpt, geworpenen op aarde!" in: Henk Oosterling, *Radicale middelmatigheid* [Radical Mediocrity] (Amsterdam: Boom, 2000), 129–32.
52. Heidegger, "The Thing," in: *Poetry, Language, Thought*, 167.
53. The concealment of a thing, its *Zuhandenheit* ("being handy," or in official jargon, "readiness-to-hand"), lies in its invisibility. In a strange paradoxical form of existence, the thing as tool disappears the more it is used, like a hammer in one's hand driving a nail into a wall. The more things are taken up in multiple networks of action, the more they tend to conceal ("withdraw") themselves. Only when broken do they return into visibility and *Vorhandenheit* ("being at hand" or, again in official jargon, "presence-at-hand"). See also: Graham Harman, *Tool-Being: Heidegger and the Metaphysics of Objects* (Peru, Ill.: Open Court, 2002), esp. 15–24.
54. "It is very necessary, in the outset of all inquiry, to distinguish carefully between Architecture and Building." VIII: 27.
55. Ruskin, *Works*, V: 201–20.
56. The old futuristic dream of fully automated homes resulted every ten or so years in a new House of the Future. The house would adapt to your habits: close the curtains, heat the bathwater, order a pizza, help you remember when to pick up the children from school – in short, live your life. It always reminds me of Joseph Losey's 1963 movie *The Servant*, in which the butler becomes the master of the house. Servility and ergonomic comfort are always tricks to remove you from control.
57. Bruno Latour, *Why Has Critique Run Out of Steam? From Matters of Fact to Matters of Concern* (*Critical Inquiry* 30 (Winter 2004), 225–48. Also available at bruno-latour.fr.
58. Heidegger, "The Thing," in: *Poetry, Language, Thought*, 172.
59. Bruno Latour, *Pandora's Hope* (Cambridge, Mass.: Harvard University Press, 1999), 183–85.
60. Latour, *Critique*, 233. Latour always tries to sever Whitehead's Bergson half.
61. Martin Heidegger, "Only a God Can Save Us," in: *Der Spiegel,* interviewed by Rudolf Augstein and Georg Wolff in 1966 (published after Heidegger's death in 1976), trans. for: *Philosophy Today* 20 (Winter 1976), 267–84.
62. Martin Heidegger, "The Question Concerning Technology," *Basic Writings,* ed. David Krell (New York: Routledge, Kegan and Paul, 1993), 308–41.
63. It started with books developing a specific focus on vitalism, such as Shirley Roe's *Matter, Life, and Generation* and Helmut Müller-Sievers's later *Self-Generation*, followed by Robert Richards's marvelous *The Romantic Conception of Life* of 2002 (which has influenced these final paragraphs considerably) and, more recently, Iain Hamilton Grant's *Philosophies of Nature after Schelling*.
64. Friedrich Wilhelm Joseph Schelling, *Sämmtliche Werke*, ed. K. F. A. Schelling, vol. III (Stuttgart: Cotta, 1856–61), 284.

5. the ecology of design

1. The "argument from design" has been made in many different ways, but generally its

formula is that whatever a thing does in its relations *after* it is made is part of the intentions *before* it is made. In short, its end and purpose are its cause, which, in the case
of natural objects, amounts to an argument for the existence of God. This was extensively discussed by the ancient Greeks, including Aristotle; during English empiricism,
by people such as David Hume (in *Dialogues Concerning Natural Religion*); and by the-
ologians like William Paley. It lives on in the contemporary notion of "intelligent design." I will be addressing some of these arguments in this chapter, but it will not be
my principal topic, which is aesthetics.

2. William Paley, *Natural theology: or, Evidences of the existence and attributes of the deity,
   collected from the appearances of nature* (Trenton: Daniel Fenton, 1824, orig. 1802), 19.
3. Mark Taylor, *After God* (Chicago: University of Chicago Press, 2007).
4. Denis Diderot, *Rameau's Nephew and D'Alembert's Dream* (London: Penguin Classics,
   1976) and "Principes philosophiques sur la matiere et le mouvement," in: *Oeuvres
   Philosophiques* (Paris: Gallimard, 2010). Diderot developed a very interesting theory on
   matter as fibrous, and fibers as sensible and irritable, which he also applied to light and
   sound. See: Andrew Clark, *Diderot's Dream* (Aldershot: Ashgate, 2008), 75–84.
5. Paley, *Natural Theology*, 188.
6. Charles Darwin, *On the Origin of Species* (London: John Murray, 1859), 490. I will usually use the edition annotated by James Costa (Cambridge, Mass.: Belknap and Harvard University Press, 2009) but will follow the original paging. Where indicated, I
   switch to the sixth edition of thirteen years later, since the two differ substantially in
   places.
7. Alfred North Whitehead, *Adventures of Ideas* (New York: The Free Press, 1967), 265.
8. "Let us adapt a sort of pluralistic monism," William James proposes in *Pragmatism*
   (New York: Longmans, Green and Co., 1907), 13.
9. DeLanda, *A New Philosophy of Society*, 10.
10. Gilles Deleuze, *Dialogues II*, trans. Hugh Tomlinson and Barbara Habberjam (Lon-
    don: Continuum, 2006), 41.
11. Gilles Deleuze and Félix Guattari, *A Thousand Plateaus: Capitalism and Schizophrenia*,
    trans. Brian Massumi (London: Athlone Press, 1988), 10.
12. Deleuze, *Dialogues II*, 39–40 and 52.
13. DeLanda, *A New Philosophy of Society*, 11.
14. Manuel DeLanda, "Emergence, Causality and Realism," in: *The Speculative Turn: Con-
    tinental Materialism and Realism*, eds. Bryant, Srnicek, Harman (Melbourne: re.press,
    2010), 385.
15. Alfred North Whitehead, *Process and Reality: An Essay in Cosmology* (New York: The
    Free Press, 1978, corrected edition, eds. David Ray Griffin and Donald Sherburne,
    orig. 1929), 162–63. And: Charles Hartshorne, *Beyond Humanism: Essays in the New
    Philosophy of Nature* (Chicago: Willet, Clark and Co., 1937), esp. Chapter XII "Mind
    and Body: Organic Sympathy."
16. Whitehead, *Process and Reality*, 162.
17. See: John Hayman, "Towards the Labyrinth: Ruskin's Lectures as Slade Professor of
    Art" in: Robert Hewison, *New Approaches to Ruskin* (London: Routledge & Kegan
    Paul, 1981), 121. See also Letter 23 in *Fors Clavigera* (XXVII, 394–416).
18. As we can learn from Alfred Gell, the anthropologist we referred to in Chapter Three
    (note 73). Before *Art and Agency*, Gell wrote articles on the topic of a conceptual over-
    lap between art and technology, showing that there was an agency in art whose most

basic example was the seductive trap and that technology, owing to its own intricacy, could never be distinct from aesthetic relations. See: Alfred Gell, "The Technology of Enchantment and the Enchantment of Technology," in: *Anthropology, Art and Aesthetics*, eds. Jeremy Coote and Anthony Shelton (Oxford: Oxford University Press, 1992) and "Vogel's Net: Traps as Artworks and Artworks as Traps," in: *Journal of Material Culture* (March 1996, 15–38). The trapping of the viewer through intricacy is first mentioned in Hogarth's *The Analysis of Beauty*, where "waving and serpentine lines" lead "the eye a wanton kind of chase" (Chapter V, "On Intricacy"). As I have argued in the previous chapters, I think aesthetic relations, "felt relations," proceed by finding points of abstraction that are structural in the case of objects and postural in the case of human beings and animals, since they occur in the form of "attuned activity," which is not exactly a trap, though the notion fits the definition of one.

19. See also Tim Ingold's *Lines: A Brief History* (London: Routledge, 2007), 96–101. There are many similarities between his book and this one, especially in the examples and references – not only the labyrinths but also Semper, Riegl, weaving, and even the cracked mud in Chapter Two. However, there are also many differences, too many to properly discuss in the small space of a note.

20. Ruskin, *Works*, XIX: xlv and XXV: xlvi.

21. Ibid., XXV: 11–189.

22. Ibid., XXV: 197–552.

23. Ibid., XXV: xli.

24. Jonathan Smith, *Charles Darwin and Victorian Visual Culture* (Cambridge: Cambridge University Press, 2006).

25. See: Philippe Descola, *Par-delà nature et culture* (Paris: Gallimard, 2005). See also note 67, Chapter Three.

26. J. W. Goethe, *Morphologie*, quoted from: Robert Richards, *The Romantic Conception of Life: Science and Philosophy in the Age of Goethe* (Chicago: University of Chicago Press, 2002), 454.

27. Sean Carroll, *Endless Forms Most Beautiful: The New Science of Evo Devo and the Making of the Animal Kingdom* (London: Weidenfeld & Nicolson, 2006), 26.

28. Aristotle, *Physics*, trans. Hardie and Gaye, (Oxford: Clarendon, 1930), 198 b 23–27.

29. R. H. Brady, "Form and Cause in Goethe's Morphology," in: *Goethe and the Sciences: A Re-appraisal*, ed. Amrine, Zucker and Wheeler (Dordrecht: Reidel, 1987).

30. See note 68, Chapter Three.

31. Charles Darwin, *The Descent of Man, and Selection in Relation to Sex*, 2 Vols. (London: John Murray, 1871 reprinted in facsimile in 1998 for The Classics of Science Library), II: 72–73.

32. Gerry Webster and Brian Goodwin, *Form and Transformation: Generative Relational Principles in Biology* (Cambridge: Cambridge University Press, 1996), 111.

33. Darwin, *Descent*, II: 233.

34. Darwin, *Origin*, 88.

35. Immanuel Kant, *Critique of Judgment*, trans. James Meredith (Oxford: Oxford University Press, 2007, orig. 1790), § 68, 383/211.

36. Darwin, *Descent*, II: 142.

37. Grant Allen, "Aesthetic Evolution in Man," *The Popular Science Monthly*, January 1881, 339–56.

38. Darwin, *Descent*, II: 353.

39. Darwin, *Origin*, 6th edition (1872), 162. With every new edition of *Origin*, Darwin seems to comment on the new views in *Descent*.
40. Ruskin, *Works*, XXV: 263.
41. Ibid., XXV: 263.
42. Darwin, *Descent*, II: 72–73.
43. Ibid., II: 292.
44. Ibid., II: 293.
45. "Everything must take a detour" sounds like a direct quote from Baudrillard's *De la séduction* (Paris: Galileé, 1979). All relations are labyrinthic in Baudrillard, and I would make much more use of his concept of seduction were it not founded in semiotics. Basically, it is always signs that seduce. Seduction makes extensive use of veils and ornament as well, obviously, but it always leads to the void behind the veil, by means of the fatal strategy of irony, what Baudrillard called reversibility.
46. Jean Baudrillard, "The Animals: Territories and Metamorphoses," in: *Simulacra and Simulations*, trans. Sheila Faria Glaser (Ann Arbor: University of Michigan, 1994, orig. 1981), 139.
47. Ruskin, *Works*, XXV: 264.
48. Ibid., XXV: 268.
49. The connecting of sentences through decoration is based on the same reason why books should be illuminated, according to Ruskin (*Works*, V, 139): "It is with a view (not the least important among many others bearing upon art) to the reopening of this great field of human intelligence, long entirely closed, that I am striving to introduce Gothic architecture into daily domestic use; and to revive the art of illumination, properly so called; not the art of miniature-painting in books, or on vellum, which has ridiculously been confused with it; but of making *writing*, simple writing, beautiful to the eye, by investing it with the great chord of perfect colour, blue, purple, scarlet, white, and gold, and in that chord of colour, permitting the continual play of the fancy of the writer in every species of grotesque imagination, carefully excluding shadow; the distinctive difference between illumination and painting proper, being, that illumination admits *no* shadows, but only gradations of pure colour." This passage, quoted by Marshall McLuhan in *The Gutenberg Galaxy* (Toronto, 1962: 266–67), also explains, according to McLuhan, how Rimbaud arrived at the title for his *Illuminations* during the period when he lived in London.
50. Ibid., XXV: 267.
51. Ibid., XXV: 249–50.
52. Martin Heidegger, "The Origin of the Work of Art," in: *Poetry, Language, Thought*, trans. Albert Hofstadter (New York: Harper & Row, 1971), 173.
53. Immanuel Kant, *Critique of Judgment*, trans. James Meredith (Oxford: Oxford University Press, 2007, orig. 1790), § 64, 371–72/199–200.
54. Ibid., § 65, 372/200.
55. See also: Michael Ruse, *Darwin and Design: Does Evolution have a Purpose?* (Cambridge, Mass.: Harvard University Press, 2003), 46–50.
56. See: David Skrbina, *Panpsychism in the West* (Cambridge, Mass.: MIT Press, 2007). Lev Vygotsky is very clear in his *The Psychology of Art* (1925, Chapter 9) that feelings are by nature always conscious, which would mean panexperientialism and panpsychism cannot be separated. In any case, my position would amount to a panaestheticism.

57. Samuel Butler, *Life and Habit* (London: Fifield, 1910, orig. 1878), 134.

58. David Hume, "Of the Standard of Taste" in: *Four Dissertations* (London: Millar, 1757), 208–9.

59. From: christianhubert.com/writings/nature.

60. Darwin, *Origin*, 6th edition (1872), 160–61.

61. Darwin, *Origin*, 67. For his elaborations and corrections back and forth, see James Costa's annotations.

62. Ruskin, *Works*, VII: 203–17.

63. Richard Dawkins, *The Selfish Gene* (Oxford: Oxford University Press, 1976), Preface.

64. Peter Kropotkin, *Mutual Aid* (London: William Heinemann, 1907, orig. 1902). For an excellent discussion, see: Stephen J. Gould, "Kropotkin Was No Crackpot," in: *Natural History* 106 (June 1997): 12–21.

65. V. C. Wynne-Edwards, *Animal Dispersion in Relation to Social Behavior* (Edinburgh: Oliver and Boyd, 1962). For a comparison between Dawkins and Wynne-Edwards, see: Stephen J. Gould, "Caring Groups and Selfish Genes," in: *The Panda's Thumb* (London: Penguin Books, 1990, orig. 1980), 72–78.

66. Darwin, *Descent*, I: 98.

67. Joan Roughgarden, *The Genial Gene: Deconstructing Darwinian Selfishness* (Berkeley: University of California Press, 2009).

68. Lynn Margulis, *Symbiotic Planet: A New Look at Evolution* (Amherst: Basic Books, 1998).

69. Ruskin, *Works*, VII: 205.

70. Alfred North Whitehead, *Modes of Thought* (New York: The Free Press, 1968), 119.

71. "Boids" is the term Craig Reynolds of the famous Sante Fé Institute gave to his cyber-birds, which operate according to the four-rule algorithm.

72. DeLanda, "Emergence, Causality and Realism," 386.

73. Generally, feeling and especially sympathy are postulated only in the case of tightly organic or so-called unified wholes. We already find this notion in Stoic theology, and in Sextus Empiricus (who distinguishes between unified, conjoined and separate wholes – see P. A. Meijer's *Stoic Theology*, 86–87) and even in Hartshorne's "organic sympathy." I shy away from anything close to organicism and argue that all types of entities – loose and tight, perfect and imperfect, and all those in between – are constituted by sympathy, mainly because my form of sympathy cannot be identified with the final entity but only with what the parts feel it necessary to agree on. To be sure, this is an organic relationship, but its local organicity never makes it all the way to the whole, turning it into an infra- or suborganicism. It is a sort of reversal of the Deleuzian "body without organs": there are organs, but no body is ever finalized. An entity can be composed of many sympathies working simultaneously, ranging from strong bonds to very weak links. The fact that an entity has been composed does not mean that all the parts experience exactly the same amount of sympathy. The parts intend a composition, though its existence lies in the future; the actuality is not the sympathizing of parts with a whole of any sort but with neighboring parts. With sympathy, we never encounter any form of an overall structure or strength; by its nature, it creates fragile objects.

74. In *Panpsychism in the West*, David Skrbina explains the concept of panpsychism principally as an alternative to the emergence of mind: consciousness cannot be emergent in the sense of being built out of non-mind parts. All parts, in whatever quantity or quality, must contain something of consciousness, or else it cannot exist in any other quan-

tity. Skrbina refrains, however, from proclaiming panpsychism the alternative to all emergence - for instance, the emergence of humans in history or of planets in space. But the fact that a new species or planet "emerges" does not make it reliant on emergence for its instantiation; on the contrary. "Clearly a cubic Earth would produce a different gravitational field than a spherical one," he writes. Yes, but the fact is that there is no cubic earth, and gravity in each little chunk of matter preceded the planet and made it round. It seems to me that if we accept the presence of feeling (or experience, or mind) at every scale of existence (panaestheticism), it plays a role in all part-whole relations, not only in the emergence of consciousness.

75. See note 15, Chapter Two.
76. Whitehead, *Process and Reality*, 102.
77. Though Whitehead's process-theologist followers Charles Hartshorne (in *Beyond Humanism*) and David Ray Griffin (in *Unsnarling the World Knot*) made more of this distinction between true individuals and mere aggregates. We might state that not all entities have the same feelings, or that if they do they experience them in various gradations, but never that one entity has the capacity to feel and the other does not, as process theology has it. Everything feels, and everything feels as much *as it possibly can*, a grain in a heap of sand as much as a cell in kidney tissue, and as much a ballet dancer during *Sleeping Beauty*. But are these feelings more complex the more complex the internal structure is? Certainly. And does this increased complexity lead to more freedom, to a wider variation of actions and sympathies? Yes, that too. And the next question: Does the heap of sand count as an entity itself? For us, to answer it means asking: Is it not only each grain of sand that feels but also the heap? And the answer is yes, because it acts as an entity, i.e., it has sympathetic encounters, for instance, with the ground it lies on. William James's "compound problem" (*Principles of Psychology* I, 160) – in short, the fact that we cannot add up the feelings of parts to make the feeling of a new whole – fails us at this point, because it lacks the notion of action (in a reversal of Latour's problem, which acknowledges action but not feeling). Parts feel, but as they feel they act, and while they act they build structure, that of a new whole, and the structure processes the feelings of the new entity. And the last question: Do the parts then feel the same as the whole feels but somehow less of it? No: the relations between the parts are completely different from that between the whole and its partners. What the heap of sand feels lying on the ground is not the same as what a grain in that heap surrounded by a dozen others feels, nor is it a larger form of it. The grain shares many directions with its neighbors, being multi-oriented, while the heap is singularly oriented on the plane below it. If a wooden beam is stressed, that does not mean the fibers in that beam experience the same stress, since they experience it as fibers, not as a beam. The fibers have a sympathetic relationship with each other, not with the beam, and they do not need to become beamlike to construct a beam. If they were pebbles and particles in a concrete beam, their experiences would again be different. Feelings are neither divisible nor addable. The interiors of the parts are not wholly continuous with the interior of the whole, since the exteriors of the parts come in between, sharing their abstract points, and it is these exteriors that construct the interior of the whole. So yes, there is continuity of feeling, but not of *a* feeling. I think a major difference between Gothic ontology and the ontologies of Hartshorne, the early James and sometimes even Whitehead, lies in the fact that the latter's entities are mostly based on Leibniz's monads and are therefore atomistically *point-like*, while entities in Gothic

ontology are always ribs or ribbons and *line-like*. If it is linelike, an entity cannot be distinguished from force or orientation. Ribs are always oriented; when they feel, they act with intention. Ribs not only move but also change, as points cannot, and points therefore cannot combine qualitative and quantitative variables. The latter point is crucial, as without it we can never bridge the gap left by emergence, with pure quantity on the side of the many and pure quality on the side of the one.

78. Whitehead, *Process and Reality*, 113. See also: Steven Shaviro, *Without Criteria: Kant, Whitehead, Deleuze, and Aesthetics* (Cambridge, Mass.: MIT Press, 2009), Chapter Three.

79. Erwin Schrödinger, "The Present Situation in Quantum Mechanics," in: *Quantum Theory and Measurement*, ed. John Wheeler and W. H. Zurek (Princeton: Princeton University Press, 1983, orig. 1935). See also: Karen Barad, *Meeting the Universe Halfway: Quantum Physics and the Entanglement of Matter and Meaning* (Durham: Duke University Press, 2007), Chapter Seven.

80. Bruno Latour, *Pandora's Hope* (Cambridge, Mass.: Harvard University Press, 1999), Chapter Six.

81. Ibid., 179: "I use(d) translation to mean displacement, drift, invention, mediation, the creation of a link that did not exist before and that to some degree modifies the original two."

82. That marvelous word of James J. Gibson's; see: *The Ecological Approach to Visual Perception* (Boston: Houghton Mifflin, 1986, orig. 1979). Performance and performativity are terms used in earlier actor-network theory, e.g., by Bruno Latour and John Law, and applied mostly to technical objects that express themselves in "ecological" clusters of agency between institutes, organizations, people and machinery. Both "performance" and "affordance" signify an entanglement of subject and object, an inextricable codependency between them, though the terms are descriptive of a practice rather than being explicative, like our notions of feeling and sympathy.

83. Marcel Mauss, *The Gift: Forms and Functions of Exchange in Archaic Societies,* trans. Ian Cunnison (London: Cohen & West, 1966, orig. 1924), 3–5. Mauss, however, meant it as the subjectivity exceeding the object – "… the thing itself is a person or pertains to a person" – while I view it more as an object exceeding itself with feeling.

84. Ibid., 8–12.

85. Latour, *Pandora's Hope*, 182: "Action is simply not a property of humans but of an association of actants"; by actants, Latour means "humans and nonhumans" sharing an activity.

86. Heidegger, *Being and Time*, § 15–17.

87. See note 14.

88. Charles Hartshorne, *Born to Sing: An Interpretation and World Survey of Bird Song* (Bloomington: Indiana University Press, 1973).

89. Karl von Frisch, *Tanzsprache und Orientierung der Bienen* (Berlin: Springer Verlag, 1965).

90. Gregory Bateson, *Steps to an Ecology of Mind*, 455–57. To illustrate the fact that there is no clear boundary between organism and environment, Bateson uses some examples in the chapter "The Cybernetics of 'Self': A Theory of Alcoholism": one of a man felling a tree with an axe, one of someone hitting a billiard ball, and one of a blind person walking with a cane (317–18). These are all examples of haptic feelings extending into

objects (hand into cane) and through objects into other objects (cane into pavement),
close to extension in the McLuhanian sense and similar to the examples of the whisk
and the cream in the third chapter and the chimpanzee with the stick in this one.
At first sight, Bateson's argument seems to suggest a distinction between feeling-*into*
and feeling-*through* an object, between *mimetic* objects of art and *prosthetic* objects of
technology, but such a distinction would not be tenable, since we saw in the third
chapter that lines of feeling tend to proceed and objects should be viewed as stations,
not termini. If we again take up one of our typical examples from art, the Gothic
hinge, we see that there is sympathy not only between the door and the hinge but between the door frame and the hinge as well, between the wall and door frame, the
door and handle, etc. In short, there always exists a larger meshwork of sympathies,
since sympathy is based on aesthetic relations. From a prosthetic point of view, the
wall extends itself through the frame into the hinge, or the frame through the hinge
into the door; from a mimetic point of view, the wall acts like the door's edge in the
shape of a frame, and the door acts like a hand in the shape of a handle.

91. Eldridge Adams, "Territory Size and Shape in Fire Ants: A Model Based on Neighbourhood Interactions," in: *Ecology* 79, 1998: 1125–34.

92. Tijs Goldschmidt, "Every Species is the Embodiment of Experience with the World,"
in: *Feelings Are Always Local*, eds. Joke Brouwer and Arjen Mulder (Rotterdam:
V2_Publishing, 2004), 136–50. See also: Tijs Goldschmidt, *Darwin's Pond: Drama in
Lake Victoria* (Cambridge, Mass.: MIT Press, 1996).

93. To understand this technical argument somewhat better, let us try to imagine it as a
procedure. If one first were to lay out the oranges in the bottom of the box, packed as
tightly as possible, three of them would always meet at a node. Then, when one
placed a second layer on top, one would need to shift the whole pattern: an orange
does not go on top of the previous ones but in between, to fit exactly in the pocket
created by the node in the first layer. Looking at it three-dimensionally, this means
four oranges always meet at one (virtual) point – and so on, until the box is filled.
Now, if one were to replace the oranges with balloons and pour plaster over the whole
system, let it harden, and then puncture all the balloons, one would see all the empty
space replaced by legs in a structural system, something very close to a bone structure,
and each node would consist of four legs.

94. Jakob von Uexküll, *A Foray into the Worlds of Animals and Humans*, trans. Joseph
O'Neill (Minneapolis: University of Minnesota Press, 2010), passim.

95. Ibid., 190–91.

96. Georges Canguilhem, *Knowledge of Life* (New York: Fordham University Press, 2008),
104. He quotes Xavier Bichat from 1834.

97. Scott Turner, *The Extended Organism: The Physiology of Animal-Built Structures* (Cambridge, Mass: Harvard University Press, 2000), 194–200. Turner chose his title in direct contradistinction to Dawkins's *The Extended Phenotype* (1982).

98. Peter Sloterdijk, *Im Weltinnenraum des Kapitals: für eine philosophische Theorie der Globalisierung* (Frankfurt a.M.: Suhrkamp, 2005).

99. Ibid., Chapter 33.

100. Mario Praz, *Il patto col serpente* [The Pact with the Snake] (Milan: Mondadori, 1972).
Referenced to the Dutch edition: "De interieurs van Proust," in: *Het Verdrag met de
Slang* (Amsterdam: De Arbeiderspers, 1972), 476–95. Similarly, in his *The History of*

Furnishing (Braziller, 1964), Praz advocates only a single strategy as valid in interior decoration: stuffing it as completely as possible with objects and leaving no space for architecture.

101. In my *The Architecture of Continuity*, 252–53.
102. Rem Koolhaas, *The Harvard Design School Guide to Shopping* (Berlin: Taschen, 2002), 337–59.
103. Richard Buckminster Fuller, *Operating Manual For Spaceship Earth* (Carbondale: Southern Illinois University, 1970).
104. Peter Sloterdijk, *Sphären, 3 vols. I: Blasen, II: Globen, III: Schäume* (Frankfurt a.M.: Suhrkamp, 1998–2004).
105. See: Bruno Latour, *Pandora's Hope*, Chapter Nine. Latour starts the final chapter of his book with the disturbing suggestion that "something is missing" from his analysis (267) and proceeds to work from (scientific) facts and (religious) fetishes toward a mergence for which he coins the name "factishes." Latour is always close to Whitehead, and so he is here, when he extends the notion of event by accepting facts as constructed, but at the same time he excludes Whitehead's concepts of aim and beauty. And, if you seek to merge knowledge and belief, as Latour attempts to, you can hardly avoid Bergsonian intuition, which, as we discussed in Chapter Three, is part of the procedure of sympathy and aesthetics. Beauty is factual value. In this light, Frederick Ferré's *Living and Value* (Albany: SUNY Press, 2001) could be of interest. Ferré is another Whiteheadian process theologist, but one much more willing to accept beauty as ethics than, for instance, Griffin; he calls it "kalogenesis," combining the Greek roots for beauty (*kalós*) and creation (*genesis*): "the intrinsically satisfying experience … what Whiteheadians mean by beauty" (109). And, on page 136, he says: "… My environmental ethic will be neither biocentric nor anthropocentric, but *kalocentric*. The main ethical concerns will be support for creation of beauty in experience …"
106. Graham Harvey, *Animism: Respecting the Living World* (London: Hurst & Co., 2005).
107. Ruskin, *Works*, XVII: 84.
108. Ibid., XVII: 164. This is my final word in the proof of Ruskin being a vitalist.
109. See: *The Politics of the Impure*, eds. Joke Brouwer, Arjen Mulder and Lars Spuybroek (Rotterdam: V2_Publishing, 2010).
110. Marshall McLuhan, *Understanding Media: The Extensions of Man* (New York: Signet Books, 1964), 103.

bibliography

Abraham, Pol. *Viollet-le-Duc et le rationalisme médiéval*. Paris: Vincent, Fréal et Cie., 1934.

Adams, Eldridge. "Territory Size and Shape in Fire Ants: A Model Based on Neighbourhood Interactions," in: *Ecology*, 79:4 (June 1998), 1125–34.

Adamson, Glenn, ed. *The Craft Reader*. Oxford: Berg, 2010.

———. *Thinking Through Craft*. Oxford: Berg, 2007.

Agamben, Giorgio. *Potentialities: Collected Essays in Philosophy*. Edited and translated by Daniel Heller-Roazen. Stanford: Stanford University Press, 1999.

———. *The Open: Man and Animal*. Translated by Kevin Attell. Stanford: Stanford University Press, 2004.

Allen, Grant. "Aesthetic Evolution in Man" in: *The Popular Science Monthly*, 18 (January 1881), 339–56.

———. *Physiological Aesthetics*. New York: D. Appleton and Co., 1877.

Anthony, P. D. *John Ruskin's Labour*. Cambridge: Cambridge University Press, 1983.

Aristotle. *Physics*. Translated by Hardie and Gaye. Oxford: Clarendon, 1930.

———. *The Nichomachean Ethics*. Translated by David Ross. Oxford: Oxford University Press, 1984.

Armstrong, Charles I. *Romantic Organicism: From Idealist Origins to Ambivalent Afterlife*. Houndmills: Palgrave Macmillan, 2003.

Arnheim, Rudolf. *New Essays on the Psychology of Art*. Berkeley: University of California Press, 1986.

Arscott, Caroline. *Interlacings: Willliam Morris and Edward Burne-Jones*. New Haven and London: Yale University Press, 2008.

Artaud, Antonin. *The Theatre and Its Double*. New York: Grove Press, 1958.

Aschenbrenner, Karl, and Arnold Isenberg, eds. *Aesthetic Theories: Studies in the Philosophy of Art*. Englewood Cliffs: Prentice-Hall, 1965.

Atterbury, Paul, ed. *A. W. N. Pugin: Master of the Gothic Revival*. New Haven and London: Yale University Press, 1995.

Auerbach, Jeffrey A. *The Great Exhibition of 1851: A Nation on Display*. New Haven and London: Yale University Press, 1999.

Babbage, Charles. *On the Economy of Machinery and Manufactures*. Teddington: The Echo Library, 2008.

———. *The Exposition of 1851*. London: John Murray, 1851.

Bailey, Andrew R. "Beyond the Fringe: William James on the Transitional Parts of the Stream of Consciousness," in: *Journal of Consciousness Studies*, 6:2/3 (February/March 1999), 141–53.

Bain, George. *Celtic Art: The Methods of Construction*. London: Constable, 1951.

Baker, Derek W. *The Flowers of William Morris*. London: Barn Elms Publishing, 1996.

Baljon, Cornelis J. "Interpreting Ruskin: The Argument of the Seven Lamps of Architecture and the Stones of Venice," in: *The Journal of Aesthetics and Art Criticism*, 55:4 (Autumn 1997), 401–14.

Ball, Philip. *The Self-Made Tapestry: Pattern Formation in Nature*. Oxford: Oxford University Press, 1999.

———. *Universe of Stone: A Biography of Chartres Cathedral*. New York: Harper-Collins, 2008.

Ballantyne, Andrew. *Architecture, Landscape and Liberty: Richard Payne Knight and the Picturesque*. Cambridge: Cambridge University Press, 1997.

Banta, Martha. *Henry James and the Occult: The Great Extension*. Bloomington: Indiana University Press, 1972.

Barad, Karen. *Meeting the Universe Halfway: Quantum Physics and the Entanglement of Matter and Meaning*. Durham: Duke University Press, 2007.

Barzun, Jacques. *A Stroll with William James*. Chicago: University of Chicago Press, 1983.

Basch, Victor. *Essai critique sur l'esthétique de Kant*. Paris: Félix Alcan, 1896.

Bateson, Gregory, and Mary Catherine Bateson. *Angels Fear: Towards an Epistemology of the Sacred*. New York: Macmillan Publishing, 1987.

———. *Mind and Nature: A Necessary Unity*. New York: E. P. Dutton, 1979.

———. *Steps to an Ecology of Mind: Collected Essays in Anthropology, Psychiatry, Evolution, and Epistemology*. New York: Chandler, 1972.

Bateson, William. *Problems of Genetics*. New Haven and London: Yale University Press, 1979, orig. 1913.

Baudrillard, Jean. *De la séduction*. Paris: Galilée, 1979.

———. *L'Échange symbolique et la mort*. Paris: Gallimard, 1976.

———. *Simulacra and Simulations*. Translated by Sheila Faria Glaser. Ann Arbor: University of Michigan, 1994, orig. 1981.

Bennett, Jane. *Thoreau's Nature: Ethics, Politics, and the Wild*. Walnut Creek: Altamira Press, 2000.

Bentley, W. A., and Humphreys, W. J. *Snow Crystals*. New York: Dover Publications, 1962.

Bergson, Henri. *Creative Evolution*. New York: Dover Publications, 1998, orig. English translation 1911.

———. *Creative Mind: An Introduction to Metaphysics*. New York: Citadel Press, 1946, orig. 1903.

Besant, Annie, and Charles Leadbetter. *Thought-Forms*. Wheaton, Ill.: Quest Books, 1999.

Billings, Robert William. *The Power of Form*. Edinburgh: William Blackwood and Sons, 1851.

Bisgrove, Richard. *The Gardens of Gertrude Jekyll*. London: Francis Lincoln, 1992.
———. *William Robinson: The Wild Gardener*. London: Francis Lincoln, 2008.

Bizup, Joseph. *Manufacturing Culture: Vindications of Early Victorian Industry*. Charlottesville: University of Virginia Press, 2003.

Blau, Eve. *Ruskinian Gothic: The Architecture of Deane and Woodward*. Princeton: Princeton University Press, 1980.

Boas, Franz. *Primitive Art*. Mineola, New York: Dover Publications, 1983.

Bony, Jean. *French Gothic Architecture of the 12ᵗʰ & 13ᵗʰ Centuries*. Berkeley: University of California Press, 1983.
———. *The English Decorated Style: Gothic Architecture Transformed, 1250–1350*. Ithaca: Cornell University Press, 1979.

Brady, R. H. "Form and Cause in Goethe's Morphology," in: *Goethe and the Sciences: A Re-appraisal*. Eds. F. Amrine, F. J. Zucker and H. Wheeler. Dordrecht: Reidel, 1987.

Brett, David. *On Decoration*. Cambridge: The Lutterworth Press, 1992.
———. *Rethinking Decoration: Pleasure and Ideology in the Visual Arts*. Cambridge: Cambridge University Press, 2005.

Brooks, Michael W. *John Ruskin and Victorian Architecture*. New Brunswick: Rutgers University Press, 1987.

Brouwer, J., A. Mulder and L. Spuybroek, eds. *The Politics of the Impure*. Rotterdam: V2_Publishing, 2010.

Brownlee, David B. *The Law Courts: The Architecture of George Edmund Street*. Cambridge, Mass.: MIT Press, 1984.

Buchanan, Brett. *Onto-Ethologies: The Animal Environments of Uexküll, Heidegger, Merleau-Ponty, and Deleuze*. Albany: SUNY Press, 2008.

Buckley, Jerome Hamilton. *The Victorian Temper: A Study in Literary Culture*. London: George Allen, 1952.

Buckminster Fuller, Richard. *Operating Manual for Spaceship Earth*. Carbondale: Southern Illinois University, 1970.

Buffon, Georges-Louis Leclerc, Comte de. "Histoire naturelle des animaux," in: *Oeuvres Complètes de Buffon*. 14 Vols. Paris: Imprimerie Royale, 1885.

Burd, Van Akin, ed. *Christmas Story: John Ruskin's Venetian Letters of 1876–1877*. Newark: University of Delaware Press, 1999.
———, ed. *John Ruskin and Rose La Touche: Her Unpublished Diaries of 1861 and 1867*. Oxford: Clarendon Press, 1979.
———, ed. *The Ruskin Family Letters*. 2 vols. Ithaca: Cornell University Press, 1973.

Burke, Edmund. *A Philosophical Enquiry into the Origin of our Ideas of the Sublime and the Beautiful*. Oxford: Oxford University Press, 1998, orig. 1757.

Butler, Samuel. *Life and Habit*. London: Fifield, 1910, orig. 1878.

Callicot, J. Baird, and Michael P. Nelson, eds. *The Great New Wilderness Debate: An Expansive Collection of Writings Defining Wilderness From John Muir to Gary Snyder*. Athens: The University of Georgia Press, 1998.

Canguilhem, Georges. *Knowledge of Life*. New York: Fordham University Press, 2008.

Cannon, Jon. *Cathedral: The Great English Cathedrals and the World That Made Them, 600–1540*. London: Constable, 2007.

Carroll, Sean. *Endless Forms Most Beautiful: The New Science of Evo Devo and the Making of the Animal Kingdom*. London: Weidenfeld & Nicolson, 2006.

Channell, David. *The Vital Machine: A Study of Technology and Organic Life*. New York: Oxford University Press, 1991.

Christie, Archibald. *Pattern Design: An Introduction to the Study of Formal Ornament*. New York: Dover Publications, 1969.

Clark, Andrew. *Diderot's Part*. Aldershot: Ashgate, 2008.

Clark, Kenneth. *Ruskin Today*. London: John Murray, 1964.

———. *The Gothic Revival: An Essay in the History of Taste*. London: Constable and Co., 1928.

Colebrooke, Henry Thomas. "On Presenting the Gold Medal of the Astronomical Society to Charles Babbage," in: *Memoirs of the Astronomical Society*, 1 (1825), 509–10.

Collier, Bruce, and James MacLachlan. *Charles Babbage and the Engines of Perfection*. Oxford: Oxford University Press, 1998.

Collingwood, W. G. *The Art and Teaching of John Ruskin*. New York: G. P. Putnam's Sons, 1891.

———. *The Life and Work of John Ruskin*. 2 vols. Boston and New York: Houghton, Mifflin and Co., 1893.

Conner, Patrick. *Savage Ruskin*. London: Macmillan Press, 1979.

Cook, E. T. *Homes and Haunts of John Ruskin*. London: George Allen, 1912.

———. *The Life of John Ruskin*. 2 Vols. London: George Allen, 1912.

Coyle, John. "Ruskin, Proust and the Art of Failure," in: *Essays in Criticism*, 56:1 (2006), 28–49.

Coyne, Richard. *Technoromanticism: Digital Narrative, Holism, and the Romance of the Real*. Cambridge, Mass.: MIT Press, 1999.

Crinson, Mark. *Empire Building: Orientalism and Victorian Architecture*. London and New York: Routledge, 1996.

Crook, J. Mordaunt. "Ruskinian Gothic," in: *The Ruskin Polygon*. Eds. John Dixon Hunt and Faith Holland. Manchester: Manchester University Press, 1982.

Darwin, Charles. *On the Origin of Species*. Annotated by James Costa. Cambridge, Mass.: Belknap and Harvard University Press, 2009, orig. 1859.

———. *The Descent of Man, and Selection in Relation to Sex*. 2 vols. London: John Murray, 1871, reprinted in facsimile for *The Classics of Science Library* in 1998.

————. *The Power of Movement in Plants*. New York: Da Capo Press, 1966, reprinted from the 1881 edition.

Davenport, Guy. "The House That Jack Built," in: *The Geography of the Imagination*. London: Picador, 1984.

Davies, Erik. *Techgnosis: Myth, Magic and Mysticism in the Age of Information*. New York: Harmony Books, 1998.

Dawkins, Richard. *The Extended Phenotype*. Oxford: Oxford University Press, 1982.

————. *The Selfish Gene*. Oxford: Oxford University Press, 1976.

De Hamel, Christopher. *A History of Illuminated Manuscripts*. London: Guild Publishing and Phaidon, 1986.

Dearden, James. *John Ruskin: A Life in Pictures*. Sheffield: Sheffield Academic Press, 1999.

DeLanda, Manuel. "Emergence, Causality and Realism," in: *The Speculative Turn: Continental Materialism and Realism*. Eds. L. Bryant, N. Srnicek, G. Harman. Melbourne: re.press, 2010.

————. *A New Philosophy of Society: Assemblage Theory and Social Complexity*. London and New York: Continuum, 2006.

Deleuze, Gilles, and Félix Guattari. *A Thousand Plateaus: Capitalism and Schizophrenia*. Translated by Brian Massumi. London: Athlone Press, 1988.

Deleuze, Gilles. *Bergsonism*. Translated by Hugh Tomlinson and Barbara Habberjam. New York: Zone Books, 1991.

————. *Dialogues II*. Translated by Hugh Tomlinson and Barbara Habberjam. London and New York: Continuum, 2006.

————. *Essays Critical and Clinical*. Translated by Daniel W. Smith and Michael A. Greco. New York: Verso, 1998.

————. *Francis Bacon: The Logic of Sensation*. Translated by Daniel W. Smith. London and New York: Continuum, 2003.

————. *Pure Immanence*. Translated by Anne Boyman. New York: Zone Books, 2001.

————. *The Fold: Leibniz and the Baroque*. Translated by Tom Conley. Minneapolis: University of Minnesota Press, 1993.

Descola, Philippe. *Par-delà nature et culture*. Paris: Gallimard, 2005.

Desmond, Adrian, and James Moore. *Darwin*. London: Penguin Books, 1992.

Diderot, Denis. *Oeuvres Philosophiques*. Paris: Gallimard, 2010.

————. *Rameau's Nephew and D'Alembert's Dream*. London: Penguin Classics, 1976.

Dixon Hunt, John, and Faith M. Holland, eds. *The Ruskin Polygon: Essays on the Imagination of John Ruskin*. Manchester: Manchester University Press, 1982.

Dixon Hunt, John. *Gardens and the Picturesque: Studies in the History of Landscape Architecture*. Cambridge, Mass.: MIT Press, 1994.

Donahue, Neil H., ed. *Invisible Cathedrals: The Expressionist Art History of Wil-*

helm Worringer. University Park, Penn.: Pennsylvania State University Press, 1995.

Dresser, Christopher. *Principles of Decorative Design*. London: Academy Editions, 1973, reprinted from 1873.

―――. *The Art of Decorative Design*. New York: American Life Foundation, 1977, reprinted from 1862.

Driesch, Hans. *The History and Theory of Vitalism*. Translated by C. K. Ogden. London: Macmillan and Co., 1914.

Dyson, George B. *Darwin Among the Machines: The Evolution of Global Intelligence*. Reading, Mass.: Perseus Books, 1997.

Eastlake, Charles L. *A History of the Gothic Revival*. New York: American Life Foundation, 1975, orig. 1872.

Eck, Caroline van. *Organicism in Nineteenth-Century Architecture: An Inquiry into Its Theoretical and Philosophical Background*. Amsterdam, Architectura & Natura Press, 1994.

Eco, Umberto, ed. *History of Beauty*. Translated by Alistair McEwen. New York: Rizzoli, 2004.

Ellmann, Richard. *Oscar Wilde*. London: Penguin Books, 1988.

Emery, Elisabeth. *Romancing the Cathedral: Gothic Architecture in Fin-de-Siècle French Culture*. New York: State University of New York Press, 2001.

Erlande-Brandenburg, Alain. *The Cathedral Builders of the Middle Ages*. London: Thames and Hudson, 1995.

―――. *The Cathedral: The Social and Architectural Dynamics of Construction*. Translated by Martin Thom. Cambridge: Cambridge University Press, 1994.

Essinger, James. *Jacquard's Web: How a Hand Loom Led to the Birth of the Information Age*. Oxford: Oxford University Press, 2004.

Evans, Joan. *Pattern: A Study of Ornament in Western Europe, 1180-1900*. 2 vols. *I: Middle Ages* and *II: Renaissance to 1900*. New York: Da Capo Press, 1976.

Fechner, Gustav Theodor. *Das Unendliche Leben*. München: Matthes & Seitz Verlag, 1984.

―――. *Religion of a Scientist*. Translated by W. Lowrie. New York: Pantheon, 1946.

Ferré, Frederick. *Living and Value: Towards a Constructive Postmodern Ethics*. Albany: SUNY Press, 2001.

Fitchen, John. *The Construction of Gothic Cathedrals: A Study of Medieval Vault Erection*. Chicago and London: Chicago University Press, 1981, orig. 1961.

Focillon, Henri. *The Art of the West*. 2 vols. *I: Romanesque Art* and *II: Gothic Art*. Translated by Donald King. London: Phaidon, 1963.

―――. *The Life of Forms of Art*. Translated by Charles Hogan and George Kubler. New York: Wittenborn, 1948, republished by Zone Books, 1992.

Fox, Daniel M. *The Discovery of Abundance: Simon N. Patten and the Transformation of Social Theory*. Ithaca: Cornell University Press, 1967.

Frampton, Kenneth. *Studies in Tectonic Culture: The Poetics of Construction in Nineteenth and Twentieth Century Architecture.* Cambridge, Mass.: MIT Press, 1995.

Francé, Raoul Heinrich. *Die Pflanze als Erfinder.* Stuttgart: Kosmos, Gesellschaft der Naturfreunde, 1920.

———. *Germs of Mind in Plants.* Translated by A. M. Simons. Chicago: Charles H. Kerr & Co., 1905.

Frank, Isabelle, ed. *The Theory of Decorative Art: An Anthology of European and American Writings, 1750–1940.* Translated by David Britt. New Haven and London: Yale University Press, 2000.

Frankl, Paul. *Gothic Architecture.* London: Penguin, 1962, republished by Yale University Press, 2000.

———. *The Gothic: Literary Sources and Interpretation through Eight Centuries.* Princeton: Princeton University Press, 1960.

Frazer, James. *The Golden Bough: A History of Myth and Religion.* London: Chancellor Press, 1994.

Frisch, Karl von. *Tanzsprache und Orientierung der Bienen.* Berlin: Springer Verlag, 1965.

Fry, Paul. *Wordsworth and the Poetry of What We Are.* New Haven and London: Yale University Press, 2008.

Gamble, Cynthia. "John Ruskin, Viollet-le-Duc and the Alps," in: *Alpine Journal,* 104:348 (1999), 185–96.

———. *John Ruskin, Henry James and the Shropshire Lads.* London: New European Publications, 2008.

———. *Proust as Interpreter of Ruskin: The Seven Lamps of Translation.* Birmingham, Alab.: Summa Publications, 2002.

Gardner, John Starkie. *Ironwork, Part I and II.* London: Chapman and Hall, 1893.

Garrigan, Kristine Ottesen. *Ruskin on Architecture: His Thought and Influence.* Madison, Wis.: University of Wisconsin Press, 1973.

Geddes, Patrick. *Cities in Evolution.* London: Williams & Norgate, 1949, revised edition from 1915.

———. *John Ruskin, Economist.* Edinburgh: William Brown, 1884.

Gell, Alfred. "The Technology of Enchantment and the Enchantment of Technology," in: *Anthropology, Art and Aesthetics.* Eds. Jeremy Coote and Anthony Shelton. Oxford: Oxford University Press, 1992.

———. "Vogel's Net: Traps as Artworks and Artworks as Traps," in: *Journal of Material Culture,* 1:1 (March 1996), 15–38.

———. *Art and Agency: An Anthropological Theory.* Oxford: Oxford University Press, 1998.

Gerard, Alexander. *An Essay on Taste.* Edinburgh: J. Bell, 1758.

Gibson, James J. *The Ecological Approach to Visual Perception.* Boston: Houghton Mifflin, 1986, orig. 1979.

Gladstein, Gerald A. "The Historical Roots of Contemporary Empathy Research," in: *Journal of the History of the Behavioral Sciences*, 20:1 (January 1984), 38–59.

Goldschmidt, Tijs. "Every Species is the Embodiment of Experience with the World," in: *Feelings Are Always Local*, 136–50. Eds. Joke Brouwer and Arjen Mulder. Rotterdam: V2_Publishing, 2004.

———. *Darwin's Pond: Drama in Lake Victoria*. Cambridge, Mass.: MIT Press, 1996.

Gombrich, Ernst. *The Sense of Order: A Study in the Psychology of Decorative Art*. London: Phaidon, 2006.

Gould, Stephen J. "Kropotkin Was No Crackpot," in: *Natural History*, 106:7 (June 1997), 12–21.

———. *The Panda's Thumb*. London: Penguin Books, 1990, orig. 1980.

Grant, Iain Hamilton. *Philosophies of Nature After Schelling*. London and New York: Continuum, 2006.

Greeno, James G. "Gibson's Affordances," in: *Psychological Review*, 101:2 (1994), 336–42.

Griffin, David Ray. *Unsnarling the World Knot: Consciousness, Freedom, and the Mind-Body Problem*. Eugene, Oreg.: Wipf and Stock, 2007, orig. 1998.

———. *Whitehead's Radically Different Postmodern Philosophy: An Argument for Its Contemporary Relevance*. New York: SUNY Press, 2007.

Grodecki, Louis. *Gothic Architecture*. New York: Rizzoli, 1985.

Haddon, Alfred. *Evolution in Art*. London: Walter Scott, 1895.

Hague, Angela. *Fiction, Intuition, and Creativity: Studies in Brontë, James, Woolf, and Lessing*. Washington: Catholic University of America Press, 2003.

Halén, Widar. *Christopher Dresser: A Pioneer of Modern Design*. London: Phaidon Press, 1990.

Haraway, Donna Jeanne. *Crystals, Fabrics, and Fields: Metaphors that Shape Embryos*. Berkeley: North Atlantic Books, 2004, orig. 1974.

Harman, Graham. *Prince of Networks: Bruno Latour and Metaphysics*. Melbourne: re.press, 2009.

———. *Tool-Being: Heidegger and the Metaphysics of Objects*. Peru, Ill.: Open Court, 2002.

Hartshorne, Charles. *Beyond Humanism: Essays in the New Philosophy of Nature*. Chicago: Willet, Clark and Co., 1937.

———. *Born to Sing: An Interpretation and World Survey of Bird Song*. Bloomington: Indiana University Press, 1973.

Harvey, Charles, and Jon Press. *William Morris: Design and Enterprise in Victorian Britain*. Manchester: Manchester University Press, 1991.

Harvey, Graham. *Animism: Respecting the Living World*. London: Hurst & Co., 2005.

Hayman, John. "Towards the Labyrinth: Ruskin's Lectures as Slade Professor of

Art" in: Robert Hewison, *New Approaches to Ruskin*. London and New York: Routledge & Kegan Paul, 1981.

Heft, Harry. *Ecological Psychology in Context: James Gibson, Roger Barker, and the Legacy of William James's Radical Empiricism*. Mahwah, N. J.: Lawrence Erlbaum, 2001.

Heidegger, Martin. "Only a God Can Save Us," in: *Der Spiegel*, interviewed by Rudolf Augstein and Georg Wolff in 1966. Published after Heidegger's death in 1976, translated for *Philosophy Today*, 20 (Winter 1976), 267–84.

———. *Basic Writings*. Ed. David Krell. New York: Routledge & Kegan Paul, 1993.

———. *Being and Time*. Translated by John Macquarrie and Edward Robinson. New York: Harper and Brothers, 1962.

———. *Poetry, Language, Thought*. Translated by Albert Hofstadter. New York: Harper & Row, 1971.

Helmreich, Anne. "Re-presenting Nature: Ideology, Art, and Science in William Robinson's 'Wild Garden,'" in: *Nature and Ideology: Natural Garden Design in the Twentieth Century*, ed. Joachim Wolschke-Bulmann. Washington: Dumbarton Oaks, 1997.

Helsinger, Elisabeth K. *Ruskin and the Art of the Beholder*. Cambridge, Mass.: Harvard University Press, 1982.

Henning, Brian G. "On the Possibility of a Whiteheadian Aesthetics of Morals," in: *Process Studies*, 31:2 (2002), 97–114.

———. "Trusting the Efficacy of Beauty," in: *Ethics & the Environment*, 14:1 (2009), 101–28.

Herder, Johann Gottfried. *Sculpture: Some Observations on Shape and Form from Pygmalion's Creative Dream*. Translated by Jason Gaiger. Chicago and London: Chicago University Press, 2002.

Hewison, Robert, ed. *New Approaches to Ruskin*. London and New York: Routledge & Kegan Paul, 1981.

Hewison, Robert, Ian Warrell and Stephen Wildman. *Ruskin, Turner and the Pre-Raphaelites*. Catalogue to the exhibition. London: Tate Gallery Publishing, 2000.

Hewison, Robert. *John Ruskin: The Argument of the Eye*. Princeton: Princeton University Press, 1976.

———. *Ruskin's Artists: Studies in Victorian Visual Economy*. Aldershot: Ashgate Publishing, 2000.

Heyman, Jacques. *The Stone Skeleton: Structural Engineering of Masonry Architecture*. Cambridge: Cambridge University Press, 1995.

Hill, Rosemary. *God's Architect: Pugin and the Building of Romantic Britain*. London: Penguin Books, 2008.

Hilton, Tim. *John Ruskin: The Early Years*. New Haven and London: Yale University Press, 1985.

————. *John Ruskin: The Later Years*. New Haven and London: Yale University Press, 2000.

Hipple, Walter John. *The Beautiful, the Sublime and the Picturesque*. Carbondale: Southern Illinois University Press, 1957.

Hogarth, William. *The Analysis of Beauty*. Introduced by Ronald Paulson. New Haven and London: Yale University Press, 1997, orig. 1753.

Holheim, W. Wolfgang. *The Hermeneutic Mode: Essays on Time in Literature and Literary Theory*. Ithaca: Cornell University Press, 1984.

Horne, Clare E. *Geometric Symmetry in Patterns and Tilings*. Cambridge: Woodhead Publishing, 2000.

Hrvol Flores, Carol A. *Owen Jones: Design, Ornament, Architecture and Theory in an Age of Transition*. New York: Rizzoli, 2006.

Hugo, Victor. *Notre-Dame de Paris*. Translated by Alban Krailsheimer. Oxford: Oxford World's Classics, 1993.

Huizinga, Johan. *The Autumn of the Middle Ages*. Chicago: University of Chicago Press, 1996, orig. 1919.

Hulme, T. E. *Further Speculations*. Ed. Sam Hynes. Lincoln: University of Nebraska Press, 1962.

————. *Speculations: Essays on Humanism and the Philosophy of Art*. London and New York: Routledge & Kegan Paul, 1987, orig. 1924.

Hume, David. *Four Dissertations*. London: Millar, 1757.

————. *Treatise on Human Nature*. 2 vols. London: J. M. Dent & Sons, 1911, orig. 1739.

Humphreys, Henry Noel, and Owen Jones. *The Illuminated Books of the Middle Ages*. London: Bracken Books, 1990, orig. 1849.

Hussey, Christopher. *The Picturesque: Studies in a Point of View*. London: G. P. Putnam, 1927.

Ierodiakonou, Katerina. "The Greek Concept of Sympatheia and Its Byzantine Appropriation in Michael Psellos," in: *The Occult Sciences in Byzantium*. Eds. P. Magdalino and M. Mavroudi. Geneva: La Pomme d'Or, 2006.

Ihde, Don. *Heidegger's Technologies: Postphenomenological Perspectives*. New York: Fordham University Press, 2010.

Ingold, Tim. *Lines: A Brief History*. London and New York: Routledge, 2007.

————. *The Perception of the Environment: Essays on Livelihood, Dwelling and Skill*. London and New York: Routledge, 2000.

Jahoda, Gustav. "Theodor Lipps and the Shift from 'Sympathy' to 'Empathy,'" in: *Journal of the History of the Behavioral Sciences*, 41:2 (Spring 2005), 151–63.

James, William. *A Pluralistic Universe*. Cambridge, Mass.: Harvard University Press, 1977, orig. 1909.

————. *Essays in Radical Empiricism*. Lincoln: University of Nebraska Press, 1996, orig. 1912.

————. *The Principles of Psychology*. 2 vols. New York: Dover Publications, 1950, orig. 1890.

Jantzen, Hans. *Die Gotik des Abendlandes*. Köln: DuMont, 1962. Translated as *High Gothic* by James Palmes (Princeton University Press, 1984).

Johnston, John. *The Allure of Machinic Life*. Cambridge, Mass.: MIT Press, 2008.

Jones, Alun R. *The Life and Opinions of T. E. Hulme*. Boston: Beacon Press, 1960.

Jones, Owen. *The Grammar of Ornament*. London: Day and Son, 1856, with 100 folio plates. The later edition with 112 folio plates was published by Bernard Quaritch in 1865 (reprinted by Studio Editions in 1986).

Jung, Carl-Gustav. *Psychological Types*. Translated by H. G. Barnes and revised by R. Hull. Princeton: Princeton University Press, 1976.

Kane, Robert and Stephen H. Phillips, eds. *Hartshorne: Process Philosophy and Theology*. Albany: SUNY Press, 1989.

Kant, Immanuel. *Critique of Judgement*. Translated by James Meredith. Oxford: Oxford University Press, 2007, orig. 1790.

Katz, Robert L. *Empathy: Its Nature and Uses*. London: The Free Press of Glencoe, Collier-MacMillan, 1963.

Kemp, Wolfgang. *The Desire of My Eyes: The Life and Work of John Ruskin*. New York: Noonday Press, 1992.

Kirschner, Marc, and John Gerhart. *The Plausibility of Life: Resolving Darwin's Dilemma*. New Haven and London: Yale University Press, 2005.

Koolhaas, Rem. *The Harvard Design School Guide to Shopping*. Berlin: Taschen, 2002.

Kropotkin, Peter. *Mutual Aid: A Factor of Evolution*. London: William Heinemann, 1907, orig. 1902.

La Sizeranne, Robert (Monier) de. *Ruskin and the Religion of Beauty*. Translated by the Countess of Galloway. London: George Allen, 1899.

Lamprecht, Karl. *Initial-Ornamentik des VIII. bis XIII. Jahrhunderts*. Leipzig: Alphons Dürr Verlag, 1882.

Landow, George, ed. *Ladies of Shalott: A Victorian Masterpiece and Its Contexts*. Catalogue for the exhibition in Bell Gallery, List Art Center, Providence, 1985.

Landow, George. *Elegant Jeremiahs: The Sage from Carlyle to Mailer*. Ithaca: Cornell University Press, 1986.

———. *John Ruskin*. Oxford: Oxford University Press, 1985.

———. *The Aesthetic and Critical Theories of John Ruskin*. Princeton: Princeton University Press, 1971.

———. *William Holman Hunt and Typological Symbolism*. New Haven: Yale University Press and the Paul Mellon Centre for Studies in British Art, 1979.

Lapoujade, David. "From Network to Patchwork," in: *The Pragmatist Imagination: Thinking About "Things in the Making."* Ed. Joan Ockman. Princeton: Princeton Architectural Press, 2000.

———. "From Transcendental Empiricism to Worker Nomadism: William James," in: *Pli*, 9 (2000), 190–99.

Latour, Bruno. "Can We Get Our Materialism Back, Please?" in: *Isis*, 98 (2007), 138–42.

Latour, Bruno. "Why Has Critique Run Out of Steam? From Matters of Fact to Matters of Concern" in: *Critical Inquiry*, 30 (Winter 2004), 225–48.

———. *Pandora's Hope: Essays on the Reality of Science Studies*. Cambridge, Mass.: Harvard University Press, 1999.

Lawrence, D. H. *Studies in Classic American Literature*. Harmondsworth: Penguin Books, 1981.

Lee, Vernon. *Beauty and Ugliness*. London: John Lane, 1912.

———. *Laurus Nobilis: Chapters on Art and Life*. London: John Lane, 1909.

———. *The Beautiful*. Cambridge: Cambridge University Press, 1913.

Levine, George. *Realism, Ethics and Secularism: Essays on Victorian Literature and Science*. Cambridge: Cambridge University Press, 2008.

Links, J. G. *The Ruskins in Normandy: A Tour in 1848 with Murray's Hand-book*. London: John Murray, 1968.

Lipps, Theodor. "Empathy and Aesthetic Pleasure," in: *Aesthetic Theories: Studies in the Philosophy of Art*. Eds. Karl Aschenbrenner and Arnold Isenberg. Englewood Cliffs: Prentice-Hall, 1965.

———. "Empathy, Inner Imitation, and Sense-Feelings," in: Melvin Rader, *A Modern Book of Esthetics: An Anthology*. New York: Holt, Rhinehart and Winston, 1979.

———. *Ästhetik: Psychologie des Schönen under der Kunst*. 2 vols. Leipzig: Leopold Voss Verlag, 1914.

———. *Raumästhetik*. Amsterdam: E. J. Bonset, 1966, reprint from 1897.

Listowel, The Earl of (William Hare). *Modern Aesthetics: An Historical Introduction*. New York: Teachers College Press, 1967.

Loos, Adolf. *Ornament and Crime, Selected Essays*. Ed. Adolf Opel. Translated by Michael Mitchell. Riverside: Ariadne Press, 1998.

Lucie-Smith, Edward. *The Story of Craft: The Craftsman's Role in Society*. Oxford: Phaidon, 1981.

Lutyens, Mary, ed. *Effie in Venice: Unpublished Letters of Mrs. John Ruskin Written from Venice between 1849 and 1852*. London: John Murray, 1965.

Lutyens, Mary. *Millais and the Ruskins*. New York: Vanguard Press, 1967.

MacArthur, John. *The Picturesque: Architecture, Disgust and Other Irregularities*. London and New York: Routledge, 2007.

MacCarthy, Fiona. *William Morris: A Life of Our Time*. London: Faber and Faber, 1995.

Mallgrave, Harry Francis, and Eleftherios Ikonomou, eds. *Empathy, Form, and Space: Problems in German Aesthetics, 1873–1893*. Santa Monica: Getty Center Publications, 1994.

Mandelbrot, Benoit. *The Fractal Geometry of Nature*. New York: Freeman and Company, 1983.

Margulis, Lynn. *Symbiotic Planet: A New Look at Evolution.* Amherst: Basic Books, 1998.

Maritain, Jacques. *Art and Scholasticism.* Translated by J. F. Scanlan. London: Sheed & Ward, 1946.

Massumi, Brian. "The Ether and Your Anger: Toward a Pragmatics of the Useless," in: *The Pragmatist Imagination: Thinking About "Things in the Making."* Ed. Joan Ockman. Princeton: Princeton Architectural Press, 2000.

———. "The Thinking-Feeling of What Happens," in: *Interact or Die!* Eds. Joke Brouwer and Arjen Mulder. Rotterdam: V2_Publishing, 2007.

Mauss, Marcel. *The Gift: Forms and Functions of Exchange in Archaic Societies.* Translated by Ian Cunnison. London: Cohen & West, 1966, orig. 1924.

Mayeroff, Milton. *On Caring.* New York: Harper & Row, 1971.

McCullough, Malcolm. *Abstracting Craft: The Practical Digital Hand.* Cambridge, Mass.: MIT Press, 1997.

McDermott, John J. *Streams of Experience: Reflections on the History and Philosophy of American Culture.* Amherst: University of Massachusetts Press, 1986.

McLuhan, Marshall. *The Gutenberg Galaxy.* Toronto: University of Toronto Press, 1962.

———. *Understanding Media: The Extensions of Man.* New York: Signet Books, 1964.

Meijer, P. A. *Stoic Theology: Proofs of the Existence of the Cosmic God and of the Traditional Gods.* Delft: Eburon, 2007.

Meurant, Georges. *Shoowa Design: African Textiles from the Kingdom of Kuba.* London: Thames and Hudson, 1986.

Meyer, Franz Sales. *Handbook of Ornament: A Grammar of Art, Industrial and Architectural Designing in All Its Branches for Practical as well as Theoretical Use.* New York: Dover Publications, 1957, reprint from 1888.

Meynell, Alice. *John Ruskin.* New York: Dodd, Mead and Co., 1900.

Middleton, Robin. "Viollet-le-Duc et les Alpes: la dispute du Mont Blanc," in: *Viollet-le-Duc: Centenaire de la Mort à Lausanne.* Cat. Exposition au Musée historique de l'Ancien-Evêché, 1979.

Morris, William. *Gothic Architecture: A Lecture for the Arts and Crafts Exhibition Society.* Hammersmith: Kelmscott Press, 1893.

———. *News from Nowhere and Other Writings.* London: Penguin Books, 1993.

———. *Some Hints on Pattern-Designing.* London: printed at the Kelmscott Press, Hammersmith, and published by Longmans & Co., 1899.

Morrison, P., and E. Morrison, *Charles Babbage and his Calculating Machines.* New York: Dover, 1961.

Müller-Sievers, Helmut. *Self-Generation: Biology, Philosophy, and Literature Around 1800.* Stanford: Stanford University Press, 1997.

Naylor, Gillian, ed. *William Morris by Himself: Designs and Writings.* London and Sydney: Macdonald and Co., 1988.

Ockman, Joan, ed. *The Pragmatist Imagination: Thinking About "Things In The Making."* Princeton: Princeton Architectural Press, 2000.

Oelschlager, Max. *The Idea of Wilderness: From Prehistory to the Age of Ecology.* New Haven and London: Yale University Press, 1991.

Oosterling, Henk. *Radicale middelmatigheid.* Amsterdam: Boom, 2000.

Oudolf, Piet, and Henk Gerritsen. *Planting the Natural Garden.* Translated by Susanne Tonkens-Hart. Portland: Timber Press, 2003.

Paley, William. *Natural theology: or, Evidences of the existence and attributes of the deity, collected from the appearances of nature.* Trenton: Daniel Fenton, 1824, orig. 1802.

Panofsky, Erwin. *Gothic Architecture and Scholasticism.* New York: Meridian Books, 1951.

————. *Studies in Iconology: Humanistic Themes in the Art of the Renaissance.* New York: Harper & Row, 1967, orig. 1939.

Parry, Linda, ed. *William Morris.* London: Philip Wilson Publishers in association with the Victoria and Albert Museum, 1996.

Paz, Octavio. *In Praise of Hands: Contemporary Crafts of the World.* Greenwich, Conn.: New York Graphic Society, 1974.

Penny, Nicholas. *Ruskin's Drawings in the Ashmolean Museum.* Oxford: Phaidon and Christie's, 1989.

Perry, Ralph Barton. *In the Spirit of William James.* New Haven and London: Yale University Press, 1938.

————. *The Thought and Character of William James.* Cambridge, Mass.: Harvard University Press, 1948.

Pevsner, Nikolaus. *Ruskin and Viollet-le-Duc: Englishness and Frenchness in the Appreciation of Gothic Architecture.* London: Thames and Hudson, 1969.

Pinkney, Tony. *William Morris in Oxford: The Campaigning Years, 1879–1895.* Grosmont: Illuminati Books, 2007.

Pissaro, Joachim. *Monet's Cathedral: Rouen 1892–1894.* New York: Alfred A. Knopf, 1990.

Praz, Mario. *An Illustrated History of Furnishing: From the Renaissance to the 20ᵗʰ Century.* Translated by William Weaver. New York: G. Braziller, 1964.

————. *Il patto col serpente.* Milan: Mondadori, 1972.

Prettejohn, Elizabeth. *The Art of the Pre-Raphaelites.* London: Tate Publishing, 2007.

Price, Uvedale. *On the Picturesque.* Otley: Woodstock Books, 2000 facsimile, reprint from 1796.

Proust, Marcel. *On Reading Ruskin: Prefaces to La Bible d'Amiens and Sésame et les Lys.* Translated and edited by Jean Autret, William Burford and Philip J. Wolfe. New Haven and London: Yale University Press, 1987.

Pugin, Augustus Welby Northmore. *Contrasts; or, A parallel between the noble edifices of the fourteenth and fifteenth centuries, and similar buildings of the present day; shewing the present decay of taste; Accompanied by appropriate Text*. London: printed for the author, 1836.

Raaijmakers, Dick. *CAHIER-M: A Brief Morphology of Electronic Sound*. Leuven: University Press of Leuven, 2000, revised edition 2005.

Rader, Melvin. *A Modern Book of Esthetics: An Anthology*. New York: Holt, Rhinehart and Winston, 1979.

Recht, Roland. *Believing and Seeing: The Art of Gothic Cathedrals*. Translated by Mary Whittall. Chicago: University of Chicago Press, 2008.

Reill, Peter Hanns. *Vitalizing Nature in the Enlightenment*. Berkeley: University of California Press, 2005.

Reiss, John O. *Not By Design: Retiring Darwin's Watchmaker*. Berkeley: University of California Press, 2009.

Richards, Robert. "Michael Ruse's Design for Living," in: *Journal of the History of Biology*, 37:1 (2004), 25–38.

———. *The Romantic Conception of Life: Science and Philosophy in the Age of Goethe*. Chicago: University of Chicago Press, 2002.

Riegl, Alois. *Problems of Style*. Translated by Evelyn Kain. Princeton: Princeton University Press, 1992, orig. 1893.

Risatti, Howard. *A Theory of Craft: Function and Aesthetic Expression*. Chapel Hill: University of North Carolina Press, 2007.

Robinson, William. *The English Flower Garden*. Sagaponack: Sagapress, 1984.

———. *The Wild Garden, or the Naturalization and Natural Grouping of Hardy Exotic Plants*. Illustrated by Alfred Parsons. London: John Murray, 1870.

Roe, Shirley. *Matter, Life, and Generation*. Cambridge: Cambridge University Press, 1981.

Rosenberg, John D. *Elegy for an Age: the Presence of the Past in Victorian Literature*. London: Anthem Press, 2005.

———. *The Darkening Glass: A Portrait of Ruskin's Genius*. New York: Columbia University Press, 1980, orig. 1961.

Rosenberg, John D., ed. *The Genius of John Ruskin: Selections from His Writings*. New York: G. Braziller, 1963.

Roughgarden, Joan. *The Genial Gene: Deconstructing Darwinian Selfishness*. Berkeley: University of California Press, 2009.

Rowe, Colin, and Robert Slutzky. "Transparency: Literal and Phenomenal," in: *Perspecta*, 8 (1963), 45–54.

Ruse, Michael. *Darwin and Design: Does Evolution Have a Purpose?* Cambridge, Mass.: Harvard University Press, 2003.

Ruskin, John. *The Nature of Gothic: A Chapter of The Stones of Venice*. Printed at the Kelmscott Press, Hammersmith, and published by George Allen, London, 1892.

———. *The Works of John Ruskin*. 39 vols. Library edition. Eds. E. T. Cook and Alexander Wedderburn. London: George Allen, 1903–12.

Russell, Bertrand. *The Analysis of the Mind*. London: George Allen & Unwin, 1921.

Rykwert, Joseph. *The Necessity of Artifice*. New York: Rizzoli, 1982.

Sacks, Oliver. *An Anthropologist on Mars*. New York: Alfred A. Knopf, 1996.

Santayana, George. *The Sense of Beauty: Being the Outline of Aesthetic Theory*. New York: Dover Publications, 1955, orig. 1896.

Sawyer, Paul L. *Ruskin's Poetic Argument: The Design of the Major Works*. Ithaca: Cornell University Press, 1985.

Schama, Simon. *Landscape and Memory*. London: HarperCollins Publishers, 1995.

Scheler, Max. *The Nature of Sympathy*. Translated by Peter Heath. Hamden, Conn.: Shoe String Press, 1970, orig. 1954.

Schelling, Friedrich Wilhelm Joseph. *Sämmtliche Werke*, ed. K. F. A. Schelling. Stuttgart: Cotta, 1856–61.

Schneider, Norbert. "Form of Thought and Presentational Gesture in Karl Popper and E. H. Gombrich," in: *Human Affairs*, 19:3 (2009), 251–58.

Schrödinger, Erwin. "The Present Situation in Quantum Mechanics," in: *Quantum Theory and Measurement*. Eds. John Wheeler and W. H. Zurek. Princeton: Princeton University Press, 1983, orig. 1935.

Schumacher, E. F. *Good Work*. London: Abacus, 1980.

Scruton, Roger. *Beauty*. Oxford: Oxford University Press, 2009.

Semper, Gottfried. *Style in the Technical and Tectonic Arts; or, Practical Aesthetics*. Translated by Harry Mallgrave and Michael Robinson. Los Angeles: Getty Publications, 2004, orig. 1860.

———. *The Four Elements of Architecture and Other Writings*. Translated by Harry Mallgrave and Wolfgang Herrmann. Cambridge: Cambridge University Press, 1989, orig. 1851.

Sennett, Richard. *The Craftsman*. New Haven and London: Yale University Press, 2008.

Shapiro, Meyer. *The Language of Forms: Lectures on Insular Manuscript Art*. New York: The Pierpont Morgan Library, 2005.

Shaviro, Steven. "Self-Enjoyment and Concern: On Whitehead and Levinas," in: *Beyond Metaphysics?: Explorations in Alfred North Whitehead's Late Thought*. Eds. R. Faber, B. Henning, and C. Combs. Amsterdam: Rodopi, 2010.

———. *Without Criteria: Kant, Whitehead, Deleuze, and Aesthetics*. Cambridge, Mass.: MIT Press, 2009.

Sherburne, James Clark. *John Ruskin, or the Ambiguities of Abundance*. Cambridge, Mass.: Harvard University Press, 1972.

Simondon, Gilbert. *L'individu et sa genèse physico-biologique*. Paris: Presses Universitaires de France, 1964.

Simson, Otto von. *The Gothic Cathedral: Origins of Gothic Architecture and the Me-*

dieval Concept of Order. Princeton: Princeton University Press, 1988, orig. 1956.

Skrbina, David. *Panpsychism in the West*. Cambridge, Mass.: MIT Press, 2007.

Slote, Michael. *The Ethics of Care and Empathy*. London and New York: Routledge, 2007.

Sloterdijk, Peter. *Im Weltinnenraum des Kapitals: für eine philosophische Theorie der Globalisierung*. Frankfurt a.M.: Suhrkamp, 2005.

———. *Sphären,* 3 vols. *I: Blasen, II: Globen, III: Schäume.* Frankfurt a.M.: Suhrkamp, 1998–2004.

Small, I. C. "Vernon Lee, Association and 'Impressionist' Criticism," in: *The British Journal of Aesthetics*, 17:2 (1977), 178–84.

Smith, Jonathan. *Charles Darwin and Victorian Visual Culture*. Cambridge: Cambridge University Press, 2006.

———. *Fact and Feeling: Baconian Science and the Nineteenth-Century Literary Imagination*. Madison, Wis.: University of Wisconsin Press, 1994.

Spuybroek, Lars, ed. *Research & Design: Textile Tectonics*. Rotterdam: NAi Publishers, 2011.

———. *Research & Design: The Architecture of Variation*. London: Thames and Hudson, 2009.

Spuybroek, Lars. *The Architecture of Continuity: Essays and Conversations*. V2_Publishing, 2008.

Steenbergen, Clemens, and Wouter Reh. *Architecture and Landscape*. Bussum: Thoth, 1996.

Stein, Edith. *On the Problem of Empathy*. Translated by Waltraut Stein. Washington: ICS Publications, 1989.

Stokes, Adrian. *Stones of Rimini*. New York: Schocken Books, 1969.

Summerson, John. *Heavenly Mansions and Other Essays on Architecture*. New York: W. W. Norton, 1963.

Swade, Doron. *The Difference Engine: Charles Babbage and the Quest to Build the First Computer*. New York: Viking, 2000.

Taussig, Michael. *Mimesis and Alterity: A Particular History of the Senses*. New York: Routledge, 1993.

Taylor, Mark. *After God*. Chicago: University of Chicago Press, 2007.

Thompson, Paul. *William Butterfield: Victorian Architect*. Cambridge, Mass.: MIT Press, 1971.

Thornton, Peter. *Form and Decoration: Innovation in the Decorative Arts, 1470–1870*. London: Weidenfeld and Nicolson, 1998.

Titchener, Edward B. *Lectures on the Experimental Psychology of the Thought-Processes*. New York: Macmillan, 1909.

Townsend, Dabney. *Hume's Aesthetic Theory: Taste and Sentiment*. London and New York: Routledge, 2001.

Trilling, James. *Ornament: A Modern Perspective*. Seattle: University of Washington Press, 2003.

Tuinen, Sjoerd van. "Air-Conditioning Spaceship Earth: Peter Sloterdijk's Ethico-Aesthetic Paradigm," in: *Environment and Planning D: Society and Space*, 27:1 (2009), 105–18.

Turing, Alan. "Computing Machinery and Intelligence," in: *Mind*, 59:236 (October 1950), 433–60.

———. "The Chemical Basis of Morphogenesis," in: *Philosophical Transactions of the Royal Society of London*, 237:641 (August 1952), 37–72.

Turk, Greg. "Generating Textures on Arbitrary Surfaces using Reaction-Diffusion," in: *Computer Graphics*, 25:4 (July 1991), 289–98.

Turner, J. Scott. *The Extended Organism: The Physiology of Animal-Built Structures*. Cambridge, Mass: Harvard University Press, 2000.

———. *The Tinkerer's Accomplice: How Design Emerges from Life Itself*. Cambridge, Mass.: Harvard University Press, 2007.

Tweedale, Martin. *Scotus vs. Ockham: A Medieval Dispute over Universals*. 2 vols. Lewiston: Edwin Mellen Press, 1999.

Uexküll, Jakob von. *A Foray into the Worlds of Animals and Humans*. Translated by Joseph O'Neill. Minneapolis: University of Minnesota Press, 2010.

Unrau, John. "Ruskin, the Workman and the Savageness of the Gothic," in: *New Approaches to Ruskin*. Ed. Robert Hewison, London and New York: Routledge & Kegan Paul, 1981.

———. *Ruskin and St. Mark's*. London: Thames and Hudson, 1984.

Van der Post, Lucia. *William Morris and Morris & Co*. London: V&A Publications, 2003.

Verbeek, Peter-Paul. *What Things Do: Philosophical Reflections on Technology, Agency, and Design*. Translated by Robert P. Crease. University Park: Pennsylvania State University Press, 2005.

Viljoen, Helen Gill, ed. *The Brantwood Diary of John Ruskin*. New Haven and London: Yale University Press, 1971.

Viljoen, Helen Gill. *Ruskin's Scottish Heritage: A Prelude*. Urbana: University of Illinois Press, 1956.

Villard de Honnecourt, *The Sketchbook of Villard de Honnecourt*. Ed. Theodore Bowie. Westport: Greenwood Press, 1982.

Viollet-le-Duc, Eugène Emmanuel. *Discourses on Architecture*. Translated by Benjamin Brucknall. New York: Grove Press, 1959, orig. 1858–72.

———. *Le Massif du Mont Blanc*. Paris: Baudry, 1876.

Waal, Frans de. *The Age of Empathy: Nature's Lessons for a Kinder Society*. New York: Harmony Books, 2009.

Waggoner, Diane, ed. *The Beauty of Life: William Morris and the Art of Design*. London: Thames and Hudson, 2003.

Walton, Paul H. *Master Drawings by John Ruskin*. London: Pilkington Press, 2000.

―――. *The Drawings of John Ruskin*. New York: Hacker Art Books Inc., 1985.

Washburn, Dorothy, and Donald Crowe, eds. *Symmetry Comes of Age: The Role of Patterns in Culture*. Seattle: University of Washington Press, 2004.

―――. *Symmetries of Culture: Theory and Practice of Plane Pattern Analysis*. Seattle: University of Washington Press, 1988.

Webster, Gerry, and Brian Goodwin. *Form and Transformation: Generative Relational Principles in Biology*. Cambridge: Cambridge University Press, 1996.

Wettlaufer, Alexandra K. *In the Mind's Eye: The Visual Impulse in Diderot, Baudelaire and Ruskin*. Amsterdam: Rodopi, 2003.

Whitehead, Alfred North. *Adventures of Ideas*. New York: The Free Press, 1967, orig. 1933.

―――. *Modes of Thought*. New York: The Free Press, 1968, orig. 1938.

―――. *Process and Reality: An Essay in Cosmology*. Corrected edition. Eds. David Ray Griffin and Donald Sherburne. New York: The Free Press, 1978, orig. 1929.

Wild, K. W. *Intuition*. Cambridge: Cambridge University Press, 1938.

Wilde, Oscar. *Complete Works of Oscar Wilde*. London: Book Club Associates, 1976.

Williams, Raymond. *Culture and Society: 1780–1950*. New York: Columbia University Press, 1983.

Willis, Robert. *Remarks on the Architecture of the Middle Ages, Especially of Italy*. Cambridge: Pitt Press, 1835.

Wilson, A. N. *The Victorians*. New York and London: W. W. Norton & Co., 2004.

Wispé, Lauren, ed. *Altruism, Sympathy, and Helping: Psychological and Sociological Principles*. New York: Academic Press, 1978.

Wispé, Lauren. "The Distinction between Sympathy and Empathy: To Call Forth a Concept, a Word Is Needed," in: *Journal of Personality and Social Psychology*, 50:2 (August 1986), 314–21.

―――. *The Psychology of Sympathy*. New York: Plenum Press, 1991.

Wolschke-Bulmahn, Joachim, ed. *Nature and Ideology: Natural Garden Design in the Twentieth Century*. Washington: Dumbarton Oaks, 1997.

Wordsworth, William. *The Major Works*. Oxford: Oxford's World Classics, 2000.

Worringer, Wilhelm. *Abstraction and Empathy*. Translated by Michael Bullock. Chicago: Elephant Paperbacks, 1997, orig. 1908.

―――. *Form in Gothic*. Translated and introduced by Herbert Read. New York: Schocken Books, 1957, orig. 1911.

―――. *Lukas Cranach*. München: R. Piper & Co., 1908.

Wynne-Edwards, V. C. *Animal Dispersion in Relation to Social Behaviour*. Edinburgh: Oliver and Boyd, 1962.

index

Abraham, Pol, 46

abstraction, 17, 24, 38, 41, 44, 77, 100, 101, 118, 128, 129, 135, 194, 199, 215, 230, 299, 311, 318; abstract centerline, 123; abstract matching, 277, 313; abstract materialism, 95, 96, 106; and retraction, 191; and subtraction, 191; as the exclusion of life, 190; generalized, 53, 131, 190, 191, 192; life and, 48, 123, 126, 199, 227; pure abstraction (synonym with generalized), 140, 163, 172, 186, 187, 189, 199, 263, 333; related to cruelty, 78, 133, 225; related to sympathy, 177, 190, 206, 259; Ruskin's abstract lines, 115, 117, 119, 123, 126, 138, 180, 248, 277; sheet of, 139, 227, 276, 315; specified abstraction as opposed to schematism, 116, 182, 271; specified, 54, 62, 72, 182, 190, 191, 196, 205; temporary (synonym with specified), 165, 196; time abstracted, 218; twentieth-century concept of, 131, 171, 176, 262; Worringer's concept of, 186, 188, 202, 327; *See also* pattern, posture, points, figure, code

Adams, Eldridge, 323

Aestheticism, 86, 130, 272

aesthetics, 9, 46, 48, 54, 86, 96, 98, 146–48, 171–75, 205, 229, 256, 261, 265, 269, 274, 279, 294, 298–305 passim, 309, 310, 314, 319; as a spectrum, 209; aesthetic ontology, 209, 255; and pleasure, 293; Darwin's, 281; definition of, 145, 271, 282, 291; ethics and, 234, 308; evolutionary aesthetics, 290; Gothic, 68; happiness and, 249; Hume's, 228; Lipps's, 178–82; of advertising, 258; of beauty, 211, 212; of massing, 76; of relief, 249, 305, 313; of territories, 321–22; of texture, 83; of the picturesque,

208, 215–22, 230; of the sublime, 213, 263; Ruskinian, 40, 80, 222, 227, 228, 272, 281, 283; speculative, 94; vitalism as, 282, 331; Worringer's, 188–90; *See also* panaestheticism, beauty, sublime, picturesque

affect, 204, 277, 278 "back to back," 277, 312, 315; compared to feeling, 210, 278; definition of, 209–10; DeLanda and, 277, 320, 321; Deleuze and, 276, 352n44

agency, 42, 48, 139, 203, 255, 259, 271, 273, 280, 287, 300, 304, 319, 359n18, 364n82; *See also* work

Alberti, Leon Battista, 34, 44, 211, 252

Allen, Grant, 289, 290, 292

Ammophila wasp (example of sympathetic encounter), 162–65, 170, 177, 183, 191, 228, 261, 276, 352n48

animacy, 203, 354n76

animation, 42, 122, 178, 190, 203, 252, 253, 282, 286

animism, 74, 231, 282, 325; compared to naturalism, 353n67; compared to vitalism, 282, 330

Aristotle, 21, 64, 284, 296–98, 301–4

Art Nouveau, 12, 130, 272, 327, 328; and sleep, 326; and tendrils, 155, 327; oneiricism, 130, 326

Artaud, Antonin, *The Theatre of Cruelty*, 133

assemblage, 220, 271, 275, 316, 321; assemblage meshwork, 320; assemblage theory, 275, 312–14

assembly, 38, 175, 207, 221; assembly network, 320; gathering, 255; Latour and, 255; *See also* thing: *Thing*

awareness, 72, 158, 165, 202, 203, 259

Babbage, Charles, 8, 52–54, 57, 58, 65, 78, 135, 141; Difference Engine, 53

Bain, Alexander, 307

Ball, Philip, 340n17, 349n64

Bateson, Gregory, 96, 135, 284, 322, 365n90

Baudrillard, Jean, 50, 264, 293, 361n45

beauty, 9, 10, 40, 44, 47, 51, 57, 68, 85, 114, 140, 177, 178, 189, 211–15, 223, 232, 269, 271–73, 282, 329; "a beauty that works," 9, 45, 304; as activity of the parts, 182, 291, 316; beauty as aim, 86, 182, 287, 299, 300, 311, 319, 330; compared to the sublime, 9, 145, 211, 215, 235, 265; compared to ugliness, 188, 210, 213, 281, 285, 294; Darwin's concept of, 64, 271, 280–81, 286–90, 305; definitions of, 182, 210, 257; glowing and, 74, 327, 328; gracefulness, 50, 211, 232, 257, 312, 319; Herder's concept of, 147; Hume's concept of, 182, 305; objective vs subjective, 305; pleasure as opposed to, 292; radiating and, 74, 205, 311, 314, 318; Ruskin's concept of, 222, 227, 232, 266, 283, 331; Ruskin's typical beauty, 222; Ruskin's vital beauty, 146, 209, 222, 223, 227, 229, 232, 270; variety and, 19, 98; Whitehead's concept of, 223, 271–72, 282, 309; *See also* Hogarth, William: *The Analysis of Beauty*, Aestheticism

Benjamin, Walter, 326

Bergson, Henri, 9, 22, 119, 147, 149, 159–77, 180, 189, 191, 201, 202, 205, 221, 228, 270, 276, 278, 282, 319; "in the making," 119, 123, 129, 133, 160, 166, 177, 195, 197, 218, 351n26; definition of intuition, 161; divining sympathy, 164; interpenetration, 160, 177, 184, 277, 319; intuition, 41, 139, 159–72, 177, 190, 203, 234, 257, 282, 316, 366n105; on art, 170–71, 282; sympathy, 161, 163, 170

Bernini, Gianlorenzo, 223, 347n34

braiding, 25, 29, 36, 38, 44, 54, 91, 92, 139, 141, 157, 184, 195, 202, 224, 321, 345n10

Brown, Lancelot "Capability," 219, 237

Buffon, Comte de, 55, 56

Burne-Jones, Edward; *Perseus Cycle*, 234; *The Legend of Briar Rose*, 232

Butterfield, William, 80

care, 9, 11, 75, 129, 143, 152, 164, 170, 173–75, 200, 205, 239, 243, 260, 305; and aesthetics, 257; as being careful, 49, 97, 119, 166, 170, 219; as keeping, 134, 195, 240; compared to concern, 255, 258; definitions of, 134, 248; *Fürsorge*, 249; Latour's denial of, 257; Ruskin on, 134, 251, 309, 313

Carroll, Sean, 284

causality, 284, 297, 317; efficient cause, 299, 301, 304, 309, 313; final cause, 284, 296, 297, 299, 304, 309, 313; linear, 299, 315; non-linear, 297

changefulness 16, 19–41, 51, 53, 58, 59, 61, 83, 138, 140, 195, 216, 232, 286; related to the young picturesque, 216; Ruskin's definitions of, 14, 19; related to savageness, 16, 30, 34, 38; as variation, 19, 21

Channell, David, 25

Clark, Kenneth, 8

computing, 22, 48, 52, 54, 67, 68, 117, 135, 136, 139, 242, 267, 312; Charles Babbage and, 57; Difference Engine, 52; not necessarily electronic, 22, 65; *See also* Turing, digital

code, 52, 53, 56–58, 69, 117, 227, 295; as internal mold, 161; genetic code, 35, 56, 118; Gothic code, 58–60, 62–63; *See also* digital, growth: algorithm

composition, 32, 46, 52, 76, 221, 282, 291, 308, 311; Bergson and, 162; defined by Ruskin, 252, 306, 309; defined by Whitehead, 309; Latour and, 319; Uexküll and, 324–25; *See also* configuration, aesthetics, beauty

concern, 9, 173, 249, 255, 259, 260, 328, 331; as weighted, 249; Heidegger and, 250; Latour and, 257, 318; *Sorge*, 249; *See also* care, cura

configuration, 21, 26, 32, 57, 60, 101, 106, 119, 140, 153, 195, 272; definition of, 44; configurational variation, 20, 61, 68; configurationalism, 217; compared to construction, 26, 68, 103, 309; compared to composition, 308; reliant on figural behavior, 44, 57, 59, 117, 126; and Gestalt, 111; and pattern, 96; and order, 111; specific to the Gothic, 20, 47, 70, 89, 150, 243, 267, 286; *See also* composition

crystallization, 32, 42, 57, 59, 87, 97, 98, 110, 112, 173, 194, 221, 230, 232, 296, 317, 329, 347n34; related to abstraction, 110, 173, 187, 189; related to the sublime, 230, 262, 331; Riegl and, 187; Ruskin's girls holding hands, 62, 306, 312, 315; Viollet-le-Duc and, 47, 187; Worringer and, 189, 190

cura, 173, 249, 257, 260; Heidegger and, 173, 250; myth of Cura, 248

daidallein, 279, 300; as cunning, 279, 321, 325, 330; as embellishment, 94, 279, 300, 318, 321, 330

Darwin, Charles, 8, 64, 142, 235, 271, 278, 280; "Law of Battle," 306; adaptationism, 284, 285, 290; concept of decoration, 280, 289, 306; Darwinism, 163, 281, 283, 292–307; natural selection, 163, 272, 280, 284–87, 298, 304, 307, 308; relationship with Ruskin, 280; sexual selection, 235, 281, 286, 287, 288, 292, 306; *The Descent of Man*, 280, 281, 286, 289, 306, 307; *The Origin of Species*, 271, 280, 281, 286, 289, 306

decoration, 24, 34, 132, 139, 140, 197, 199, 201, 203, 231, 261, 280, 323, 327, 361n49; definitions of, 235, 295, 302; Dresser's concept of, 131; generalized, 196; Jones's concept of, 106; Mario Praz and, 365n100; related to transition, 96; Ruskin's concept of, 78–81, 295; strong decoration, 129, 141, 252, 257, 304; weak decoration, 129, 141, 258; *See also* ornament, pattern, wall veil

deformation, 20, 136–38, 194, 198, 223, 297; as changefulness; 136; as gradualism, 138

DeLanda, Manuel, 277, 312, 320; assemblage theory, 312, 321; emergence, 67, 315, 316, 362n74, 364n77; relations of exteriority, 275

Deleuze, Gilles, 153, 157, 206, 231, 276, 316, 322, 362n73; affect, 276; and sympathy, 167, 276, 352n44; Hume and, 275; *Immanence: A Life …*, 206; James and, 154, 206, 351n17; nonorganic, 30, 32; relations of exteriority, 275, 313, 314; the fold, 66; vitalist, 12; Worringer and, 30–31, 340n26

delicacy, 16, 38, 42, 47, 66, 70, 71, 86, 110, 129, 174, 209, 216, 217, 232, 235, 251, 256, 258, 261, 272, 273, 279, 293, 302, 310, 319; definitions of, 45, 81; Ruskin and, 38, 113, 132, 341n35, 345n10. *See also* fragility, vulnerability

design, 9, 14, 20, 26, 31, 35, 54, 61, 67, 76, 96, 99–102, 113, 118, 128, 129, 132, 140, 173–76, 183–86, 196, 200, 202, 220, 226, 248, 249, 252, 259, 272, 295, 311, 322, 329; argument from, 67, 269, 270, 298; as distinct from engineering, 47, 175, 186, 241, 250, 254, 266, 318, 328, 329, 331; definitions of, 139, 205, 240, 250; design and execution, 14, 38, 52, 57, 58; design and work, 17, 30, 38, 52, 242; design principle, 19, 253; design technique, 19, 38, 54, 58–60, 69, 70, 91, 240; design without a designer, 240, 271, 300, 333; designer, 54, 61, 67, 99, 106, 111, 120, 176, 200, 219, 237, 242, 249, 260, 267, 269, 288, 294, 298, 299, 328; difference between Heidegger and Ruskin, 254; God, 65, 68, 192, 250, 253, 269, 270, 271, 300; Jones's rules of, 106; Kant and, 287, 297; landscape design, 218, 219; Morris's rules of, 120, 122; picturesque design rules, 220–22; quality of design, 174–76, 256, 259, 314; rule and rule-based, 29, 32, 57, 58, 82, 89, 103, 106, 107, 120, 126, 129, 130, 139, 140, 195, 208, 221, 242, 312, 342n51, 362n71; self-design, 42, 271; teleology, 192, 223, 271–72, 284–87, 296–302; territory as designed, 231, 323, 324; time of design, 217, 220, 238, 239, 266; *wabi-sabi*, 129, 257; wild garden design, 235, 237–40; *See also* pattern, composition, configuration, well-being, well-becoming, digital: digital design

Dickens, Charles, 244; *Our Mutual Friend*, 206

digital, 9, 12, 17, 54, 56, 57, 65, 99, 128, 135–40, 142, 242, 242, 263; digital design, 9, 267; digital Gothic, 22, 48, 59, 61, 62, 99, 175, 267; Gothic nature of the digital, 68; minimum difference, 135; *See also* code, computing

Dresser, Christopher, 110, 130, 131, 133, 196

dressing, 77, 81, 86, 91, 93, 95, 111, 133, 134, 137, 255, 273, 293; as cloaking, 204, 205, 251, 258, 273; as drapery, 80–82, 87, 89, 93, 94, 102, 137, 237, 259, 327, 328; as veiling, 9, 81, 87, 89, 95, 133, 139, 205, 227, 229, 254, 257, 259, 273, 275, 277–89, 302, 304, 321, 330; dress code, 295; *See also* wall veil, Earth Veil, *Gewand*

Earth Veil, 130, 197, 273, 330–32; as horizontality, 87, 273, 274, 278, 279, 321, 332; as the sectional plane, 183, 273; as the veil of strange intermediate being, 87, 143, 216, 235, 257, 316, 317, 330; Ruskin's definition of, 87; *See also* labyrinth

ecology, 9, 132, 143, 258, 278, 318, 319, 332, 364n90; actor-network, 319, 321, 364n82; ecology without environment, 246; Latour's network, 184, 317–21; meshwork, 320; network of sympathy, 317; *See also* milieu, environment

Einfühlung, 9, 147, 172, 177–79, 183, 187, 188, 190, 291, 320, 350n4; definitions of, 171, 300; history of, 171–72; translation of, 169, 172; *See also* empathy, feeling-into

Einklang, 178, 274; *See also* harmony

elasticity, 46, 94, 114, 146, 155, 159, 163, 166, 180, 191, 295, 313, 315, 316, 320, 321, 327; *See also* flexibility

Ellul, Jacques, 49, 262, 263

empathy 24, 44, 147, 164, 169, 172, 176–78, 187, 190, 197–202, 209, 216, 230, 314, 327, 341n31; as interrupted sympathy, 172, 184; conceptual difference between Worringer and Lipps, 188–90; related to naturalism, 171, 189, 197; related to sympathy, 172, 177, 252, 258, 259; sympathy starts with, 169, 171, 184, 197, 353n48; See also *Einfühlung*, feeling-into

entanglement, 71, 119–21, 143, 173, 176, 184, 232, 250, 258, 279, 280, 298; definition of, 317; diagram of, 319–20; difference with actor-network theory, 319, 331; difference with assemblage theory, 275, 321; entanglement theory, 175, 317; *Tangle Carpet*© project, 242, 266, 267, 333; *See also* labyrinth, interlacing, knotwork

environment, 79, 143, 246, 285, 286, 295, 296, 298, 311, 322–25, 331, 364n90; See also *Umwelt*, *Welt*: Heidegger's Open

ethics, 9, 16, 61, 229, 310; as related to aesthetics, 146, 234, 282, 308, 309, 366n105

eudaimonia (well-being), 210, 232, 240, 250, 254, 256, 296, 304, 310, 312; as happiness, 181, 232, 249, 250, 252; as well-being, 232, 296, 297, 298, 301, 302, 308, 311; feelings of enjoyment, 249; *See also* flourishing

euprepeia (well-becoming), 295, 296; as proper, 181, 182, 184, 294, 295

experience, 40, 52, 71, 72, 145, 161, 165, 171, 178, 179–81, 186, 189, 206, 213, 214, 249, 256, 262, 272, 276, 278, 280, 287, 290, 298, 320; as basis of Radical Empiricism, 152–59, 228; pure experience, 149, 152, 200

Expressionism, 11, 24, 51, 65, 69, 80, 95, 135, 138, 147, 171, 172, 187; *Die Brücke*, 187; Ruskin as proto-expressionist, 30, 79, 115

fabricism 129, 176, 252, 261, 274, 330; and constructivism, 252; and fabrication, 329; as related to mosaicism, 274, 322; definition of, 175

Fechner, Gustav, 203, 231, 274, 291, 328, 354n77

feeling, 51, 75, 111, 131, 133, 134, 143–50, 155, 156, 183, 210, 228, 256, 277, 282, 291, 295, 302, 311, 312, 325; actuality of, 313; and aesthetics, 145, 177, 272, 299, 305, 319, 321; apathy, 314; Art Nouveau and, 328; compared to affect, 210, 276, 278; critique of pure feeling, 316; definitions of, 165, 271, 273, 313; design and, 205; elasticity and, 146, 155, 180, 295, 313, 315, 320, 321; fel-low-feeling, 227; entanglement and, 317, 330; example of the stick, 300, 318; example of the whisk, 168; fatigue, 191; feeling of feeling, 277; felt abstrac-tion, 177, 191, 271, 275, 276, 278, 299, 314; felt necessity, 277; felt objectivity, 170, 182, 305; felt relations, 152, 169, 171, 175, 182, 204, 256, 276, 291, 298, 300, 313, 317, 325, 330, 360n18; felt transition, 155, 156, 160, 184, 191; jovi-ality, 312, 313, 316; longing, 314, 320; orientation and, 165, 316; see-feel, 171, 183, 184; sympathy as the original, 161, 162, 205; things and, 175, 183, 184, 257, 271, 300; Vischer's versions, 172; *See also* feeling-into, feeling-with, *Ein-fühlung*, entanglement

feeling-for, 231, 317

feeling-into, 169, 184, 189, 242, 256, 311, 319, 324, 365n90; derived from Dutch *invoelen*, 169; *See also* empathy

feeling-through, 365n90

feeling-with, 169, 186, 189, 197, 231, 256, 291; derived from Dutch *meevoelen*; 169; *See also* sympathy

figure, 9, 20–22, 31, 35, 36, 42, 43–44, 51, 53, 59, 60, 62, 66, 68, 88, 101, 103, 106, 117, 123, 126, 140, 179, 194, 195, 198, 202, 242, 243, 252, 286, 302; definitions of, 21, 111; Y-figure (bifurcation), 88, 100, 110, 117, 126, 136, 347n48; T-fig-ure (branching), 110, 117, 123, 126; Z-figure (zigzag or chevron), 88, 126, 194; J-figure (ogive or tendril), 21, 22, 88, 116, 117, 126; C-figure (lobe or cusp), 21, 22, 126, 136; S-figure (ogee or ser-pentine line), 21, 22, 44, 123, 126; as motif, 21, 51, 59, 88, 99, 126, 194, 195, 324

Flamboyant (late Gothic style), 36, 38, 40, 41, 82, 139, 349n67; Ruskin's struggle with; 341n35, 344–45n10

flexibility, 20, 26, 38, 41–45, 50, 52, 59, 65, 67, 102, 123, 137, 140, 169, 191, 195, 221, 312, 341n35, 342n51, 345n10, 347n34, 349n67; as bending, 38, 43, 50, 59, 62, 88, 117, 119, 126, 137, 207, 242, 256, 299, 301; *See also* elasticity

flourishing, 9, 49, 210, 227, 231, 232, 235, 239, 257, 266, 302, 304, 309, 333; See also *eudaimonia*

Focillon, Henri, 13, 41, 70

fractal, 31, 74, 81, 107, 117, 123, 246, 257

fragility, 8, 70, 86, 174, 175, 208–9, 235, 261, 273, 302, 304, 310, 362n73

Frampton, Kenneth, 95, 346n29

Francé, Raoul Heinrich, 299

Frankl, Paul, 13, 69, 340n21

Frazer, James, 164, 352n39, 352n48

freedom, 9, 21, 30, 41, 49, 66, 67, 140, 208, 210, 232, 262, 265, 266, 301, 363n77; movement and, 234; free man vs. free hand, 234

Friedrich, Caspar David, 189, 213

fringe, 148, 153, 155, 160, 180, 205, 257, 273, 274, 275, 279, 302, 314, 320, 322, 351n15; as feeling, 155; as frayed, 157, 256

Frisch, Karl von, 321

furnishing, 174, 205, 243, 323, 328

Gehry, Frank, 54, 61

Gell, Alfred, 203, 205, 213, 359n18

gift, 134, 201, 251, 318, 327; generosity, 174, 257, 312, 313, 318, 332; gift economy, 40; Heidegger's concept of the, 250–53, 257; Marcel Mauss's concept of the, 318; prestation, 318; Ruskin's concept of the, 9, 251; *See also* sacrifice, work: extra work

Gilpin, William, 218, 219, 230

Goethe, Johann Wolfgang von, 283, 285, 286, 288

Gogh, Vincent van, 209, 244–46, 253, 257

Gombrich, Ernst, 11, 30, 78, 98, 110, 111, 116, 131, 291; searchlight theory of the mind, 111; *The Sense of Order*, 98, 111, 116, 131, 341n31

Goodwin, Brian, 284

Gothic (twelfth- to fifteenth-century style), 11–48, 54, 82, 86, 89, 99, 102, 118, 128, 130, 138, 140, 147, 150, 156, 161, 176, 184, 187, 195, 198, 202, 209, 223, 235, 242, 243, 250, 252, 257, 267, 272, 286, 304, 309, 321, 327, 333; cathedrals, 17, 32, 58–60, 63, 66, 68–72, 98, 116, 118, 139, 168, 201, 202, 250, 255, 261, 327; Gothic age, 17–19; Decorated, 35; English Gothic, 63; French Gothic, 41, 63, 72–73, 116; Gothic architecture, 24, 25, 32–33, 44, 201; Gothic line, 12, 30, 340n26; Gothick, 12; historians of the Gothic, 13, 21, 69–71; neo-Gothic or Gothic Revival (nineteenth-century), 11, 12, 64, 117, 122, 295, 327; poulaines, 41; Rayonnant, 35; relation between structure and ornament, 25, 44; relation to the Romanesque, 34, 36, 44, 68; rose windows, 23, 26, 286, 300; Ruskin's six characteristics of, 14–16; use of wooden templates, 18, 30; Worringer on the Gothic, 12, 24, 33, 34, 41, 64, 71, 187, 201, 202; *See also* Flamboyant, grouped shaft, tracery, ontology: Gothic ontology

Gothic hinge (example of sympathetic encounter), 116–19, 130, 131, 139, 142, 168, 227, 228, 273, 277, 278, 304, 348n61, 353n67, 365n90

Gould, Stephen Jay, 35, 90, 284, 291

Griffin, David Ray, 159, 298, 363n77, 366n105

grotesqueness, 16, 30, 60, 103

grouped shaft (Gothic column), 19, 20, 26, 59, 72; as bundle, 14, 26, 34, 41, 45, 52, 347n34; as compound pier, 20, 186

growth, 31, 33, 34, 51, 55, 56, 59, 97, 101, 128, 129, 135, 179, 218, 240, 301, 320, 348n48; algorithm, 60, 117, 226, 242, 267; Aristotle and, 297; *Bildung*, 216; generation, 59, 64, 117, 139, 139, 226, 242, 266, 267, 268, 312, 348n48; Jones and, 106; Kant and, 297; Morris and, 122, 123, 126, 346n30; overgrowth, 30, 129, 135, 231, 238, 240; picturesque and, 220, 221; Ruskin and, 9, 29, 114, 226, 232, 247, 252, 266; Salisbury and Bourges Cathedral as generated, 63; *See also* flourishing, *eudaimonia*

Haeckel, Ernst, 26, 112, 283, 328

harmony, 107, 110, 113, 182, 211, 221, 228, 274, 291, 305, 311; See also *Einklang*

Hartshorne, Charles, 363n77, 362n73; *Born to Sing*, 321; on aggregations, 361n77; on sympathy, 277

Heidegger, Martin, 9, 173, 209, 243–61, 302, 319, 323, 328; *Bestand*, 263; concealment, 251, 253, 256, 273, 319, 358n53; cura, 173, 248, 250; Dasein, 250, 257, 324; *ergon*, 210, 254; gift, 251; Open, 247, 324; *The Origin of the Work of Art*, 246; thing, 174, 243, 255; tool, 251, 257, 319

Hogarth, William, 19, 116, 239, 279, 340n19; serpentine line, 23, 115, 216, 217; *The Analysis of Beauty*, 19, 216, 355n3, 355n5, 360n18

Hugo, Victor, 133, 344n2

Hulme, T. E., 24, 135, 172

Hume, David, 146, 182, 227, 228, 281, 305; association, 228; Darwin and, 305; Deleuze and, 275; James's deviation of, 152; *Treatise on Human Nature*, 182

Hunt, William Holman, 86, 342n41; *The Scapegoat*, 85, 350n67; *The Lady of Shalott*, 345n11

Hutcheson, Francis, 227

Illumination, 24, 36, 126, 216, 347n34, 348n53; method of construction, 127; Rimbaud's *Illuminations*, 361n49; Ruskin's view of, 361n49

indeterminacy, 58, 160, 175, 192, 202, 203, 205, 241, 296, 299, 302, 320

interlacing, 20, 24, 41, 47, 59, 62, 77, 82, 93, 101, 106, 119, 122, 126, 128, 134, 195, 304, 321 intuition, 41, 139, 159–72, 177, 180, 190, 203, 221, 234, 282, 316, 351n26, 366n105; definition of, 161; distinct from sympathy, 167; Latour against, 257; related to sympathy, 161

James, William, 9, 119, 147–62, 167, 169, 171, 179–84, 190, 192, 196, 197, 200, 203, 205, 206, 221, 228, 237, 257, 273, 279, 302, 320, 322, 351n19, 351n26, 354n77, 354n78; *A Pluralistic Universe*, 160, 351n26; Dyak's head, 153, 157, 168, 184, 202, 302; experience, 72, 74, 149–61, 170–73, 178–81, 186–91, 200, 206, 213, 228, 249, 256, 272, 276, 278, 280, 282, 286, 290, 298, 320; intimacy, 150, 169, 228, 231, 319; mosaic philosophy, 152; *See also* fringe

James, Henry, 204, 354n78

Jekyll, Gertrude, 237

Jones, Owen, 13, 75, 77, 82, 87–89, 99, 102–13, 115, 119, 120, 131, 138, 189, 198, 326, 327; and Christopher Dresser, 130; and Jules Goury, 103; compared with Morris, 123, 128; concept of bloom, 111; principle of repose, 107, 126, 190; principle of variety, 98; *The Grammar of Ornament*, 102

kalogenesis, 366n105

Kant, Immanuel, 111, 150, 191, 243, 281, 298, 301; apriority, 191, 237, 252, 297, 351n17; judgment, 146, 212, 285, 287–89; on beauty, 212, 291; on growth, 297; on teleology, 287, 297, 298; on the sublime, 213, 214; schematism, 98, 107, 123, 237, 283

Kierkegaard, Soren, 250, 295

Kirschner, Marc, 285

Klein, Yves, 197, 198, 203, 204

Knight, Richard Payne, 221, 230

knotwork, 24, 30, 38, 93, 106, 156, 202, 224, 275, 321, 322, 328; Celtic, 36, 77, 157; Semper and, 44, 95, 346n29

Koolhaas, Rem, 327

Kropotkin, Peter, 307

labyrinth, 38, 314, 321, 326, 327, 361n45; and Daedalus, 279, 298, 318; *See also* Earth Veil

Landow, George, 145, 146, 227

Lamprecht, Karl, 24, 36

Latour, Bruno, 8, 209, 260, 267, 318, 321, 329; assembly, 320; definitions of translation, 318, 319; entanglement, 317; on black boxes, 184, 255, 319; on exploded views, 209, 240; opinion on Bergson, 257; opinion on Heidegger, 254; *Pandora's Hope*, 317; use of Heidegger's Thing and gathering, 255

Lawrence, D. H., 276; critique on Whitman's concept of sympathy, 231, 317, 352n44

Lee, Vernon, 24, 172, 204, 291

life, 14, 24, 25, 29, 31, 34, 41, 47, 57, 111, 114, 129, 147, 151, 157, 160, 170, 182, 192, 198, 199, 202, 217, 223, 226, 227, 230, 238, 259, 271, 282, 294, 296, 304, 308, 310, 325, 331; a specific life, 199, 203; abstract life, 48, 123, 126; definitions of, 32, 48, 229; Deleuze and, 206; indetermination in matter, 160, 202, 205; James and, 206; life in general, 198, 203; life is artificial, 229; Lipps and, 178; nonorganic life, 12; Ruskin and, 14, 62, 86, 200, 330–31, 339n11; techniques and, 95; Wordsworth and, 228; Worringer and, 25, 189, 201; *See also* vitalism

Lipps, Theodor, 9, 172, 177–88, 205, 223, 228, 256, 270, 291, 331; and posture, 190, 223, 235, 304; and sympathy, 176, 180, 188, 249; compared to Schmarsow, Wölfflin and Vischer, 147, 178; compared to Worringer, 187–88, 190; related to Hume, 182; *See also Einfühlung*, willow tree

live-with, 169, 173, 188, 199, 243, 256, 311, 314, 328; as acting within the act of sympathy, 166; derived from Dutch *meeleven*; 169; *See also* sympathy

Loos, Adolf, 76, 133, 141

Lorrain, Claude, 218

Loudon, John, 220, 237

Lovelace, Ada, 53, 65

Mandelbrot, Benoit, 246; *The Fractal Geometry of Nature*, 81

matter, 31, 34, 38, 42, 52, 54–57, 63, 68, 71, 87, 90, 96, 97, 101, 117, 139, 150, 159, 160, 179, 300; and hylomorphism, 267, 304; and substance, 76; as active, 95, 168, 170, 194, 201, 202, 270, 316; as inert, 270; as opposed to mass, 76, 77, 90, 97, 137; heterogeneity of, 192; immaterial, 57, 70; *See also* Semper, Gottfried: *Stoffwechselthese*, mold

Marey, Etienne-Jules, 165–67, 183, 184, 198, 204, 352n42, 354n78

Mauss, Marcel, 318, 364n83

McLuhan, Marshall, 173, 212, 329, 333, 361n49, 364n90

Margulis, Lynn, 307, 308

Mies van der Rohe, Ludwig, 62, 81, 92, 141, 208, 342n47, 344n9

milieu, definition of; 325

Mill, John Stuart, 40

Millais, John Everett, 42, 45, 62, 83–86, 342n41, 350n67; *Design for a Gothic Window*, 43; *Mariana*, 83, 138, 224, 345n11; working on Ruskin's portrait, 41

mold, 30, 32, 54–56, 95, 97, 161, 253, 298, 301; as hylomorphic, 267, 304; variable mold, 56, 267; internal mold, 55, 56, 161; as template, 18, 30, 99, 128; as schema, 21, 35, 50, 53, 98, 107, 114, 116, 123, 131, 135, 162, 165, 184, 191, 237, 283, 285

Moleschott, Jacob, 93

Monet, Claude, 72–74, 131

Morris, William, 8, 11, 77, 99, 118–30, 138, 141, 142, 199, 243, 261, 304, 327; *Acanthus* wallpaper, 119–25; *Bullerswood* carpet, 184; compared to William James, 151, 156, 184, 197, 314, 322; design principles as digital, 242, 267; Morris & Co., 184, 200, 310; *Myrtle* wallpaper, 119–21; opinion on classicism, 44, 250; opinion on the gothic, 71; *Pimpernel* wallpaper, 121–24; *Some*

Hints on Pattern Designing, 122, 134; theory of pattern design, 119, 122, 123, 346n30

mosaic, 102, 103, 153–58, 198, 220, 285, 288, 347n34, 348n61; as tessellation, 101; Darwin's model of nature as, 306; James's philosophy as, 148, 152, 273, 322; mosaicism, 274, 322; Owen Jones and, 77; relation between fabric and, 156, 157, 160, 306; Semper and, 94; wild gardens as, 237; *See also* tessellation, Owen Jones, pattern: Voronoi pattern

Mumford, Lewis, 49, 262, 263

naturalism, 16, 60, 83, 118, 123, 126, 129, 130, 190, 197, 199, 215, 240, 259; as mimesis, 325, 352n48; as opposed to animism, 325, 330, 353–54n67; as related to empathy, 186, 197, 230, 258, 327; as related to sympathy, 171, 186, 190, 199; naturalist outline, 123; psychology of, 129; Ruskin and, 14, 113; supernaturalism, 354n67

Naturphilosophie, 210, 264; for machines, 143, 265, 300

Nordicism, 12, 34, 255

ontology, 62, 86, 158, 217, 267, 274, 279, 282, 297, 302, 332, 363n77; aesthetics and, 9, 209, 282; Baroque ontology, 44, 65, 242; definition of, 43, 209; Gothic ontology, 9, 67, 74, 143, 155, 209, 216, 241, 250, 266, 313, 317, 326, 363n77; Greek ontology, 43, 65, 74, 242, 250, 267

organicism, 32, 34, 123, 274, 311, 313; and mechanism, 264, 297, 317; Hartshorne and, 362n73; nonorganic, 12, 25, 30–32, 34, 194, 227; suborganicism, 362n72; superorganism, 316

orientation, 165, 276, 278, 316, 363n77

ornament, 16, 19, 25, 34, 48, 64, 168, 196, 232, 258, 274, 295, 302, 330; as abstract making, 129, 266; as artificial texture, 77; as drapery, 81, 82, 93, 94, 137, 237; as encrustation, 77, 80, 82, 85, 87, 93,

101, 137; as patterned materiality, 96–100, 130; as related to structure in classicism, 44, 201; as related to structure in the Gothic, 25, 38, 44, 201, 252; as related to textile techniques, *see* Semper, ribbon ornament; as strong decoration, 257; classicist, 41, 47, 82; compared to texture, 129; Darwin's concept of, 280, 289, 306; decline of, 76, 129, 133; definitions of, 77, 81, 129, 130, 231; diaper, 82, 103, 107, 118, 123, 198, 209; distinguished between tessellation and ribbon, 101, 102; Dresser's concept of, 130; for our own age, 139–43, 268; Gothic ornament, 14, 45; Jones's concept of, 102–6, 107–12; Maori tattoo, 88, 89; Morris's concept of, 122; Northern, 24, 25, 31, 37; not related to the joint, 44, 95, 129; related to sympathy, 128, 129; Ruskin's concept of, 81, 114, 115, 132, 137, 140, 174, 232, 234, 252, 295; Semper's concept of, 90–95; uselessness and, 40, 134, 174, 234, 251, 252, 304; *See also* tessellation, ribbon ornament, wall veil

Oudolf, Piet, 237, 238

Paley, William, 67, 240, 269, 270, 271, 280, 300; *Natural Theology*, 299; watch on a heath allegory, 67, 241

panaestheticism, 361n56, 363n74

panexperientialism, 159, 298, 361n56

Panofsky, Erwin, 69, 70, 343n64, 343n71; *Gothic Architecture and Scholasticism*, 64

panpsychism, 299, 361n56, 362n74

pattern, 22, 24, 47, 51, 77, 83, 88, 89, 94, 97, 98–103, 107–13, 117–23, 152, 156, 165, 166, 196, 217, 258, 267, 272, 288, 293, 295, 302, 312, 321; as construction, 129, 252; as transitional, 102, 117, 118, 184, 195; cracked mud pattern, 83, 97, 100, 101, 107, 322, 323; definitions of, 57, 96, 227; digital patterning, 135–38, an image is not a, 126; drystone wall, 153, 154, 157; periodicity of pattern, 107, 120, 122, 126, 128, 284–86; Shoowa-Kuba cloth patterns, 192–96; Voronoi

pattern, 112, 154, 295, 323; *See also* configuration, tessellation, abstraction: sheet of abstraction

Penrose, Roger, 112

Piano, Renzo, 48, 54

picturesque, 13, 49, 64, 80, 143, 147, 214–22, 229, 247, 257, 261, 272, 281, 302, 304, 329, 331; additive technique of the, 221; as between beauty and sublime, 214–15, 230; as related to landscaping, 218–20; definitions of, 210, 218, 230, 246, 261; examples of the, 207, 208, 260; Heidegger and the, 244; old (erosive), 215–17, 229; Ruskin's high picturesque as parasitical to the sublime, 222, 230, 247, 270; Ruskin's low picturesque, 225, 228; Ruskin's noble or high picturesque, 225, 227; the cottage as a model of, 220, 221, 247; the problem of the, 208, 222; wild garden and the, 235, 239; young (constitutive), 215–17, 223, 229, 266

Poe, Edgar Allan, 327

points (of sympathetic encounter), 22, 42, 50–52, 59, 66, 116–18, 126, 165, 169, 191, 276, 299, 316, 319, 347n48; abstract points, 313, 318; Marey points, 183; points of abstraction, 118, 360n18; points of agreement, 189, 299, 351n17, 352n48, 353n67; postural points, 182

polished (aspect of sublime objects), 75, 76, 142, 199, 259, 357n29; the armored knight, 234

Pollock, Jackson, 208, 345n13, 347n34, 348n58

posture, 181, 182, 191, 202, 223, 235, 277, 291, 304, 319, 321, 353n67, 360n18; Lipps and, 183, 190; Uexküll and, 324

Praz, Mario, 327, 365n100

Price, Uvedale, 214, 221, 230

Proust, Marcel, 8, 327, 344n2, 356n14

Pugin, Augustus Welby, 11, 12, 29, 74

Read, Herbert, 24

realism, 83, 85, 103, 123, 126, 227, 229, 343n64, 353n67

redundancy, 16, 58, 59, 67, 140, 175, 250,

272; spelled as redundance by Ruskin, 16

rib, 19, 20, 25, 45–47, 50, 59, 70, 81, 122, 138, 140, 186, 304, 327, 363n77; and perpetual novelty, 20; as opposed to fold, 66; as related to the ribbon, 34–38, 347n34; definition of, 21; ribbed vault, 14, 340n21; ribs enacted by angels, 42; stones vs., 68; tool of changefulness, 26

ribbon ornament, 34–41, 77, 82, 93, 115–19, 136, 141, 142, 156, 195, 216, 235, 274, 330, 348n53, 348n58, 363n77; ribboning as main technique of Morris, 119–28, 184; definitions of, 101–2, 347n34; filigree, 81, 261, 272, 345n10; knitting, 57, 85, 96, 202, 320; plaiting, 24, 90, 93, 106, 184; related to tiling, 128; related to vegetal ornament, 126; ribboning, 138, 302; *See also* braiding, interlacing, knotwork, weaving

Riegl, Alois, 98, 230, 347n34, 360n19; Riegl's influence on Worringer, 187, 190, 194; *Problems of Style*, 346n24, 346n30; *Stilfragen*, 95, 187

rigidity, 16, 17, 43–47, 59, 66, 67, 119, 202, 252; active rigidity, 86, 235, 250, 345n10; Ruskin's definition of active rigidity, 45

Rimbaud, Arthur, 361n49

Robinson, William, 209, 230, 231, 235–39, 332; concept of the wild, 237; Gravetye Manor, 238, 240, 357n38; *The English Flower Garden*, 237; *The Wild Garden*, 235–39

Roughgarden, Joan, 307

Rowe, Colin, 81

Ruskin, John, 11–17, 17–47, 55, 58, 78–83, 113–15, 174, 182, 222–35, 247–54, 260, 292–305, 315; "Law of Help," 48, 252, 306, 308; "The Flamboyant Architecture of the Valley of the Somme," 36, 341n35; "The Material of Ornament," 114; "The Nature of Gothic," 11, 12–13, 17, 45, 48, 58, 78, 138, 146; "The Poetry of Architecture," 220; and Babbage, 52, 53; and Christianity, 14, 269, 309; and Effie Gray, 41; and Hogarth, 19, 23; and Millais, 41, 42; and political economy, 174, 200, 234, 331; and Pugin, 12; and the Gothic, 9, 13, 17–47, 64, 140; and the pathetic fallacy, 178; as a vitalist, 14, 200, 208; criticism of industrialism, 54, 243; fictitious dialogue with Heidegger, 253; Guild of St. George, 61, 268; holiday in Scotland, 41; linear vs. surface Gothic, 82; *Love's Meinie*, 235, 281; *Modern Painters*, 14–15, 78, 83, 86, 224, 226, 227, 246, 281, 306; *Munera Pulveris*, 331; on abstract lines, 114–15; on active rigidity, 45; on beauty as the end, 296; on composition, 309; on Darwinism, 292, 293–94, 294; on design, 113, 132; on growth, 29; on imperfection, 14, 80; on interlacing, 37; on life, 62, 200, 330–31; on low and high picturesque, 225, 228; on sacrifice, 40, 174; on sympathy, 16, 228; on tenderness, 129; on the Earth Veil, 87; on the Flamboyant, 139; on the Matterhorn, 78, 79; on the parasitical sublime, 230; on the wall veil, 80, 137; on variation, 18, 114; on well-becoming, 295; on work, 19, 40, 52, 232–34; opinions on Ruskin, 12, 79; *Proserpina*, 235, 281, 292; relation with Darwin, 280; relation with Viollet-le-Duc, 46, 182; *The Ethics of the Dust*, 62; *The Seven Lamps of Architecture*, 40, 64, 78, 137, 174, 230, 232, 251, 341n38, 345n10, 349n67; *The Stones of Venice*, 11, 26, 78, 114; *The Two Paths*, 113, 132; traveling, 82; *Unto This Last*, 40, 175, 330; *See also* changefulness, savageness, rigidity, wall veil, Earth Veil, picturesque: low picturesque, picturesque: high picturesque, beauty: vital beauty, variation

sacrifice, 40, 66, 86, 134, 174, 245, 250, 251, 313; "Lamp of Sacrifice," 40, 251; offering, 86, 253, 318; Ruskin's concept of, 174–75, 251; *See also* gift, work: extra work

savageness, 17, 40, 51, 58, 60, 232, 262; collective execution, 30–33; imperfection,

14, 19, 33, 51, 58, 60, 66, 80, 208, 215, 252, 331, 362n73; individual execution, 19; related to cracking, 138, 195; related to primitive, 13, 78, 92, 148, 187, 189, 190, 192, 195, 201, 203, 206, 278; related to savage, 13, 16, 20, 51, 80, 103, 136, 206, 229, 232, 331; related to the old picturesque, 216; Ruskin's definition of, 13

Schelling, Friedrich Wilhelm Joseph, 264–66, 333; *Bedingung*, 210, 265; condition(ing), 101, 118, 128, 139, 143, 155, 174, 239, 266, 311, 312, 326, 329; productivity, 260, 265, 266, 333; *unbedingt*, 210, 265

Scholasticism, 64, 65, 70, 343n63, 343n64; Worringer's opinion on, 64

Schumacher, E. F., 49

Scott, George Gilbert, 64, 295

Sedlmayr, Hans, 70

Semper, Gottfried, 38, 44, 64, 74, 75, 77, 87, 89–97, 106, 107, 114, 129, 131, 133, 138, 156, 168, 194, 326–28, 345n16, 346n29; *Bekleidungsprinzip*, 91, 92, 94, 106; description of the four elements, 90; *Gewand*, 91, 93, 130; *Mauer*, 91, 92, 129; *Stoffwechselthese*, 77, 93, 94, 97, 102, 117, 129, 168; *Style*, 93; *Wand*, 91, 92, 129

Sennett, Richard, 8, 17, 48, 50, 54

Simondon, Gilbert, 56

Simson, Otto von, 69

Sloterdijk, Peter, 323, 326, 328, 329; *Anthropotechnik*, 329; *Sphären*, 328

Smith, Adam, 146, 227, 307

Smith, Jonathan, 281

snow crystals, 26, 28, 80, 89, 97–101, 117; as ice crystals, 32, 72, 101, 139, 217, 248, 264, 345n10

spirits, 74, 203, 232, 248, 250, 256, 313, 331; art and, 203; as *daimon*, 259; as satellite-spirit, 204, 282; compared to soul and eidos, 204; demon, 203, 205, 210, 259; design and, 205; ghosts and, 204; spirit(uality), 25, 41, 42, 71, 72, 85, 158, 188, 197, 229; veiling and, 205; *Weltseele*, 274; world mind, 203; See also *eu-daimonia*, animism

Stein, Gertrude, 154, 192

Stokes, Adrian, *Stones of Rimini*, 55

Street, George Edmund, 64, 80

sublime, 9, 186, 189, 213, 214, 225, 231, 253, 265, 281, 310, 324, 329, 332; as infrastructure, 254; as opposed to beauty, 215; as pure structure, 189; compared to ugliness, 213; definitions of, 210, 332; Heidegger and the, 245, 246, 250; Heidegger's and Ruskin's opposite use of the, 9, 247; Kant and, 213; related to abstraction, 230; shock and/or awe, 134, 186, 189, 213, 231, 245; style of technology, 214, 261, 263; sublime objects, 234–35, 211, 254, 259; technological sublime, 145, 214, 264, 331; the ruin and, 220; twentieth century and, 8, 75, 134, 145, 214, 261–62, 270; wet sublime, 232; *See also* polished, *Welt*: Heidegger's Open, Schelling: *unbedingt*

sympathy, 9, 60, 69, 71, 72, 128, 146, 147, 161–77, 184, 189, 203, 205, 206, 218, 249, 258, 266, 275–78, 282, 305, 310, 311, 314, 317, 322; (felt) immediacy, 128, 146, 175, 177, 179, 228, 257, 300; and contemporary art, 131–32; art and, 170, 171, 177, 197–200, 226, 229, 245; as an encounter, 131, 151, 174, 191, 204, 223, 226, 227, 228–31, 245, 249, 256, 273, 274, 282, 300, 305, 308, 310, 313, 314, 320, 321, 329, 331, 348n61, 363n77; as attunement, 182, 210, 272, 348n61; as opposed to relations of exteriority, 275, 351n23; as opposed to sentiment, 222, 226, 244; as related to tenderness, 78, 129, 131–34, 164, 189, 195, 199, 248, 348n61; as resonance, 134, 146, 174, 178, 182, 210, 229, 266, 272, 277, 282, 291, 305; based on dissolving dualisms, 183, 229; Bergson and, 161, 163, 164, 170; between feeling and thinking, 162, 165; compared to empathy, 169, 172, 184; compared to love, 162, 167, 231; compared to pity, 134, 224–26; Darwin and, 307; definitions of, 9, 129, 148, 174, 177, 181, 191;

dependent on both abstraction and empathy, 177, 184, 188, 209, 259; example of Kuni the bonobo, 170; Hartshorne and, 277; Hume and, 146, 182, 227, 228; immediate sympathy, 259; in relation to ornament, 128, 129, 258, 261; Lipps and, 180–81; longing and, 314, 320; mediated sympathy, 259; relations of interiority, 163, 276, 317, 352n44; risk of sympathy, 166, 189; Ruskin and, 16, 228, 253, 257; self-sympathy, 197; separated in abstraction and empathy, 190, 215, 259; starts with naturalism, 171, 353n48; Stoic concept of, 164, 362n73; sympathetic magic, 164, 352n39, 352n48, 353n67; three-step procedure of, 169; Whitehead and, 278; Whitman and, 231; *See also* specified abstraction, Gothic hinge, Ammophila wasp, willow tree, points

Teilhard de Chardin, Pierre, 274

teleology, 192, 223, 271, 284, 299; Aristotle and, 296, 297, 301; as related to morphology, 285; as-if teleology, 287, 297, 298, 300, 301; bent or curved path, 299, 302, 318; entelechy, 301, 302, 304; Kant and, 287, 297; purposiveness, 210, 223, 263, 286, 287, 304; Ruskin and, 296, 300, 302; U-turn teleology, 298; Whitehead and, 271–72; *See also* causality: final cause

Tennyson, Alfred, Lord, 83, 85, 86

terminus, 45, 156, 202, 365n90; James's concept of, 351n19; slowing down, 156, 212; stillness, 86, 100, 106, 214, 223; stations, 83, 95, 101, 156, 184, 214, 321, 328, 365n90; stopping, 10, 59, 85, 117, 240, 242; *See also* rigidity

territory, 231, 274, 293, 310, 328, 332; aesthetics of, 321; as interior decoration, 323; closed interior, 326, 329; deterritorialize, 12, 31; open interior, 325; packed structure of, 323; shape of countries, 322

tessellation, 89, 102–12, 129, 138, 153, 154, 157, 216, 302, 323; as pattern of outlines, 101, 136; compared to encrustation, 101; cracking, 34, 51, 83, 97, 100–2, 112, 134, 137, 138, 195, 257, 315, 322, 323; definition of, 77, 102; diagrid, 107, 110, 120; grid, 107, 110, 120, 128, 156; lattice, 24, 100, 107, 110, 112, 128; mineral ornament, 126; quasi-crystal, 112; tiling, 77, 91, 99, 101, 111, 119, 120, 121, 126, 128, 135, 156, 274, 279; types of, 107, 111; *See also* mosaic, Owen Jones, crystallization, pattern: Voronoi pattern, territory

texture, 77, 80, 94, 138; as texture mapping, 136, 140; as weak decoration, 129, 141, 257; definition of, 83; Pre-Raphaelites and, 85, 86, 119

thing, 9, 43, 53, 57, 62, 71, 72, 75, 86, 133, 142, 146, 148–77, 178, 196, 204, 215, 217, 218, 221, 251–56, 265–67, 275, 276, 287, 297, 300, 302, 311, 313, 317, 318, 331; as a thing in the making, 129, 133, 160, 195; as a thing made, 74, 97, 160; as cause or *chose*, 296; as Celtic knotwork, 157; as different from the object, 174, 175, 251; as equal to the object, 83, 254; as line-like (ribs, fibers, fringes, string theory, strings), 68, 86, 175, 182, 359n4, 363n77; as Morrisian rugs, 314; as point-like (atomism, monadism, punctualizations, blackboxing), 184, 255, 319, 363n77; as sake or *Sache*, 296, 304, 309; as stones, 155; as stuff, 148, 151, 155, 158, 174; as whats, 148, 157, 196, 202; bad thing, 259; definitions of, 173, 175; design and, 133, 139, 145, 205; Gothic things, 66, 68, 72, 184, 242, 272; Heidegger and, 174, 243, 255; Latour and, 254; no-thing, 245, 254; rape of things, 133; Scholasticism and, 64–66; *Thing* and, 255; thing-action, 66, 243, 251, 256, 304, 309; thing-feeling, 176, 271; unthing, 210, 258, 259; wild things, 210, 260, 265, 267; *See also* ontology, furnishing

Thoreau, Henry David, 230, 231, 247, 262

Titchener, Edward, 172

Titian, 140, 196–98, 202

tracery, 14, 19, 26, 29, 36, 40, 44, 65, 81, 82, 121, 139, 198, 203, 208, 216, 261, 286, 328, 345n10, 349n67; bar and plate tracery, 35; mullion, 25, 41, 121; techniques of, 18, 19; tracing house, 18; *See also* Decorated, Rayonnant, Flamboyant, Gothic

transformation, 25, 81, 91, 94, 97, 137, 160, 170, 199, 201, 230, 241, 242, 271, 283, 297, 304, 345n10; as incrementalism, 136; as related to deformation, 136, 194, 297; *See also* savageness

transition, 82–85, 90, 100–2, 115, 122, 129, 131, 132, 159, 160, 168, 184, 191, 195, 197, 202, 230, 252, 257, 304; between empathy and abstraction, 198–99; from concrete to abstract, 118; in James, 149, 152, 155, 156; in Semper, 91–97; main characteristic of ornament, 96

Turing, Alan, 65, 78, 135–39, 141, 295

Turner, J. M. W., 213, 225, 227, 280

Turner, Scott, 325

Uexküll, Jakob von, 324, 325, 330, 352n48

Umwelt, 325; Sloterdijk and, 330; Uexküll and, 324

value, 199, 200, 329; exchange value, 40, 200; intrinsic beauty, 271, 316, 366n105; intrinsic value, 330, 331; user value, 40, 134, 175

variation, 19–34, 50–60, 88, 98–106, 116, 126, 128, 142, 195, 262, 268; as change, 14, 19–20, 25, 32, 34, 64, 67, 94, 116, 156, 160, 165, 176, 179, 191, 195, 204, 215, 217, 240, 252, 276, 278, 283, 297, 314, 363n77; as dependent on repetition, 99, 113, 284; as related to uniformity, 98, 135, 142, 283, 301; biased variation, 192, 285; configurational, 20, 61, 68; Darwin's concept of, 271, 285, 286, 306; endless variation, 280; experiential variation, 155; Goethe and, 283; gradual variation, 106, 136, 138, 194, 195, 196, 283, 288, 315; Hogarth's concept of, 19, 115, 340n19; Jones's concept of, 106; perpetual novelty, 19,

20, 29, 68, 286; proportional, 20; random variation, 64, 140, 153, 156, 284, 285; related to differentiation, 31; Ruskin's concept of, 14, 16, 19, 83, 87; threshold of, 31, 195; *See also* changefulness, deformation, elasticity, flexibility, design: rule and rule-based

Viollet-le-Duc, Eugène, 46, 186, 240; concept of structure, 47; crystallization, 187

Vischer, Robert, 147, 172, 178

vitalism, 12, 135, 147, 208, 228, 229, 231, 269, 270, 285, 301, 330, 339n11; as aesthetic theory, 282; as the wrong conclusion, 282; Bergson's concept of, 192, 282; *élan vital*, 192; Lipps's concept of, 178; Ruskin's concept of, 14, 200, 331; *Trieb*, 31, 215, 301; vital machine, 25, 62; vital materialism, 68; vital movement, 24; vital power, 331; vital principle, 14; vitality, 25, 63; vitalized geometry, 24, 30, 45, 47, 102, 120, 128, 195, 232, 340n26; *See also* beauty: Ruskin's vital beauty

vulnerability, 129, 163, 170, 174, 208, 245, 261, 262

Waal, Frans de, 169, 205

wall veil, 80, 87, 89, 137, 273, 332; definition of, 78

Wallace, Alfred Russell, 281

weaving, 25, 29, 45, 53, 58, 66, 70, 77, 83, 89, 101, 102, 106, 132, 138, 155–57, 167, 176, 184, 191, 195, 202, 209, 274, 328, 345n10; Semper and, 91–96; tracery and, 35–42 passim

Welt, 245, 250, 324, 328; Heidegger's Open, 247, 324, 329

Whitehead, Alfred North, 159, 223, 249, 255, 277, 278, 282, 316, 331; concept of beauty, 271–72; concept of composition, 309

Whitman, Walt, 231, 352n44

wild, 230–32, 278, 331; as the home of decoration, 231, 232, 234; made up of interiors, 323; Robinson and, 235–40; technological wild, 243, 261–68; Thoreau and, 231; wilderness, 142, 262, 332; *See also* growth: overgrowth, flourishing

Wilde, Oscar, 130, 250, 272, 348n55

Williams, Raymond, 8

Willis, Robert, 21

willow tree (example of sympathetic encounter), 178, 181–83, 187, 190, 204, 256

Wordsworth, William, 72, 219, 220, 228, 356n18

Worringer, Wilhelm, 9, 11, 12, 25, 31–38, 41, 51, 64, 69, 71, 147, 177, 186–203, 230, 327, 340n23, 347n34; *Abstraction and Empathy*, 24, 172, 187, 201; *Abstraktion und Einfühlung*, 171, 172; *Form in Gothic*, 64, 201; northern line, 23–24

work, 14, 35, 38, 42, 48, 54–57, 74, 117, 130, 140, 142, 164, 168, 182, 212, 217, 226, 234, 253, 279, 293, 300; as craft, 14, 18, 38, 42, 49, 54, 57, 58, 96, 129, 139, 141, 142, 162, 195, 243, 251, 266, 333; as elaboration, 30, 54, 58, 123, 140, 141, 168, 174, 194, 261, 272, 279, 280, 292, 293; as opposed to labor, 40; as related to force, 50, 97, 250; as related to structure, 42–43, 44, 130, 140, 250; as related to sympathy, 174; carving, 13, 17, 18, 30, 40, 42, 55–57, 70, 94, 96, 120, 139, 168, 174, 232, 250, 349n67; casting, 48, 50, 55–61, 93, 95, 139, 223, 298, 304; conflation of design and, 17, 30, 38, 52, 332; definition of, 40–41, 279, 313; extra work, 40, 86, 134, 152, 166, 234, 250; leisure, 40, 142, 272; Oscar Wilde at, 130, 250, 348n55; robotics, 17, 54, 57, 58, 141, 142; Ruskin's concept of, 40, 41, 182, 272; servility, 254, 300, 319; task, 53, 234; *Werkform*, 44; *See also* agency, freedom: free man vs. free hand, beauty: "a beauty that works"

Wynne-Edwards, V. C., 307, 308

colophon

Production and design: Joke Brouwer
Copy editor: Laura Martz

Cover image: digitally altered image of William Morris's *Acanthus* wallpaper (1875), designed for Morris & Co.

This publication was financially supported by the Netherlands Architecture Fund

Available in North, South and Central America through D.A.P./Distributed Art Publishers Inc, 155 Sixth Avenue 2nd Floor, New York, NY 10013-1507, tel +1 212 627 1999, fax +1 212 627 9484, dap@dapinc.com

Available in the United Kingdom and Ireland through Art Data, 12 Bell Industrial Estate, 50 Cunnington Street, London W4 5HB, tel +44 208 747 1061, fax +44 208 742 2319, orders@artdata.co.uk

Printed and bound in The Netherlands

ISBN 978-90-5662-827-7

http://www.v2.nl/publishing